THE UNIVERSITY REFORM
OF TSAR ALEXANDER I
1802-1835

JAMES T. FLYNN

THE UNIVERSITY REFORM
OF TSAR ALEXANDER I
1802-1835

THE CATHOLIC UNIVERSITY
OF AMERICA PRESS
WASHINGTON, D.C.

Library of Congress Cataloging-in-Publication Data

LIBRARY OF CONGRESS CATALOGING-IN-PUBLICATION DATA

Flynn, James T., 1932–
 The university reform of Tsar Alexander I, 1802–1835 / James T.
Flynn.
    p.   cm.
 Bibliography: p.
 Includes index.
 ISBN 0-8132-0653-7
  1. Education, Higher—Soviet Union—History—19th century.
 2. Russkoe bibleĭskoe obshchestvo (Saint Petersburg, Russia)
 I. Title.
 LA837.F59   1988
 378.47—dc19   88-3184

CONTENTS

ACKNOWLEDGMENTS

ONE ASPECT or another of Russia's "University Question" has occupied my scholarly attention, off and on, for many years. Over those years I have benefitted from the support and advice of many institutions and individuals. I am particularly grateful for my students and colleagues at Holy Cross, whose interest and questions have repeatedly not only reawakened my own interest but provided also the insights that only the interested non-specialist can offer, helping me to distinguish the proverbial forest from the trees. It has been my good fortune also to meet and work with many, perhaps most, of the specialists, the scholars who have worked on themes related to my subject during the past decade or so. My debt to these colleagues and friends I have indicated where possible in citation of their published works or, in cases where that was not possible, in footnotes where most suitable. The support of the Russian Research Center of Harvard University has been essential for all aspects of my work. I am deeply grateful for the International Research and Exchanges Board (IREX) and Fulbright fellowships, which permitted work in Leningrad, and for the faculty fellowships from Holy Cross, which enabled me to work in the Library of Congress, the New York Public Library, and several other major collections. To Professor Marc Raeff of Columbia University I owe much, not only for his scholarly advice but also for the willing and generous spirit in which he offered it. I wish to record my gratitude to the journals that have published my earlier formulations of some problems taken up in this study, listed in the bibliography and notes, and also to their unnamed readers whose critiques often were especially helpful in refining my notions of the subject.

vii

Finally, my wife Nancy has given over these many years the sort of support for which any thanks within my poor powers of expression must be inadequate. To her in affection and gratitude this study is dedicated.

J.T.F.

INTRODUCTION

THE FOUNDATION of the university system in Russia was among the more important and enduring of the many reforms undertaken in the early years of the reign of Alexander I. It was, moreover, a program that initially expressed well one of the more striking aspects of the heterogeneous collection of ideas and assumptions called "enlightened absolutism."[1] The reformers planned to use the power of the state, not to force change on people, but rather to remove the obstacles to change, to free people from the burdens and constraints of the past, in order to permit them to pursue freely their own goals and interests. Naturally, enlightened reformers assumed that the pursuit of individual goals, when free from the political, legal, economic, intellectual, and even spiritual bonds maintained by interests and institutions rooted in the past, would in fact promote the common good. One of the reformers, M. M. Speranskii, in September 1803 stated the proposition well: "Reforms which are made by the power of the state generally are not lasting, especially in those cases when state power must struggle against centuries old traditions. . . . Therefore, it is better and easier to lead [people] to improvement by simply opening to them the path to their own improvement. Supervising from a distance the peoples' activities, the state can arrange matters to assist them to take the path to improvement without using any kind of force. . . . As little restriction as

1. Grete Klingenstein, "Despotismus und Wissenschaft: Zur Kritik norddeutscher Aufklärer an der österreichischen Universität 1750–1790," *Formen der europäischen Aufklärung*, Friedrich Engel-Janosi, others, eds., in *Wiener Beiträge zur Geschichte der Neuzeit*, Bd 3 (1976), 127–157, provides a particularly insightful discussion, much broader than the title suggests, of the uses of "enlightened absolutism" in the reform of university systems.

possible, as much freedom as possible, these are the principles for all reform in society."[2] In 1847, S. S. Uvarov, arguably the most important of the reformers who worked to implement university reform, sounded a note of alarm. "The half-century [sic] old idea," he wrote, "that every Russian owes service to the crown . . . is weakening, without doubt. Though it remains usual still for a young man to begin by giving some years to state service, when no opportunity opens to him the path he wants . . . the young man decides not to stay long. . . . In such a time, there forms quickly a new sort of people, with their own understanding, their own private judgments and dreams, not concerned so much with the government's goals as with their own success."[3] Much of what had been planned in 1803 had been achieved. Yet Uvarov expressed alarm, not satisfaction. What had happened? The conventional explanation is that the original "liberal" goals, even when they were achieved only in part, proved not only unwelcome but even threatening because they undermined autocratic Russia's state and social structure, prompting both the rise of reaction, in several guises and stages, and the rise of the opposition intelligentsia, if not indeed the Decembrist revolt against autocracy.[4]

But that is not what happened. The original reform was planned to have a significant impact on the state services and on society, not least by providing new cadres of university-trained civil servants

2. M. I. Shugurov, "Doklad o evreiakh imperatoru Aleksandru Pavlovichu, 1812," *RA*, 1903 (No. 2), 254–255. This is a copy of a report of September 1803 (unfortunately lost in a fire in 1862) from the Committee on the improvement of the Jews, one of the many committees appointed by Alexander I in the early years of his reign to plan one reform or another. This committee included, in addition to Speranskii, Czartoryski, Kochubei, and several others who also served on the committees that planned educational reform. For analysis of this committee's work, see John D. Klier, "The Origins of the Jewish Minority Problem in Russia 1772–1812" (Ph.D., University of Illinois, 1975), 231–248.

3. "Vsepoddanneishaia zapiska, predstavlennaia gosudariu imperatoru Nikolaiu I, byvshim ministrom Narodnago Prosveshcheniia grafom Uvarovym, v fevrale 1847 goda," *Grazhdanskoe chinoproizvodstvo v Rossii*, V. A. Evreinov, ed. (SPB, 1887), 84.

4. Two recent studies have done much to illuminate the shift in the uses of state power in the reign of Nicholas I. Neither, however, pays much attention to the impact of university reform. For more extended discussion, see my reviews of N. V. Riasanovsky, *A Parting of Ways: Government and the Educated Public in Russia 1801–1855* (Oxford, 1976) in *Russian History*, v.4 (1977), 78–79, and W. B. Lincoln, *Nicholas I: Emperor and Autocrat of All the Russias* (Indiana, 1978), in *Slavic Review*, v.38 (1979), 109–110.

and through the universities' direction of a public-school system extended into the villages all over the empire. Instead, after nearly four decades the universities' impact on the state services, let alone on the villages, remained slight. Thus, although the university reform had successes, a significant impact on state or society was not yet among them. Moreover, "reactionaries" had not managed to frustrate the original reform. Uvarov, indeed, did not attempt to do that. He worked hard, long, and in the end successfully, to keep in place the essentials of the original "liberal" university reform, convinced that in the long run it would prove the best path for Russia.

The basic aim of this study, then, is to describe what happened, to make clear the choices made by the policy makers, and to understand why they made those choices. As a history of the efforts of the Ministry of Education to establish the university system, this study takes seriously the administrators' perceptions of the issues. Study of the policies proposed, accepted, and rejected illuminates not only the complexity and difficulty of the issues but also the problems the administrators had in grasping the issues and the possibilities open to them.

Focus on policy is not the only useful approach to the study of educational systems. One might investigate pedagogy, or the role of schools as agents of cultural or social change, or as agents of stability in the transmission of values and skills. Though the impact of the universities in all these areas proved slight, they are important areas and thus are given much attention. Yet, focus on policy helps to make clear that much in the history of the Russian universities is best understood as a subset of political history. Moreover, this focus permits appreciation of a remarkable element in the success that was achieved. The reform effort that founded the Russian university system was marked by three decades of struggle among men as diverse in outlook and goals as Czartoryski and Stroganov of Alexander's Secret Committee, Catherinian conservatives such as Razumovskii and Shishkov, pietists of the Bible Society such as Golitsyn and Magnitskii, and, most important, the codifier of "Official Nationality," Uvarov. These struggles were bitter, long-lasting, and costly. Nonetheless, in the end the statute of 1835 retained the essential elements of the original reform statutes of 1804. Thus, it marked in one sense the success of the original reform. But it also marked the failure of many attempts to improve, or defeat, the original 1804 reform. A close examination of this Russian experience in founding a university system drawn from Western models, in both its successes and failures, tells much of the ways in which Western-inspired reforms proved both useful and irrelevant in meeting Russian needs as perceived by reformers and reactionaries alike.

ABBREVIATIONS

Abbreviations. In bibliography and footnotes the following abbreviations are used:

SPB	*St. Petersburg*
RA	*Russkii Arkhiv*
RS	*Russkaia Starina*
SEER	*Slavonic and East European Review*
VE	*Vestnik Evropy*
VLU	*Vestnik Leningradskogo Universiteta*
VMU	*Vestnik Moskovskogo Universiteta*
ZhMNP	*Zhurnal Ministerstva narodnago prosveshcheniia*

THE UNIVERSITY REFORM
OF TSAR ALEXANDER I
1802-1835

CHAPTER I

THE ISSUES

IN MAY 1802, not much more than a year after the murder of his father elevated him to the throne of Russia, Tsar Alexander I paid a visit to Dorpat and took part in a ceremony that marked the formal opening of a new university. Both the assembled local nobles, who founded and financed the new institution, and the newly recruited professors, who disagreed sharply with the nobles on most matters touching university policy, expected the tsar to make clear his support for their position. In his address of welcome, the professors' spokesman promised that he and his colleagues would take "special concern for the poor."[1] In reply, Alexander seemed to go out of his way to signal support for the professors' desire to open the university to all academically qualified candidates, without regard to social class. His reply delighted the professors and horrified most nobles. Delighted or horrified, both professors and nobles before long had reason to doubt whether the tsar meant what he seemed to say. Confusion and doubt about his intentions may have been sown deliberately by Alexander in order to confuse and disorganize those who would oppose his plans. By design or not, confusion and doubt came to the new institution at Dorpat as to many, perhaps most, reforms attempted in Alexander's time. The many reforms attempted not only had in common the doubt and confusion they often occasioned; they also had common origins in the reformers'

1. Friedrich Bienemann, *Der Dorpater Professor Georg Friedrich Parrot und Kaiser Alexander I* (Reval, 1902), 115–116. This address is reprinted also in E. V. Petukhov, *Imperatorskii Iurevskii, byvshii Derptskii, Universitet 1802–1865* (Iurev, 1902), 112–113 and in N. K. Shil'der, *Imperator Aleksandr I, ego zhizn' i tsarstvovanie*, 4 v. (SPB, 1904–05), II, 32–36.

expectations and experience, and also in aspects that seem not to have occurred to the reformers.

1. The Question of Reform

The reign of Alexander was clearly the reign of a reformer. The times, the era of the French Revolution and Napoleon, and Russia's situation, poised between Catherine the Great's accomplishments and Paul I's attempts to reverse them, made some sort of far-reaching change all but inevitable. Moreover, the young tsar clearly thought of himself as a reformer and meant to carry out that role. Yet the end of Alexander's reign was marked by confusion and doubt so strong that some advocates of reform were near despair. Part of the reason was the reforms' failure to achieve their stated goals. That failure only partly explained the doubt and confusion, however, for in some ways some reforms achieved their goals but nonetheless were regarded as failures. The personal characteristics of the tsar played a role, but the question of reform in the Russia of Alexander I was confusing not only because the tsar was enigmatic, or possibly himself confused, but also because the situation was complex and every problem multifaceted. Russia faced many challenges that crowded together, requiring that something, often something quite far-reaching, be done, and done quickly, to change or to fortify basic political and economic institutions. The challenges came in the sharply threatening form of military peril as well as in the benign form of aspirations to make significant improvement in economic development, health, and welfare. Additional complexity stemmed from the reformers' need to choose among many competing concepts of reform that often were mutually contradictory if equally plausible and well recommended. Not surprisingly, the reformers often found it difficult to decide which model to follow, and they tried to combine more than one approach in meeting one need or another. Most important, the reform plans were not undertaken as desperate emergency measures to ward off danger. They were taken up in a spirit of optimism, as the paths to a better future, established on the certainties of science and reason and marked with the highest human values, whether of secular-minded humanism or otherworldly pietism. Naturally, therefore, many looked forward with confidence to the development of reform. Failure in these circumstances was so unexpected that it seemed especially disappointing.

In some areas success was achieved, if at a very high price. The Russian army was entirely transformed. In tactics, organization, training, and equipment the army came to match the best of the relatively small professional armies that had been fundamental to successful modernization, particularly in central Europe. In recruitment and relation to civil society, the army kept its Petrine ways, traditional by this time. But in the strikingly high percentage of the population directly engaged in the military, the Russian army more than matched the new mass armies of the era of the French Revolution and Napoleon. These changes proved not temporary responses to wartime emergencies, but became permanent transformations. During the reign of Alexander I an army whose strength was not quite 400,000 troops became a peacetime standing army of a good deal more than a million.

In some other areas Alexandrine reforms clearly failed. Serfdom was a basic feature, perhaps the basic feature, that sharply distinguished Russia from the progressive Europe whose successes the reformers wanted to emulate. Alexander's government, in particular the group of personal friends and advisers who formed his "Secret Committee," had no difficulty in agreeing that serfdom was an economic and political anachronism that retarded economic growth and social development, and that it was a moral outrage as well, inescapably producing both misery and disorder. There was no lack of ideas for reform. The so-called Free Farmers Act in February 1803 launched a program intended to try capitalism as an answer to serfdom by encouraging those peasants who could, as individuals or even as communal organizations, to purchase their lands and freedom, showing the way that the pursuit of self-interest would promote the common good by undermining serfdom. Other solutions were tried, at least in part as pilot programs for the whole empire. In the Baltic province of Livland in 1804 serfs were granted hereditary rights to the land, but not personal freedom. In neighboring Estland in 1811 serfs were granted personal freedom without rights to the land. Either procedure seemed to many to promise to undermine serfdom, though neither did. The military colonies program, begun in 1810 and pushed vigorously after 1816, approached the problem from the opposite end. No longer relying on the motivation of self-interest, the government would transform peasant lives by the use of state power and military discipline. There was a better way of life for rural Russia, and the government knew what that way was, if it could but find the way to motivate people to pursue it. These and other programs and policies showed that there were many possible solutions to the problems of serfdom, though all proved deficient in practice.[2]

The reform that produced the foundation of the Russian university system had its origins, then, in a time of wide-ranging change. Dwarfed by comparison with the scope and vast numbers involved in the changes in the military, and seldom meeting problems as intractable as those rooted in serfdom, the university reform shared with other aspects of the reform effort the sort of goals Alexander formulated, and the variety in sources and resources available to meet them. In general terms, two quite different concepts of the path to reform coexisted, that of enlightened absolutism and that of constitutionalism. At Alexander's accession, Russia already had long experience in attempting to choose between them. An important part of that experience was the frustration inherent in the paradox that Russia's reformers repeatedly found it necessary to turn to state power, if not arbitrary despotism, in order to achieve constitutional gains.[3] Paul I, and Peter III at mid-eighteenth century, made especially noteworthy attempts to follow the example of the great Peter, using state power to make Russia more efficient and more just. Both had reigns cut short by assassination. Their use of state power seemed to many merely arbitrary, capricious abuse that justi-

2. Allen McConnell, "Alexander I's Hundred Days: The Politics of a Paternalist Reformer," *Slavic Review*, 28 (1969), 373–393, and the same writer's *Tsar Alexander I: Paternalistic Reformer* (New York, 1970), 1–44, 138–147, are excellent introductions to the question of reform in the early years of the reign and to serfdom and the military. For legal and institutional reform, see Marc Raeff, *Comprendre l'ancien régime russe* (Paris, 1982), 124–132. For the army, see John L. H. Keep, "The Russian Army's Response to the French Revolution," *Jahrbücher für Geschichte Osteuropas,* 28 (1980), 500–523. Nothing comparable exists for the problem of serfdom. Among the better brief discussions are Jerome Blum, *Lord and Peasant in Russia* (Princeton, 1961), 539–545; George Yaney, *The Systematization of Russian Government: Social Evolution in the Domestic Administration of Imperial Russia 1711–1905* (Urbana, 1973), 162–164.

3. This point is particularly well made in David L. Ransel, *The Politics of Catherinian Russia: The Panin Party* (New Haven, 1975), 269–289, and its terms learnedly discussed in Marc Raeff, *The Well-Ordered Police State: Social and Institutional Change through Law in the Germanies and Russia 1600–1800* (New Haven, 1983), 195–250. See also Raeff's "The Domestic Policies of Peter III and His Overthrow," *American Historical Review,* 75 (1970), 1289–1310. V. O. Kliuchevskii, *Kurs Russkoi Istorii* in *Sochineniia* (8 v., Moscow, 1958), V, 186–193 remains a useful summary analysis of Paul's reign as one of principled reform, rather than merely despotic arbitrariness.

fied the most extreme forms of resistance to what otherwise had to be regarded as legally constituted authority. This circumstance gave Alexander significant advantages in the early months and years of his reign. Since his grandmother, Catherine the Great, had removed him from his father's house and care, he was not associated with Paul's reputation for cruel caprice. For many, the end of Paul's caprice was the definition of reform. The news of Paul's murder, at which "people cried with joy and embraced one another as on Easter Sunday," therefore made it possible for Alexander to appear the reformer without making hard choices but by merely repealing some of Paul's more obnoxious edicts.[4]

It was not long, however, before Alexander had to begin making choices. Some of those choices seemed to indicate that he appreciated the need not only to avoid gross excesses in the abuse of power but to develop institutions that could restrain such abuse by promoting constitutional growth on something like the British model. There were men, often with high-level experience in Catherine's government, who well understood enlightened reform in such terms. Alexander appeared to encourage them by founding a "permanent council" in which some of them could provide legal advice to the tsar, and by establishing a "commission on the composition of the law" to plan revision of the legal system. He asked A. P. Vorontsov, whose appreciation of British political and legal practice was well known, to draw up a model constitution, the "Charter of the Russian People." Expressing concern for the Senate's "traditional" rights, Alexander also asked it to draw up a constitutional proposal for itself. In the manifesto issued at his accession, moreover, Alexander promised to rule in the spirit of his grandmother Catherine, a promise that naturally called up visions in the minds of gentry of the constitutional guarantees of gentry rights of person and property made in the charter of 1785. Such steps might have developed institutions and practices to promote something comparable to the constitutional government of the British model. They would foster the growth of liberty by protecting the interests and rights of at least some segments of society. Preserving a balance be-

4. Quotation: *Karamzin's Memoir on Ancient and Modern Russia*, Richard Pipes, ed. and trans. (New York, 1966), 136. There was, of course, much in Peter III and especially Paul I that was obnoxious, cruel, capricious, and despotic. In that, at least, they were like the ruler whose tradition they meant to carry on: Peter the Great.

tween the central government and other institutions and groups, such steps meant developing constitutional government in the sense of limiting the power of the central government by requiring it to govern through, or at least with the consent of, institutions devoted to maintaining the rights of established groups. In Russia that clearly meant, in the first place, respecting the rights and interests of the higher nobility, with attention too for the Orthodox Church and the provincial gentry. Many therefore regarded such steps, not as hopeful reforms, but as fundamentally unsound. The stable excellence of a British constitution was not the only outcome of such policies. Montesquieuian balance could promote a reactionary defense of vested interests against the common good, as witnessed in the *Parlements* of pre-revolutionary France, blocking all responsible reform until they too were swept away in the great 1789 revolution. Alexander, in any event, was no amiable, or lazy, Louis XVI, knuckling under to the selfish defenders of private interests, and therefore he did not seriously countenance for long any of these constitutional steps. By late 1804 all these attempts at reform had been abandoned or crushed, most spectacularly when the tsar angrily rejected the Senate's attempt to exercise its "right" to protest new laws that enfringed upon established gentry rights.[5]

It would say too much, nonetheless, to argue that Alexander had thus revealed himself as despotic or hypocritical. There was something ambiguous in both theory and practice to pursuing liberty, justice, or even simple efficiency by granting to established groups or institutions the right to promote their own interests as the common good. Enlightened absolutism was the way out of that particular dilemma, using the power of the state to remove obstacles to liberty, justice, or efficiency, including the obstacles formed by the traditional rights of established groups and bodies, such as the nobility and clergy. Enlightened absolutism had its own dilemma,

5. O. A. Narkiewicz, "Alexander I and the Senate Reform," *SEER*, XLVII (1969), 115–136, thoroughly presents the issues, concluding that it is "doubtful" in any case that the Senate reforms ever could have led to "genuinely democratic reforms." Karamzin protested on another occasion, citing Montesquieu to point out that "It is bad when a servant obtains mastery over a weak lord, but a prudent lord respects his choice servants, and considers their honor his own. The rights of the well-born are not something apart from monarchical authority—they are its principal and indispensable instrumentality by means of which the body politic is kept in motion." Pipes, *Karamzin's Memoir*, 200.

demonstrated poignantly in the career of the ruler who was perhaps the most serious and principled of those called enlightened absolutists. Joseph II found it necessary to organize an efficient secret police, whose arbitrary exercise of power was itself a denial of liberty, to combat those citizens of the Habsburg realms who seemed ready to use their newly gained freedoms from traditional constraints to pursue their own goals, which often were in fact at odds with those set by the reforming monarchy. A way out of this dilemma seemed offered by the notions of *Rechtsstaat*. The reforming state formulated goals in terms of an order of society both just and efficient, knowable by science and reason, and thus attacked the order of society founded on tradition, or indeed on any concept of reason inconsistent with the mechanistic assumptions of the *philosophe*. The *Rechtsstaat* was enlightened absolutist in its use of the state's power to pursue those goals, but it also committed itself to the law it formulated, guarantee that the arbitrary exercise of state power would not undermine liberty and justice. Alexander was open to this notion, which lay behind much of the institutional and legal reform, including the educational, undertaken in the early years of his reign.[6]

The enlightened *Rechtsstaat* clearly stood in need of men able and willing to formulate and implement programs to achieve its goals. Not surprisingly, every state in enlightened Europe during the age of Enlightenment made some effort to develop an educational system that could provide such men for its services. Reform in higher education became indeed both means and end, required in order to pursue reform goals and so necessary that it was pursued as one of the essential reforms. Three among these efforts proved particularly important in the development of university reform in Alexander's Russia: the development of German universities, especially Göttingen; the struggle between secular reformers and clerical, es-

6. For good discussions, sensitive to the ambiguities in both these ideas on constitution and Alexander's approach to them, see Marc Raeff, *Michael Speransky, Statesman of Imperial Russia* (The Hague, 1957), 29–46; Patricia K. Grimsted, *The Foreign Ministers of Alexander I* (Berkeley, 1969), 49–55. Reflecting their importance for the whole history of Imperial Russia, these questions have become the focus of an extensive literature in both the West and the Soviet Union. A lucid and learned discussion of the questions and the literature is in David Christian, "The Political Views of the Unofficial Committee in 1801: Some New Evidence," *Canadian-American Slavic Studies*, v. 12 (1978), 247–258.

pecially Jesuits, for a new school system in Poland; and the academic reforms of the Habsburg Empire, as introduced into Russia under Catherine the Great.

Göttingen's great success made it uncommonly influential. Though relatively new, founded in 1734 in a small and not very important town, Göttingen soon made its mark. It fostered university autonomy rooted not so much in the traditional defense of the rights and liberties of established institutions and classes as in the results achieved by a faculty that worked in academic freedom for both teachers and learners, and whose scholarship contributed to the community the constant development of knowledge. These results, moreover, bore fruit in the utilitarian sense of providing the best training for men who would carry forward the *Rechtsstaat*'s programs. Such a combination of virtues made the model of Göttingen all but irresistible, particularly as they were brought into the Russian reformers' discussions by M. N. Murav'ev, who was personally close to Alexander and to academic leaders at Göttingen. Jesuits and the Polish National Education Commission sharply disagreed about many important issues, but both worked hard to develop schools whose graduates could compare well with Europe's best in both up-to-date competence in their fields and in motivation to use their gifts for the good of the wider community. Moreover, in the details of organization and curriculum, both came closer to agreement than either seemed likely to admit. Adam Czartoryski, who was especially close to Alexander personally, was both well informed on the achievements of educational reformers in Poland and intent on fostering their further development.[7]

Murav'ev was particularly important becase his influence tended to encourage some choices while precluding others. He, and Czartoryski as well, took very seriously the development of the university in fostering reform. In many ways this was a minority view in the late eighteenth century. Enrollment in most universities in western Europe was declining sharply. Some centuries-old institutions closed forever. Many enlightened critics sought to help mankind achieve liberation from the dead hand of the past by encouraging

---

7. On the appeal of Göttingen's example, see Klingenstein, "Despotismus und Wissenschaft," *Wiener Beiträge zur Geschichte der Neuzeit*, Bd 3 (1976), 127–155. On the Jesuits and the National School Commission, see Stanislaw Litak, "Das Schulwesen der Jesuiten in Polen: Entwicklung und Verfall," *Wiener Beiträge zur Geschichte der Neuzeit*, Bd 5 (1978), 124–137.

the development of new institutional forms for education. Many argued that the university was among the decaying institutions rooted in the past that should be replaced with more rationally conceived ways of providing education for a new, progressive, era. As often as not, such critics were quite right to argue that many universities had become centers of pedantry, not of learning, whose academic autonomy was most useful for faculty nepotism, securing jobs for friends and relatives, not for the defense of professional values. Göttingen, and Halle and some others, were exceptional not only in their academic excellence but also in making the traditional university an institution to foster reform rather than an obstacle in the way of enlightenment.[8]

The institutional and intellectual legacy of Catherine the Great's work in educational reform matched the importance of Göttingen's example. The school system Catherine founded in 1782 was based on the "decreed Enlightenment" characteristic of Catholic Europe, though it was first worked out and made successful in Protestant Prussia. The "Allgemeine Schulordnung" of Johann Felbiger was first successfully applied in Prussian Silesia, then throughout the domains of Frederick the Great, then throughout the Habsburg Empire. The fundamentals of the system were the development of a series of textbooks for all the basic subjects, from reading, writing, arithmetic, and basic religious and moral doctrine through advanced, gymnasium and/or *realschule*, courses in mathematics, sciences, languages, and social studies as well as in religion and morality. Training programs for teachers in the most efficient methods of getting the contents of this series of texts into the heads of pupils stressed oral drill and memorization. Up-to-date command of the essentials of a modern, useful education, thus, could be efficiently delivered to ever-wider segments of the population. Obviously wildly different in tone and temper from the Göttingen notion of what education was about, this system had achieved noteworthy success in the villages of the Habsburg Empire, even as Göttingen-minded reformers attained some success in reform of the empire's universities. Catherine, ever impressed with success, brought to Russia one of the officials who had played a major role in devel-

---

8. R. Steven Turner, "University Reformers and Professorial Scholarship in Germany 1760–1806," *The University in Society*, L. Stone, ed. (2 v., Princeton, 1974), II, 495–531, provides a judicious introduction to the problem of university reform in eighteenth-century Germany.

oping the system in the Habsburg lands with Slavic populations: Teodor Jankovic de Mirievo.[9]

Mirievo joined the School Commission (*Komissiia ob uchrezhdenii uchilishch*) Catherine founded in 1782 to plan and supervise the development of a new system. In a decade of work, the commission introduced into Russia the essentials of the Felbiger system. At the village level its quite uniform basic curriculum aimed at providing general literacy and numeracy, together with indoctrination in religious and social values likely to foster loyalty and cooperation. Graduates of the village school were prepared for advancement to the middle school (*malaia* in the designation adopted in Russia) to be opened in each county seat, which prepared its graduates for the "main" secondary school to be located in each provincial capital. The teachers' college that the commission opened in St. Petersburg provided training in the curriculum and methods of the system.

Mirievo, and the commission, tried to do more than duplicate the Austrian model. In the Habsburg lands, the secondary school in each province (called the "Normal School") was the top of a three-step ladder, designed primarily to train teachers for the lower schools and people equipped with enough of the basics of a general liberal arts education to make useful candidates for the lower echelons of the public services or of private enterprises. Such people were not eligible for admission to universities, to prepare for careers in the senior levels of the public services or the church. Mirievo proposed that the main secondary school do just that, becoming in effect (and as it turned out often in name as well) the gymnasium, the secondary school that trained students for university admission. The top of the ladder in Russia, then, would be a network of universities that Mirievo proposed would join Russia's only existing university at Moscow. Most striking, in the context of the authoritarian sort of enlightened school system Mirievo helped to build, was his proposal that the projected universities should have Göttingen's academic freedom, the "right of free teaching." Moreover, he ar-

9. Max J. Okenfuss, "Education and Empire: School Reform in Enlightened Russia," *Jahrbücher für Geschichte Osteuropas*, Bd 27 (1979), 41–68, and Isabel de Madariaga, "The Foundation of the Russian Educational System by Catherine II," *SEER*, v. 57 (1979), 369–395, are superior, well-informed discussions that make entirely obsolete such earlier treatments as Nicholas Hans, *History of Russian Educational Policy 1701–1917* (London, 1931) and W. H. E. Johnson, *Russia's Educational Heritage* (Pittsburgh, 1950).

gued that, unlike the system in the Habsburg lands, the system should make no class or "age" distinctions.[10]

Mirievo also put forward proposals for the universities from former colleagues in Austria who wanted law taught, not as professional training in the faculty of Russian law, but in the philosophy faculty, as a system of logic derived from fundamental first principles. To provide genuine learning, then, as distinct from mere utilitarian vocational training for bureaucrats, Mirievo thought law students in Russian universities should study German law rather than Russian, for German law could provide not only good "examples" but also the distance to encourage objectivity, and thus reliance on reason rather than on tradition as the standard for law. Göttingen, and many other universities, in central and eastern Europe had fostered reforms that did both, providing vocational training at a high professional level for bureaucrats in *Staatswissenschaft*, without surrendering either philosophic studies of the enlightened empiricist and/or idealist sort or, for that matter, the values of the old classics curriculum, especially Latin philology.

Many members, including P. A. Zavadovskii, one of Catherine's favorites whom she appointed chairman of the commission, argued against these recommendations from Mirievo, since they required distinctions and priorities that did not need to be made and overlooked some points that did need stressing, such as the need to develop a curriculum that used the Russian language as the most efficient means to promote the "spread of learning" in Russia. Remarkably few objections, however, were raised against the notion that not only should the system provide the rudiments of literacy for all, but that the village school should form the foundation stage, open to all, in a single system that extended up through the univer-

10. George M. O'Brien, "Maria Theresa's attempt to Educate an Empire," *Paedagogica Historica*, v. 10 (1970), 542–565, provides a useful introduction to the system's development in the Habsburg lands. The changes from the Austrian system that Mirievo introduced in Russia had echoes in the programs and practices of the Polish National Education Commission, of the Jesuit network, and of French reformers both before and after 1789. None, however, seem to have directly influenced Mirievo, who came to propose changes from the Austrian system through his own experience in applying the Felbiger system to the Slavic-speaking, Orthodox villages of the Habsburg empire. For details on Mirievo's work in Russia, see Peter Polz, "Theodor Jankovic und die Schulreform in Russland," in *Die Aufklärung in Ost-and Südosteuropa*, Erna Lesky, others, eds. (Koln, 1972), 119–174. See also J. L. Black, *Citizens for the Fatherland: Education, Educators, and Pedagogical Ideas in Eighteenth Century Russia* (Boulder, 1979), 130–151. On Mirievo's work under

sity. One of the commission's projects endorsed the view of the renowned Lomonosov that the only requirement for admission to a university in Russia should be adequate academic preparation. The commission explicitly defended the rights of peasants to higher education, quoting Lomonosov that "everyone may become a student no matter what his rank or age." While none could doubt that in Russia as elsewhere the goals of this enlightened reform were practical, even utilitarian, their moral dimension was underscored by the commission's declaration that the Russian nobility no more risked "degradation" in attending schools in common with other classes than "when they hear the word of God together with the unfree in the churches."[11]

In some ways, the commission's proposals and plans were not new or original. Catherine had received many plans for an empire-wide educational system offering a basic general education to all, including a very detailed one that she solicited from Diderot in 1777. Indeed, she had published one herself a decade earlier. A curriculum that stressed general education, rather than vocational training, had been the rule rather than the exception in all Russia's modern schools since the great reformer, Peter I, founded them at the beginning of the century. Nonetheless, in 1782 an empire-wide system still did not exist and, though most schools offered general education, or liberal arts and sciences at the gymnasium or at other more advanced schools, most were also professional schools, sponsored by one or another agency to train for itself recruits who were chosen from one or another social class. Despite the emphasis on general education, or liberal arts, most curricula in Russian schools had developed as "professional" education, offered as training for one or another vocation or profession, normally to members of the social class for which that vocation or profession constituted the usual way of life. Indeed, that education came to form an important part of the definition of that class.[12]

Maria Theresa, see Philip J. Adler, "Habsburg School Reform Among the Orthodox Minorities, 1770–1780," *Slavic Review*, v. 33 (1974), 23–45.

11. M. I. Sukhomlinov, *Izsledovaniia i stat'i po russkoi literature i prosveshcheniiu*, 2 v. (SPB, 1889), I, 56. S. V. Rozhdestvenskii, "Universitetskii vopros v tsarstvovanie imp. Ekaterina IIoi i sistema narodnago prosveshcheniia po Ustavam 1804 goda," *Vestnik Evropy*, 1907 (No. 7), 29.

12. The best discussion of the "class-professional" character of the schools remains S. V. Rozhdestvenskii, *Ocherki po istorii sistem narodnago prosveshcheniia v*

The commission that Mirievo chaired developed able staff members, such as N. I. Fuss, who was well versed in the plans and proposals and seriously interested in realizing them in practice. Not surprisingly, much remained only plan or proposal. No new universities, for example, were founded. Nonetheless, a good deal was achieved in practice. The commission founded a teachers' college in St. Petersburg that recruited sons of Orthodox clergy to train as teachers in the new system. In the early 1780s there existed in Russia not many more than 50 state-supported schools, enrolling fewer than 5,000 students. At the end of Catherine's reign, Russia had at least 550 such schools, enrolling 62,000 pupils. It was especially important that the new secondary schools had been placed in towns that previously had no school at all. In sum, at the turn of the century, educational reformers in Russia had to deal not with a *tabula rasa* but with the beginnings of an enlightened system already in place.[13]

2. Planning a New System

Tsar Paul, as in much else, attempted to undo his mother's work in education. During his brief reign the number of schools and students declined. Perhaps the main consequence of his effort was the stimulation of a sense of urgency, underscoring for many the importance of further reform in education. Many were convinced of the importance of the work and were confident that Alexander would provide the necessary leadership. Friedrich LaHarpe, one of the

Rossii v XVIII–XIX vekakh, I (SPB, 1912), 264–281. The combination of general and liberal with technical and vocational education is well described at its beginnings by Max J. Okenfuss in "The Jesuit Origins of Petrine Education," *The Eighteenth Century in Russia*, John Garrard, ed. (Oxford, 1973), 106–130, and "Technical Training in Russia under Peter the Great," *History of Education Quarterly*, 13 (1973), 325–345. Undoubtedly the best analysis of the role of class-professional education in defining, and tightening, class lines in eighteenth-century Russia is Gregory L. Freeze, *The Russian Levites: Parish Clergy in the Eighteenth Century* (Cambridge, 1977), 78–106.

13. M. T. Beliavskii, "Shkola i sistema obrazovaniia v Rossii v kontse XVIII stoletiia," *Vestnik Moskovskogo Universiteta*, 1959 (No. 2), 105–120, concludes that Catherine's reforms were more successful than previously realized. See, e.g., P. Miliukov, *Ocherki po istorii russkoi kul'tury*, II (4th ed., SPB, 1905), 327, which gives for the year 1796 a total of 316 schools with 17,341 students. For these Miliukov figures, see also Hans, *Russian Educational Policy*, 32; Johnson, *Russia's Educational Heritage*, 60, 263.

tutors provided for Alexander by his grandmother Catherine, left Russia when Paul became tsar, returning to his native Switzerland with a French army. In August 1801 he gladly accepted Alexander's invitation to return to Russia to assist his former pupil in the great work of reform. At the same time, Alexander asked another former tutor, Murav'ev, to begin a study for the reform of Moscow University. A minor official, V. N. Karazin, in March 1801 wrote a long letter to Alexander, praising what he presumed was the new tsar's intention to undertake reform. Alexander responded by asking Karazin to draw up some proposals for reform in education. He responded to a suggestion made by P. A. Stroganov by calling together a small group of friends, the so-called Secret Committee, to begin discussion of what needed to be done. In the first months of his reign, then, Alexander found it easy to gather advisors on educational affairs, as on other matters too, who had confidence in him and in the prospects for reform.[14]

In December 1801 the Secret Committee took up the question of education. The committee began its discussion with a detailed proposal from LaHarpe. LaHarpe's draft argued that Russia badly needed an empire-wide educational system, since progress was possible only in societies whose citizenry was literate. He called for the foundation of a ministry of education to supervise the work of a network of universities, which would train the teachers needed to staff a complete school system down to the primary grades. Russia, said LaHarpe, had (or soon could have) three universities, at Moscow, Dorpat, and Vilna. He proposed three more, at St. Petersburg, Kazan, and Kiev. The universities, under the supervision of the ministry, would be the top of the educational ladder, reaching down to the local level, providing control and supervision as well as trained teachers for all the schools in their areas. To facilitate control, LaHarpe suggested that the universities, not any police agency, have censorship authority in all parts of the empire. The Secret Committee all but ignored LaHarpe's plan, in part because the members did not share Alexander's personal esteem for LaHarpe, but also because his proposal was so unexceptional. It closely resembled Mirievo's plans, and many others too, and expressed no better than

14. Arthur Boehlingk, *Friedrich Caesar LaHarpe*, 2 v. (Bern, 1925), II, 40–41; Sukhomlinov, *Izsledovaniia*, II, 116–117; Nikolai Mikhailovich, *Graf Pavel Aleksandrovich Stroganov*, 3 v. (SPB, 1903), II, 5–7, 26–29 (hereafter cited as Stroganov); Shil'der, *Aleksandr*, II, 32–36.

many others the goals and principles and general ideas on organization and curriculum shared by nearly all in enlightened Europe who agreed that state authority was needed to foster progress in education. Since that was a diverse, as well as large, circle, LaHarpe's proposal did not advance the discussion very far.[15]

The Secret Committee's own discussion advanced the argument not much further. Novosiltsev agreed to write up a proposal to flesh out LaHarpe's rather general statement. Stroganov said that, important though the details would be, it was especially important to understand the main goals. Russia needed especially, not "particular reforms" providing better vocational or professional training at one thing or another, but general education for the masses. The masses needed to have the general education that would permit them to become members of society, capable of exercising the full rights of citizenship. On the other hand, Stroganov thought it obvious that Russia needed better professional training as well. He drew upon his knowledge of French practice, which he had studied extensively, attempting to sketch a system that could meet both needs, providing enlightenment through general education for all while also providing specialized curricula for special vocational needs. A bit hazy on detail, Stroganov nonetheless was clear on insisting that a clear distinction needed to be made between education aimed at general enlightenment and education aimed at professional training. Czartoryski agreed that it was important to make that distinction, and suggested that therefore the schools run by the army, to cite one obvious example, should offer technical training in their specialties and not be a concern of the ministry of public education. Alexander thought it difficult, if not impossible, to draw that line in Russia. Army schools, such as the cadet corps, had to offer general education along with professional training, since the students were unlikely to acquire the necessary general education elsewhere, while the schools that provided basic general education also had to offer vocational training in order to be useful to their localities. Stroganov seemed at various times to see the wisdom of both points of view.[16]

15. The notes kept by Stroganov are the main source for the committee's work. For the committee's discussion of LeHarpe's plan, see Stroganov, II, 144–148.

16. *Stroganov*, II, 26–29, 40–44, 208–212, 225–226. The members of the Secret Committee, N. N. Novosiltsev, V. P. Kochubei, Adam Czartoryski, and P. A. Stroganov, had in common not only personal friendship with Alexander, but relative

Vague and meandering though it was, the Secret Committee's discussion outlined a general plan that closely resembled that of LaHarpe, or of Mirievo, or of others. They projected a ministry of education to supervise a system of universities that supervised schools organized in a ladder down to the villages of the whole empire. The schools would operate on a classless, or all-class, basis, providing enlightenment for all by offering general education leading up to a liberal arts curriculum and at the same time the development of improved vocational and professional training. The committee spent little time or energy in providing details. The drafting of detailed plans was left to others, who could take up the work upon the foundation of the ministries. An *ukaz* of 8 September 1802 founded the ministries, including the ministry of education. Novosil'tsev contributed the draft, but the law on the ministry expressed the general ideas agreed upon by the whole committee. The Ministry of Public Education (*Ministerstvo narodnogo prosveshcheniia*) would provide "enlightenment" (*prosveshcheniia*) to the whole "people" (*narod*). The minister's full title was "Minister of public education, of the training of youth and the spread of learning," a title expressing well, if in a general way, the overlapping goals of the new ministry.[17]

Alexander at once introduced a note of confusion by naming Zavadovskii to the office of minister. Zavadovskii had few of the qualities of character or intellect that distinguished many of his colleagues who had served the government of Catherine II, such as A. P. Vorontsov. A "favorite" who served Catherine as chairman of the School Commission, Zavadovskii had shown little interest in pushing forward the reforms proposed. LaHarpe and others complained that Zavadovskii was not a suitable choice, for he was not likely to prove zealous in moving in the direction the reformers had in mind. Alexander saw no difficulty in the appointment, telling LaHarpe that it was no more than a gesture to mollify conservative opinion, while his colleagues in the ministry saw to it that Zavadovskii did not "block the good we are trying to do."[18]

youth (Novosiltsev was the eldest, born in 1761) and yet considerable experience in government. E. E. Roach, "The Origins of Alexander I's Unofficial Committee," *The Russian Review*, v. 28 (1969), 315–326.

17. *Polnoe sobranie zakonov rossiiskoi imperii*, 243–248 (No. 20406).

18. Nikolai Mikhailovich, *Imperator Aleksandr I* (Petrograd, 1914), 363 (Alexander to LaHarpe, 7 July 1803).

Chief among those colleagues was Murav'ev, who was appointed assistant minister on 8 September. On the same day a new agency was founded, the Commission on Schools (*Kommissiia uchilishch*) to serve as the ministry's planning board. Murav'ev was joined on the commission by Czartoryski of the Secret Committee and his friend Count Potocki, one of the ablest of those engaged in the struggle for reform in Poland before the last partition; General Klinger, the director of the First Cadet Corps; and three members of Catherine's old commission, including Fuss. A newcomer, V. N. Karazin, was named chairman. This commission's chief assigned task was to "found universities where they do not yet exist." The universities were to supervise all schools in their areas. The commission was also to work out the details for the schools' "dependence" on the universities and the relationship to the ministry of all the institutions placed under it, including the Academy of Sciences, the Russian Academy, all schools (with the insignificant exception of those under the direct patronage of the dowager empress), all presses, public libraries, laboratories, museums, and all other institutions for the "spread of learning" and, finally, the organization of censorship, now the responsibility of the ministry of education.[19]

This commission had a short career, in good measure because much of its work was well advanced, if not already accomplished in principle. The noble assemblies of the Baltic provinces in early 1802 sent the tsar their plan for a new university in Dorpat. Alexander approved the plan, but changed it almost completely from what the noble planners had in mind. Far from dominated by the nobles, the plans were turned about by the tsar, to provide academic freedom for a self-governing faculty, which was to cooperate with the central government's ministry in providing the education soon to be required of all candidates for places in the state services, regardless of the candidate's social class. In May 1802 Alexander, on a visit to Dorpat, again made clear his support for the faculty's idea of enlightened reform. In September, when the commission began its work, the Dorpat faculty's leader, Parrot, hastened to St. Petersburg to contribute his proposals. Zavadovskii, "bringing up a new objection every day, indeed every hour," did all he could to delay the work, but when Parrot complained to the tsar, Alexander at once

19. *Sbornik postanovlenii po ministerstvu narodnago prosveshcheniia*, 15 v. (SPB, 1875–1902), I, 4–5.

issued orders to implement Parrot's plan. The commission began its work, then, with a detailed draft for a university statute worked out and approved by the tsar.[20]

The contributions of Murav'ev reenforced both the general idea and many of the details of the Parrot drafts for Dorpat. In March 1802 the Secret Committee asked Murav'ev to chair a committee (Potocki, Fuss, and Karazin were the members) to study Moscow University, comparing it to the "best foreign examples" in order to propose reforms for the Russian university. Murav'ev, for whom the best foreign example was without question Göttingen, collected testimony from well-known Göttingen professors. All stressed the importance of academic freedom, made possible by the institutional autonomy of the university, and devotion to the development of the higher learning. Nearly all denounced the evil influence of directives from without, especially from the government or church, and also the danger of offering training and professional education rather than leading the student into the self-development nourished by liberal, humane, studies. Professor Brandes argued that a university must not be an institution for training or "upbringing" but a "scholarly corporation" devoted to higher learning. Moreover, it could not maintain "schoolboy discipline," for in the university the student "learns to walk by himself." August Ludwig Schlözer, who knew Russia well at first hand, warned particularly against the evils of state control, which, he said, stifled scholarship and thus defeated the true purpose of the university.

Christopher Meiners, a well-known historian of higher education, amplified Schlözer's points. He recommended, indeed, that universities be located away from the capital and that the government official in charge of the university not reside in the university town—all measures in hopes of minimizing government influence on the internal workings of the university. Meiners was especially insistant that the university devote itself to higher learning in the liberal arts, avoiding professional, applied training as much as possible, for he was convinced that in the long run humane studies produced better men, men whose values made them also the better

20. Parrot's work in St. Petersburg is carefully described in E. E. Martinson, *Istoriia osnovaniia tartuskogo (b. Derptskogo—iurevskogo) universiteta* (Leningrad, 1954), 53–61. His plan, issued as an "akt" by the ministry, 12 December 1802, is in *Sbornik postanovlenii*, I, 6–12, Bienemann, *Parrot*, 164, prints his complaint to Alexander about Zavadovskii's stalling.

specialists. He wanted particularly to avoid training in law, theology, and medicine, but urged that these faculties stress their history and philosophy. Even in medicine, the student should get as much pure theory as possible, avoiding applied training. Meiners was convinced that the wisdom of his views had been demonstrated in the Habsburg lands, concluding that the failure of much of the reform in higher education on the Göttingen model resulted from tight government and church control in a program that tried to use learning as the path to developing efficiency in state services.[21]

No member of the Murav'ev committee questioned Meiners' assertion that university reform in Austria failed because it was a Roman Catholic state, and succeeded elsewhere in Protestant states. Nor did any wonder whether failure in some measure was inevitable for a reform that tried to combine the absolutist's interest in training efficient and loyal civil servants with self-directed academic freedom, and tried to use the autonomous university itself as the agency to manage a system of lower schools that offered a curriculum prescribed by the central government and stressed drill and memorization in its teaching methods. Murav'ev shared the views of his Göttingen friends and declared that academic freedom was "necessary not only for the development of education . . . but also for raising popular morals." At Murav'ev's request, Moscow University loaned one of its senior professors to the committee. Professor Bause, a Saxon with a doctorate from Leipzig, had long preached that Russians were too ready to borrow from the West and should now concentrate on development of native values, specifically a university curriculum that used the students' native language, Russian, as the medium of instruction. This, naturally enough, was a welcome proposal. The Murav'ev committee then contributed plans that stressed the patriotic, as well as the practical, goal of developing instruction in Russian at the same time that it recommended the corporate autonomy of Göttingen as the best model for university organization.[22]

21. Rozhdestvenskii, *Istoricheskii obzor*, 56−57; Sukhomlinov, *Izsledovaniia*, I, 42−56. Schlözer spent much time in Russia; his first visit was in 1771, and he taught Russian history at Göttingen from 1772. Edward Winter, ed., *August Ludwig v. Schlözer und Russland* (Berlin, 1961), 1−41.

22. Murav'ev quoted in Rozhdestvenskii, *Istoricheskii obzor*, 39. On Bause, see *Biograficheskii slovar professorov i prepodavatelei Imperatorskago Moskovskago universiteta*, 2 v. (Moscow, 1855), I, 68−85.

Parrot and Murav'ev supplied the materials that the Commission on Schools took up at its first meeting in September 1802. The chairman, Karazin, was not present. He had Alexander's consent to locate one of the new universities in Kharkov, his home town, and had already left to begin the preparations there. Murav'ev and Mirievo were not appointed to the commission but took part in all its meetings. The group parceled out the work: Klinger to work out the details of the proposals for the lower schools, Parrot for Dorpat, Czartoryski for Vilna, and Fuss for the other universities. Mirievo argued for a university in Kiev, but after the meeting of 4 October gave up, agreeing to a university in Kharkov instead, together with Moscow, St. Petersburg, Dorpat, Vilna, and Kazan. In late October Karazin returned to St. Petersburg and presented a plan for the university in Kharkov completely different from the Göttingen model, since "everything in Russia should be new and self-developed." His plan was ignored. The commission met for the last time on 22 October, discussing Murav'ev's materials on Moscow University.[23]

The personnel of the commission were also members of the ministry's governing board, titled the Main School Administration, which summed up the commission's work in the first major piece of legislation of the educational reform, the "Preliminary regulation for public education," issued on 24 January 1803.[24] The regulation announced that "Public education in the Russian Empire is a special state department, entrusted to the minister of that department and under his direction managed by the Main School Administration." In order to provide "for the moral formation of the citizenry, corresponding to the duties and needs of each class, four kinds of schools are established, namely (1) village [*prikhodskiia*], (2)

23. The record of the Commission's meetings, printed in S. F. Platonov, ed., *Opisanie del arkhiva Ministerstva nardonago prosveshcheniia* (Petrograd, 1917), 88–90, suggests that the members planned further discussion on Moscow University and offers no hint that they realized that the 22 October meeting would be the last. Members continued to submit materials for the commission's files as late as July 1804. The proposals made by Fuss and Mirievo are printed in Rozhdestvenskii, *Materialy*, 380–395. Sukhomlinov, *Izsledovaniia*, I, 56–58, discusses the various plans, stressing the features and language that appeared in the final legislation in 1803–1804. The best discussion of the commission is Rozhdestvenskii, "Universitetskii vopros," *VE*, 33–37.

24. *Sbornik postanovlenii*, I, 13–21. Many summaries are available, including Rozhdestvenskii, *Istoricheskii obzor*, 50–51; Hans, *Educational Policy*, 37–38. Perhaps the best is in M. F. Shabaeva, ed., *Ocherki istorii shkoly i pedagogicheskoi mysli narodov SSSR: XVIII v.—pervaia polovina XIX v.* (Moscow, 1973), 198–199.

county [*uezd*], (3) provincial or gymnasia [*gubernskiia ili gimnazii*], and (4) universities." Though this definition seemed to call for a class-differentiated system, in detail the system described called for a ladder system, each school leading to the one above, open equally to all classes, and stressing general education at the village level leading to liberal arts at the gymnasium and university levels. The village school stressed reading, writing, arithmetic, and a course based on the text that Catherine the Great's commission provided for the purpose of moral formation, *The Duties of Man and Citizen*. The two-year county school pursued the same goals, introducing the rudiments of history, geography, philosophy, political economy, and natural history. The four-year gymnasium course took all these subjects further, adding modern and classic languages, and taking mathematics through trigonometry. The schools were to follow not only this prescribed curriculum, but even prescribed hours, students spending thirty hours a week in class in a six-day week (half-days on Wednesdays and Saturdays), teachers responsible for twenty class hours each week. The village school was under the direction of an inspector from the county school, who held the ninth rank in the Table of Ranks, only one step from achieving heriditary nobility in the system that Peter the Great created to supplement if not to replace nobility of birth with aristocracy of talent and achievement. The village school inspector, therefore, was meant to be a figure of importance, as was the inspector for county schools provided by the provincial gymnasium, who held the seventh rank and was empowered to "require" the assistance of the local marshal of nobility.

3. The University Statutes

This sytematic embodiment of the "decreed enlightenment" in education led the student up the educational ladder to the university, which was in its curriculum and organization modeled after the quite different sort of enlightenment provided by Göttingen. The regulation divided the empire into six educational districts (*okrugi*), in which all schools were under the control of the six "universities founded for the teaching of sciences at the highest level; besides those already in existence at Moscow, Vilna, and Dorpat, others are founded in the St. Petersburg, Kazan, and Kharkov districts. . . ."

Each university's administration was to be headed by a rector elected by and from among the professors in their "general university meeting." Professors too were to be elected by the faculty and, like the rector, "confirmed" by the ministry. Professors received the seventh rank, rectors the fifth, in the Table of Ranks. The university was required to supervise the work of all lower schools in its district, providing at least one on-site inspection for each school each year, and reporting annually to the ministry's Main School Administration. The Main School Administration was made up of the "curator" (*popechitel'*) of each district and others named by the tsar. The curator was responsible for the good order of all schools in his district and was required to visit his university at least once every two years. Put another way, he was to live in the capital and thus, if the expectations of the Göttingen advisors worked out, would not unduly influence the ordinary process of the university's work and life.[25]

The enlightened absolutist's goal of increased efficiency was stated in section 24. "Five years from the opening of the schools in his district," it read, "no one will be admitted to civil service which requires legal or other knowledge who has not completed study in a state or private school." The next section empowered the universities to grant degrees, the first, *Kandidat,* requiring successful completion of a three-year course and bringing with it the twelfth rank, i.e., "officer" status. The autonomy of the university was furthered by the provision that each university have its own court for its own members, from which appeals could go only to the Senate. The universities were organized into faculties, each to elect its own dean. The four deans and the rector made up the administrative board to manage the university. This autonomous university was required to maintain a "teachers or pedagogical institute" to prepare students for teaching the required curriculum prescribed for the lower schools. These students would be state-supported and upon graduation would be required to serve at least six years in teaching.

25. Alexander named to the first Main School Administration all the members of the School Commission. For all personnel of the Main School Administration for Alexander's reign, see Sukhomlinov, *Izsledovaniia,* I, 490–491. Catherine's old School Commission continued to function until March 1803, carrying out a number of tasks at Zavadovskii's direction and preparing reports on the lower schools. Professor Beliavskii has found that the reports contained much misinformation. S. V. Rozhdestvenskii, "Komissia ob uchrezhdenii narodnykh uchilishch 1783–1803 g. i

On the same day, 24 January 1803, a law "on the establishment of academic districts" listed the provinces to make up each district and appointed the six curators: Murav'ev for Moscow, Czartoryski for Vilna, Klinger for Dorpat, Novosiltsev for St. Petersburg, Potocki for Kharkov, and Manteuffel for Kazan.[26] This law promised separate "statutes" for each of the universities. The Main School Adminstration held an organization meeting that very day. It agreed that Parrot should provide the statute for Dorpat, Czartoryski that for Vilna, and a "general" statute worked out for the others. In March they issued a proposed budget for the universities, agreeing that each should have twenty-eight professors (at 2,000 rubles each), and forty state student stipends (at 200 rubles each), the same figures as Parrot's plan for Dorpat the previous December. Czartoryski submitted a preliminary "akt" for Vilna in mid-April and a final statute that became law on 18 May 1803. Parrot's statute for Dorpat was issued in September. The draft statute for Moscow was ready in May 1803.[27] It was not promulgated, however, until November 1804. Stroganov ascribed the delay to Zavadovskii's sloth, though something more significant may have been at issue. In August 1803 Zavadovskii revised Parrot's draft statute for Dorpat, making it read that the university accept students from "every free class" rather than "every class." The Main School Administration protested that this revision produced "unacceptable conclusions." They argued to Alexander that "abuses which might arise from unlimited acceptance into the university of persons of all classes are prevented by the very rules written into the statute," since before acceptance the student must "present information about his legal status." The Main School Administration's statement was a good deal less clear than Zavadovskii's revision, for it did not indicate what use the university was to make of information about the stu-

---

ministerstvo narodnago prosveshcheniia," *ZhMNP*, 1906 (May), 17–18; Beliavskii, "Shkola i sistema," *VMU*, 1959 (No. 2), 111.

26. *Sbornik postanovlenii*, I, 21–22. Manteuffel was the leader of the noble opposition to Parrot at Dorpat and had been elected "president" of the university by the noble assembly. Alexander abolished the office of university "president" as "unnecessary." Manteuffel knew nothing whatever about Kazan and was soon replaced as Kazan curator. It seems likely that he was appointed simply to keep him busy in St. Petersburg while Parrot and the faculty completed the organization of the new university at Dorpat.

27. Tsentral'nyi gosudarstvennyi istoricheskii arkhiv (Leningrad), fond 733, opis' 28, delo 23, listy 1–11. Hereafter TsGIAL.

dents' legal status. Nonetheless, Alexander favored their explanation, and Zavadovskii was overridden.[28]

Despite the occasional ambiguity, the university statues were in most matters both similar and clear enough on the main goals. All called for universities organized into four faculties and a pedagogical institute. All provided for university autonomy and academic freedom; rectors and deans to be elected from and by the professors and the faculties to set their own standards in teaching, examinations, and all other aspects of the life of each university, as well as forming the censorship authority for each district. All called upon the faculties to teach their subjects at the highest levels, while at the same time extending knowledge through their research and writing. All incorporated the Preliminary Regulation, calling upon the universities to manage the schools of their districts. All made similar statements on goals. Czartoryski's "akt" of 19 April 1803 said that Vilna University served "for the formation of useful citizens, for all classes and all types of state service." The Vilna statute (18 May) declared that the university taught "the sciences useful for the citizen of every class in the various types of state service." Parrot's statute for Dorpat (12 September 1803) said that the university was founded for the "common good" and ". . . therefore accepts as students people from every class of native Russians and foreigners. . . ." The Moscow statute (5 November 1804), and the nearly identical ones for Kazan and Kharkov issued on the same day, defined the university as "the highest learned organization, founded for the dissemination of learning. In it youth prepare for entrance into the various branches of state service. . . . Among the sciences taught in the university are those necessary for all who wish to be useful to themselves and to the Fatherland, no matter what role in life or which service they choose."[29]

The Moscow statute added to the Preliminary Regulation's de-

28. S. V. Rozhdestvenskii, "Soslovnyi vopros v russkikh universitetakh v pervoi chertverti xix veka," *ZhMNP,* 1907 (May), 84–85; Rozhdestvenskii, "Universitetskii vopros," *VE,* 41. For Stroganov's comment on Zavadovskii, see Stroganov to Novosiltsev, 28 October 1804, in A. N. Pypin, *Die Geistigen Bewegungen in der ersten Hälfte des XIX Jahrhunderts,* B. Minzes, trans. (Berlin, 1894), 143.

29. The statutes are printed in *Sbornik postanovlenii,* I, 39–46 (Vilna), 139–199 (Dorpat), 295–331 (Moscow, Kharkov, and Kazan). The reasons that St. Petersburg's statute was not forthcoming are discussed in chapter II. Most differences among the other five statutes proved inconsequential. The exception was the different treatment of theology. At Dorpat the theology faculty was a Lutheran seminary. At Vilna the theology faculty was a Catholic seminary. At the others no provision

scription of the *kandidat* degree, for those who completed the three-year course, a provision for an *attestat* for students who did not successfully complete the course but who "have had the courses for all the necessary knowledge and wish to leave the university. . . ." The *attestat* would show the time spent in study, the courses taken, the recommendation of the professors in those courses, and a statement of conduct signed by the officers of the university. The *attestat* carried with it no right to any level in the Table of Ranks, but it was clearly aimed at providing admission to the services for those who had made some progress in the new system. It was, then, a concession to practicality, for it was obvious that the new system could not soon meet the manpower needs of the services with candidates who had completed the *kandidat*. There were other concessions too. The village school was the base of the new system. Thus, every village, or two, depending on population, "should have" a village school that took in "every class of children, without discrimination by sex or age." The school year in the village was to run "from the end of field work, continuing until the beginning of field work in the next year." The Moscow statute did not repeat the Dorpat statute on accepting students from "any rank or class," but the description of the village school and its place in the ladder system made clear enough the intent to open the system to all classes. However, the village school was not funded by the central government. The universities and other schools were, but it was impractical to attempt funding village schools throughout the empire. In the hope, perhaps, of stimulating local support to make good this lack, the village schools were allowed to teach agriculture, in addition to the required general education subjects. Similar considerations led to other concessions, such as accepting proposals from merchant guilds to add optional courses in "commercial sciences" to the required courses in gymnasia.[30]

4. The Questions Ahead

The concessions did not go so far as to attempt to meet the objections of those who opposed the main thrust of the reform planned.

was made for a theology faculty. Courses in Orthodoxy were listed for the faculty of moral-political science, but no effort to offer these courses was made for many years.

30. Rozhdestvenskii, "Universitetskii vopros," *VE*, 446; Rozhdestvenskii, *Isto-richeskii obzor*, 51–52. Franklin A. Walker, "Popular Response to Public Education

Not all such objections came from defenders of the established elites. Ivan Pnin, for example, was an outspoken foe of serfdom and a well-known advocate of "liberty." Yet his book, *An Essay on Enlightenment with Reference to Russia*, published in 1804, attacked not only serfdom but also the system of education outlined in the Preliminary Regulation.[31] Pnin argued that the goal of education must be to provide the individual with the knowledge that he needed to take his place in society. A single unified curriculum, therefore, was a mistake, for education "can not be the same for everyone, since society is made up of various classes." Thus, the individual should "receive an education appropriate for his estate, occupation, and way of life." The Preliminary Regulation was wrong to provide a single general education program for all. Pnin went into considerable detail, outlining an alternative. He wanted, for example, two different schools at the county level, one offering training in manual arts for craftsmen, another giving accounting and other commercial subjects for merchants. Pnin proposed a completely class-orientated system, for the utilitarian reason that Russia needed sound professional-vocational training at all levels, which he thought more progressive than pursuing some abstract notion of justice in a single system open to all. The proposed classless system, he wrote, showed the influence of the *philosophe* doctrine on the "natural man," a creature "we can conceive only in our minds." Far from a blueprint for progress, such doctrine "contains more metaphysical disquisitions than simple intelligible truths."

Objections such as those from Pnin had no discernable influence on the planning or legislation of the new system, even though some objections were raised by men who held important posts within the new ministry.[32] Nonetheless, they were important objections be-

---

in the Reign of Alexander I (1801–1825)," *History of Education Quarterly* (Winter, 1984), 527–543, based on the periodical press, particularly *Moskovskiia vedomosti* and *Severnaia pochta*, finds much evidence of favorable local response to the government's plans, including donations from many individuals and noble, merchant, and clergy groups interested in founding and assisting village schools in their communities.

31. Pnin's book is reprinted, with helpful notes, in I. Ia. Shchipanov, ed., *Russkie prosvetiteli: ot Radishcheva do dekabristov*, 2 v. (Moscow, 1966), I, 179–231. A generous portion is translated in Marc Raeff, ed., *Russian Intellectual History: An Anthology* (New York, 1966), 126–158. Rozhdestvenskii, "Universitetskii vopros," *VE*, 440–446, describes Pnin's objections and those of others who made similar points.

32. I. I. Martynov, for example, a priest's son close to both Novosiltsev and

cause they expressed the fear of well-educated people, well disposed toward enlightened reform, that the new system could not meet Russia's true need in education. No one in 1804, to be sure, needed to fear that Russia would soon face the consequences of "unlimited" admission to universities of persons of "all classes," as the Main School Administration responded to Zavadovskii in August 1803. The system did not yet exist. Clearly much needed to be done before it could have any consequences, hopeful or fearful. The immediate question was whether the state could and would indeed carry out its plans to develop a set of universities, native institutions staffed by Russians and devoted to higher learning in an unconditioned pursuit of truth. A second question was the ability of such universities to train teachers and provide the supervision necessary for general education, and hence enlightenment, for the whole nation right down to the villages. A third question was the ability of such universities to provide professional training for the servicemen, the bureaucrats, needed to staff an enlightened imperial service, all on an all-class basis to offer not only an enlarged talent pool but a measure of justice as well. These, it hardly needed saying, were difficult questions, not least because they were interlocked, each requiring a measure of success for progress to be made in working out the others.

Perhaps most important, the planners did not say that these were difficult questions, requiring the use of state power to overcome obstacles of many kinds. Instead, the enlightened absolutist plans of Alexander I, unlike those of Peter the Great, did not require that anyone of any class attend any school. Alexander's reformers intended "to lead [people] to improvement by opening paths to their own happiness. . . ." The reformers hoped, indeed seemed confident, that by opening paths to happiness they could allow, not force, Russia to take progressive steps. This meant accepting the Göttingen professor's notion that universities were institutions where the individual learned to "walk by himself" and that had no need, or use, for schoolboy, or military, discipline. It meant reliance on the self-motivation of students and faculty alike to make a success of the reform, for autonomous self-governing institutions were

Stroganov, served as staff director in the ministry while he founded a journal, *Severnyi vestnik,* in 1804 whose first issue published a critique of the new system much like Pnin's.

to cooperate voluntarily in the task of spreading learning to ever-widening circles of people in all walks of life, providing expert scholars and well-trained bureaucrats, both able and willing to advance the country's ability to meet its needs not only in military security and economic development but in patriotic and religious values, and in justice too. It was a high-minded, indeed magnanimous, hope.

CHAPTER II

THE EXPERIENCE OF THE FIRST DECADE

BY THE END of the first decade the six institutions planned were
operating soundly enough to seem worth some praise. Yet, the experience of the decade so disappointed many of the reformers that
they began calling for major changes—in effect, for a reform of the
reform. The two ministers of the period, Zavadovskii (1803–1810)
and A. K. Razumovskii (1810–1816), gave so little active leadership that each university was left to its own devices to work out its
foundation and development. This circumstance magnified the importance of each curator, as well as the particular local situation,
and minimized the importance of the statutes and the ministry. It
was assumed during the planning that Vilna and Dorpat were special and should be treated separately. It was surprising that the differences among the other four institutions proved as significant as
those which made Vilna and Dorpat distinct. It was most surprising
that local conditions, and the details of which individuals did what,
proved more important in the development of universities in autocratic Russia than the directives of the central administration. A
decade that saw the establishment of the Université de France and
the initiation of Humboldt's reforms in education in Prussia was an
age in which Russia's presumed models in education, the advanced
states of the West, pursued centralization. More by default than
intent, Russia did not.

1. Moscow University

Moscow was transformed into a growing institution already making an important contribution in all the areas the reformers had in mind. Moscow thus set the standard by which the other universities' success might be measured, and it proved strong enough to overcome the enormous calamity of 1812. The reform plan, the statute of 1804, was implemented at Moscow a year before its promulgation, for Moscow University was ready for change. Founded in 1755, the university had not grown rapidly. Enrollment rarely reached ninety and was usually about fifty students. Foreign scholars, usually Germans who knew little Russian, predominated on the faculty. Nonetheless, Moscow had become an important institution, realizing one of the goals of Catherine's reformers by making the university the only significant Russian institution of learning that was not a class-professional school. While gentry (and "officers' sons") provided a substantial number of the students, more often than not the majority were non-gentry. Moreover, the life work of many of Russia's best-known "enlightened" figures, preeminently Lomonosov, was intimately connected with the university. The secondary schools attached to the university provided a modern education for substantial numbers of gentry and others. The university press produced works of all kinds, *belles-lettres* as well as textbooks and newspapers. The "circles" of university-connected people were the vehicle for a significant part of Russia's intellectual and cultural life. Most important, Lomonosov's spirit continued, for the university took seriously its commitment to values he cherished in scholarship, academic freedom, Russian patriotism, and all-class education.[1]

When Murav'ev took up his post as curator of Moscow University, therefore, the university's many strengths gave him advantages, while the deficiencies were so clear that nearly everyone agreed that changes were needed. A graduate of the university himself, Murav'ev was a well-known, highly regarded member of the community. The university gladly cooperated with his committee, which

1. For Moscow University in the eighteenth century, see *Istoriia Moskvy v shesti tomakh: tom vtoroi: period feodalizma XVIII v.* (Moscow, 1953), 484–495. N. A. Penchko, *Osnovanie moskovskogo universiteta* (Moscow, 1953), stresses Lomonosov's role. M. N. Tikhomirov, *Istoriia moskovskogo universiteta*, 2 v. (Moscow, 1955), I, 1–75, is especially valuable for bibliography.

studied university organization and, upon Murav'ev's appointment as curator, speedily carried out the installation of a new administration, electing Professor Chebotarev rector.[2]

Murav'ev's task, as he saw it, was to fill out the faculty as rapidly as possible, to encourage and promote scholarly work, to recruit students, to implement the new system by providing the required secondary and lower schools for the district, and to encourage as much community support as possible. The easiest task proved the promotion of community support. Murav'ev sponsored a program of public lectures in which faculty members gave evening courses open to all. The lectures drew overflow crowds of people from all classes. Professor Strakhov's physics course, with experiments performed before the audience, was a special favorite, but all the lectures—on history, literature, and much else—were well received and focussed interest and local pride in the university. There was an outpouring of gifts of money, books, and laboratory equipment. The Ural industrialist Demidov gave 100,000 rubles, intended to aid poor students from Iaroslavl' province. Other gifts made possible the foundation of ten new gymnasia and many county and village schools. By the end of 1804, faculty members had traveled throughout the district, inspecting schools, overseeing the opening of new ones, and implementing the new program.

Murav'ev's efforts in recruiting faculty benefitted from his connections in Göttingen, which enabled him to bring in many able German scholars. Equally important, those connections facilitated efforts to upgrade the work of the Russians. A. F. Merzliakov, for example, the son of a poor merchant from Perm, entered Moscow University in 1799, assisted by a group of nobles that included Zavadovskii. When Merzliakov finished the kandidat exams in 1804, he was appointed to the faculty, as teacher of rhetoric and poetry. Murav'ev took him under his guidance in St. Petersburg, preparing him to undertake doctoral studies. He initiated a program that took in a number of recent Moscow graduates and sent them to western universities, principally Göttingen, to prepare for university teaching. Murav'ev's efforts were successful. Fifteen new

2. E. V. Petukhov, "Mikhail Nikitich Murav'ev," ZhMNP, 1894 (No. 8), 267–269. Unless otherwise noted, the information used in the following discussion of Moscow is derived from Tikhomirov, Istoriia, I, 77–144; Biograficheskii slovar' moskovskago universiteta; and Stepan Shevyrev, Istoriia Imperatorskago Moskovskago Universiteta (Moscow, 1855), 319–412.

men joined the faculty in 1804 alone, four of them Russians. Moscow quickly acquired more than enough to meet the statute requirements in faculty and had few problems of quality.[3] Many of the new faculty members knew little Russian and saw little point in learning. This caused some hard feelings among the Russians as well as difficulties for students, whose grasp of foreign languages was often minimal. Murav'ev was well aware of the problem. His first curator's report to the ministry argued the need to make Russian the language of instruction as soon as possible. By 1812 this problem was all but resolved, for Moscow then had a faculty of thirty-nine, including twenty-five Russians. There were problems, however. Professor of Chemistry F. F. Reis, for example, who came from Göttingen in 1804, could not be persuaded to broaden the coverage of his subject, but persisted in teaching courses limited in large part to exploration of the properties of mineral waters. Yet, in the main, Murav'ev's efforts in providing a quality faculty succeeded well, as Christian August Schlözer, one of Murav'ev's additions to the history staff, proudly reported to his father in Göttingen.[4]

Murav'ev also sponsored the foundation of a number of learned societies and the publication of many new journals and other works. Many of the societies and journals involved the faculty in relationships with other members of Moscow society. Nearly every physician in the area took some part in the work of the new medical society. The new Society for the Study of Russian History and Antiquities, under Professor Chebotarev, drew upon the community interest in the Russian past, stimulating gifts to the library, which rapidly came to hold 20,000 volumes. These books and document collections soon made Moscow a center of historical studies. The work of such organizations helped the development of the university and placed the resources of the university at the service of the district. The physics society sponsored many scholarly "expeditions" that surveyed the district, doing mapping and research into

3. Nikolai Muzko, "Aleksei Fedorovich Merzliakov 1778–1830 gg.," RS, 1879 (January), 113–115; Markus Wischnitzer, Die Universität Göttingen und die Entwicklung der liberalen Ideen in Russland in erstern Viertel des 19 Jahrhunderts (Berlin, 1907), 25–29, 34–36.
4. Schlözer was a good example of the language problem. Students protested when he lectured in German or Latin, laughed at him when he tried to lecture in Russian. D. N. Sverbeev, "Iz vospominanii," Moskovskii universitet v vospominaniiakh sovremenikov, R. A. Kovnator, ed., (Moscow, 1956), 13.

water resources, soil properties, and minerals. In this way, professors I. A. Dvigubskii and P. I. Strakhov became widely known and esteemed figures.

Students were the chief problem. Enrollment increased, to 215 by 1812, and the percentage of non-nobles remained high, seldom less than half the student body. Given the university's obvious strengths, this was a disappointingly small student body. Moreover, the number who graduated were but a fraction of those who entered. Murav'ev, in a special circular issued in 1805, pointed out that students who finished the course were guaranteed officer status, at least the twelfth rank for the *kandidat*, but few were willing or able to stay long enough to meet the requirements of the *kandidat*. To meet this problem, Murav'ev made plans for changes. He continued to insist on thorough entrance examinations, but he dropped Latin as an entrance requirement, apparently a concession to gentry students who found it difficult to match students from the clergy in that subject. He promised a new curriculum for the university's own gymnasium, which he described as a "very useful institution until now," and also for the gentry *pansion,* a boarding school for nobles whose curriculum went from very basic reading and writing through gymnasium- or even university-level introductory courses in most academic disciplines. Murav'ev planned to eliminate basic courses and reduce the size of both schools, in an effort to produce graduates more likely to prove able and willing to succeed at the university *kandidat* level.

Little came of these efforts. Faced with the Napoleonic wars, the government opened a series of military training programs that promised university students commissions in the army, sometimes in as little as six months.[5] Not surprisingly, many students left to enter these programs. In the period from 1808 to 1810, Moscow produced one doctorate, three "masters," and six *kandidats*. The statute provided twelve stipends (4,800 rubles) for those working toward the doctorate and twelve stipends (3,600 rubles) for holders of the *kandidat* working toward the masters degree. There were so few candidates at either level that most of these stipends went unused year after year.

Most students were very pleased with the university, and with themselves for being there. They especially appreciated the atten-

5. *Sbornik postanovlenii,* I, 447, 471, 482.

tion that many faculty members gave them, offering nearly private tutorial instruction. State students, those housed and fed at government expense, lived in the university building under the supervision of a faculty-elected "inspector." Self-supporting students, those who paid for their board and room, often lived in the homes of faculty members. In either case, they received close supervision and help with their studies. Merzliakov was particularly well known, and valued, as the friend and helper of lower-ranking students. For many years he had the first class of the day for first-year students, rhetoric at 8:00 a.m. In the cold and dark, the "candle-light lecture series" the students called it, he would appear with a large mug of hot tea, which the students were sure had been fortified with stronger drink. He began by calling upon a student to hand him a book for the day's lesson, "any book you want." Taking whatever choice the student proffered, Merzliakov would find examples of just what he was looking for and launch into his exposition. Most of his students were charmed, as well as instructed, by Merzliakov's performances.[6]

The same students received much advice from family and friends to leave the university as soon as possible and, especially for gentry, had the way smoothed to a place in a ministry by letters of recommendation from family and friends, if not from the university. Family connections, as well as the government's need for large numbers of new junior officers for the army, made it likely that few students would stay long enough to satisfy the *kandidat* requirements. The statute provided an *attestat* for those leaving for service who had "taken all the courses for the necessary knowledge." Though the statute did not use the term, such men soon came to be designated "actual student" (*deistvitel'nyi student*), and the *attestat* became in effect the degree sought by most students, especially those of gentry origins. At Moscow, attaining the *attestat* required success in examinations given each June. The students found it a worthy goal, for, as one put it, the student *attestat* made one "already an officer, an important man."[7] The failure to produce large numbers of *kan-*

6. E. T. Timkovskii, "Moskovskii universitet v 1806–1810," *Russkie universitety v ikh ustavakh i vospominaniiakh sovremennikov*, I. M. Solov'ev, ed., (SPB, 1914), 69; Zhikharev, "Dnevnik moskovskogo studenta s 1805 po 1807 god," *Ibid.*, 64, 67; Sverbeev, "Iz vospominanii," *Moskovskii universitet* (Kovnator, ed.), 8.

7. Timkovskii, "Moskovskii universitet," *Russkie universitety* (Solov'ev, ed.), 69.

didats, despite the disappointment of some of the reformers, did not mean that Moscow failed to produce better-prepared servicemen, for the university became a sound institution at the student diploma level.

Murav'ev's accomplishment became increasingly evident after his death in July 1807. Neither of his immediate successors, A. K. Razumovskii and P. I. Golenishchev-Kutuzov, had anything like Murav'ev's ability or standing in Moscow society, yet the momentum gained in the Murav'ev years carried the university to steady growth and progress, cut short only by the catastrophe of its nearly total physical destruction in 1812. Razumovskii came from a Ukrainian family well situated in wealth and position, rewards for assistance to empresses Elizabeth and Catherine II. He was among those Murav'ev drew into university circles, serving as president of the university's Society for the Study of Nature and making substantial gifts to it as well as to the university library.[8]

Razumovskii appointed a very able man as his "chancellerist" in the university, Professor M. T. Kachenovskii, who kept things running smoothly. Since Zavadovskii had reduced the schedule of meetings of the Main School Administration to one a month, at most, there was not much business transacted with the ministry. Razumovskii worked on a project to extend the term of the university rector from one to three years, so that the university might benefit from the experience rectors gained by service. The faculty readily approved, but it took years (until September 1809) to gain ministry approval for the idea, not because any opposed it but simply because that was Zavadovskii's pace. Other changes during these years owed little to Razumovskii or to the ministry. In October 1808 the faculty, distressed with some student habits, promulgated a new set of regulations for student behavior. The new rules called upon students to attend class, to study, and to go to church on Sundays. Students would be allowed to leave the university premises on class days only after dinner, and then for no more than two hours. The

---

Henceforth, *deistvitel'nyi student* will be translated as "student diploma." The difference between the diploma and the *kandidat* included more than years in the university but also the degree of success on the annual exams and the preparation and defense of a thesis for the *kandidat.*

8. A. A. Vasil'chikov, ed., *Semeistvo Razumovskikh,* II (SPB, 1880), 1–48, provides details for Razumovskii's life to 1807.

gates would close at 10:00 each night. Any student out after that hour could be sentenced by the university court to a jail term.[9]

Another change was introduced by neither the university nor the ministry. Michael Speranskii, Alexander's chief worker in the effort to reform the state services, planned a program that he hoped would encourage formal study as preparation for state service. His project became law in August 1809. Speranskii pointed out that a goal of the university reform was the production of better-trained men for the state services but that this part of the reform ". . . was not yet achieved in practice." Speranskii's program called for examinations in academic subjects, first of all in Russian and one foreign language, for promotion to rank of "collegiate assessor." The universities were to give special summer courses from May to October. Moscow offered these "civil service" courses in philosophy, history, Roman law, economics, statistics, and languages to prepare *chinovniki* for the examinations. The courses were taught by the regular faculty, indeed were no more than hurried versions of the regular courses. *Chinovniki* were horrified at the law and for a time refused to believe that it was meant to apply to men already in the service. But, in the summer of 1810 about one hundred men took the courses at Moscow, coming to the university after work "tired and hungry," as one of them put it. So few could pass the examinations in the fall that the university substituted for the exams an *attestat* issued by the professor in each course, testifying that the student had studied the material and was "qualified."[10]

In 1810 Zavadovskii requested retirement. Alexander, after some hesitation, turned to the curator of Russia's senior university to replace him as minister, and named Kutuzov in Razumovskii's stead at Moscow. The change in ministers had little immediate consequence for the university. There was a rumor that Razumovskii would clean house in the ministry, starting with the discharge of the staff direc-

9. N. P. Barsukov, "Mikhail Trofimovich Kachenovskii, professor moskovskogo universiteta, 1775–1842," *RS*, 1889 (October), 199; Rozhdestvenskii, *Istoricheskii obzor*, 42; *Sbornik postanovlenii*, I, 596–597; Vasil'chikov, *Semeistvo Razumovskikh*, II, 237–241 (Reinhard to Razumovskii, 13 October 1808). The university did not offer instruction in religion, but the faculty expected that the students would meet the ordinary obligations of communicants of the Orthodox Church.

10. *Sbornik postanovlenii*, I, 582–589; M.[A.] Korf, *Zhizn' grafa Speranskogo*, 2 v. (SPB, 1861), 176–186; "Imperatorskii moskovskii universitet v 1799–1830 v vospominaniakh Mikhaila Prokhorovicha Tret'iakova," *RS*, 1892 (July), 129–130. "Collegiate assessor" was the eighth rank in the Table of Ranks, and brought with it promotion to hereditary nobility.

tor, Martynov. Nothing of the kind happened. Instead, Razumov-skii warmly supported Martynov and used his influence to foster education on the class-professional lines that Martynov, Pnin, and others favored from the beginning. Razumovskii supported the foundation of the new Tsarskosel'skii Lycee, to train nobles for places in the higher civil service ranks, and arranged independence from the state system for the schools run by the Jesuits in St. Petersburg and throughout the western provinces, which were in practice if not law schools for gentry. He supported the introduction of religion into many schools (though not the universities) and the use of clergy as teachers in the lower schools. Clearly, Razumov-skii lacked sympathy for many of the goals and assumptions of the original reform. Yet, for the most part he let alone the universities, the key institutions in the original reform.[11]

Razumovskii's successor at Moscow was an enthusiastic supporter of Shishkov and well known in Moscow's literary circles, where he did what he could to harrass Karamzin, whose "cosmopolitanism" offended most Shishkovites. He arranged the appointment of P. F. Timkovskii as Professor of History. Timkovskii, who completed his doctorate at Moscow in 1808, was a charter member of the university's history society, whose work concentrated on editing old chronicles, seldom touching post-Petrine topics. Kutuzov also secured the addition of a new chair in Slavonic for the university. "The Slavonic language," he argued, "is the root and source of our language. Without a full knowledge of it, one can hardly become a writer." Moreover, for "inexperienced youth" a knowledge of Slavonic "as with a knowledge of religion and our history, is an absolute requirement."[12]

Kutuzov also sought tightened censorship and urged replacing the faculty-elected censorship committee with one appointed by the curator. He spent much effort in trying to ingratiate himself with Razumovskii and in writing absurdly self-congratulatory reports on his work with the university. He also liked to work short hours at

11. Rozhdestvenskii, *Istoricheskii obzor*, 41–42; Vasil'chikov, *Semeistvo Razumovskikh*, II, 64–87; Dmitri Kobeko, *Imperatorskii tsarskosel'skii litsei: nastavniki i pitomtsy 1811–1843* (SPB, 1911), 11–21; J. T. Flynn, "The Role of the Jesuits in the Politics of Russian Education 1801–1820," *Catholic Historical Review*, LVI (1970), 256–259.

12. TsGIAL, f. 733, op. 28, d. 1528, *listy* 1–2 (Kutuzov to Razumovskii, 2 August 1810). The initiative for founding the chair of Slavonic came from Kutuzov, not Razumovskii.

irregular intervals. Yet, as if in spite of himself, Kutuzov contributed to the university's progress. His interest in Slavonic and in Russian national values, while clearly reactionary from the point of view of many of the reformers of 1803–1804 and certainly ungenerous compared with Murav'ev's attitudes, led him to foster the appointment to the faculty of Russians of nationalist views, a fact that helped to continue support for the university, for patriotic views were well received in Moscow society. In 1811 Zhukovskii, who had taken over the editorship of *Vestnik Evropy* from Karamzin, declared that Kutuzov's appointments showed that Moscow University "day by day" came nearer its goal, the making of a "Russian university." [13]

Kutuzov's national feeling led him also, in his own way, to support social mobility. In September 1811 he reported to Razumovskii that a census by the local government had uncovered three teachers in the university who lacked documents to prove that they had legally left their original low classes. Unless they could produce such evidence, the local government intended to return them to their original classes. Kutuzov pointed out that these men were "Russians whose talents give honor to our Fatherland." Hinting darkly that otherwise they might be replaced with foreigners, Kutuzov requested that the ministry take whatever steps were necessary to provide "officer" rank for these men, in recognition of their "long and faithful service." Razumovskii soon obtained Senate approval for commissions for Kutuzov's three teachers. [14] Two "conservatives," faced with the need to choose between promoting Russians from lower classes or seeing academic posts go to foreigners, unhesitatingly chose to support the promotion of Russians.

Neither Kutuzov nor Razumovskii helped the university during the calamity of the French invasion in 1812. [15] Razumovskii joined

13. Vasil'chikov, *Semeistvo Razumovskikh*, II, 64–65: "Universitet v vospominaniiakh Tret'iakova," *RS*, 1892 (July), 128. Zhukovskii quoted in Shevyrev, *Istoriia*, 411. When S. S. Uvarov, Razumovskii's son-in-law, returned from diplomatic duty in Vienna, Kutuzov promptly arranged his election as "honorary member" of Moscow University, in recognition, he explained, of Uvarov's "scholarly attainments." Vasil'chikov, *Semeistvo Razumovskikh*, II, 335 (Kutuzov to Razumovskii, 2 August 1811).

14. TsGIAL, f. 733, op. 28, d. 147, list 1 (Kutuzov to Razumovskii, 25 September 1811), list 11 (Razumovskii to Senate, 16 November 1811), list 14 (Razumovskii to Kutuzov, 6 December 1811).

15. The literature on Moscow in 1812 is immense. The most useful sources for

the Committee of Ministers, the army, and several other agencies in issuing orders to the university to close, or stay open; to stay in Moscow or evacuate to Nizhnii Novgorod, Kazan, or several other places; to return to Moscow, or not return, and so on. Kutuzov, when the French drew near, took 2,000 rubles of university money and fled. Others struggled more courageously. The rector, Professor Heim, managed to evacuate a contingent of faculty and students. Professor Strakhov saved the physics laboratory. Little else was saved. The fire of early September destroyed the main building and with it the 20,000 volumes of the library. Most of the professors' apartments, with their personal libraries, were destroyed. Professor Reinhard was killed in the fires. Strakhov collapsed and died. Others simply disappeared. Its facilities destroyed, its personnel scattered, Moscow University ceased to exist in September 1812.

In October adjunct Druzhinin returned to the city and took it upon himself to send a report on the damage to the ministry. Kutuzov returned in November. Meanwhile, returning faculty members resumed publication of the university newspaper, putting out "back issues" to replace those missed, and promising speedy reopening of the university. The returnees ignored the instructions they kept receiving from St. Petersburg: to go to, or stay in, Simbirsk, Vladimir, and other places. They concentrated on locating members of the university, finding quarters and acquiring the means to reopen for the academic year 1813–1814. To plan the reconstruction, in early January 1813 five professors formed a "commission," since they could not yet locate enough faculty members to constitute a quorum for meetings of the faculty council. By mid-July enough members had returned to resume council meetings. In late August the council published an announcement of the reopening of the university, listing the faculty and the courses to be given. In short, Moscow University reconstituted itself, with no help from the ministry or from other agencies of the central government. While the ministry could do no more than issue meaningless orders,

our purposes are Shevyrev, *Istoriia*, 413–428; Tikhomirov, *Istoriia*, I, 85–94; I. A. Fedosov, "Moskovskii universitet v 1812 godu," *Voprosy istorii*, 1954 (No. 6), 106–117; N. Likin, "Moskovskii universitet v Nizhnem-Novgorode v 1812 gody," *ZhMNP*, 1915 (No. 6), 206–215; Nil Popov, "Moskovskii universitet posle 1812 goda," *RA*, 1881 (No. 1), 386–421; A. N. Popov, "Moskva v 1812 gody," *RA*, 1875 (No. 8), 369–402.

local society provided effective aid. The university's requests for support, published in its newspaper, quickly brought in gifts of money, books (over 12,000 volumes by 1815), use of buildings, and much else. Merzliakov took charge of running volunteer drives, collecting gifts for the university, and he had no difficulty in tapping the city's pride in the university to provide substantial support.

The reopened university was, naturally, much weakened. Many who would not have qualified in 1811 were appointed to the faculty. Some were experienced gymnasium teachers, such as G. I. Miagkov, who became teacher of mathematics. Others were recent *kandidats* of the university, such as I. I. Davydov, appointed adjunct in philosophy. Instruction in French was given part time by the pastor of the local Roman Catholic church. Many chairs were combined, others left vacant. Lacking facilities for them, the university had to turn away many students, though some stayed on as self-supporting "auditors." The state students were reduced to quarters that made study very difficult.[16] Since the university needed its building, the university gymnasium was closed. Nonetheless, 129 students resumed study in Moscow University in September 1813. In the face of the total destruction of 1812, the faculty's cohesion and much local support for the university made possible a remarkable recovery.

2. The New Foundations

In striking contrast with the situation at Moscow, the foundation of new universities at Dorpat and Vilna were the occasions of bitter quarrels, while those at Kharkov and Kazan met an extraordinary combination of hostility and indifference.

The Baltic provinces were ruled by a German-speaking nobility whose provincial diets elected marshals of the nobility who were actually significant figures in local government. Repeated confirmation of their "rights," since Peter the Great wrested the provinces from Sweden in 1710, meant that the nobility ruled. The towns, similarly, were ruled by councils controlled by German-speaking burgers, descendants of the great days of the Hanseatic League. It

16. Kutuzov requested a one-hundred ruble increase (from two hundred) in support for each state student, since many "lacked beds to sleep in or tables to work at," competing with the "other inhabitants" of the city for housing and resources that the destruction of 1812 made very scarce. TsGIAL, f. 733, op. 28, d. 212, listy 1–6 (Kutuzov to Razumovskii, 25 October 1814).

seemed obvious to some that noble diets and merchant town councils were the sort of institutions that could nourish the development of something like constitutionalism. But this was an Old Regime society that was threatened by many aspects of the Enlightenment. It felt itself threatened in the late eighteenth century, when increasing numbers of Lutheran clergymen risked, and often lost, their "livings" by attacking serfdom. One, Garlieb Merkel, became particularly well known for his anguished moral indictment of serfdom, *Die Letten,* published in Leipzig in 1797. Moreover, many forward-looking nobles, including Count Friedrich von Sievers, Livonian marshal of nobility in 1797, agitated against serfdom on the ground that the chronic inefficiency of unfree labor stifled economic improvement.[17]

Defense against such attacks included an attempt to found a university under noble control, to foster the views of the conservative elites, and, by providing higher education at home, to keep youth from the corruption of new doctrines in German or other western universities.[18] In October 1798, with Tsar Paul's permission, the three noble diets drew up a plan for a Protestant "Landesuniversität," under the supervision of a board of curators elected by the nobles. The curators were to elect one of their number to serve as president of the university. Quarrels among the nobles over the location of the university and over faculty appointments caused much delay. In April 1801 Alexander issued an *ukaz* choosing Dorpat as the site, and in May he sent an order forbidding further delay. Count Manteuffel, marshall of the Livonian nobility and noble elected president of the university, brought to Alexander in St. Petersburg the nobles' plan for his approval. In January 1802 Alexander approved the plan, but made some striking changes: the election of a noble "president" was "unnecessary," the faculty would supervise the selection of faculty members and regulate the university's teaching, and would elect a faculty committee to exercise censorship power in the provinces. Finally, two years after the university's opening, inhabitants of the Baltic provinces would be eligible for appointment to the state services only upon completion of two

17. Reinhard Wittram, *Baltische Geschichte* (Munich, 1954), 125–157, remains the superior introduction to the Baltic provinces in the eighteenth century.

18. Unless otherwise noted, the discussion of the foundation of Dorpat University is based on Petukhov, *Derptskii universitet,* 92–309; Martinson, *Istoriia osnovaniia,* 18–120; Bienemann, *Parrot,* 97–160.

years' study in the university. These features foreshadowed the final university reform legislation of 1804. In 1802 at Dorpat they were especially striking, for the main point of the noble plan—noble control—had been pointedly eliminated. The reform made a particularly clear example of enlightened absolutism in practice: the use of state power against the traditional rights of established elites, in pursuit of both utilitarian and moral goals, all for the good of society.

The faculty members engaged at various times over the past years began meeting in the home of one of their number, Georg Parrot.[19] They agreed with the curators to hold a ceremonial opening of the university in April 1802, but agreed on little else, for the meeting became a quarrel over what the tsar really meant by his January statement. At the opening, five professors and nineteen students and the assembled noble curators heard Manteuffel warn the students to avoid "noisy games" and assail those who attacked the social order. Parrot's answering speech offered the students a sympathetic description of the plight of the peasants and urged them not to forget the people whose labors made possible their study. In May Alexander visited Dorpat, which occasioned another ceremonial meeting. While polite with the curators, Alexander warmly congratulated Parrot on his welcoming address, making a point of asking him to send him a written copy. Parrot's speech assured Alexander of the devoted loyalty of the people of the provinces and promised that the university would make no distinction between rich and poor, powerful or weak, except to assure the poor of special concern.

Despite this clear signal from the tsar, the curators continued to argue that the tsar did not mean to displace them as the authorities responsible for the university. In October Parrot decided to go to St. Petersburg to secure a resolution of the struggle. The curators voted

19. Parrot came from Germany to Livonia in 1795, invited by Count Sievers to tutor his son. Parrot was a very enthusiastic exponent of enlightened rationalism of the sort associated with the *Encyclopédie*. He helped Sievers found an Economic Society, modeled after the Free Economic Society founded by Catherine the Great, to work for social and economic reform. As permanent secretary of this organization, Parrot through his writing was well known throughout the provinces. When the noble curators began searching for faculty, his name was naturally proposed, and, with the support of Sievers and his friends, Parrot was appointed professor in January 1801. Bienemann, *Parrot*, 3–94. See also Pethukhov, *Derptskii universitet*, 122–123; Martinson, *Istoriia osnovaniia*, 42–47; Wittram, *Baltische Geschichte*, 170–171.

to refuse him permission to go, but Parrot went and contributed much to the ministry discussions on the new statutes. Returning to Dorpat in December 1802 with Alexander's signature on an "*akt*," which spelled out clearly the university's independence from noble control, Parrot was promptly elected rector by his faculty colleagues. The victory of Parrot and the faculty was inescapably a defeat for local interests. In consequence, the early years of Dorpat University saw nothing comparable to the outpouring of gifts, money, books, and so on, at Moscow. Money donated for scholarships, indeed, was usually restricted to the benefit of noble students, a remarkable development for an institution dedicated to special concern for the lowly. The professors did not seem to mind. As one put it, the arrangements for the new university were a "great triumph for good!" [20]

The "Main School," which was reorganized as Vilna University in 1803, was the product of even more extended struggle for reform than Dorpat. Poland, whose military and constitutional weakness in 1772 made possible if not invited partition, was jolted into reform by partition. Poland's military and constitutional weakness was rooted in traditional institutions and practices, among them the schools. A National Education Commission formed in 1773 directed a major effort to modernize the educational system. The commission, one of whose leading supporters was Adam Czartoryski's father, drew its inspiration from the Enlightenment in France, particularly from the physiocrats. Every working member of the commission, indeed, had spent time, at least a year, studying in France at one time or another. There was in this French-rooted approach to enlightened reform a good deal of secularism, some anticlericalism, and much utilitarianism. On the other hand, the goal of this enlightenment in Poland was not *ecrasez l'infâme*, for many of

20. J. W. Krause, "Das Erste Jahrzehnt der Ehemaligen Universität Dorpat," *Baltische Monatsschrift*, LIII (1902), 242. These are the memoirs, written in 1827, of one of the first professors. The noble curators were recognized in the statute (September 1803) as part of a committee on finances, and the funds collected by the nobles for their planned university were accepted. Klinger, the ministry's curator for Dorpat, argued against any role for the noble curators, but Parrot and the faculty found it useful to have the nobles' official participation, as well as their funds. The faculty member elected rector had the right to decide all questions on which the noble and faculty members of the committee could not agree. M[aximilian] Rieger, *Friedrich Maximilian Klinger: Sein Leben und Werke* (2 v., Darmstadt, 1880–1896), II, 571; *Sbornik postanovlenii*, I, 142, 188.

the leading reformers were churchmen. The president of the commission, indeed, was Ignacy Massalski, the Roman Catholic Bishop of Vilna. Among those who long argued the need for the monarchy to take the lead in sponsoring significant reform were the Jesuits, whose schools were an important part of the educational system and who began the reform process themselves in their schools decades before the first partition.[21]

The commission was fortunate in its beginnings, for 1773 was also the year that the pope suppressed the Jesuit order. Few in Poland, from the most conservative nobles to the most ardent reformers, favored that act. But, when it was accomplished for reasons having nothing to do with Poland, the Polish reformers gained for the use of the new commission the Jesuit schools, the capital investment and supporting funds that went with them, and a pool of trained professional educators, many of whom were sympathetic to many reform goals. Thus the commission was spared the need to persuade the nation that it should at once shoulder a major new tax burden to support a reformed school system. Instead, the commission's schools provided many men, trained and motivated, who helped carry out reforms that eventually included a more just and effective tax system. The commission not only made use of the former Jesuit schools and teachers, but also maintained their administrative system and much of their curriculum as well. The Jesuit academy at Vilna, founded in 1579, was the administrative center for Jesuit schools in the Lithuanian component of the Polish Commonwealth. At its secularization—i.e., assumption by the National Education Commission in 1780—it continued to function as the administrative center for the schools in Poland's eastern provinces. The formal ceremony marking the opening of the academic year 1781–1782 at Vilna featured an address by a former Jesuit, now a lay professor, to the assembled nobles on "not fearing" the new

21. Ambrose Jobert, *La Commission d'éducation nationale en Pologne, 1773–1794* (Paris, 1941), remains the fullest account of the commission's work. A useful up-to-date summary of the whole reform effort is Daniel Stone, *Polish Politics and National Reform 1775–1788* (Boulder, 1976). An incisive discussion, particularly strong on the Jesuits' contribution, is Mark F. O'Connor, "Cultures in Conflict: A Case Study in Russian-Polish Relations: The University at Wilno" (Ph.D., Boston College, 1977), 68–166. On the Jesuits, see also Daniel Beauvois, "Les Jésuites dans l'Empire Russe 1772–1820," *Dix-Huitieme Siècle*, No. 8 (1976), 257–272; Litak, "Das Schulwesen der Jesuiten," *Wiener Beiträge*, Bd 5, 124–137.

curriculum, which he argued was not in fact all that new, but instead the appropriate culmination of changes long under way.[22] In other ways, to be sure, the changes were very great. The commission's basic work, the statute of 1783, divided Poland into two "districts," each supervised by a senior academic center, Vilna for the east, Cracow University for the west. The system, not surprisingly, called for a ladder system down to the village elementary schools, in a pattern quite similar to that brought to Russia by Mirievo. Perhaps more important was the effort of the commission's most able workers, such as Hugo Kołłątaj, to promote a new curriculum that focussed on Polish language, literature, and history as well as on other modern languages and the natural sciences. The commission clearly meant to foster social mobility through education.

Such developments in the goals and scope of education provoked growing opposition, particularly in the eastern provinces, for they were in part at least attempts to alter the essentially religious goals of many older schools and to facilitate important social change. On both counts they were resisted. By 1793 more than half the former Jesuit faculty members at Vilna had departed, many finding that the new curriculum departed too far from their concept of sound reform. Many nobles obviously feared the success of reform. More interested in defending the traditional noble-dominated society than in patriotic renewal of the Polish state, many supported the Confederation of Targowica and Russian intervention, the second partition. In the lands taken by Russia in the partitions, moreover, at least eighty percent of the population was neither Polish nor Polonized, but Lithuanian, Belorussian, or Ukrainian peasants. In these eastern provinces, then, a rise in national feeling among Poles undercut some of the reformers' efforts to extend citizenship, participation in public life and avenues of social advancement, to the low classes, who were also the non-Polish nationalities.

These national, social, and religious tensions were rubbed raw in the second partition and especially in Poland's war against it, which culminated in the total defeat of the third partition in 1795. Catherine the Great in 1773 forbade promulgation of the papal suppression of the Jesuits in the lands taken in the first partition.

22. O'Connor, "Wilno," 104–05.

Thus there remained an independent Jesuit system. Tsar Paul in 1797 announced that he planned to turn all schools in Russian Poland over to the Jesuits. Nothing came of that threatening promise, except acerbation of an already tense situation. Bishop Massalski had been hung in 1793 by Polish patriots who found him too ready to see the wisdom of cooperating with the Russians. Kołłątaj languished in prison, victim of the Russian victory. When the Jesuits from their administrative center at Polotsk, in the zone of the first partition, tried to send an inspection team to the academy (or "Main School" in the education commission's terminology) at Vilna, the rector resisted so acrimoniously that he too was imprisoned. His assistant, the former Jesuit Poczobut, managed to persuade the Polotsk Jesuits not to carry out inspections at Vilna. But at the time of Alexander's accession tension remained high. Educational reform in such circumstances inescapably focussed intense controversy over the encouragement to be given Polish patriotism, religious values, and the justice of the class system.

Alexander determined which camp in the many-sided struggle would have the upper hand. He gave Czartoryski complete freedom as curator of the new Vilna district. Czartoryski made no effort to hide his sympathy for the work of the former National Education Commission. Kołłątaj returned, joined by other able members of the commission, such as Tadeusz Czacki and Jan Śniadecki. Vilna University, the key institution in these reformers' hands, was obviously weak. The frequent turnover in personnel and the legal reorganizations that marked the period of the partitions kept the numbers of experienced faculty low and tended also to keep down student numbers. Though the city grew to a population of more than 25,000 in the early years of the century, and saw considerable advances in economic development, the school did not share in the advances. Indeed, by 1802 student enrollment was but half of that for 1792. Nonetheless, Czartoryski, responsible for producing the new university statute (which was drafted for the most part by the rector, Strojnowski), provided preambles to the foundation *akt* and the statute that called the "rich experience" of the "ancient" Vilna University a special strength upon which the reformers could build. Indeed, it was obvious that the experience of enlightened reformers in Poland, especially the National Education Commission and the Jesuits, made a contribution to the development of the reform statutes. Still, the reformers in Vilna could not doubt that they faced difficult problems in trying to translate the plans into practice. It was simply assumed that the "Main School" staff would remain, the nucleus of the university faculty, and that Strojnowski would continue as rector.[23]

Parrot and Klinger at Dorpat and Strojnowski and Czartoryski at Vilna faced difficult tasks, but the task at Kharkov and Kazan was much more demanding. In neither could the tsar intervene to choose which contending party in a reform effort to support. Instead, at Kharkov and Kazan the reform effort came as an intrusion imposed from the capital, meeting local indifference when it did not provoke hostility.

Karazin was chiefly responsible for the selection of Kharkov, convinced that his home town was bursting with interest in learning. The chief evidence for that interest was a vote by the provincial gentry assembly in September 1801 to provide 100,000 rubles in support of a cadet corps, a military academy, for the education of gentry sons. Overjoyed at gaining Alexander's agreement to locate one of the new universities in Kharkov, Karazin addressed the gentry assembly. He pointed out that the foundation of a new university gave Kharkov the opportunity to become for Russia what Athens had been for ancient Greece.[24] This extravagant estimate of Khar-

23. These developments are given brief treatment (I, 17–25) in what is in other respects the most thorough history of Vilna University and its district, Daniel Beauvois, *Lumières et Société en l'Europe de l'Est: l'Université de Vilna et les ecoles polonaises de l'Empire russe (1803–1832)*, 2 v. (Paris, 1977). The most important Polish account remains Józef Bielinski, *Uniwersytet Wileński, 1579–1831*, 2 v. (Cracow, 1899–1900), which (II, 13–20) outlines developments from 1783 to 1798. A. Bendzius, *Vilnianus universitetas* (Vilna, 1966), 69–101, provides a good summary-outline for developments from 1780 to 1803. For assistance with Lithuanian materials, I am indebted to the late Adolphas Venclauskas of the Clark University library. Czartoryski's role in bringing the Polish experience to the educational reform in the Russian empire clearly was important. The Vilna statute was the first promulgated. Nonetheless, assertions that the Russian reform was little more than a copy of the Polish (e.g., Hans, *Educational Policy*, 37–41) exaggerate that role.

24. "Rech' V. N. Karazin v sobranii Khar'kovskogo dvorianstva 11 augusta 1802 g.," *Russkie universitety* (Solov'ev, ed.), 77. For details see J. T. Flynn, "V. N. Karazin, the Gentry, and Kharkov University," *Slavic Review*, v. 28 (1969), 209–220. Karazin has been the subject of many laudatory works. Among the most useful are Ia. V. Abramov, *V. N. Karazin, osnovatel' Kharkovskogo universiteta: ego zhizn' i obshchestvennaia deiatel'nost'* (SPB, 1891); D. I. Bagalei, *Prosvetitel'naia deiatel'nost' Vasiliia Nazarovicha Karazina* (Kharkov, 1893); N. Tikhi, *Vasilii Nazarovich Karazin; ego zhizn' i obshchestvennaia deiatel'nost'* (Kiev, 1905); A. G. Sliusarskii, *V. N. Karazin: ego nauchnaia i obshchestvennaia deiatel'nost'* (Kharkov, 1955). Two recent accounts of his role in the university's foundation are also very favorable to Karazin: Iurii Lavrinenko, *Vasil' Karazin, Arkhitekt Vidrodzhennia* (Munich,

kov's potential impressed the local gentry no more than Karazin's recommendation that they raise a million rubles for the new institution. After a month's negotiations, the assembly agreed to provide 400,000 rubles for a school that Karazin described as "one of the highest schools in the empire," preparing "youth for social and state service." It would have nine departments, including military science, and would operate "two schools for the low classes, one for agriculture, one for crafts and trade." Kharkov would not, then, be a copy of a German university, for "in Russia everything should be new and self-formed as she is herself." The gentry assembly would elect the rector and a commission for the university's administration. These arrangements, and the gentry's 400,000 rubles, would make the university "independent," Karazin said.[25]

Clearly, Karazins's plans had little in common with the ministry's. Karazin, a member of Murav'ev's committee on universities and chair of the ministry's Commission on Schools, knew well enough the ministry plans. But he proposed something quite different: expanding and improving vocational and professional training in the occupations traditional for each class. There were many, both in Russia and the West, for whom this was a perfectly acceptable "enlightened" goal, as the success of the Felbiger system, among others, testified. Yet, when Karazin returned to St. Petersburg, he found all doors closed to him. None of the reformers, nor any member of the ministry, would consent to discuss the arrangements he had made. In January 1803 the Preliminary Regulation declared the foundation of a university in Kharkov and named as curator Count Seweryn Potocki, Czartoryski's coworker. Karazin was not mentioned. Nonetheless, Karazin spent the next several months traveling back and forth between Kharkov and the capital, trying hard to get the university launched. His efforts included hiring personnel, making purchases for the library, and spending a good deal of university money. In June 1804 Zavadovskii finally made a formal com-

---

1975), 54–78; Orest Pelech, "Toward A Historical Sociology of the Ukrainian Ideologues in the Russian Empire of the 1830s and 1840s" (Ph.D., Princeton, 1976), 44–49. For a judicious introduction, see Ludwig Janowski, "Uniwersytet Charkowski w początach swego istnienia (1805–1820)," *Rozprawy Akademii Umiejętności: Wydział Filologiczny:* serya III, tom IV (Cracow, 1911), 128–136.

25. "Vasilii Nazarovich Karazin, osnovatel' Khar'kovskogo universiteta," *RS*, 1875 (No. 12), 337–338, (No. 13), 61–67. Quotations 62, 76.

plaint to Alexander at the steps taken by Karazin "without any sort of permission." Alexander at once ordered Karazin not to "meddle" further in the university's affairs, and indeed to stay away from it altogether.[26] Karazin's resignation, submitted soon thereafter, was immediately accepted. A number of various sources and ideas were available to those making the university reform, but Karazin's experience showed that the reformers welcomed only concepts congruent with Göttingen's organization and curriculum and at least potentially open to all classes.

Potocki, returning from an inspection trip to Kharkov in June 1804, reported that the university could open at once, for the faculty and buildings were ready. Unfortunately, there were no students. Kharkov was a trade and administrative center with a population of perhaps 10,000. It had a church school, Kharkov College, for clergy, but no gymnasium or other kind of secondary school. Despite Karazin's praise for its intellectual promise, Kharkov could produce no students willing and able to make use of the new "German"-style university. Potocki recommended postponing the university opening until January 1805, while he tried to recruit an entering class.[27]

Kazan was far larger than Kharkov, nearly three times more populous, and had a gymnasium founded in 1758.[28] As in Kharkov, the gentry assembly had recently voted to support a proposal for a cadet corps in the area. The gentry's advice was neither sought nor accepted in St. Petersburg. When the Preliminary Regulation declared a university was founded in Kazan in January 1803, Manteuffel, the gentry elected president of Dorpat University, was named curator. He knew nothing whatever about Kazan, but in that he was not unique. None of those who planned Kazan University knew Kazan, nor did S. Ia. Rumovskii, who replaced Manteuffel as curator in June 1803.

26. N. A. Lavrovskii, "Vasilii Nazarevich Karazin i otkrytie Khar'kovskogo universiteta," ZhMNP, 1872 (January), 91.

27. D. I. Bagalei, Opyt istorii Khar'kovskogo universiteta, 2 v. (Kharkov, 1893–1904), I, 780. On the city, see D. I. Bagalei, D. P. Miller, Istoriia goroda Khar'kova za 250 let ego sushchestvovaniia, 1655-go po 1905-i god (Kharkov, 1912), especially 685–721, on Kharkov College and the district's schools before 1804.

28. N. N. Bulich, Iz pervykh let Kazanskago universiteta 1805–1819, 2 v. (SPB, 1904), I, 18–38; N. P. Zagoskin, Istoriia Imperatorskago Kazanskago universiteta za pervyia sto let ego sushchestvovaniia 1804–1904, 4 v. (Kazan, 1902–04), I, 23–44.

The son of a village priest from Vladimir, Rumovskii won selection for the Aleksandro-Nevskii seminary in St. Petersburg. His talent in mathematics attracted the notice of Lomonosov himself, who arranged an appointment to the Academy of Sciences and study in Berlin. Scholarly contacts with German mathematicians, and the fact that he had once made a trip to Iakutsk, now part of the Kazan educational district, seemed to make Rumovskii the best available candidate for curator of Kazan. Still, he was over seventy years of age and had not been anywhere near Kazan, or indeed anywhere outside the city of St. Petersburg, in at least twenty years.

The quality of Rumovskii's curatorship was soon established. For six months he did nothing whatever. In February 1804 he hired a professor, P. A. Zapëlin, a Mecklenburger with a recent doctorate in history from Göttingen. Zapëlin began teaching world history in the Kazan gymnasium in September 1804. The university's statute was published in November. The statute called for a chair in astronomy, reflecting Rumovskii's interest, but otherwise was identical with Moscow's. Shortly, Rumovskii wrote to the director of the Kazan gymnasium, I. F. Iakovkin, appointing him director of the university. Iakovkin went right to work, reporting to Rumovskii in December 1804 that the university had been "organized." In February 1805 Rumovskii made his first, and last, visit to Kazan. There was no public ceremony, or even announcement, but Rumovskii met with Iakovkin and the faculty, assigned rooms 7 and 8 of the gymnasium to the university, read the statute, and on the next day left for St. Petersburg, leaving Iakovkin in charge. Kazan University had been founded, but not many people were likely to know about it.

3. Faculty

The great differences in the situations of the universities naturally influenced faculty recruitment. Dorpat and Vilna matched Moscow in recruiting well-prepared staffs of professional academics who agreed on the main goals and assumptions of the reform. Kharkov and Kazan added some able individuals, but remained badly understaffed. Worse, their faculties sharply divided on important issues. The ministry offered no assistance in recruiting and no curator requested it, for all seemed willing to handle the matter by themselves.

At Dorpat, Klinger had only to pass on appointments sent up by

Parrot. The faculty that began the year 1802–1803 numbered ten
men, who had been engaged by the gentry curators.[29] Typical was
J. L. Müthel, a pastor's son born in Livonia in 1763. He studied law
at Göttingen before serving in a number of government posts in
Riga. Parrot had no difficulty in filling all vacancies by 1804. The
new men differed in no significant way from those appointed by the
gentry curators. With the exception of Glinka, the professor of Russian, all were Germans or German-speaking natives of the Baltic
provinces and most were sons of Lutheran clergymen. All studied in
German universities, where more than half earned their doctorates.

Vilna matched Dorpat in faculty development, but took longer to
do so. Rector Strojnowski engaged Kołłątaj and several others in a
vigorous discussion in 1803–1804. Strojnowski wanted to recruit
foreigners. He was soon persuaded to go as slowly as necessary to
find qualified Poles for as many positions as possible. With the exception of the medical faculty, most positions in the end were reserved for Poles.[30] Consequently, it took Vilna nearly a decade to fill
out its staff to the statute requirements. Most of the men appointed
had studied in Western universities, more often in France than in
Germany.

Many faculty members at both Dorpat and Vilna thought they
were much overworked. All were required to teach at least two lecture courses each term and to "keep abreast" of their disciplines.
Vilna required each faculty member to present a scholarly paper
to the faculty assembly each year. Moreover, autonomous self-
governing universities required that faculty members assume responsibility for all administrative work, including supervision of
maintenance and security. Service on the district censorship committee, or school committee, or university court, were usually time-

29. A. V. Levitskii, ed., *Biograficheskii slovar' professorov i prepodavatelei Imperatorskago Iur'evskago, byvshago Derptskago, universiteta,* 2 v. (Iur'ev, 1902–
03), contains biographical sketches of all members, short histories of each faculty,
lists of service dates and of courses taught. See also Petukhov, *Derptskii universitet,*
159–161.

30. Czartoryski in 1807 advised the faculty to be open to appointing foreigners,
since continued preference for even "mediocre" Poles over "eminent" foreigners
would "necessarily retard the progress of learning in our country." Beauvois, *L'Université de Vilna,* I, 161. For the additions to the faculty, see *ibid.,* 87–90, 104–116;
Bielinski, *Uniwersytet Wileński,* II, 24–48. Many of the medical professors came
from Vienna, but the outstanding addition was L. H. Bojanus, an Alsatian with an
M.D. from Jena, who became a prolific researcher and writer. Jan Rostanfiński,
"Ludwik Henryk Bojanus," *Księga Pamiątkowa Uniwersytetu Wileńskiego,* Ferdynand Ruszązyc, ed. (Vilna, 1929), 129–134.

consuming and difficult assignments. Both Dorpat and Vilna saw much faculty grumbling at the appointment of professors for the Russian language. Klinger ordered the Dorpat faculty to accept G. A. Glinka, who proved nearly as incompetent as he was lazy. He was replaced in 1810 by A. S. Kaisarov, an able teacher-scholar who soon became one of the most respected members of the faculty. Nonetheless, his appointment was held against Klinger as an act of "despotism." In all other matters, Klinger carefully respected the faculty's statutory rights. Still, many complained at his repeated demands that the faculty do something to curb student violence. Such demands, they thought, showed that the curator was a "creature of the Russians," too ready to stress "discipline." Parrot, several times reelected rector, missed few opportunities to protest what he regarded as violations of faculty rights.[31]

No one at Vilna thought to charge Czartoryski with despotism, for he intervened little in the university's work. The faculty promptly accepted his recommendation to appoint I. I. Cherniavskii as professor of Russian. His colleagues found ludicrous Cherniavskii's repeated complaints of the poor housing and pay he endured in Vilna, and were not amused by his lecture before the faculty assembly, in which he praised the record of the Russian empire in the promotion of religious liberty. Rector Śniadecki sent to Czartoryski a protest at the "capricious" behavior of his Russian professor. But, although Cherniavskii had few students, did little teaching and less scholarship, his faculty colleagues accepted his appointment without protest because they understood the need to have a Russian well placed on the faculty. In other matters the Vilna faculty was quick to defend its rights. Strojnowski, the first rector, was forced out of office because many faculty members came to believe that he overstepped his authority, particularly in showing partiality to appointment of clergy to the faculty.[32]

Dorpat and Vilna offered formal instruction in religion. Both the

---

31. "Wegen Glinka," Klinger explained to Parrot, "es war unsere Pflicht als Auslander der Nation in ihm ein Kompliment zu machen." E. V. Petukhov, *Kafedra russkago iazyka i slovesnosti v Iur'evskom (Derptskom) universitete* (Iur'ev, 1900), 27. See also B. G. Glinka-Mavrin, "Grigorii Andreevich Glinka," *RS*, v. 17 (1876), 75–105. On Klinger's dealings with Parrot and the faculty council, see Martinson, *Istoriia osnovania*, 62–63; Petukhov, *Derptskii universitet*, 169–175, 182–183; Smoljan, *Klinger*, 99–114.

32. Beauvois, *L'Université de Vilna*, I, 58–69, 167–168, describes the work of the faculty council; *ibid.*, 117–123, 139–143, Professor Cherniavskii's career.

Lutheran Church in the Baltic provinces and the Roman Catholic Church in Poland were challenged by the secularizing tendencies that were part of the Enlightenment. For that reason, the foundations of the universities occasioned much anxiety about the organization of state universities that were to provide the training for the next generation of clergy. These anxieties soon subsided. The Lutheran theology faculty at Dorpat was composed of self-confessed "rationalists," for that was what the faculty wanted. Despite initial misgivings, that fact proved no problem for the church in practice. After 1810 the Lutheran Church required candidates for clerical posts from Dorpat University to pass special church-administered examinations testing their command of Latin, Estonian, and other languages, but not theology, Scripture, or doctrine. It was their practical competence, not their ideological-theological leanings, which the church had learned to distrust in Dorpat-trained men.[33]

The religious struggle at Vilna had been even sharper than at Dorpat. Thus, the announcement of the Vilna Statute in 1803 produced some alarm in papal circles, especially since it required study in the seminary at Vilna University for appointment to any clerical post in the provinces of the Vilna district. The papal legate soon reported to Rome that the church had nothing to fear from the new institution, in which, he said, theology was in "good hands."[34] The seminary at Vilna was slow to organize and by 1812 had produced only six graduates. But the struggle over the appropriate balance between religion and secular concerns at the university nearly disappeared as soon as the university began to function.

Unlike the quite homogeneous faculties of Moscow, Dorpat, and Vilna, those at Kharkov and Kazan were remarkably diverse in origins and education. Moreover, neither was able to complete its staff, filling the positions listed in the statutes, at any time before 1815. In both, faculty recruitment was left almost completely to the curator.

33. Petukhov, Derptskii universitet, 297–298.

34. M. J. Rouët de Journal, ed., Nonciatures de Russie, 4 v. (Vatican City, 1952), III, 361–362 (Arezzo to Consalvi, 21 November 1803). Some were distressed by these developments. Professor Frank of the medical faculty became a sharp foe of Strojnowski because he thought that theology was unscientific and thus unworthy of a place in a decent university. When Strojnowski's successor as rector, the world-famous mathematician Sniadecki, also proved a moderate on religious issues, Frank bitterly attacked him too. On one occasion Frank requested Czartoryski to abrogate the rector's election and to apoint him, Frank, rector. Beauvois, L'Université de Vilna, I, 63, 268, 332–333; Bielinski, Uniwersytet Wileński, I, 108–114.

Potocki began his search by making offers to a number of scholars at Cracow. All declined the chance to move to Kharkov. Potocki obtained most of the early recruits in Vienna. Of the twenty-one engaged by the end of 1805, eleven had the rank of professor and seven were Russians. Among the Russians the best known were I. S. Rizhskii, professor of Russian literature who was repeatedly elected rector until his death in 1811, and I. F. Osipovskii. Rizhskii, educated in the seminary at Pskov, was a former teacher in the cadet corps in St. Petersburg and secretary of the Holy Synod; he had published a good deal on various topics in literature and linguistics. Osipovskii was also a seminary graduate who completed study at the Teachers College founded in St. Petersburg by Catherine the Great's School Commission, where he particularly distinguished himself in mathematics and was soon appointed professor. These men represented the best of the old system, which the new universities were designed to replace: sons of clergymen, seminary-educated, with advanced training quite abreast of the best European practice in teaching secular subjects.

Potocki also recruited from two other groups: Slavs from the Habsburg Empire and Germans from German universities. The mathematician A. I. Stoikovich was the leader among the Habsburg Slavs. A Serb, graduated from Pressburg Academy, he took a doctorate at Tübingen. In 1803, under increasing pressure from Habsburg authorites to convert to Roman Catholicism if he wished to continue his career as an educator, Stoikovich gladly accepted Potocki's offer to escape this dilemma by moving to Kharkov. The largest group consisted of the Germans, among whom was I. E. Schad, a Franconian with a degree from Ghent. Born a Roman Catholic, Schad received his early education in Catholic seminaries, but left them and his Catholicism to become a prolific exponent of Kantian idealism. The havoc in Germany caused by the Napoleonic wars drove many to Kharkov, including the best known, C. F. Rommel of Marburg University, who turned down Potocki's offer in 1803 but was glad to have it renewed in 1810.[35]

35. Bagalei, *Opyt istorii*, I, 485–539, provides biographical sketches of the faculty members for this period. Sukhomlinov, *Izsledovaniia*, I, 64–99, and Janowski, "Uniwersytet Charkowski," *Rozprawy*, 189–218, discuss many of the leaders and Potocki's role. For details, M. G. Khalanskii, D. I. Bagalei, *Istoriko-filologicheskii fakul'tet Khar'kovskago universiteta za pervyia 100 let ego sushchestvovaniia 1805–1905* (Kharkov, 1908); I. P. Osipov, D. I. Bagalei, *Fiziko-matematicheskii fakul'tet Khar'kovskago universiteta za pervyia sto let ego sushchestvovaniia 1805–1905*

Potocki's success in recruiting Germans was behind some of the university's most serious problems. First, the Germans taught in German or Latin, thus making much of their work inaccessible to most Kharkov students. Second, turnover was very high. The staff never came up to the statutory number because many Germans left as soon as possible. Most important, the university's statutory autonomy did not work well, for it was undermined by the faculty's inability to agree. The Kharkov district included all of "left bank" Ukraine and the three provinces fashioned from the territories conquered from the Turks by Catherine the Great. Providing inspections of the schools of this huge area kept many faculty members out on the none-too-developed highways for long periods of time. The Germans found this a particularly onerous task, for which they had little training or desire, a fact that led to much friction between them and their faculty colleagues. The Germans wanted the faculty council to insist on better academic preparation and work from the students. The Russians in turn often accused the Germans of making academic demands irrelevant for students preparing for entry to the Russian state services. Osipovskii, for example, forcefully denounced Schad's teaching of Kantian philosophy, which he thought forced students to contend with a dream world of idle speculation, entirely out of contact with anything "real." [36] Another point of contention was the Russians' usual solution to controverted issues: sending them to the curator in St. Petersburg for resolution. The Germans thought that no way to run an autonomous university.

On Rizhskii's death in 1811, Stoikovich took the lead in urging the ministry to appoint the rector, since he thought that allowing the election called for by the statute likely would mean the election of a German, which would split irreparably an already divided faculty. Potocki refused to take that step. Instead, the statute was

(Kharkov, 1908); L. N. Zagurskii, *Opyt istorii Iuridicheskago fakul'teta Imperatorskago Khar'kovskago universiteta* (Kharkov, 1906).

36. Bagalei, *Opyt istorii,* I, 701–702. For his fight against "reactionary Kantism" Osipovskii has been well regarded in Soviet accounts. See, e.g., I. N. Kravets, "T. F. Osipovskii, vydaiushchiisia Russkii filosof-materialist i estestvoispytatel'," *Voprosy filosofii,* 1951 (No. 5), 111–120. Bagalei, *Opyt istorii,* I, is a very detailed account of the university up to 1815. See, *ibid.,* 282–292, on the working of the faculty council. A useful summary of Bagalei's massive work is the same writer's *Kratkii ocherk istorii Khar'kovskago universiteta za pervyia sto let ego sushchestvovaniia* (Kharkov, 1906), 1–115, which is itself summarized in S. M. Korolivskii, *Khar'kovskii gosudarstvennyi universitet im. A.M. Gor'kogo za 150 let* (Kharkov, 1955), 7–53.

changed, conforming to Moscow's precedent by lengthening the rector's term to three years and, it was hoped, reducing the friction that arose at election time. Stoikovich was elected to the new three-year term. His election set off the sort of bitter controversy he had feared. Charged, among other things, with unfair treatment of Russians, excessive unauthorized absences, poor teaching, and illegal trade in imported wines, Stoikovich vigorously defended himself, in large measure by attacking others. In 1813 Razumovskii invited Stoikovich to apply for a leave. Instead, Stoikovich requested retirement on full pension, received it (for reasons of "health"), and left permanently.[37]

Life in the town of Kharkov did not lighten the German professors' burdens. The town's xenophobia was strong and mounted as the Napoleonic wars progressed. Many Germans were also alarmed at local standards in food, housing, and especially in sanitation. Noting that annually births in Kharkov were exceeded by deaths, including the deaths of seven German faculty members in five years, they asked the university medical faculty to conduct an investigation of the reasons for the high death rate, especially of "healthy middle-aged people, in large measure foreigners," in short, themselves.[38]

The faculty situation at Kazan was perhaps worse than at Kharkov. After Curator Rumovskii appointed Iakovkin director of the new university, there followed no election of a rector or of deans, nor organization into the faculties described in the statute. Meetings of the faculty soon became little more than quarrels in which faculty members, to no avail, demanded their statutory rights. They could not persuade Iakovkin, or Rumovskii, to recognize a faculty vote. Zapëlin, the first professor, compared his Ph.D. from Göt-

37. Bagalei, *Opyt istorii*, I, 301–302, 338–339. Potocki pointed out that all faculty members with the rank of professor were eligible for election to the rectorship, but urged the election of a Russian who would "know the language and customs of the country." *Ibid.*, 300. See also N. Lavrovskii, "Epizod iz istorii Khar'kovskago universiteta," *Chteniia v Imperatorskom obshchestve istorii i drevnostei Rossiiskikh pri Moskovskom universitete*, 1873 (No. 4), smes, 2–35.

38. Bagalei, *Istoriia goroda*, 91; Khalanskii, *Istoriko-filologicheskii fakul'tet*, 150–159; "Iz vospominanii professora Rommelia o Khar'kovskom universitete," *Russkie university* (Solov'ev, ed.), 79–83. The low quality of life had one advantage for the university. In 1806 the provincial governor arranged to turn over to the medical faculty for instructional purposes the bodies of "unknown suicides found in the streets," which provided an average of five cadavers a year for the medical faculty's work.

tingen with Iakovkin's meager credentials and concluded, loudly and often, that he should be rector and Iakovkin dismissed. Zapëlin was the one dismissed. Iakovkin reported that he was a "disorderly" individual who caused trouble. The original faculty appointed in 1804, six men, had short careers. By 1807 two had died and four were dismissed, charged with causing "disorder."[39]

Rumovskii not only took Iakovkin's advice on personnel matters, but in June 1805 warned the faculty that "the council is not a court over the director." It was wrong, he said, for the faculty to "take votes after the director has left the room," for that was "contrary to the statute confirmed by His Majesty."[40] Rumovskii's view, clearly inconsistent with both the letter and the spirit of the statute, was repeatedly challenged by newly arrived faculty members. By 1812 Rumovskii had hired enough men to meet the statute's authorized number of professors at least twice over, but turnover was so high that at no time did the faculty approach that number. In 1812 Kazan had seventeen professors, eleven short of the statute number, all but two of whom were foreigners.

Typical of those who stayed more than briefly was M. I. Herman, a well-known philologist who had completed a doctorate at Göttingen but in the turmoil of the Napoleonic years could find no secure position in Germany. He came to St. Petersburg in 1805, uninvited, and applied to Rumovskii for appointment to Kazan. Rumovskii personally gave him a little test in Latin, as he did with nearly all applicants. At Kazan, Herman at once joined the opposition, astonished to find that he had been misled by Rumovskii into believing that the statute "ruled" in Kazan when it was obvious that such was not the case. He was unhappy too that the gymnasium provided so little effective language teaching, so that students were ill equiped to begin university study. At Iakovkin's suggestion, Rumovskii warned Herman to restrain his "vivacité," which was unsuitable in a "place where tranquility and good order should rule." Otherwise, Rumovskii concluded, "it may turn out to

39. E. V. Petukhov, "Peter Tseplin, pervyi professor Kazanskogo universiteta, 1772–1832," *ZhMNP*, 1902 (No. 2), 352, argues that Zapelin's "very highly developed self-love" was as much responsible for his dismissal as Iakovkin's "indefensible behavior." Details on careers of all Kazan faculty members are in N. P. Zagoskin, ed., *Biograficheskii slovar' professorov i prepodavatelei Imperatorskago Kazanskago universiteta 1804–1904*, 2 v. (Kazan, 1904).

40. Bulich, *Iz pervykh let*, I, 288.

your disadvantage."[41] Herman fell silent. The threat in Rumovskii's advice was clear to a man who had travelled far to secure appointment to a university faculty. Rumovskii, prodded by Minister Razumovskii to "follow the example of Moscow University," i.e., implement the statute, in 1810 told Iakovkin to organize faculty elections for rector and deans, though the elections took place only after Rumovskii's death and the arrival of a new curator, M. A. Saltykov, in 1813. The decade-long struggle to establish faculty governance in accord with the statutes showed how difficult it was in places such as Kazan and Kharkov for many Russians, even those whose educations included experience in the West as well as in St. Petersburg, to grasp the intent of the statute on such matters. Many educated Russians had long since internalized the standards and aspirations implicit in the plans developed from Göttingen's model, as the careers of men such as Murav'ev well illustrated, but that process clearly had not yet spread in the provinces beyond St. Petersburg and Moscow. This was a problem no more intractable, perhaps, than that of developing a faculty of native Russians at Moscow. Nonetheless, after a decade's experience, it remained a problem not yet solved.[42]

There were many faculty members for whom their Russian colleagues' unwillingness, or inability, to implement the statute was not the most severe difficulty. Most foreigners found Kazan a difficult, even dangerous, place to live, regardless of the university situation. Kazan spread over a huge area (the squares were really "steppes," one of the Germans declared), whose streets were axle-deep quagmires in rainy seasons and stifling dust-bowls in dry. Constructed almost entirely of wood, Kazan frequently suffered devastating fires. A high death rate resulted from almost continuous epidemics of one kind or another. Moreover, the Germans found themselves unwelcome outsiders, never invited to dinner or to any social occasion. Local officials persisted in talking down to them, using the personal form "ty" even in official business. Local authority responded to the threat of the Napoleonic wars by organizing a commission in 1806 to watch out for subversives. This commission re-

41. Bulich, *Iz pervykh let*, I, 73–79. Quotations 75, 78. See also Zagoskin, *Biograficheskii slovar'*, I, 208–209.

42. Razumovskii's attempts to encourage Rumovskii's understanding of the need for faculty elections included sending him a model ballot box. Bulich, *Iz pervykh let*, II, 272.

quired the foreign professors, there being few other potential subversives to watch along the Volga, to surrender their passports, to submit to prolonged questioning and to much rude treatment. Iakovkin protested at the unfair, indeed deliberately humiliating, treatment of the foreign faculty members, but he had no success in moderating it. Local hostility to the university, combined with low faculty morale, often complicated by excessive use of alcohol, contributed to the faculty's inability to make much impact on the quality of life in Kazan.[43]

The university faculties obviously faced widely differing situations, but only Vilna faced serious competition for control over the schools of its district. In the eastern third of the Vilna district, which was made up of the provinces taken from Poland in the first partition, the Jesuits had been protected by Catherine the Great and continued to run a successful school system. In the towns with both a Jesuit academy and a public gymnasium, the Jesuit school always had more students than its neighbor. In 1811, for reasons having nothing to do with education, the Jesuits' *de facto* independence was granted legal recognition. Meanwhile, in the southern third of the district, one of the former National School Commission's more nationalistic reformers, Czacki, organized a lycée at Krzemieniec that he hoped to develop into an independent university. The lycée did not get that far, but it went well beyond the regular gymnasium course and functioned as the administrative center *de facto* of an autonomous district within the district. Vilna's rector, Śniadecki, tried hard to get both the Jesuits and Czacki to accept the lead of the Vilna program, but with little success. The Jesuits found it incredible that anyone would presume to offer them instruction on how to run schools, and Czacki persisted in concentrating on developing Polish language, literature, and historical studies. Vilna stressed science and mathematics, which Śniadecki and a clear majority of the faculty were convinced was the most effective use of their resources. Neither the Jesuits nor Czacki agreed, and both ran effective systems that competed with that supervised by Vilna University. Śniadecki repeatedly protested these developments to Czartoryski, but could not persuade the curator to intervene. All three sets of schools

43. Bulich, *Iz pervykh let*, I, 93–94; N. P. Zagoskin, ed., *Sputnik po Kazani* (Kazan, 1895), 473–500. Zagoskin points out that between 1775 and 1832 Kazan experienced no major famine, but the city's "reputation for epidemics" and serious fires remained well deserved.

offered up-to-date science and social studies, together with patriotic
and religious-moral values, if in varying proportions and emphases.
Czartoryski apparently found that the variety provided richness and
strength rather than cause for alarm.[44]

4. Students

The other universities might have envied Vilna its competitors,
for no other district had to be concerned with a proliferation of
schools. It was instead a particularly burdensome task for each to
stimulate the development of lower schools at all. The most important problem was the scarcity of students. Vilna had relatively little
trouble attracting students with the ability, preparation, and motivation to take advantage of its offerings. Starting with an enrollment of 150, by 1810 Vilna regularly had more than 500 students.
The crisis of the war in 1812 drove that number down to fewer than
200, which was no reflection on the university. Magisters and doctorates were few, but more than half of Vilna's students stayed long
enough to earn a student diploma. No other university, including
Moscow, came close to this rate of success in the decade. Dorpat by
1812 enrolled 259 students, more than Moscow but far fewer than
Vilna. More than half of Dorpat's students stayed less than a year,
thus keeping very low the number of diplomas awarded and, in fact,
making it impossible to offer the three-year course sequence for the
kandidat outlined in the statute, for there were too few students to
undertake the upper-division courses. At Vilna the overwhelming
number of students were nobles. At Dorpat all but a handful were
nobles or sons of German merchants or clergymen.[45]

44. The struggle between the Jesuits and Vilna is detailed in Beauvois, "Les
Jésuites," *Dix-Huitieme Siècle; A. Sapunov, Zametka o kollegii i akademii iezuitov v
Polotske* (Vitebsk, 1890), and A. Beletskii, *Istoricheskii obzor deitel'nosti Vilenskago uchebnago okruga,* otdel tretii (Vilna, 1908), which is devoted to developments in Vitebsk and Mohilev provinces. For discussion of Czacki's "district within
a district," see D[aniel] Beauvois, "École et société en Ukraine occidentale 1800–
1825," *Revue du Nord,* No. 225 (1975), 173–184.

45. Beauvois, *L'Université de Vilna,* I, 314–317, discusses student enrollment
and the sources bearing on that topic. E. V. Petukhov, *Statisticheskiia tablitsy i lichnye
spiski po imperatorskomu iur'evskomu byvshemu derptskomu universitet* (Iur'ev,
1902), provides details on Dorpat students. Martinson, *Istoriia osnovaniia,* 111–
120, argues that Dorpat provided the means for advancement of Estonians and Lat-
vians. The paucity of examples, only two belonging to the period before 1815,
suggests that the case is overstated. There was an exceptional Latvian serf, whose
outstanding academic record made him almost a celebrity. He made a career for

Kharkov in the fall of 1805 had fifty-seven students. Enrollment grew to 118 in 1812. Most were from the clergy and enrolled as "state" students. Except at Dorpat, the reformers had not considered charging students with tuition. All were either "self-supporting" or "state," i.e., housed and fed at state expense. State students were obligated to serve six years, most in teaching in the lower schools of the district, upon graduation. Few, as it turned out, actually took up teaching, in part because few finished the student diploma course, let alone the *kandidat*. Gentry and merchants, the classes that might have provided self-supporting students, did not do so, while townsmen, craftsmen, or peasants and other low "obligated" classes seldom could qualify academically. Potocki worked at some steps to meet these problems. In 1806 he secured increases in the number of state student stipends and opened a new *pansion* to house and feed fifty gentry students at state expense while they did diploma course work in the university. These students were not to be held to six years in teaching. Potocki was astonished that gentry of the Kharkov region could not imagine that a fourteen-year-old should consider any alternative to immediate entrance to service, usually military. He hoped the economic need that undergirded much of this attitude could be met by increased financial aid for students. In the short run, however, these steps seemed to have had no effect on local society's continued indifference, and sometimes hostility, to the kind of education the new university offered. The Kharkov gentry had voted to support a military training school, a cadet corps, and then agreed, if a bit grudgingly, to Karazin's proposal for expanded professional-vocational schooling. The gentry's expressed desires and expectations in education were not being met by a "German" university.[46]

Kazan was perhaps even more indifferent than Kharkov. In 1804

himself as manager of a mirror factory in Vyborg. See also Petukhov, *Derptskii universitet*, 231; A. Hasselblatt, G. Otto, eds., *Album Academicum der Kaiserlichen Universität Dorpat* (Dorpat, 1889), 9.

46. Bagalei, *Opyt istorii*, I, 788–810. Precision is not possible in discussing student numbers at Kharkov, or for that matter at the other universities. For example, at Kharkov in 1809 enrollment reported by status, state or self-supporting, totaled 91, by class origins 88. Bagalei doubts that either figure was correct, since subtracting departures during the year brought enrollment down to something like 72. The second qualification for admission to the *pansion*, after noble status, was certifiable poverty, indicating that Potocki's goal was to meet the gentry's economic need in order to attract them into the system. *Sbornik rasporiazhenii*, I, 108–109, 117.

Iakovkin simply designated the senior class of the gymnasium as university students, producing a student body of forty-one, all gentry and all but six state students. Enrollment grew to forty-nine, the peak, in 1807. In that year twenty-four left to enter a new officer-candidate program in the army. Few degrees or diplomas were given, nor were more than a handful held to the obligation to serve six years as teachers. On the rare occasion when an effort was made, the student's family invariably managed to get some official in another agency to support application for an exemption, which the Ministry of Education always granted.[47]

With the notable exceptions of Moscow and Vilna, all the faculties filled their reports to the ministry with complaints not only at the paucity of students but particularly at the weak ability, preparation, and motivation of those they had. At Kazan the faculty once refused to certify an able student for assignment to a teaching position in a district school, instead sending a less-qualified candidate, because they wanted to keep the able student in the university.[48] Naturally, such problems contributed to each other. If the districts could provide few students to the universities, the universities could provide few teachers for the district schools. Each university faculty gave much time and effort to organization of a Pedagogical Institute, whose academic program was offered by the regular faculties, and to visiting all the schools of the districts.[49] Since the faculties could do little to provide teachers, the assistance they could offer was discouragingly minimal. The Dorpat faculty, which was able to provide only nine teachers in ten years, in 1807 reported

47. For the delighted reaction to their sudden promotion to university status, see memoirs of two members of the first class, S. T. Aksakov, "Vospominaniia," *Sobranie sochinenii*, S. Mashinskii, ed., 4 v. (Moscow, 1955), 121–124; V. I. Panaev, "Vospominaniia," *Vestnik Evropy*, 1867 (No. 3), 219–225. Panaev fell deeply in love with one of Iakovkin's daughters and remembered her and her family with genuine affection for the rest of his life. This doubtless contributed to his warmly positive picture of the university, which is contradicted by Aksakov and all others. See also Bulich, *Iz pervykh let*, I, 140–145.

48. Bulich, *Iz pervykh let*, I, 395.

49. A good summary discussion of the institutes is in Shabaeva, *Ocherki istorii shkoly*, 270–273. Shabaeva points out that "we have very little information on what actually went on in the pedagogical institutes" and suggests that means that little went on. Useful detail may be found in A. M. Tkachenko, *Rol' Khar'kovskogo universiteta v razvitii shkoly v pervom tridtsatiletii sushchestvovaniia universiteta* (Avtoreferat dissertatsiia, Kharkov, 1950), 4–29; T. V. Shurtakova, *Rukovodstvo Kazanskogo universiteta razvitiem nachal'nogo i srednogo obrazovaniia v uchebnom okruge v 1805–1836 gg.* (Avtoreferat dissertatsii, Kazan, 1959), 5–17; Petukhov, *Derptskii universitet*, 201–207.

that the university school committee's task was impossible. Dorpat assigned one of its most able and respected members, Professor Morgenstern, to head the Pedagogical Institute, and saw much effort by many able men.[50] That much hard work by able people should produce so little result was especially frustrating. But similarly discouraged reports also came from other faculties, which had not made so great an effort in teacher-training but were nonetheless disappointed at the meager results. Though none wanted to spell it out too clearly, it seemed obvious that the reform was failing in other ways too. The universities, as each complained, produced so few teachers that it was hopeless to look for signs of the enlightenment in the countryside that was envisioned by LaHarpe and many others. Equally discouraging, if not often noted in the reports of university faculties, the universities had too few students to make much impact on the talent pool available to the state services and, since the great majority of the students came from the established elites, the impact of the all-class principle seemed hard to notice.

Discouragement at the minimal results achieved was not universal. Curator Klinger, for example, usually filed quite optimistic reports, noting that things went well in the Dorpat district. Klinger may have been more correct than he realized for, though there could be no doubt that deficiencies persisted, it was also true that worthwhile steps were taken. The number of students in the lower schools of the Kharkov district, for example, doubled in the decade 1803–1813. While the Kazan faculty could not provide many new teachers, they were able to assist several communes of state peasants in organizing their own schools. In short, there were signs of progress.

The signs were hard for many to see, not only because faculty members were often struck by the low quality of their students and especially by their lack of motivation, which made student discipline a serious issue in every university except Vilna. Moscow's new discipline code of 1808 was matched in each of the others by 1813. After years of complaints that students failed to study, or come to class, or disrupted classes, or filled their time with fighting with

50. Morgenstern, German-born and Halle-educated, was a respected teacher and scholar who also served as university librarian. Under his direction, the library grew to 65,000 volumes, the largest and perhaps the best in the university system. *Uchenye zapiski tartuskogo gosudarstvennogo universiteta*, No. 262 (1970), is a special issue devoted to Morgenstern's career, including articles on his work as director of teacher training (28–39) and as librarian (48–60).

both townspeople and each other, drunkenness, stealing, cheating, lying, gambling, and so on and on, the Kazan faculty council in 1813 appointed a special committee to write new regulations. They were promulgated in 1815 in two versions, a "long" one and "short" one designed so that each student could have his own copy.[51] The short version informed students that they were "obliged to pay attention in classes" and be "diligent and careful in their work." They should avoid "drunkenness, immodesty, and deceitfulness" and were forbidden to gamble for money, or to leave the university without first informing the faculty and paying their bills. The long version provided the rationale for the new rules, pointing out that students had privileges in society because they were students, preparing themselves both morally and academically to serve society. They should strive to be worthy of their privileges by fulfilling their academic obligations, by being religious, and by avoiding drunkenness, fighting, cheating, and so on. A similar set of new rules at Dorpat also warned against firing guns in the university buildings or going about the town in disguises.

Detailed rules were not much help. Even Dorpat University loomed large in a town of four thousand. Students, proud of their special status, which set them above others, and little distracted by academic work, found outlets for their energies in almost constant rounds of window-breaking, setting off fire alarms, harassing townspeople, and fighting with both townspeople and each other. The student body was well beyond the capacity of the faculty, or local police, to control. Klinger, in 1811, suggested that professors would be well advised not to have windows on the street side of their homes, since there was no way to prevent students from repeatedly breaking them. In 1815 some students, sixty or more, on a prank attacked some local people, killing one and badly injuring several others. The next day, enraged townsmen chased students off the streets, beating any they could catch. The tense situation eased only when the university court turned over seven alleged ring-leaders to the local authorities for a criminal trial.[52]

The violently destructive fun with which many students brightened their lives was quite innocent of any political, or perhaps even

51. The "short" version is printed in Zagoskin, *Istoriia*, I, 542–543; the "long" in *Sbornik rasporiazhenii*, I, 266–270.

52. Petukhov, *Derptskii universitet*, 244–257, 275–286; E. Cheshkhin, "Studencheskiia bezchinstva v Derpte 1804," *RA*, 1887 (No. 10), 265–281.

moral, significance. Neither *fronde* nor *pugachevshchina*, it was no more than the entertainment that appeals to the less than sophisticated in many times and places.[53] Nonetheless, it did contribute to doubts about the worth of the reform, for an essential element of the reform was reliance on the voluntary self-motivated cooperation of all, including students, to make a success of the enterprise. Since the path that students chose did not seem to include taking on careers in teaching but did include wild destructiveness, some questioned the value of the reform itself. Some, indeed, gave up. Professor Rommel at Kharkov University, for example, was an able scholar. He published a number of textbooks designed to improve language training in the district. He served most of the faculty committees that administered the university and chaired the school committee, which served also as Kharkov's pedagogical institute. In his courses he found few students could keep up, while the few with adequate ability and preparation were nonetheless not interested. They wanted only an *attestat*, a certificate enabling them to enter a service career as soon as possible. Rommel found too that most provincial and county school officials were retirees from the military who wanted as little contact with him as they could manage. Rommel married a Kharkov woman, the daughter of an army major, but still found himself regarded as an unwelcome outsider. In 1814 he resigned and, while a typhoid epidemic raged in Kharkov, left the district, never to return.[54]

53. That the rewards for such behavior were more social and psychic than economic or political does not mean it was without importance. There was, to be sure, much violence in late-eighteenth and early-nineteenth century Russia that was purposeful response to political and economic pressures. For introductions see George L. Yaney, *The Systematization of Russian Government: Social Evolution in the Domestic Administration of Imperial Russia 1711–1905* (Urbana, 1973), 102–111; Richard Pipes, *Russia Under The Old Regime* (New York, 1974), 155–157. This sort of purposeful, even rational, use of violence was not the problem at Dorpat, or the other universities. Valuable discussions of the place of non-rational—perhaps better, sub-rational—violence in the culture of premodern rural peoples (though some of them live in cities in the twentieth century) include Lawrence Stone, *The Crisis of the Aristocracy 1558–1641* (Oxford, 1965), 223–234, and Peter N. Stearns, *Be A Man! Males in Modern Society* (New York, 1979), 127–145, especially 142–143. An interesting discussion of this phenomenon in the American South, Elliot J. Gorn, "Gouge and Bite, Pull Hair and Scratch: The Social Significance of Fighting in the Southern Backcountry," *American Historical Review*, 90 (1985), 18–43, wisely rejects (39, note 70) the assertion, sometimes made in the literature of the subject, that this sort of violence is somehow peculiar to the Irish and Scots.
54. "Vospominaniia Rommela," *Russkie universitety* (Solov'ev, ed.), 80–83.

5. St. Petersburg

No university was founded in St. Petersburg until 1819. Instead, Novosiltsev, district curator, arranged the reorganization of Catherine the Great's teachers' college, renamed the Pedagogical Institute. In January 1804 he secured a new budget for the staff and one hundred state students. With the able assistance of Stroganov, he outmanuevered several government agencies to obtain the historic "building of the twelve colleges," which gave the institute an excellent location, directly across the Neva from the Winter Palace.[55] Novosiltsev delayed the foundation of a university in the capital because he did not want a university organized on the terms agreed upon for the others. He wanted a university in St. Petersburg, but he sought a quite different sort of institution and, unlike Karazin at Kharkov, had the political sense to delay the foundation until it was likely that his views might prevail.

Novosiltsev's regulation was far more detailed than the university statutes' sections on their pedagogical institutes, and required a much stricter regime.[56] The chief officer of the school, under the curator, was a director appointed by the curator, not a rector elected by the faculty. Indeed, all officials were appointed, none elected. The faculty was required to meet twice monthly to discuss the school's academic affairs, but all financial, disciplinary, and administrative affairs remained the concern of appointed officials. Novosiltsev gave firm guidelines to the faculty. The university statutes listed the subject areas to be taught and required each faculty mem-

---

55. Czartoryski, *Memoirs*, I, 309–310, says that Novosiltsev decided "for the present" to delay the foundation of a university. V. V. Grigor'ev, *Imperatoriskii S.Peterburgskii universitet v techenie pervykh piatidesiati let ego sushchestvovaniia* (SPB, 1870), 3, suggests that "one may think" that the reformers thought that it was too difficult to recruit faculty for four new universities at once, but could safely postpone St. Petersburg's university, since the city had other institutions giving advanced instruction. Grigor'ev was careful to note that this is only a suggestion, for there is no evidence that the planners held this view. Since it was not too difficult in fact to recruit new faculty and since new faculty were recruited for the institute, Grigor'ev's suggestion is not persuasive. See also M. V. Iogansen, "Istoriia Zdaniia 12 kollegii vo vtoroi polovine XVIII veka i pervoi polovine XIX veka," *Ocherki po istorii Leningradskogo universiteta* (N. G. Sladkevich, ed., Leningrad, 1962), 191.

56. Novosiltsev's "regulation" is in *Sbornik postanovlenii*, I, 233–255. A good summary account of the institute's development is in Shabaeva, *Ocherki istorii shkoly*, 270–273. See also L. N. Dudareva, *Podgotovka uchitelia i razvitie pedagogicheskoi nauki v Peterburgskom-Petrogradskom universitete v period s 1819 po 1917 god* (Avtoreferat dissertatsii, Leningrad, 1969), 3–8.

ber to offer two courses each term in his area. Novosiltsev prescribed the courses, and gave directions on the method. "It is forbidden to dictate lectures in class," he wrote.[57] The students also received clear directions. They could leave the institute building only with a pass from the inspector of discipline. On Sundays all were required to attend church, in a body under the direct supervision of the inspector. At ten o'clock, all were to "lie down to sleep." Clearly, Novosiltsev accepted neither university autonomy nor the Göttingen view that higher learning had no place for "school boy discipline."

The institute's mission was the training of teachers for the gymnasia of the district. It recruited its students from the clergy and offered them a two-year general liberal arts course, with "strict" examinations at the end of each year. In the third year, the student took courses in the area he proposed to teach and did supervised practice teaching in St. Petersburg schools. In the university institutes, students practiced teaching also, but almost always by preparing lesson plans and giving occasional lectures in their professors' courses in the university. In the first decade, the institute provided 330 reasonably well-prepared teachers for its district. None of the universities came close to that record. Novosiltsev might well have argued that the results showed that he was right to insist on strictly controlled, "decreed enlightenment," on a traditional class-professional basis.

Novosiltsev did not trumpet success, for he left government service in 1810, a deeply troubled man whose problems with alcohol, whether cause or consequence of his other problems, seemed to end his career. His place at St. Petersburg was taken by S. S. Uvarov, Minister Razumovskii's son-in-law. One of Uvarov's first steps was to appoint Christian Friedrich Gräfe, a Saxon with a Leipzig doctorate, professor of classics. An accomplished classicist himself, Uvarov thought that a "future university" needed such scholars. The faculty Gräfe joined was composed of men recruited from two sources, Slavs from the Habsburg Empire, usually graduates of Vienna University, and Russians from the clergy, often graduates of Catherine the Great's teachers' college.

I. S. Orlai, himself a native of "Carpatho-Ruthenia" who entered service in Russia in 1791, helped Novosiltsev recruit Habsburg

57. *Sbornik postanovlenii*, I, 241.

Slavs, who, he pointed out, were able teachers and scholars whose native language and religion made them sympathetic to Russia, "their ancient fatherland."[58] To the scholars he contacted, Orlai stressed the advantages of "scholarly service" in Russia, describing the rank, 2,000-ruble salary, pension benefits, and education of children at state expense. These men served the institute well. M. A. Balugianskii, for example, son of Uniate clergy and educated at Vienna, taught law and economics, served in the Ministry of Finance and with the "Second Section" of the tsar's chancery, which produced the Imperial law code under Nicholas I. No other "Carpatho-Ruthenian" rose so high, but several held post in many government agencies while also teaching in the institute.

The Russians, clergy-born graduates of the old teachers' college, had careers in teaching but also served some agency or another in which they wrote a book, establishing themselves as the specialist on one matter or another. E. F. Ziablovskii was typical. A former seminarian, he graduated from the old teachers' college, then spent several years teaching in various schools in Siberia. He wrote a book on the lumber trade and served with several agencies, including the Ministry of Commerce. At the institute, Ziablovskii was placed in charge of the program for state officials required by the 1809 law. Obviously, Novosiltsev did not take Göttingen as his model. He brought in no German nor German-trained Russian for his faculty.[59] Uvarov changed that, adding Gräfe to his staff and encouraging the appointment of several institute graduates who were sent abroad in 1808, such as D. S. Chizov, who returned from Göttingen in 1811 to teach mathematics.

In 1811 Uvarov began a program of public lectures, doubtless modeled after the successful program at Moscow, which soon drew

58. Orlai studied medicine at the St. Petersburg Medical-Surgical Academy and served several agencies, including the army. The facts of his life before entering Russia are not well established, but it appears that he was a classmate in the Uniate seminary at Lvov of P. D. Lodii and others he helped to recruit for the institute's staff. Tamara Baitsura, *Zakarpatoukrainskaia intelligentsiia v Rossii v pervoi polovine XIX veka* (Bratislava, 1971), 23–29, 39–46, 150–157. See also E. M. Kosachevskaia, "M. A. Balugianskii v Petersburgskom universitete," *Ocherki* (Sladkevich, ed.), 40–43. In their official papers (*formuliarnie spiski*) both Balugianskii and Lodii, sons of Uniate clergy, wrote that they came from "noble Hungarian" families. E. M. Kosachevskaia, *M. A. Balugianskii i Peterburgskii universitet pervoi chetverti XIX veka* (Leningrad, 1971), 28.

59. Grigor'ev, *S.Peterburgskii universitet*, 11–26, provides brief biographies of all faculty members in this period.

audiences of one hundred or more to systematic expositions on public law, state finance, and other subjects unlikely to draw crowds for entertainment value. In short, at St. Petersburg serious work was going on and, though a university had not yet been founded, St. Petersburg Institute by 1815 had made progress toward the development of a high-level academic institution. Nonetheless, in 1813 Uvarov was dissatisfied. The "hopes" he held when taking up his curatorship had proved "illusions," he wrote.[60] The scion of an aristocratic family, Uvarov studied at Göttingen from 1803 to 1806 and thereafter entered the diplomatic service, posted to Vienna. He wrote a book in French, calling for development of a Russian center for Oriental studies, which contained a sophisticated analysis of Russia's strengths and needs in education. Translated into German and Russian, appearing in Moscow's *Vestnik Evropy*, his work attracted the notice of the academic community as well as of the tsar. Though a generation younger, Uvarov's intellectual development and values were very close to those which animated the work of the reformers in 1802–1804.[61] Named St. Petersburg's curator, he worked diligently, reorganizing the gymnasia program, adding faculty and courses to the institute, arranging that institute graduates qualify for entrance to the Academy of Sciences, writing a book on the teaching of history, and much else.

Yet Uvarov was unhappy, not so much that progress was slow but that in order to get along in the ministry, he found it necessary to "compromise" with "extremists," some of whom "lumped together French books and Napoleon." The turmoil of the war years provided the setting, and part of the cause, of bitter quarrels in which Uvarov often found both sides "wrong." He remained convinced that the reform of 1802–1804 was in essentials the best path to

60. For discussion of Uvarov's situation and views 1810–1813, see J. T. Flynn, "S. S. Uvarov's 'Liberal' Years," *Jahrbücher für Geschichte Osteuropas*, v. 20 (1972), 482–483.

61. Uvarov's exact status at Göttingen is not established. For a judicious weighing of all the evidence, see Cynthia H. Whittaker, *The Origins of Modern Russian Education: An Intellectual Biography of Count Sergei Uvarov, 1786–1855* (DeKalb, 1984), 13–14. This superior work became available after the completion of my study. It is rich and thorough, making obsolete in almost all respects all previous accounts of Uvarov's career. It is gratifying for me, therefore, to see that my view of Uvarov is congruent, though not of course identical, with Professor Whittaker's. For analysis of Uvarov's book and its implications, see *ibid.*, 19–29, and Cynthia H. Whittaker, "The Impact of the Oriental Renaissance in Russia: The Case of Sergej Uvarov," *Jahrbücher für Geschichte Osteuropas*, v. 26 (1978), 503–524.

follow. Uvarov's growing sense of being out of step with colleagues in the ministry helped make clear an important development. A decade of experience with the new system had convinced many that the reform had not worked out and that the reform itself needed reforming.

CHAPTER III

THE BIBLE SOCIETY REFORM:
THE DUAL MINISTRY

"THE FOUNDATION of our universities," wrote Kochubei in December 1814, "has not produced the beneficial results which the government expected."[1] Kochubei's observation was part of a veritable avalanche of reform proposals made during the years 1814–1820. Many were solicited by Alexander, but many more were submitted unbidden, for many Russians remained confident that the tsar was open to ideas for change. The proposed reforms ranged from basic constitutions to minor alterations in local government, from the abolition of serfdom to strengthened police and censorship. The decade of the Bible Society's influence, then, saw little thought given to abandoning reform. The era dominated by the great struggle with Napoleon was instead a time when the nature and direction of reform in Russia was vigorously debated.[2]

1. "Zapiska grafa V. P. Kochubeia o polozhenii Imperii i o merakh k prekrashcheniiu i bezporiadkov vvedenii luchschago ustroistva k raznyia otrasli, pravitel'stvo sostavliaiushchiia," *Sbornik Imperatorskago Russkago Istoricheskago Obshchestva*, v. 90 (1894), 12. Hereafter *SIRIO*.

2. S. Frederick Starr, *Decentralization and Self-Government in Russia 1830–1870* (Princeton, 1972), 92 points out that the term "constitution" is often inappropriate. "The government was bombarded with proposals for localized administration, many of which received the rather confusing title of constitutions." A generous selection of the proposals with which the government was bombarded is printed in *SIRIO*, v. 90 (1894) and in *Sbornik istoricheskikh materialov, izvlechennykh iz Arkhiva Sobstvennoi Ego Imperatorskago Velichestva Kantseliarii*, v. 7 (SPB, 1895). For discussion of several proposals printed here, and several that are not, see A. V. Predtechenskii, *Ocherki obshchestvenno-politicheskoi istorii Rossii v pervoi chetverti XIX veka* (Moscow, 1957), 295–417; Kosachevskaia, *Balugianskii*, 216–258; Helma Repczuk, "Nicholas Mordvinov (1754–1845): Russia's Would-be Reformer" (Ph.D., Columbia University, 1962), 67–120. For Alexander's address to the

Alexander himself outlined a far-reaching reform plan in 1818 in his address to the Parliament of Congress Kingdom Poland. The notion of adopting a parliamentary system, one of the highlights of the address, clearly appealed to the tsar, though he thought it necessary first to build up an efficient administration. The hostile reaction of much of Russian society to this speech may have helped to convince Alexander that the time for constitutional reform remained yet some considerable distance in the future. The "revolt" of the Semenovskii guards regiment in 1820, the news of which reached him at Troppau, where he and Metternich were meeting to consider the threat posed by recent revolts in Spain and Naples, seemed genuinely to frighten Alexander, making postponement of reform even more likely. In any event, though Alexander did not abandon the goal of reform, few of the particular reforms projected were attempted in practice. The last decade of Alexander's reign came to be regarded as a period of reaction.

But it was not meant to be so, as the changes made in the university reform help to make clear. Kochubei argued that the reforms of the previous decade were "preliminary steps, requiring completion or strengthening so that Russia, having made great strides towards enlightened reform . . ." might continue to make progress. He proposed the merger of the Ministry of Education with the Directorate of Spiritual Affairs in order to achieve benefits of "unmatched importance." He recommended recruiting students from the clergy, not because of their superior morality but because the clergy seemed the only class likely to provide students in numbers adquate to "develop a learned class." Still, morality was the key issue. "Our universities," he wrote, "are similar to German universities and are filled with professors brought in from Germany." From that, Kochubei concluded, "no little disquiet follows." Such men "cannot direct the moral formation of the youth entrusted to their care. The main goal of education is the development of morality. Experience shows that morality has no firmer foundation than religion. Therefore, religion should be the first guide for the education of youth." Consequently, "it is certain that uniting the Ministry of Education with the Directorate of Spiritual Affairs would have great benefit for education."[3]

Congress Kingdom Parliament, see Frank W. Thackeray, *Antecedents of Revolution: Alexander I and the Polish Kingdom 1815–1825* (Boulder, 1980), 44–47.

3. "Zapiska Kochubeia," *SIRIO*, quotations 6, 12, 13.

Kochubei's remarks were hasty and lacked detail. Indeed, he said that "this is not the place for a lengthy discussion of this matter." That was unfortunate, for a discussion of some details might have been helpful. It was not true, for example, that the universities were "filled" with German professors. Moscow had long since solved that problem, which had never existed at St. Petersburg and Vilna. At Dorpat a German faculty was entirely appropriate, while Kharkov and Kazan could not hold many of their Germans for very long. In short, there were problems in this area, but Kochubei did not seem well informed about them. Similarly, his complaint that "we do not need universities modelled after those of Germany . . . ." especially "when no one studies in them," not only overstated the paucity of students but gave no hint of a solution. There were, clearly enough, problems yet to be met in recruiting students. But neither in the planning stages, 1802–1804, nor after a decade's experience did Kochubei, or any of his colleagues in the Secret Committee or ministry, take up questions that could give a note of precision to the reform's goals. No goals for student enrollment had been set, either in total numbers, or by class origins, or in graduates to be provided for civil service posts or any other. Thus, the complaint that the universities had too few students always had to be a general complaint, for it had never been considered, let alone agreed upon, how many would be enough to suggest that the reform was a success.[4]

Kochubei's remarks well illustrated the state of mind of many among the original reformers, showing little knowledge of developments in the universities and a deeply felt sense of disappointment. Most important was the expression of hope in the power of religion. In May 1812 Alexander said that he was "persuaded that religion is the most powerful instrument in raising the morals of a people and that, when maintained in purity, it is the strongest pillar of support for the State."[5] This persuasion dominated the course of the universities in the decade to follow.

4. Kochubei and Speranskii seemed to agree that the universities might be replaced with a "system of lycees" that would be "the very best system [of schools] which Russia could adopt." Rozhdestvenskii, Istoricheskii obzor, 76. While a "system" of lycees, "gymnasia of higher learning, giving both university and gymnasia courses" (ibid., 75), was not developed, several were opened, chief among them the Tsarskosel'skii lycee that Speranskii proposed in 1808. Rozhdestvenskii (ibid., 74–77) discusses the lycees, private schools for gentry, and other alternatives to the universities in 1810– 1815, none of which became serious rivals to the universities.

5. Judith Cohen Zacek, "The Russian Bible Society 1812–1826" (Ph.D., Columbia University, 1964), 30.

Whether it was confidence in religion or despair at the failure of enlightenment made little difference. Most reform proposals presented to Alexander in 1814 to 1820, including Kochubei's, said that change was needed because of "abuses" in the system. The abuses included crime, bribery, and stealing, as well as incompetence, sloth, and stupidity. The basic problem, then, lay with the men in the system, not with the design of the system itself. What needed reforming was the motivation of those who entered public service. Religion seemed the likely path to that reform, especially since the secularism or rationalism of the enlightenment, the apparent alternative, had been tried and found wanting.[6]

Turning to religion in the universities was attractive also because it was easy. Few opposed it. The university faculties, especially at Kharkov and Kazan, had called repeatedly for the introduction of religion into the curriculum precisely because, they said, training for the public services was inescapably a moral enterprise.[7] Also, they had discipine problems with students that they hoped could be addressed by inculcating some religion into student lives. Moscow and St. Petersburg had required church attendance from the beginning, while Vilna and Dorpat had full theology programs. Hence, stress on religion in the universities promised no more than a shift in emphasis, not the need to strike off in new directions.

Despite the universities' long interest, the turn to religion in education did not arise from the universities. It was, rather, the consequence of a general movement. The religious revival that swept post-Napoleonic Europe took many forms, from new appreciation of the values of traditional churches to a new Romantic mysticism of nature. Among the more significant figures to respond to the new mood was the tsar, who was deeply stirred by the great crisis of the Napoleonic invasion, the most deadly peril for Russia's national existence in centuries, and then by the stupendous victory over France that made him the Tsar Liberator of Europe. Turning to reli-

6. Speranskii was a good example. He told Alexander in 1815 that he "wrote the statute" for the Tsarskosel'skii lycee, which "without immodesty" he thought "incomparably" better planned "than all our universities." Nonetheless, the heart of the matter, he wrote to Alexander in 1816, was that "all right-thinking people have long since realized that the basis of our so-called public education is very inadequate." The "doctrine of Christ," he concluded, must become the "rule for education." Kobeko, *Imperatorskii Tsarskosel'skii litsei*, 7; Rozhdestvenskii, *Istoricheskii obzor*, 106.

7. For examples, see *Sbornik rasporiazhenii*, I, 212–214, 266–270.

gion led Alexander to found the Holy Alliance and the Russian Bible Society. Given the strength of the Europe-wide wave of religious enthusiasm and the intense personal participation of the tsar in it, it was surprising that the turn to religion in the Russian universities was slow to develop. It was October 1817 before the merger that Kochubei recommended in 1814 was carried out. The Ministry of Education and the Directorate of Spiritual Affairs were united in a new Ministry of Religious Affairs and Public Education. The change was less significant than it seemed. The minister, A. N. Golitsyn, gained no new authority. He had replaced Razumovskii as Minister of Education in August 1816. Since its foundation in 1810 he headed the Directorate of Spiritual Affairs, which concerned the non-Orthodox, and was procurator of the Holy Synod since 1805. The new joint ministry, then, only united in one office responsibilities that were already united in Golitsyn's hands.

Golitsyn, as head of the Bible Society, directed the agency that embodied the hope that a change of heart could provide the motivation to build a new, truly reformed, Russia. Naturally, into the work of the ministry Golitsyn brought many Bible Society people. They brought with them special difficulties. Honest, well-motivated Bible Society people thought that institutional, organizational, or, as they usually put it, merely "external," change was not important. Thus, they gave it little attention. That meant that they ignored, almost on principle, important issues, such as recruiting students, faculty governance, and teacher training. Thus, Bible Society appointments entrusted the universities to men who knew little about the schools or, more rarely, to hypocritical careerists who were not seriously interested in either the schools or religion. In either case, the problems encountered in the first decade were not likely to be met by thoughtful solutions put forward by knowledgeable educational professionals.

1. The "All-Class" Question

One question, working out in practice the implications of the "all-class" principle, was settled. It was not particularly difficult, for it had been decided in essentials before Golitsyn took office. Taken seriously, as threat or promise, in the days when Parrot and Zavadovskii struggled over its place in the new university statutes, the universities' right to admit all academically qualified candidates without regard to class origins had made little impact in practice. Dorpat and Vilna remained nearly noble preserves. St. Petersburg Pedagogical Institute recruited mainly from the clergy. Enrollments at Kharkov and Kazan were so low that they had little influence at all. Only Moscow made progress in developing an all-class student body, but Moscow had been all-class since the days of Lomonosov and remained in 1815 a small institution. Nonetheless, questions and complaints arose regarding the social class of some students.

In November 1811 the tsar made a complaint.[8] Alexander pointed out that the universities had been founded so that "all might contribute to the well-being of the nation through learning." But, no one left his class by "mere admission" to a university. Students from low classes, the "obligated," had to complete the "whole course" in order to qualify for a new status in society. Alexander thus reaffirmed the right to promotion in social class through education, while setting standards for such promotion. Too often, students from lower classes imitated gentry by getting a university *attestat*, sometimes certifying no more than admission, and using the *attestat* to secure a post with a slot in the Table of Ranks. Thus, they contributed to their advancement, not by "learning" but by manipulating bureaucratic procedures.

Razumovskii in 1813 made two important contributions to the question. First, he informed Kharkov University that admission of students from "unfree classes" should be avoided because upon graduation such men could not take up employment as teachers or civil servants since they had to meet the legal "obligations" of their classes. Two weeks later, he responded to a question posed by the Kharkov faculty council, requesting guidance on the admission of a private serf. Razumovskii replied that the university should "explain" to the serf's master, Count I. A. Bezborodko, that "for the most part students are from the gentry and other better classes. Therefore, I think it not quite appropriate to admit" a serf. "Perhaps," he went on, "it would be better to change his fate and liberate him." In that case, "notice of his liberation" should be sent to the ministry." Moreover, "in the future in similar cases, a presentation should be sent each time for the committee's decision."[9]

8. *Sbornik postanovlenii*, I, 759 (10 November 1811).
9. *Sbornik rasporiazhenii*, I, 223 (6 September 1813), 223–24 (18 September 1813). The committee, presumably, was the Main School Administration. Rozhdest-

While not models of clarity, Razumovskii's statements became the basis for the procedure for regularizing the promotion of students from obligated classes, which meant in practice all but gentry and "officers," i.e., those promoted to ennobling ranks in the services. Each had to secure written release from his authority, master, guild, commune, or whatever, to enter the university, where, upon completion of the "whole course," the university forwarded the student's papers to the Senate, which issued certification of the student's new status, and new obligations as teacher, civil servant, soldier, or whatever. Far from the social revolution some had feared, or hoped for, the all-class admission policy had developed into a modest, prudent arrangement. Those members of unfree classes who could manage to acquire the necessary academic preparation and the voluntary assent of their authority, who would sign for their release, could serve the nation through learning, and thereby secure promotion for themselves.

This system, modest though it was, went so much against the grain of ordinary practice and expectations of Russian life that it was often difficult for those in the schools to grasp. Indeed, the schools and the ministry often made decisions contrary to its letter as well as to its spirit. In July 1808, for example, the ministry ordered Kharkov University not to admit to student status an "auditor" (*vol'noslushatel'*) because he came from the merchant class (*kupechestvo*). In November the ministry refused Kazan University permission to grant student status to two men from the *kupechestvo*. As in the case at Kharkov, both men were already in the

venskii, "Soslovnyi vopros," *ZhMNP* (1907), 97, concludes that Razumovskii's point here was that henceforth "serfs (*krepostnye liudi*) could enter gymnasia and consequently also universities only as exceptions, requiring special permission from higher administration each time." It turned out that for those who managed to obtain release from their authority, master, guild, commune, or whatever, acceptance by "higher administration" quickly became routine. Sometimes the ministry bargained with lower authorities to release a member for "scholarly service." For example, in 1824 a state peasant's commune would vote to free him for admission to Kazan University only after the ministry provided the commune with a receipt which could be used to satisfy the next military draft. TsGIAL, f. 733, op. 40, d. 121, *listy*, 1–12. Peasants' reluctance to emancipate one of their fellows, though he satisfied requirements for university admission, was natural. Releasing him meant that someone else had to carry his share of the commune's obligations. Providing recruits for the military was an especially burdensome part of the commune's obligations. A credit against the draft, service for service, seemed to the commune a fair bargain. Thus, the practical needs of traditional class obligations, not the penetration of enlightenment, explain the peasants' response to this aspect of the university reform.

school and had passed their examinations with "outstanding" success. The question really asked what sort of *attestat* to grant them. The ministry forbade granting any *attestat* that called them "students." Because they came from the *kupechestvo*, their *attestat* should call them "auditors." Furthermore, the university was told that in the future the ministry did not expect to see members of "obligated" classes admitted.[10] Alexander's *ukaz* of 1811 was particularly important, then, because it clearly reaffirmed the right of the obligated to university admission and social promotion.

Nonetheless, in December 1811 the faculty of Kharkov asked for clarification of the meaning of Alexander's November 1811 *ukaz*. Granted that men from all classes could be admitted to the university, the faculty wanted to know whether those from the obligated classes had all the rights of students. The statute of 1804 granted students the "right to carry swords," a right particularly meaningful to gentry because it was so clearly connected with the gentry's traditional role as military officers. Razumovskii promptly informed the university that men from obligated classes were to be called "auditors," and thus "may not be given the right to carry swords," a right restricted to "students."[11]

In March 1814 Alexander supported Razumovskii's ruling. Though he made no mention of swords, he declared that "it will be better to call [those from the obligated classes] auditors (*vol'nye slushateli*)" rather than students. In September the ministry sent out a circular to all the districts, repeating the regulations and their goals. "The government founded universities to provide the means for youth to obtain learning at the highest level" and "to make available to the various branches of state service able and well educated servicemen (*chinovniki*)." Too many, however, stayed in the universities "for only a very short time" in order to get "some sort of university *attestat*." Henceforth, the universities should curb such abuse by following all the rules.[12]

---

10. Zagoskin, *Istoriia*, 498; Bulich, *Iz pervykh let*, I, 390; Rozhdestvenskii, "Soslovnyi vopros," *ZhMNP* (1907), 97.

11. Rozhdestvenskii, "Soslovnyi vopros," *ZhMNP* (1907), 99.

12. *Sbornik rasporiazhenii*, I, 237–38 (16 March 1814); 256–57 (30 September 1814). Assuming that these statements indicated that Razumovskii was attempting to hinder the promotion of the obligated, the rector of Vilna, Sniadecki, protested that Razumovskii worked "against the great plans of the monarch, who wishes education to be open to all." Beauvois, *L'Université de Vilna*, I, 321. Beauvois calls this "the cry of indignation of an enlightened man," but notes too that "Śniadecki's protest is somewhat rhetorical, since at Vilna the nobility seemed more in the majority

The Senate, in 1815, made some refinements in the system. First, the Senate informed the universities that the "liberation certificates," submitted to the Senate for confirmation of the new social status of "those from unfree classes" upon completion of the university course, had to be "the originals." Some months later, the Senate decided to exempt students from the clergy from presentation of their documents to the Senate upon completion of the university course. In June 1816 the Senate warned that papers submitted by the universities for men from "obligated" classes should provide "exact information," including the "year, month, and day" of completion of the university course.[13]

When Golitsyn became minister in 1816, the meaning of the all-class policy had been worked out. Nonetheless, questions about it continued to arise. They were the same questions already settled, testimony to the difficulty many, both in and out of the schools, had in grasping the concept of social mobility. In April 1819 another circular to all the universities went out from the ministry, summarizing the rules and making a special point that those "from tax-paying classes" were required to complete six years of service after graduation. This required repeating because "it is found that in many cases those who have signed [i.e., accepted aid as state students] give various excuses to avoid fulfillment of their obligations." In November the Committee of Ministers posed a question. What happens, the ministers asked, in the case of those from obligated classes who do not finish their course of studies? Golitsyn's answer was clear: "They must remain in their former rank."[14]

Shortly thereafter, in December 1819, the ministry authorized another refinement in the procedures. In the case of a Jew, there would be no requirement for the "liberation certificate" from his Jewish communal authority if the individual converted to Orthodoxy, in which case his certificate of baptism would constitute his liberation certificate. To complete his emancipation, however, he still had to "complete the whole course" in the university. Another ruling, in June 1820, upheld the established procedures. Some "au-

than anywhere else in the empire." Hulewicz, Śniadecki, li-lii, quotes the same letter, but calls it a response to Alexander's 1811 ukaz.

13. Sbornik rasporiazhenii, I, 259 (21 January 1815); 287 (27 June 1816); Sbornik postanovlenii, I, 855–56 (9 September 1815).

14. Sbornik rasporiazhenii, I, 377–78 (23 April 1819); Sbornik postanovlenii, I, 1309 (29 November 1819).

ditors" had claimed that, since they were auditors not students, university rules for students did not apply to them. The ministry ruled that the term auditor (*vol'noslushatel'*) was the term for "young people from obligated classes" who were in no other way different from other students. Specifically, auditors had to attend classes, pass examinations, and be subject to all university rules, just as any other students.[15]

The clarity of these decisions and the apparent ease with which the ministry made them masked the complexity of the issues, which were deeply intertwined in such esentially moral as well as emotionally charged issues as the very existence of serfdom. It was unlikely, for example, that a Jew who converted to Orthodoxy but failed to complete his university exams would be forced by the government of the tsar "to return to his former rank." The issues of unfreedom in Russian life were many and deeply rooted. But the question of admissions to the universities of those from unfree classes involved such small numbers that, regardless of the result in individual cases, no social upset followed. It was easy, therefore, for the Golitsyn ministry to make judgments in this area, because the essential questions had already been decided and because, whatever the hopes and doubts raised by these concerns in 1801–1804, the stakes in reality had proved very low. It was clear also that the rise of the Bible Society had no impact on the question, neither advancing nor retarding the process that made routine a modest program for university admissions for those from the unfree.

2. The Dual Ministry and Its Goals

Another area that proved easily managed was that of the organization of the dual ministry itself. The manifesto that announced the formation of the new ministry said: "Desiring to make Christian

15. *Sbornik rasporiazhenii*, I, 396–97 (13 December 1819), 416–17 (13 June 1820). Use of the term "auditor" to distinguish students of obligated classes from those of "free" classes raised complications. Sometimes gentry enrolled as "auditors," assuming that they would have an easier academic program than students, a practice the ministry denounced as abuse. The 1809 law on civil service examinations called those taking the preparatory courses "external auditors" (*postoronnye slushateli*). Universities sometimes used the terms "*vol'nouchashchie*" or "*vol'nye studenty*" to designate part-time and/or non-degree course students. Such usages naturally invited confusion. Rozhdestvenskii, "Soslovnyi vopros," *ZhMNP* (1907), 104–106, discusses some of the complications and confusions that arose.

piety always the foundation of true enlightenment, we have found it useful to unite the affairs of the Ministry of Public Education with those of all religions in one administration under the title of Ministry of Spiritual Affairs and Public Education."[16] This effort might have proved a complicated affair, for bringing the dimension of piety to all education clearly was a more subtle and demanding undertaking than simply adding religion to the curriculum. Yet, the complexity was minimized by keeping separate the two areas of concern: education and religion. The Ministry of Education carried on as the "Department of Education" in a ministry whose other half was the "Department of Religious Affairs." The two agencies were separate, not having even a joint governing board. The clerical staffs remained distinct. They had different pay scales as well as their own work regulations and seniority lists. The Department of Education differed from the organization and duties of its predecessor in only one respect, the addition of an "Academic Committee" (*Uchenyi komitet*) as a subcommittee of the Main School Administration. This new committee was charged with providing textbooks and other educational materials and with consideration of "projects, proposals, and presentations regarding academic affairs, and other similar matters."[17] In contrast with the infrequent staff meetings of the Zavadovskii and Razumovskii years, this committee was required to "meet each week, on a regular schedule." The committee, numbering but three men, was chaired by N. I. Fuss, a member of the ministry since its foundation.

Changes in personnel were more important than the limited organizational change. A. I. Turgenev became "Director" of the Department of Religious Affairs. Able, active, and well connected in literary as well as religious circles, he had little influence on education because the division of the ministry into separate compartments was so complete. V. M. Popov became director of the Depart-

16. *Sbornik postanovlenii,* I, 1058 (24 October 1817). Details on the reorganization of the ministry may be found in Rozhdestvenskii, *Istoricheskii obzor,* 105–117, and Sawatsky, "Golitsyn," 230–242.

17. *Sbornik postanovlenii,* I, 1078–79. A. I. Grigorievskii, *K istorii Uchenago Komiteta Ministerstva Narodnago Prosveshcheniia* (SPB, 1902), 3–4, suggests that the ministry needed this new committee because no textbooks had been published since 1809. V. I. Lysenko, *Nikolai Ivanovich Fuss 1755–1826* (Moscow, 1975), 22–27, reviews Fuss's career in the ministry. He was also editor of three journals published by the Academy of Sciences, editor of the Free Economic Society's publications, and author of several textbooks in mathematics.

ment of Education. Like Turgenev, Popov was a veteran of service in a number of bureaucratic agencies in the capital. Unlike Turgenev, he had never studied in a university, but he was an early and completely earnest participant in the work of the Bible Society. Popov, office director in the Ministry of Interior for some years, brought to his new post experience in bureaucratic procedures and honest dedication to evangelical Christianity. He replaced I. I. Martynov, who had worked hard and with considerable success, particularly in assisting Novosiltsev in the design and management of the St. Petersburg Pedagogical Institute, where he also taught poetry courses. He also played an important role in assisting Speranskii with the Tsarskosel'skii lycée. He was well known, too, as a scholar, especially as an editor and translator of the Greek classics. In short, when Gotlitsyn replaced Martynov with Popov, he replaced an able professional in educational affairs with an individual whose training and temperament made it unlikely that he would develop competence in academic matters.[18]

Another important change was the appointment to the Main School Administration of able Orthodox clergymen, such as Archimandrite Filaret (Drozdov), who had contributed much to worthwhile reform of church schools. A. S. Sturdza proved a particularly important addition to the ministry. A member of the diplomatic service, he assisted Alexander with drafts for important documents, including the declaration of the Holy Alliance. Having spent considerable time in Germany, working on various aspects of the peace settlements, Sturdza came to share wholeheartedly the views that led German authorities to impose the repressive Karlsbad Decrees. The murder of a Russian consul, Kotzebue, by a university student in March 1819 was frightening evidence for many that a revolutionary spirit threatened the foundations of Europe's public order. It

18. On Popov, see Sawatsky, "Golitsyn," 248–251, and Zacek, "Bible Society," 36–37. In many accounts Popov is a figure of fun. See, e.g., Peter von Goetze, *Fürst Alexander Nikolajewitsch Galitzin und seine Zeit* (Leipzig, 1882), 72–73, the work of a Baltic German who served in the Department of Religious Affairs after 1817 and who found Popov an almost laughably incompetent religious "fanatic." Popov was serious, however. When in 1837 Tsar Nicholas I ordered the supression of some private prayer groups (he feared they might prove "secret societies"), Popov accepted prison and exile rather than yield in his religious practice. For a sympathetic account, see A. El'nitskii, in *Russkii biograficheskii slovar'*, XIV (SPB, 1905), 533. Many years later, Golitsyn, without mention of Popov, explained that he replaced Martynov because he was "unfit," but gave no specific reasons. "Razskazy kniazia A. N. Golitsyna: iz zapisock Iu. N. Barteneva," *RA*, 1886 (No. 3), 135.

surprised Sturdza not at all. He had long since come to believe that the German universities were hopelessly corrupted by inroads of the secularistic enlightenment and were little more than hotbeds of revolution, plotting the destruction of the most worthwhile values of civilized Christian societies. This was the message of his *Mémoire sur l'état actuel d'Allemagne,* submitted to Alexander in preparation for the Aachen conference of 1818.

Appointed to the new Academic Committee of the ministry, Sturdza dominated its first meetings. In late March 1818 he presented a draft that he wanted the committee to issue as a guide to the ministry. Perhaps impressed by Sturdza's presumed influence with the tsar, the other members, Fuss and I. S. Laval (also a newcomer to the ministry), contented themselves with suggesting only minor stylistic changes. Sturdza's draft then was issued as an "Instruction" to all the schools. Actually it was the committee's instruction to itself, for it proposed what the committee should do in order to achieve its goal to "instill in society, in Russia, constant and redeeming harmony between faith, knowledge, and authority, or to put it differently, between Christian piety, intellectual enlightenment, and the duties of citizenship."[19] Sturdza said that this "broad, complicated and many-faceted enterprise requires a unified combination of various methods and means." Yet, censorship was the only method he recommended. The committee must examine both the "literal contents and the spirit" of all books and other materials, to see that "all which are contrary or alien to the [ministry's] goals are removed from the educational system."

Within a year ill health forced Sturdza, or gave him an excuse, to give up active participation in the ministry's work, but his instruction provided a good guide to the tone and style of the Golitsyn ministry. His was the first of a series of pronouncements that the ministry issued to declare that religion was very important and that religion, learning, and good citizenship went together. Naturally, anything opposed to such principles should be removed. But Sturdza, and most of those who followed him, gave few specific examples of what in practice would be "contrary or alien" to the ministry's goals. He stated that it was a "lie that supreme authority comes *not from God* but from agreements among men." Constitu-

19. The "Instruction" is printed in *Sbornik rasporiazhenii,* I, 321–31 (5 August 1818). Quotations 321, 327, 330. Sawatsky, "Golitsyn," 257–262, is the best presentation of Sturdza's role.

tions were the "agreements among men" most in dispute in the wake of the revolutionary struggles from which Europe was just emerging. Sturdza clearly was referring to that dispute. But he did not use the term, or explicitly conclude that God's "supreme authority" and such "agreements among men" were always mutually contradictory. More specifically, he did not argue that Alexander had been mistaken to grant a constitution in Congress Kingdom Poland. Sturdza said also that "the main goal of teaching mathematics is to lead students to applied mathematics, which is necessary for the state." He did not recommend, however, that Fuss refrain from publishing his recently completed text, *A Course in Pure Mathematics*. While there could be little doubt of where, in general, Sturdza, or Golitsyn, or the Bible Society, would like to take education, they did not get down to specific cases. What remained to be decided after the reorganization of the ministry, then, was almost everything that mattered in practice.[20]

3. The Reform Betrayed: Magnitskii at Kazan

Kazan was the smallest and weakest of the universities. Nonetheless, it became especially important in the Bible Society decade, when it became even smaller and weaker, because its curator, M. L. Magnitskii, made it so. Magnitskii deliberately courted notoriety. He succeeded in making his career as curator at Kazan so well known that he seemed to contemporaries, and succeeding generations as well, to typify what the Bible Society reform was about. In fact that was not so. Magnitskii's career as Kazan's curator was atypical. He not only undid much of what had been accomplished at Kazan, but also betrayed the Bible Society reform.

Some Kazan faculty members in 1815 thought that the university had solved its major problems. The reorganization carried out under curator Saltykov since 1813 ended the administration of "director" Iakovkin. Rector and deans were elected, as provided in the

20. Sturdza may have found it difficult to work in the Golitsyn ministry because he did not really share the minister's, or the tsar's, confidence in the non-sectarian Christianity of the Bible Society. In 1848–1849 he wrote a memoir of his work in the ministry, making clear his contempt for both the original "liberal" reformers and their successors from the Bible Society. While he particularly loathed Roman Catholicism and Lutheranism, no form of Christianity except the Russian Orthodox merited any praise in Sturdza's view. "Zapiski A. S. Sturdzy: Sud'ba russkoi pravoslavnoi tserkvi v tsarstvovanie Aleksandra I-go," *RS*, 1876 (February), 266–288.

1804 statute. The promulgation of a new code of student discipline was designed to cure the worst problems in that area. Thus, because the original reform plan was at last to be really tried in Kazan, those who believed in its promise were optimistic. They were right to believe that improvement would soon follow. Student enrollment, one obvious index of success, began to climb steadily, from 42 in 1815 to 169 in 1818. The library grew to 17,500 volumes by 1818, and the collection's accessibility to students greatly improved. Speranskii, returning from the exile to which the wartime emergency had consigned him, visited with Professor Fuchs and reported that he liked what he saw of Kazan University.[21]

Yet, by 1817 Saltykov despaired of the prospects for success at Kazan and wished to give up his curatorship. His despair stemmed partly from personal revulsion at a city whose way of life, particularly its low standards of sanitation, disgusted him. The sudden death of his wife, victim of one of Kazan's many epidemics, grieved him deeply. A great fire in September 1815 shook him too, for the dimensions of the disaster were staggering. Perhaps more important than personal antipathy toward the city was the persistence of problems in the university. The university's "autonomy," self-government by an administration of rector and deans elected by and from the faculty working through a "council" in which all faculty members took part, proved, not the mechanism for cooperative solution of problems, but the arena of constant struggle. This development had several consequences, not the least of which was to destroy Saltykov's faith in the promise of faculty self-government. The faculty irretrievably split into two contending parties, the foreigners and the Russians. The first elected administration was composed entirely of foreigners. That seemed reasonable enough to them, since they were the senior men, both in time of service and scholarship. Nonetheless, many Russians resented them. The two sides struggled over issues that were as often as not almost trivial. Serious issues, such as settlement of degree requirements and examination procedures, were completed by 1818, but took no more of the faculty's time and attention than minor issues of promotion or, as some saw it, of "nepotism."[22]

21. Zagoskin, *Istoriia,* II, 7, 43–44, provides figures on enrollment and library. On Speranskii's visit, see Korf, *Zhizn' Speranskago,* II, 190.

22. Zagoskin, *Istoriia,* I, 410, 104–123. The foreigners wanted to hold Kazan's students to a three-year "preparatory" course before allowing them to undertake the

The case of D. P. Samsonov was typical. Graduated from the university with a *magister* in 1811, he served well as a language teacher and as assistant inspector of students. The university supported him for two years of study at Moscow University. He did not complete a degree at Moscow, but no one doubted that he had made good use of his years there and was a better teacher for them. But his request for promotion to adjunct (i.e., instructor) set off a bitter discussion of faculty standards. Samsonov's promotion was eventually denied. In the process, most Russians on the staff, like Samsonov graduates of Kazan University, realized that their German colleagues would never regard them as scholarly professionals, let alone academic equals. Thus a minor matter of a promotion became a serious issue. Professor Bronner, a Swiss mathematician who was inspector of students, carried on an unusually voluminous correspondence with Saltykov, as did S. P. Kondyrev, who earned Kazan's first *kandidat* in 1807 and served as chair of the school committee for many years after joining the faculty in 1809. Both repeatedly denounced the other and urged the curator to intervene to settle one question or another. Saltykov refused to do that. In August 1816, in fact, he told Bronner that he would "not get involved in the details" of faculty business and warned that he should be sent only matters that required ministerial action.[23]

Student behavior troubled members of both parties. The newly promulgated rules for student conduct, issued in March 1815, called upon students to study to the best of their abilities and to avoid drunkenness, fighting, stealing, and gambling. Faculty members were alarmed that wild student behavior often made academic work impossible. Equally important, perhaps, the reports of wild student behavior submitted to the ministry, combined with repeated reports of the faculty's troubles within itself, made sorry reading. The chief problem was student drunkenness. When faculty members complained that students failed to appear for class, inspector Bronner had to seek them out, in their rooms or wherever he could catch them. Sometimes he found thirty or more crowded into a little

---

courses leading to the *kandidat*, or diploma, but Saltykov persuaded a majority to be content with a single "preparatory" year. Bulich, *Iz pervykh let*, II, 444. The 1815 fire destroyed at least 1,500 buildings, including nearly all those on the main street, Voskresenskaia, where the university was located. Zagoskin, *Sputnik*, 476–478.

23. Bulich, *Iz pervykh let*, II, 727. On Samsonov's career, see Zagoskin, *Biograficheskii slovar'*, I, 158–159.

room, not only drunk but sick, fouled with vomit and in no condition to take up learning. There were also problems with some who
came to class. The faculty council several times passed resolutions
condemning students' shouting and throwing things in class, or
hanging around the doors, singing and shouting. This may not have
seemed much of a problem to Bronner, who on several occasions
dealt with students who were breaking down doors to beat each
other up.[24]

Since many students who left for the summer vacation in May did
not return until the following March, the council adopted a rule
promising to expel any student who missed a half year of classes.
Bronner, who was also presiding officer of the university court, tried
to use punishments that would aid learning. His court assigned
Latin translations or mathematics problems in lieu of locking up or
dismissing many students. Students found guilty of not attending
church at Easter were assigned Latin translations, to be done at
assigned hours (usually eight to ten at night) under the supervision
of a faculty member. A student who assaulted a ten-year-old girl
received three days on bread and water, and a Latin translation to
do while in jail. The use of such assignments illustrated the Kazan
faculty's problems in dealing with attitudes deeply rooted in the
mores of local society, where drunkenness and violence were too
commonplace to seem true evils. A student who assaulted an
eleven-year-old girl defended himself before the university court
with forthright aplomb: "I am well born. My father is a colonel."[25]

Professor Braun, rector of the university, recommended a drastic
punishment for student malefactors. In 1817 he proposed to the
council that those guilty of serious violations should be assigned
immediately to careers as teachers in county schools.[26] This recommendation, illustration of the low appeal of the teachers' calling in
the provinces, was not taken up, nor was another that Braun made
repeatedly, the introduction of courses in religion into the curriculum. Most faculty members agreed with Braun that the university
should promote both the scholarly development of the students and

24. D. I. Naguevskii, *Professor Frants Ksaverii Bronner, ego dnevnik i perepiska
1785–1850 gg.* (Kazan, 1902), 1–192, reprints Bronner's diary as inspector of students. Naguevskii's introduction, xxv–cxlvi, discusses Bronner's career. Bulich, *Iz
pervykh let*, II, 441–524, is a detailed description of Kazan's student problems,
based on university and ministry records as well as on Bronner's diary.
25. Bulich, *Iz pervykh let*, II, 727.
26. Shurtakova, *Rukovodstvo*, 56–57.

their moral formation. Since students were preparing to serve society, which was the reason that society supported them and the university, their education was inescapably a moral enterprise. Therefore, Braun concluded, the university should offer instruction in religion. Saltykov did not disagree, but pointed out that introducing instruction in religion might raise more problems than it solved, for influential churchmen continued to fear the intrusion of the universities.[27]

Another element that had not changed from the early days was the crushing faculty workload. The faculty never numbered more than thirty. Most taught not only their own courses but others as well, often in a different department. Members of the physics-mathematics staff also taught courses in the medical faculty. Many also taught in the gymnasium. In addition to the heavy teaching load, and committee assignments of a self-governing faculty, the supervision of the huge Kazan district presented special problems. Faculty inspectors, usually traveling in pairs, sometimes put in eight to ten weeks at a stretch, visiting schools throughout the district, which included the distant reaches of Siberia. Naturally enough, many thought that their jobs were too much and made repeated requests to St. Petersburg for a lightening of their loads.[28]

Many lightened their loads by resignation. In 1817 five of the senior members left for positions elsewhere. Bronner sold his laboratory equipment to the university and took a semester's leave to Switzerland, where he at once secured a position. Though he had no intention of returning to Kazan, he did not resign, but kept requesting extensions of his leave. Since Bronner was only on leave, the faculty council did not elect a replacement for him as inspector of students. Obviously, no one at Kazan needed an extra job, so his position was simply left vacant.[29]

While the faculty was unhappy with much student behavior, stu-

27. Bulich, Iz pervykh let, II, 459–460.

28. Ibid., 718–719. On the district's schools, and the trials of the faculty inspectors, see Zagoskin, Istoriia, III, 179–198, 240–249; Shurtakova, Rukovodstvo, 4–61. Faculty turnover in 1816 to 1819 tipped the balance against foreigners, who outnumbered Russians 15 to 14 in 1815, but were outnumbered by Russians 18 to 10 by 1818. Braun, however, remained rector for the whole period.

29. Bulich, Iz pervykh let, II, 244, says that Bronner left because he was discouraged at the news that a friend, Professor Schad, had been dismissed at Kharkov and that this prompted his departure, but there seems to be no evidence for this. It is clear that when Bronner applied for a leave, he did not plan to return to Kazan. Naguevskii, Bronner, ccii-cciii.

dents in turn had complaints about the faculty. Some claimed that they had already taken some courses in the gymnasium, where some faculty members did indeed offer the same course they gave in the university. The teachers defended that practice, and accepting two salaries for the two positions, as the only way to keep up academic quality in both institutions.[30] Many students complained that some professors spent class hours merely "dictating" lessons for students to copy down, while others lectured in languages the students did not know. Other students reported that some faculty skipped classes as often as did students. In one typical case, students requested transfer from Lobachevskii's mathematics course to that of Nikolskii, since, they said, Lobachevskii seldom came to class, leaving his students without instruction in an important course. Discussion soon became an argument in the faculty council over what students had a right to expect. Some charged that Nikolskii was popular because he made his course easy, simply repeating the gymnasium course. Nikolskii retorted that he gave his course at the level of the students' preparation and denounced those who pitched their lectures far above the students' possibilities of comprehension.[31]

This debate, serious though it was, could not be resolved. Its importance was to underscore how much more needed to be done at Kazan before the university could function in the way the original reformers had imagined it would. Saltykov focussed this concern in a series of proposals for reform that he submitted to the ministry. He told Bronner that he talked with Golitsyn about these projects "a hundred times." Saltykov's view of what needed to be done always called for carrying out the original reform of 1804, by providing greater budget authorizations for additional faculty, for staff people, for state student stipends, for the library, for physical facilities, including new buildings as well as extensive badly needed repairs for the existing ones.[32]

No one seems to have found the reports from Kazan signs of life, of healthy contentiousness and discontent with the present that might betoken continued growth. Rather, Saltykov in January 1817

30. Bulich, *Iz pervykh let*, II, 654.
31. *Ibid.*, 450–459.
32. Zagoskin, *Istoriia*, II, 146–147, reprints a typical report by Saltykov to the ministry (August, 1816), listing deficiencies and requesting additional funding. See also *ibid.*, 106–123, 138–139 (Saltykov to Bronner, 23 October 1816), 168–172; Naguevskii, *Bronner*, 336–337.

told Bronner that some in the ministry proposed solving the Kazan problem by closing the university. Some weeks later, he told Bronner that his curatorship "was ended" but that his "successor has not yet been named."[33] The hopeful promise of 1815 had proved a mirage. The hard work of many able people over a period of years seemed to produce little but urgent requests for more aid. In October 1818 Golitsyn drafted a report that concluded that the university did "not fulfill its obligations."[34] In February 1819 the rector, Professor Braun, died. Golitsyn ordered the university to postpone electing a successor pending the completion of an inspection by the ministry. Golitsyn had recently come to know a man he thought particularly well qualified to make that inspection: M. L. Magnitskii.

Magnitskii had enjoyed a remarkable career. Graduated from Moscow University, he spent some time as a guards officer before transferring to duty in the diplomatic service. He used assignments in Western capitals not only to learn Western languages but also to become an accomplished student of political theory. Thoroughly acquainted with the doctrine and practice of the enlightened, he rose speedily in the state services, becoming the chief assistant to the tsar's chief assistant, Speranskii. Alexander in 1812 found it necessary to exile Speranskii, in an apparent effort to placate the more reactionary old-line conservatives whose willing support he thought was needed for the coming trial by fire with Napoleon. So closely identified with Speranskii's "westernizing" policies was Magnitskii that he was the only associate of Speranskii who also had to go into exile.[35]

When the military threat from the West retreated, Speranskii was readmitted to service, as was Magnitskii. Speranskii used well his years as provincial governor in Siberia, achieving important reforms in the redesign of local government. Magnitskii did not take quite so well to life in the eastern provinces. Promoted to governor of Simbirsk, he struck fear into the hearts of his subordinates, whom he regarded as "vulgar" nobodies, while he worked hard to find a

33. Zagoskin, *Istoriia*, III, 278 (Saltykov to Bronner, 12 January 1817); Naguevskii, *Bronner*, 366–367 (Saltykov to Bronner, 29 January 1817).

34. Zagoskin, *Istoriia*, III, 279.

35. The best general treatment of Magnitskii's career remains N. N. Bulich, *Ocherki po istorii russkoi literatury i prosveshcheniia s nachala XIX veka* (SPB, 1905), 259–269. For a discussion of his career at Kazan, see J. T. Flynn, "Magnitskii's Purge of Kazan University: A Case Study in the Uses of Reaction in Nineteenth-Century Russia," *Journal of Modern History*, 43 (1971), 598–614.

way back to St. Petersburg. He wrote adulatory letters to officials in St. Petersburg, among them Golitsyn, and took the lead in organizing a chapter of the Bible Society in Simbirsk. Golitsyn was delighted to learn of an intelligent, hard-working, knowledgeable official who had himself experienced that conversion of the heart at which the Bible Society aimed, and who, serving in an eastern province, had already informed himself of conditions at Kazan. In January 1819, before Braun's death, Magnitskii accepted with glad thanks Golitsyn's offer to make him special inspector of Kazan University and told the minister that he looked forward to service with a ministry that "because of the beneficence of your leadership, promises a new and wonderfully happy era in the history of our country."[36]

In later years Magnitskii more than once asserted that when he took on the job of special inspector to Kazan, the main conclusion of his report had already been decided, for Golitsyn wanted a recommendation to close the university. It was clear that one solution to the tangle of problems, discussed years before, was to close the university. Golitsyn's instructions, dated 11 February 1819, asked that Magnitskii "give his opinion on whether the university can usefully continue to exist. In the event that the university should be closed," the inspector should make detailed recommendations for the future administration of the district.[37] He was also asked to be "clear," for, though the ministry knew well that conditions were poor, "both academically and economically," university reports over the years were often confusing. Finally, Magnitskii was told that "your relationship to Kazan University and it to you will be that which holds between curators and their districts." Thus, if Magnitskii could find it possible to recommend closing the university, a curatorship, and thus assignment in St. Petersburg, was a clear prospect.

Magnitskii, arriving in Kazan on 8 March, made a short speech to the assembled faculty, asking for their assistance and promising that his visit would not interfere with their normal routine or interrupt their work. His own courtesy was matched by the faculty, who cooperated gladly with the inspector. After a week's work, Magnitskii again adressed the faculty, telling them that he had prepared

36. Zagoskin, *Istoriia*, III, 276.
37. *Ibid.*, 277.

two reports, one for them and one for the "highest authority." He told the professors that he found many deficiencies. There was no effective defense against fires, and the students' living quarters were in foul condition, evidence of lack of "system" in management. There were also academic failings. "Several professors," he said, "read lectures but do not teach," for the students did no more than copy down the lectures for rote learning, really just transferring them from "notebook to notebook." The students, moreover, needed much better preparation, especially in Latin, to do university-level work. Finally Magnitskii said that "many students do not have the required knowledge of the commandments of God." The time has come, he said, when education should be "based on" religion.[38]

Magnitskii thanked the faculty for its cooperation, extending special gratitude to the vice-rector, Professor Solntsev, "my right hand in the inspection." He thanked Nikolskii for being "very helpful" and complimented Fuchs for his "great learning." Herman and Erich were promised that their "service will be brought to the attention of the authorities" while the "great talent" of Lobachevskii, Simonov, Sreznevskii, and Perevoshchikov would also be "reported to the authorities." In the end, Magnitskii had thanked, by name, nearly every individual. Closing with the advice that it would be useful to place copies of the Bible in the students' rooms, Magnitskii took leave of Kazan.

When the faculty met the next day to discuss the inspector's report, they had reason to be pleased. Not only had most been praised and thanked by name, but most could find thir own views in the report, for it simply repeated what faculty members had been saying in council meetings for years. Naturally enough the faculty found that the inspector was quite right about the condition of the university, and agreed that steps should be taken to improve teaching and get better instruction in Latin and in religion. Finally, supervision of the students did need some "system," and so it was agreed to replace Bronner, who had departed nearly two years previously, by electing his assistant, Breitenbach, to be inspector of students. Satisfied with their response to the inspector's report, the faculty turned its attention to plans for a ceremonial observance of the fifth anniversary of the university's "full" opening.[39]

38. Zagoskin, *Istoriia*, III, 283–290.
39. *Ibid.*, 291.

Magnitskii's report to the ministry painted a bleak picture. "The council of the university," he wrote, "consists of twenty-five professors and adjuncts, of whom not more than five actually have influence." Worse, one of those with influence was Iakovkin, still director of the gymnasium, who managed to arrange admission without examinations for "children of private persons" and to confer *attestats* of the "rank of student" on people who clearly had not earned them. The suspicion of corruption, long associated with Iakovkin's handling of affairs, thus had not been eliminated as thoroughly as Saltykov had led the ministry to believe. The faculty, Magnitskii went on, was divided into two groups, foreigners and Russians. Of the foreigners, "two are very worthy men." The others "know neither our language nor our laws and way of life," while some are "very tangled up in their affairs."[40]

The buildings, too, were in terrible condition, even dangerous, a fact that made one wonder what the university had done with its maintenance budget year after year. Magnitskii recommended that the ministry send an "experienced architect" to make a detailed study of what needed to be done to save the physical plant from disintegration. In the meantime, the dirt and disorder could be cleaned up, and some rudimentary steps, at least, taken as defense against fires, if only the practice of evacuating the buildings in times of fire.

"Even worse" was the "internal police of the university. The inspector of students [sic], Professor Breitenbach, is very weak in the execution of his duties. He very seldom visits the students, . . . and therefore students live without supervision." When asked how many students there were, Breitenbach promised to try to find out. The students' rooms were foul places, with dirty clothes, dishes, and garbage strewn about. To Magnitskii's surprise, the state students were paid their stipends in cash and left to provide their own board and room. Clearly, asking students to manage their own board and room was asking too much.

All this only reported, if clearly, what the ministry already knew. Magnitskii presented something quite new in his observations on teaching in the moral-political science faculty and the "moral for-

40. The report, dated 9 April 1819, is printed in *ibid.*, 547–567. It is also given, in long quotations and paraphrases, in E. M. Feoktistov, "Magnitskii, Materialy dlia istorii prosveshcheniia v Rossii," *RV*, 51 (1864), 482–492. My quotations are from Zagoskin, 545, 546, 549, 550, 551, 552, 555–556, 563, 564–565.

mation" of the students. "In this faculty," wrote Magnitskii, "I did not find the main science—the Law of God." The records showed, Magnitskii noted, that rector Braun and others had many times appealed for the introduction of courses on religion, but "their requests remain unanswered." There was only one able member of this faculty. "Only Professor Solntsev conducts his lectures in Latin; only he does his work with diligence, maintains a collection of the authors necessary for his subject, composes his own notes, and takes steps to see that students come to his lectures. Professor Sreznevskii," by contrast, "follows the system of Jakob, which is in spirit not very useful.[41] Fortunately, his lectures are so boring that no one understands him. Having sat through his class for two hours, I asked the students what the lecture was about. Not one of them knew." Bad as that was, Magnitskii went on, "nothing could be more pitiful than Professor Wrangel's teaching. He has no knowledge of his subject or of the Russian language." Kondyrev prided himself on his translation of the work of the Göttingen professor Sartorius, which presented the teaching of Adam Smith in digested textbook form. Magnitskii reported that "Kondyrev lectures on political economy following Sartorius, which cannot serve as a guide to this subject, for it does no more than give a summary of Smith." The "moral formation" of the students was even worse than their academic training. Few students could answer simple questions about religion, showing woeful lack of knowledge. For example, Magnitskii found not one student who knew what the word "Gospel" meant. "Such men, with such educations," he said, "are the fruit of fourteen years" of effort at Kazan University. He came to the

41. L. H. Jakob, well known as a prolific exponent of Kantian idealism, taught at Halle, where he took his own doctorate, until Napoleon closed the university in 1806. Gladly accepting Potocki's invitation to move to Kharkov in that year, he became well known for his many studies explaining the doctrines of Adam Smith. Professor of Political Economy at Kharkov, he published a number of studies of Russian needs, especially in tax and banking policy, which in 1809 led Speranskii to arrange his appointment to the Ministry of Finance. Jakob's 1815 essay attacking serfdom, as both immoral and inefficient, won the Free Economic Society's prize for that year. He returned to Halle in 1816. Attacking Jakob in 1819, thus, was both safe and not very illuminating, for Jakob had left the country and was identified with a number of quite various aspects of the enlightenment, though all were "liberal" in one way or another. On Jakob's scholarly writing, see Zagurskii, *Istoriia iuridicheskago fakul'teta,* 275–277. Biographical and bibliographic introductions are in David and Karin Griffiths, trans. and eds., "M. M. Speranskii as viewed in L. H. Jakob's unpublished autobiography," *Canadian-American Slavic Studies,* IX (No. 4, 1975), 481–484.

obvious conclusion: "The university has not fulfilled its statute and is not able to carry out the obligations its statute imposes on it."

To his report Magnitskii added a remarkable final section: "My general opinion on the matter." He pointed out that Golitsyn had requested that he offer his "opinion" as to "whether [the university] can be improved" or, "if not, to suggest another method of administration for the schools of the district." He concluded that "there is no possibility of improving an institution in which, of twenty-five men, hardly more than three can be counted on." Kazan University "has in the course of several years abused all the rights and privileges" granted to it. Thus, the university should be held accountable and "in all legal severity—*sentenced to destruction*."

What it might mean to sentence the university to destruction Magnitskii undertook to explain. "If the university is closed, for lack of professors or some similar reason, then doubtless the true reason for its destruction will not come out. Europe's scholars, bitter that the evil consequences of their so-called enlightenment have been detected, will slander the government, ascribing to mere arbitrary power that closing which is done in strictest justice." But, an "*akt* of public destruction" will make clear "article by article" that the university has abused its rights and "not produced what was expected in the course of fourteen years." In consequence, "all honest and right-thinking people, now and in posterity, will side with the government."

The dramatic "sentence of destruction," thus, called for no more than an *akt*, a document to give in detail the government's reasons for closing the university. Nonetheless, the call for the university's "destruction" was important, more important than merely concluding that the university should be closed. Magnitskii presented evidence compelling enough to merit consideration of the wisdom of continuing the university, for there was evidence to suggest that a faculty capable of making the university a success was not available, that the mores of the populations of the fifteen easternmost provinces of the empire were not likely to offer support to a university, nor soon produce a competent, well-motivated student body. But Magnitskii wanted the government to issue a document to argue that such were not the "true" reasons for closing Kazan. That step was made necessary, rather, by the evil consequences of teaching Western philosophy. Magnitskii's report thus required belief in something that he knew was not true, as much of the information

contained in his report showed. Kazan students were in little danger of corruption by Western doctrines. Indeed, there was not
much chance that many Kazan students would learn anything at all
about them.

Finally, Magnitskii concluded that, with the university closed, the
district would be well administered from a restructured gymnasium, which could meet the district's needs by opening a "special
section for state-supported candidates for careers in teaching" and
a "*pansion* for gentry youth." The gentry would live in a separate
building but would study in the gymnasium with others. "I was
assured in Kazan," Magnitskii noted, "that if the government
opened such a *pansion*, the gentry of all the provinces would gladly
pay a thousand rubles to support each of its students."

Magnitskii's conclusion obviously came, not from the evidence he
marshalled at Kazan, but from Sturdza's "Instruction." Thus he reflected Sturdza's equation of rationalism with an irreligious attack
on Russian patriotic values, that "lumping together of French books
and Napoleon" that Uvarov had condemned in the ministry in
1813. Magnitskii took pains also to include points for the Bible
Society, recommending that the university printing press be given
over to printing Bibles, ending the publication of academic studies
of Islam. His appeal to conservative class consciousness was no less
obvious, for a gentry promise to spend a thousand rubles a year on
each student was news indeed. Much might have come from such a
multi-directional report and set of recommendations. But the response of Uvarov, curator of the St. Petersburg district, seemed to
preempt the ground. There was a question whether the interests of
the empire, and the common good, would be served best by closing
the university, which had been tried and found wanting. That question was ignored. Uvarov concentrated on refuting Magnitskii's
charge that the evil doctrines of the West were the "true" reasons
for closing the university. His response not only dominated the discussion but became what the discussion was about.[42]

Uvarov professed dismay that "we are to consider the destruction
of one of Russia's universities, built up with such great difficulty. I
hope," he went on, "that this will be the last, as well as first, discussion of this kind." His main point was that Magnitskii's conclusions

---

42. Uvarov's response to Magnitskii's report is printed in Feoktistov, "Magnitskii," *RA*, v. 51, 492–497. It is given also, in quotations and paraphrase, in
Zagoskin, *Istoriia*, III, 308–310.

did not come from the evidence presented. "The government," he argued, "is properly vigilant in weighing the guilt of accused individuals, and will not convict without strictly judging the quality of the evidence. . . ." Magnitskii's description of matters "long since known to the ministry," he granted, might show that the university "does not meet the government's needs, or even seems a useless institution. From that it does not follow that it is harmful, or a school of deism and immorality." Indeed, he concluded, Kazan University "in many respects requires correction. But to solemnly brand it harmful, harmful in the sense of this report, I find contrary to all justice, for there is no connection between the evidence in this report and its conclusions."

No vote was taken on Magnitskii's report, for Golitsyn apparently realized that it had few supporters in the Main School Administration. Golitsyn tried to get support outside the ministry, asking Speranskii, whose commitment to evangelical Christianity was well known, to make a recommendation on Kazan. Speranskii declined to offer an opinion, except to point out that Kazan University had able professors, such as Fuchs, and that it would be unwise to hold standards too high too soon, for the universities of the West had taken centuries, not decades, to develop.[43]

Despite his difficulty in finding support for Magnitskii's report, Golitsyn took it to the tsar. Alexander seemed puzzled. "Why destroy it when it can be improved?" he asked.[44] Golitsyn shortly recommended that the tsar name Magnitskii curator for Kazan, to carry out the improvement of the university. After some hesitation, Alexander yielded to Golitsyn's judgment and in June 1819 confirmed Magnitskii's commission as Kazan's curator. Golitsyn provided the new curator with detailed instructions on how "to lead Kazan University to good order." The steps were three. First was to appoint an official, called the "director," to be responsible for nonacademic affairs, i.e., the maintenance and "moral" supervision of students. Second, Magnitskii was to see that courses on religion were added to the curriculum and to appoint clergymen to teach them. Finally, the faculty was to be improved by releasing those "unnecessary." The "unnecessary" were to be "replaced with Russians." To be sure that there was no mistake, Golitsyn listed by

43. Sawatsky, "Golitsyn," 267–268.
44. Goetze, *Galitzin*, 80–81. See also Shil'der, *Aleksandr*, IV, 294; Zagoskin, *Istoriia*, III, 312–313.

name those to be sent away and those to be retained.[45] This was an extraordinary development. The first university to be reformed under Bible Society auspices did not see the introduction of the ecumenical, indeed, cosmopolitan, pietism of the Bible Society's foundations. Instead, it saw religion courses taught by Orthodox clergy and the purge of non-Russians, no matter what their moral practice, religious views, or professional competence as academics. This "reform" was not aimed, then, at meeting the problems that existed at Kazan. Instead, it was the expression of a Sturdza-like conviction that simply merged secularism, atheism, and rationalism with revolution, all linked in a concoction of Westernism, whose clearest specification was that it was obviously un-Russian. Thus, Zapëlin was to be dismissed because he was not Russian. Kondyrev, because he was Russian, could go on teaching political economy according to the doctrines of the physiocrats and Adam Smith.

At Kazan, meanwhile, the faculty held a splendid ceremony honoring the fifth anniversary of the university's "full" opening, and elected deans of faculty for the coming year. The deans included men already on Golitsyn's list for dismissal. Clearly, the faculty had no inkling of what was in store. The faculty met on 20 August to hear a reading of Magnitskii's instruction to them. Dated 5 August, it was nearly a verbatim copy of Golitsyn's June instruction to Magnitskii.[46]

The faculty made no effort to defend itself by calling on the rights of an autonomous university to control its own membership, nor did it protest any aspect of the ministry action. The long struggle between foreigners and Russians at Kazan was over. Magnitskii appointed director a man he had known as medical director of Simbirsk, A. P. Vladimirskii. A graduate of Moscow Medical-Surgical Academy, Vladimirskii had much military service behind him. For years he protested to Saltykov that the medical instruction at Kazan University needed change, and offered to take charge of it himself. His chief complaint was that the medical faculty at Kazan was made up of foreigners. Saltykov had not bothered to reply, but Magnitskii found Vladimirskii a useful addition.

Thus Magnitskii quickly carried out two of Golitsyn's instructions: releasing most of the foreign faculty members and appointing

45. Golitsyn's instructions to Magnitskii are printed in Zagoskin, *Istoriia*, III, 313–315.
46. Zagoskin, *Istoriia*, III, 319–321.

a director. The third charge, introducing courses on religion, proved a bit more difficult. Magnitskii nominated one of the leaders in the Bible Society chapter he founded in Simbirsk, Arkhimandrite Feofan, to teach scripture, theology, and church history. Meanwhile, the faculty council recommended to the ministry the appointment of a clergyman, A. I. Nechaev, educated in the seminary at Kazan. The bishop of Kazan enthusiastically seconded the faculty's choice. After several months of negotiations, a compromise was worked out. Both were appointed to teach religion: Feofan was assigned theology and Nechaev the courses on scripture and church history.[47]

For nearly half the faculty, such matters were of little interest. They needed to secure employment elsewhere. Almost all found Magnitskii very helpful. Wrangel's application to join the staff of the Tsarskosel'skii lycee was warmly endorsed by Magnitskii, who testified that Wrangel "was released from the university due to local conditions which in no way reflect on him morally." Though Magnitskii's April report to the ministry described Wrangel's work as "pitiful," now he wrote that Wrangel was an "excellent scholar" who "will fit into the lycée without difficulty." Most dismissed members of the Kazan faculty moved on to posts as good, in pay and rank, as those they lost at Kazan, almost all supported by Magnitskii's recommendation, which testified that they were "completely qualified" for state service.[48]

In the fall of 1819 Magnitskii began the search for new faculty. In November he received word that no graduate of Moscow Medical-Surgical Academy wished to be considered for a post at Kazan. Uvarov recommended a gymnasium teacher from Novgorod, but at the last moment the candidate changed his mind and accepted a post in a cadet corps instead. Indeed, it proved nearly impossible to recruit faculty for Kazan, though both Magnitskii and Golitsyn expended considerable energy in the effort. A great many men were appointed, but most had very short careers, some lasting but a few weeks. Such rapid turnover made it impossible to offer a curriculum close to that outlined in the statutes.[49]

Unsuccessful at recruiting faculty, Magnitskii was very successful

47. See Zagoskin, *Biograficheskii slovar'*, I, 11–13, on Nechaev; 16–18, on Feofan; *ibid.*, II, 154–155, on Vladimirskii.
48. Zagoskin, *Istoriia*, III, 322–324. Herman and Erich were retired on pension, for reasons of "age."
49. For details on the recruiting efforts, and the comings and goings of the newly appointed, see Zagoskin, *Istoriia*, III, 391–432.

in making himself famous. The letters of recommendation he wrote for the dismissed faculty members show that he did not really believe that Kazan was under assault by evil-doing atheists whose teaching of Western philosophies threatened the hearts and minds of the innocent youth entrusted to their care. Yet, in January 1820 he sent to Kazan a well-publicized "Instruction" that argued that very case.

Magnitskii's Instruction stated that "the goal of the government in the education of students is the formation of true sons of the Orthodox church, true subjects of the tsar, and good and useful citizens of the fatherland."[50] Few faculty members would have found that statement of goals objectionable, or even worthy of much note, for it merely stated the obvious. More noteworthy was Magnitskii's order to the director to check student notebooks, and visit classes often, in order to see to it that the "spirit of free thought may not, either openly or secretly, weaken the teachings of the church, in the teaching of philosophy, history, or literature." The faculty had long made clear its support for requiring that students attend church, study religion, and avoid immorality, such as drunken assaults on each other. Magnitskii was determined to locate evil, not in gross student behavior, but in the faculty's teaching. He restated the original reform goals, declaring that the university must attain the academic level of Europe's "best," publish books "useful" for Russia in all areas, and train men for effective careers in the civil and military services. He added that it was "most important" that the university graduate "Christians" and that the "evil spirit of the times, the spirit of free thought," be stopped, for "all teaching in the university must be in the same spirit as that of the Holy Gospel." Thus, for example, the historian should teach that the early twelfth-century Russia of Vladimir Monomakh far surpassed the European nations of the time in learning and spirituality.

Such linking of eternal truth with Russian nationalism naturally offended, as well as threatened, foreigners. By the fall of 1820—that is, within months of receiving this Instruction—every remaining foreign faculty member, excepting only the elderly Fuchs, had resigned and left Kazan. The losses included Bartels, the senior man in mathematics, and Verderamo, the best-trained member of the

50. Magnitskii's Instruction is printed in *Sbornik postanovlenii,* I, 1317–1337. Lengthy quotations and detailed analyses are available in many works, including Flynn, "Magnitskii," *Journal of Modern History,* 43 (1971), 610–611.

medical faculty. Moreover, since some of the best Russians, including graduates of Kazan such as Perevoshchikov, joined the foreigners in resigning, the staffing situation became desperate. As the number of teaching faculty declined, so did the number of students, down to fewer than half the peak of 169 reached in 1819.

Magnitskii tried to persuade the Main School Administration that the ministry should appoint the university rectors. Rebuffed in that, in May 1820 he called for faculty elections at Kazan. Solntsev had gladly cooperated with Magnitskii's inspection, earning his praise as "my right hand in the inspection." Now Solntsev seemed appalled at the use made of his help and asked that his colleagues not elect him rector. Bartels received the most votes, but promptly declined and submitted his resignation shortly thereafter. Finally Nikolskii was prevailed upon to accept the rectorship.[51]

Magnitskii condemned the faculty in a bitter message he sent them in October 1820. He told the professors that their actions betrayed "weakmindedness" and "childish understanding." The evidence for that was clear. In their report for the academic year 1819–1820, the faculty, failing to take any special note of Magnitskii's Instruction, had omitted saying that Magnitskii had diagnosed a serious problem and found the proper cure. Professor Gorodchaninov was the only member of the faculty publicly to agree with Magnitskii's analysis and to praise the new order at Kazan. Magnitskii therefore congratulated Gorodchaninov on his perspicacity and appointed him dean of the literature faculty.[52]

Gorodchaninov was a Moscow University graduate who served many years in the postal service and briefly as a librarian at Moscow. He wrote a good deal of literary criticism, in which he supported Shishkov's position, praising native Russian virtues, which he contrasted with the baleful results of cultural borrowing from the West. Gorodchaninov's success was matched by Lobachevskii, who also came to enjoy a long career at Kazan. In his student days (in 1811) Lobachevskii had earned citation for "first place in bad behavior." He was also the most gifted student in mathematics. Awarded the graduation prize in that subject, he was appointed to the faculty as soon as he completed his *magister*. In 1820 he began teaching the physics courses left uncovered by Bron-

51. Zagoskin, *Istoriia*, III, 370–374. Bartels accepted an appointment to Dorpat University.
52. Zagoskin, *Istoriia*, III, 362–366.

ner's departure and soon took over the courses left by Bartels, while also continuing with his own. Before his promotion to full professor in 1822, he also took on the task of university librarian and several committee assignments.[53]

The successful careers of Gorodchaninov and Lobachevskii at Kazan under Magnitskii, the one of very limited gifts and attainments, the other a genius who would make major contributions to world science, indicate that it was possible for rather disparate types to get along under Magnitskii. But it was difficult and not often done. Solntsev, the "right hand of the inspection," earned Magnitskii's enmity by rejecting the rectorship. Shortly thereafter, Magnitskii ordered an inspection of the notebooks of Solntsev's students, which doubtless would reveal "harmful" teaching that would require the curator to prefer charges. Rector Nikolskii and Director Vladimirskii tried to pass off on each other the responsibility for gathering the notebooks, while few members of the university court pushed for the speedy "trial" Magnitskii ordered. It was March 1823 before the court agreed that Solntsev taught "harmful" doctrines, by using terms such as "natural law" in political science courses, doubtless leading unwary students to conclude that "nature," not God, was the source of law. The provincial governor described Solntsev's trial as "tragicomedy" and promptly recommended him for a post with the Ministry of Justice. Within a year, over Magnitskii's vigorous objections, Solntsev was assigned to Kazan as provincial procurator, the senior official of the justice ministry in the area.

In spring 1824, as Solntsev took up his new post in Kazan, and the Golitsyn ministry drew to a close, the Bible Society reform at Kazan was a shambles and the university barely alive. This little concerned Magnitskii, who after his appointment as curator had not once returned to Kazan. But it was important, nonetheless. The original university reform attempted to foster the public good by building a university based on Western models. That first reform seemed to need reform itself because of the "moral" failings of both students and faculty. There were many students who used their positions for violently destructive fun, or to shortcut the route to

53. Lobachevskii's success under Magnitskii appeared to puzzle Professor Zagoskin, who nonetheless had no doubt that Lobachevskii "did not share [Magnitskii's] views." See Zagoskin, *Biograficheskii slovar'*, II, 410. On Gorodchaninov, see *ibid.*, I, 64–66, and Bulich, *Iz pervykh let*, II, 61–613.

service, as well as faculty who collected double salaries, or for whatever reason did not carry out the responsibilities assigned to them. All this suggested that a change of heart—getting people to accept their responsibilities by providing the inspirational motivation of religion—made sense as a second reform.

That second reform had not been tried at Kazan. The Bible Society chapter, opened under Vladimirskii in November 1820, in fact proved all but stillborn and had no consequences. Vladimirskii, soon losing trust in Magnitskii as the Solntsev trial dragged along, resigned in the fall of 1822. There was little effort to improve the moral tone of the university, and thus to provide a supportive setting for the education of well-trained and motivated public-spirited officials.[54] Few accepted the curator's contention that evil lurked at Kazan and had to be ferreted out. Indeed, some had the temerity to deny problems. Feofan, the Bible Society man who was Magnitskii's choice as professor of religion, in 1822 proudly reported not only that he taught his courses "in the Russian language" but that his students in theology were well-motivated young men who "paid attention" and "tried very hard." Magnitskii promptly urged Feofan's dismissal, for "poor teaching."[55] At Kazan under Magnitskii the Bible Society reform had little to do with religion.

54. At Magnitskii's direction, the university ceased paying the state students' stipends to the students, a practice Magnitskii found "very dangerous for good education." The funds went to the university treasury while the university housed and fed the students. TsGIAL, f. 733, op. 39, d. 92, *list* 8 (Magnitskii to Golitsyn, 3 October 1819). Magnitskii's conviction in 1826 for misappropriation of university funds suggests that this new arrangement was not primarily an effort to improve student living conditions.

55. Zagoskin, *Biograficheskii slovar'*, I, 17–18.

CHAPTER IV

UNIVERSITIES IN THE BIBLE SOCIETY DECADE

MAGNITSKII, because he was prolific, energetic, and an unscrupulous braggart, made himself so well known that it was not difficult to exaggerate his significance and that of the Bible Society he claimed to serve.[1] Nonetheless, the Bible Society connection told rather little, for good or ill. To be sure, St. Petersburg University endured a purge, as destructive as that at Kazan, directed by Magnitskii's protege, Dmitrii Runich. Vilna University too underwent a reform that included the dismissal of faculty members and of Czartoryski, who personally organized the Vilna chapter of the Bible Society. Moscow, Dorpat, and Kharkov acquired Bible Society curators who in no way followed Magnitskii's example. In each case, local circumstances were more important than the Bible Society's influence in determining each university's fate.

1. St. Petersburg: Uvarov and Runich

Uvarov, curator of St. Petersburg, had reason to expect success for the original reform. He had stood up to the "reactionaries" he described, in 1813, as those who "want education without danger, that is, fire which does not burn" and who lump together "Napoleon and Montesquieu, the French army and French books. . . ." Uvarov was an elitist, distressed that "our public wants nothing

1. The exaggerations began with his contemporaries. See, e.g., *Arkiv Brat'ev Turgenevykh: Dnevniki i pis'ma Nikolaia Ivanovicha Turgeneva za 1816–1824*, III (Petrograd, 1921), 239, 248–49, 263 (diary entries for 14 September, 10 November 1820, and 22 April 1821).

higher than Krylov's tales."[2] He was also a hard-working patriot who, in the spring of 1818, thought he shared the tsar's goals. In March 1818 Uvarov, newly appointed president of the Academy of Sciences, made a carefully crafted statement of the goals and principles of reform.[3] His statement came a week after Alexander addressed the opening of the parliament of Congress Kingdom Poland. Uvarov's speech elaborated themes in the tsar's address, convincing some that Uvarov's speech was meant to amplify the tsar's views. Uvarov's address described principles to which he remained loyal for the remainder of his life. While he could not match Magnitskii's Instruction in flamboyance or notoriety, Uvarov had before him a long career as a leading figure in Russia's educational establishment. His views had much more long-term significance than Magnitskii's.

Barely a week before Sturdza presented the draft of his Instruction to the ministry, Uvarov praised Alexander as the "generous patron of all useful knowledge" who favored "impartial investigation of all truths." Sturdza's views represented part of the impulse behind the Bible Society reform. Uvarov's speech was the argument of those who remained convinced of the essential soundness of the original reform as planned in 1802–1804. His address was delivered to the Pedagogical Institute on the occasion of the appointment of two new scholars, Professors Charmoy and Demange, whom Uvarov had recruited from Paris to begin instruction in Eastern languages. Clearly, Uvarov found no peril in recruiting foreigners or introducing non-Russian subjects.

Uvarov told the students that the tsar "requires your freely made best efforts to achieve good. . . . He wishes to implant deep in your hearts a thorough appreciation of your future role in society. You

2. "Pis'mo (Grafa) S. S. Uvarova k baronu Shteinu," *Russkii arkhiv*, 1871 (No. 9), 0129–0131 (18 November 1813); "Pis'ma k V. A. Zhukovskomu (Grafa) Sergeia Semenovicha Uvarova," *ibid.*, 0161–0162 (17 August 1813). Uvarov took part in launching the patriotic journal *Syn otechestva* in 1812. For a discussion of his role, see V. G. Sirotkin, "Russkaia pressa pervoi chetverti XIX veka na inostrannykh iazykakh kak istoricheskii istochnik," *Istoriia SSSR*, 1976 (No. 4), 81–89, 95–97.

3. *Rech prezidenta imperatorskoi Akademii nauk popechitelia Sanktpeterburgskago uchebnago okruga, v torzhestvannom sobranii Glavnago Pedagogicheskago Instituta, 22 Marta 1818 goda* (SPB, 1818). Quotations 2, 25–26, 41, 48, 53–54. For an abridged translation of this speech, see Cynthia Whittaker in *Slavic and European Education Review*, 1978 (No. 1), 32–38. Whittaker's article, "The Ideology of Sergei Uvarov: An Interpretive Essay," *The Russian Review*, v. 37 (1978), 158–176, argues Uvarov's life-long commitment to the principles expressed in this speech. For discussion of its sources and political context, see Whittaker, *Uvarov*, 45–53.

must always show your future pupils the union of all that is best in religion and in learning. . . ." In short, while Uvarov disagreed with the new members of the ministry who thought that western influence was probably dangerous, and certainly suspicious, he fully shared the view that learning required the support of religion in order to achieve the goals of the original reform.

The main body of Uvarov's address focussed on the importance of history, which he said was the "subject of first importance in public education," for it provided the guide to "true enlightenment, which is nothing else than exact knowledge of our rights and obligations, the obligations and rights of man and citizen." History performed this function because it "leaves behind the dreamy metaphysics which seeks in some sort of first principles to describe the state of man before the foundation of society." Thus, Uvarov dismissed much Enlightened "rationalism" as "dreamy metaphysics" concerned with abstractions, in contrast with history, the record of man's experience in the progressive development of civilization. From the ancient Greek republics—"the beautiful dreams of the youth of mankind"—Uvarov traced in broad outline the struggle between civilization and barbarism, freedom and slavery. The contribution of Christianity was to teach "the great lesson of moral equality, given by God to the world." The point of the story was, not how far man had come, but where he was going, if with much backsliding and tribulation. "How many unsuccessful trials there had to be before the attainment of the English constitution!" Uvarov had no doubt that the "natural course of political freedom" lay before Russia, though, since Russia was "the youngest of the many-membered European family," she had yet some way to go. Uvarov thus outlined the doctrine of historicism. While it would be too much to say that he became a Romantic, he clearly joined many of his generation, leaving behind whatever measure of confidence they held in the rationalist version of the Enlightenment, while developing a view that not only continued to provide guidelines for change but assumed its inevitability. That change, since it had to follow the "natural course" that included the great lesson of Christianity, in the end would produce in Russia something remarkably like an English constitution.

It remained to note the change's meaning for Russian educators. They had a most serious obligation to discharge, Uvarov said, for "the liberation of the soul through enlightenment must come before the liberation of the body through legal action." He concluded: "My heartfelt wish is that each of you will find in your study of history new reason to love your fatherland, your faith, your tsar . . . and that no matter what your social class and no matter what the future has in store for you, you will realize that you are a link in an immeasurable chain in which are joined together . . . all mankind." Neither xenophobic nor obscurantist, Uvarov set goals that required no turning back from the original reform, but rather set those goals in the context of an understanding of progress that echoed in many respects, including patriotic feeling, those of liberals in the West.

Uvarov's deeds were as important as his words. He showed flexibility and energy, making additions to the program of the pedagogical institute and founding a *pansion* for gentry students, offering a six-year course preparing them for university admission or for the civil service exams required by the 1809 law. The state student stipend awarded these gentry students was twice that of state students in the universities. Gentry, it was clear by now, often avoided the universities because their poverty forced them to enter service as early as possible. Uvarov planned to attract them into education by meeting that problem. At the same time, he began a new program for village schoolteachers. "It is well known," he said, "and beyond doubt that the lowest public schools are the very foundation of our public education and that it is essential that these schools reach the broadest class of people . . . providing them with the basic means to open to them the path so that they may use their talents for the good of society in every sort of endeavor."[4] Clearly, Uvarov had not given up on the original goals. He meant to use the state's power to "open paths" that the people could take, not only to improve their own lot but for the good of all. At the same time, at Golitsyn's direction, he sent four institute students to England to study the Lancaster system of primary education. The Lancaster system was sponsored by the same philanthropic people who fostered the Bible Society. The Lancaster system's chief feature, using advanced students to instruct the younger, had the double attraction of promising to help the lowly and remaining inexpensive. Uvarov praised the work of the institute men sent to Britain, but kept postponing the introduction of the system. The institute neither taught the Lan-

4. *Sbornik postanovlenii*, I, 1097–1103 (25 October 1817). Quotation 1101. For the *pansion*, see *Sbornik rasporiazhenii*, I, 293–302 (8 August 1817).

caster method nor maintained a Lancaster school. Instead, Uvarov pushed his own program to train village schoolteachers who would be regular state-supported students, qualifying for rank and civil service pay. In short, Uvarov would not willingly substitute a cheap replacement, such as the Lancaster system, but sought to find the means to carry out the original reform.[5]

Uvarov did not win Golitsyn's support. One day in early 1818 the minister called to his office Professor Ia. V. Tolmachev, a priest's son whose hard work and good luck had enabled him to escape a life of unusually severe poverty. Golitsyn questioned Tolmachev about his work on the district censorship committee, pressing him to explain how the committee passed an article that favorably discussed Western constitutional practice. Tolmachev could not answer, because he could not recall the article. Golitsyn warned him: "In future bring such pieces to me first. Do not show them to Uvarov. I know the spirit of contemporary politics better than he."[6]

Obviously, Golitsyn mistrusted Uvarov's appreciation of Western constitutionalism. Nonetheless, in January 1819 he supported Uvarov's proposal to transform the Pedagogical Institute into a university. Uvarov's proposal kept the essentials of the 1804 university statutes, but made changes to "take advantage of the experience gained in the past fifteen years." As before, academic affairs were to be managed by the faculty council, led by the rector and deans elected by and from among the professors. Unlike the 1804 statutes, responsibility for maintenance, "police," and "all matters except those reserved to the faculty council" were assigned to an official appointed by the curator, the "director." The schools of the district were to be administered by a new committee, made up of the curator, the rector, and three appointed members, one of whom would be the full-time "director of district schools." Clearly, then, management of the district schools had been removed from the faculty. Uvarov removed from faculty management those activities which

5. For the relationship between Bible Society and Lancaster schools, see Judith C. Zacek, "The Lancaster School Movement in Russia," *SEER*, 45 (1967), 343–367. The order to send students to England included the advice that "it would not be bad if they knew some English." *Sbornik postanovlenii*, I, 889. Others, including Magnitskii, by 1821 came to oppose the Lancaster system for reasons opposite those of Uvarov, for they feared that it might work to promote social mobility. See Rozhdestvenskii, *Istoricheskii obzor*, 145–148; Whittaker, *Uvarov*, 69–70.

6. "Iakob Vasil'evich Tolmachev, ordinaryi professor SPb universiteta, Avtobiograficheskaia zapiska," *RS*, 1892 (September), 716.

had proved most burdensome to the faculties. "Fifteen years of experience," he said, showed that assigning these matters to faculty committees had "consequences most inconvenient for the universities."[7]

Though its statute had not yet been approved, the new university opened in February. In March the faculty conducted elections, choosing *inter alii* Balugianskii dean of philosophy-law and Chizov dean of physics-mathematics. In April Magnitskii recommended the "destruction" of Kazan University. Uvarov's rejection of Magnitskii's recommendation marked the end of progress toward the new St. Petersburg University. Magnitskii attacked every proposal that Uvarov made, charging that Uvarov's plans did "not agree with the spirit of the government and ministry" and would bring into Russia the "anarchy of German universities." Uvarov denounced Magnitskii's charges as "slanderous insults . . . to the tsar who has supported me for ten years." Magnitskii made his own counterproposals, demanding the abolition of the election of university officials because it permitted the election of foreigners who "not only have the moral depravity which comes with education in German universities, but also practice a different religion, know no Russian, and so on." At one meeting, Dmitrii Runich, newly appointed to the ministry, declared that he "agreed with everything said [by Magnitskii] without any reservation of any kind." Few others agreed, however. Ministry discussions of Uvarov's proposed university statute simply became arguments, dragging on without result for weeks, then months and years. Uncertainty engendered by the interminable wrangling in the ministry persuaded some faculty members, Balugianskii among the first, to take leaves or resign to take up posts in one or another ministry.[8]

7. S. V. Rozhdestvenskii, ed., *S.Peterburgskii universitet v pervoe stoletie ego deiatel'nosti 1819–1919; Materialy po istorii S.Petersburgskogo universiteta* (Petrograd, 1919), I, 2, 4 (Ob'iasnenie Uvarova, 13 January 1819). Uvarov's proposal is in *ibid.*, 6–12. Rozhdestvenskii's introduction (*ibid.*, iii–cxlvii) is a detailed history of the university, 1819–1835. The main body of the volume, 1–720, is a rich collection of source materials on the university, 1819–1835. Charles S. Steinger, "Government Policy and the University of St. Petersburg 1819–1849" (Ph.D., Ohio State University, 1971), makes excellent use of Rozhdestvenskii's volume, including, 48–68, a discussion of Uvarov's role in the university's foundation.

8. Rozhdestvenskii, *Materialy*, 91–108, is Magnitskii's most detailed presentation, dated 19 September 1819. Quotations 92, 107. Uvarov's response in *ibid.*, 108–110 (Uvarov to Golitsyn, 10 December 1819). Runich's statement is in TsGIAL, f. 733, op. 39, d. 312, *listy* 61–62 (Journal, Main School Administration, 11 December 1819).

In the spring of 1821 Uvarov was driven to resignation. Runich, Sturdza's replacement on the Academic Committee of the ministry, attacked a book titled *Natural Law*, published with approval of the district censors in 1818. The author, A. P. Kunitsyn, was one of the most able young scholars on the university faculty, and the author of a laudatory review in *Syn otechestvo* of Uvarov's 1818 speech. Runich charged that Kunitsyn's book fostered doctrines "contrary to Christianity" and "good order." Uvarov's vigorous protest was supported by Fuss, Balugianskii, and several others. When the Main School Administration could reach no agreement on Runich's proposal, Golitsyn took it upon himself to issue an order banning the book, and to demand that Uvarov dismiss Kunitsyn. At the same time, some students in the *pansion* rioted, or at least held a noisy demonstration. Uvarov reported that the incident was insignificant, but Golitsyn retorted that it "clearly showed weak administration" and that the students were infected by the "general spirit of self-will" that plagued modern man. He demanded that Uvarov cooperate with a detailed investigation. Instead, exasperated, in April 1821 Uvarov resigned and departed for his country estate near Moscow.[9]

Runich, promptly appointed by Golitsyn to take Uvarov's place as St. Petersburg curator, promptly reported that he found professors "teaching in a spirit contrary to Christianity." His investigation culminated in early November in three days of faculty meetings, the last of which did not conclude until three in the morning. Runich seemed to have a wonderful time, insulting faculty members, interrupting with shouts to "sit down, stupid," and so on, threatening that some professors might soon "know Siberia" first-

9. Rozhdestvenskii, *Materialy*, xxxix–xlii, is the best of the many accounts of these episodes and is well summarized by S. B. Okun' in Mavrodin, *Istoriia Leningradskogo universiteta*, 17–27. Okun' took pains to argue that the struggle between Uvarov and Golitsyn was not between a "progressive" and a "reactionary" but only between two somewhat different sorts of reactionaries. On Kunitsyn see Barry Hollingsworth, "A. P. Kunitsyn and the Social Movement under Alexander I," *SEER*, XLIII (December, 1964), 116–128. Kunitsyn's book is summarized in I. I. Solodkin, "Ugolovno-pravovye vozzreniia A. P. Kunitsyna," *Vestnik Leningradskogo universiteta*, 1966 (No. 11), 122–127, and reprinted in Shchipanov, ed., *Russkie prosvetiteli*, II, 169–351. Runich's denunciation of Kunitsyn is quoted at length in E. M. Feoktistov, "Magnitskii, materialy dlia istorii prosveshcheniia v Rossii," *Russkii vestnik*, 51 (June, 1864), 464–481. Sawatsky, "Golitsyn," 296–316, discusses Golitsyn's handling of censorship, showing that Golitsyn often seemed to feel justified in taking arbitrary actions that exceeded any reasonable reading of his legal authority.

hand. Still, though Tolmachev and some others were frightened and tried to cooperate with Runich, the faculty could not be brought to vote condemnation of the teaching of any colleague. Moreover, those Runich accused of teaching "evil" denied it and refused to promise to change. At one point Professor Galich said that he was willing to confess, if someone could explain the charges to him. In late November, urged by Golitsyn to conclude the affair, Runich reported to the ministry, recommending the dismissal of four professors. The ministry could reach no agreement. Consequently, in January 1822 Golitsyn sent his own very detailed report to the Council of Ministers, requesting a criminal trial for the four professors. The ministers refused to allow that, but came to no other conclusion. Thus, officially at least, the case remained undecided until 1827, when Tsar Nicholas I simply declared it "closed."[10]

While Runich conducted his investigation, and denounced as "reptiles of revolution" those who dared face up to him, Uvarov returned to St. Petersburg and tried to defend the professors. He wrote to Alexander that Runich's conduct was "monstrous" and "bizarre." Runich's charge that the school taught "atheism and sedition" he declared completely false. Uvarov denounced Runich and his supporters as "provocateurs of disorder" and "cold-blooded fanatics" who "pretend to defend throne and altar from attacks which do not exist." He concluded with an urgent plea that the tsar personally involve himself in the case to see that justice was done.[11] Alexander made no reply.

The tsar's reluctance to intervene did not lessen the damage done to Golitsyn's administration by this "affair of the professors." Though he did not seem to note it, Golitsyn's standing in the government was seriously weakened by his handling of the affair with such maladroit buffoonery that the bungled "purge" attracted little support even within his ministry. Balugianskii, who was not on the list of those recommended for dismissal, resigned nonetheless and became a senior official of the ministry of finance. Chizov, who was on the list for dismissal, refused to go and continued teaching until

10. Rozhdestvenskii, *Materialy,* xlviii–lviii, is the best account of Runich's investigation. *Ibid.,* 170–215, provides minutes of the meetings, votes taken, and various statements by participants. Golitsyn's recommendation is in *ibid.,* 224–236 (Dokladnaia zapiska A. N. Golitsyna, 16 January 1822).

11. Sukhomlinov, *Izsledovaniia,* I, 378–834 (Uvarov to Alexander I, 18 November 1821).

1846, serving as dean of his faculty much of the time. Plisov resigned, but did not leave and went on teaching for many years, though he had to give up his university apartment. Galich did not resign, but did no more teaching, though he continued to occupy his apartment in a university building.[12]

This muddled situation reflected badly on the minister's competence. Grand Duke Nicholas sarcastically thanked Runich: "We badly need such people, so please throw more of them out of the university. We have places for them all."[13] The future tsar's remark underscored the most important result of the affair. While the former faculty members prospered for the most part, the institution they left did not. Replacements for the men who left could be found only among recent graduates of the institute or of seminaries. None had academic credentials comparable to those leaving, with one exception. O. S. Senkovski came from Vilna University to teach Eastern languages, replacing both Charmoy and Demange, who joined the ministry of foreign affairs. Since he was replacing two men, Senkovski demanded, and received, double salary. Many vacancies were not filled at all. Student enrollment dropped rapidly, down to forty-eight by February 1823. At the end of the spring term, 1823, the university moved from its river-front location opposite the Winter Palace into the *pansion* building in center city. In consequence of the Golitsyn-Runich reform, the newly founded university could fit easily into much reduced quarters.

2. Vilna: Czartoryski and Novosiltsev

The crisis of the war did remarkably little damage to the university at Vilna. Within hardly more than a year of the end of hostilities, the university recovered its full complement of faculty and enrollment came close to its prewar peak. Yet, for reasons having little to do with the Bible Society, Vilna too suffered a "purge," with consequences significant for the outcome of the university reform and others as well. The trouble began soon after the war. Czartoryski, like Alexander, Kochubei, and many of the original reformers, had

12. On the fates of those who incurred Runich's enmity, see Rozhdestvenskii, *Materialy*, lxii–lxiii; Grigor'ev, *S. Peterburgskii universitet*, 39–43; A. V. Nikitenko, "Aleksandr Ivanovich Galich, byvshii professor S. Peterburgskogo Universiteta," *ZhMNP*, 1869 (No. 2), 57–59.

13. Rozhdestvenskii, *Materialy*, lxxvii.

paid little attention to educational matters for some time. Śniadecki, the rector, worked with skill and energy, but it was not possible to compensate for Czartoryski's absence, particularly since the minister of education, Razumovskii, distrusted Śniadecki. He demanded, indeed, that Śniadecki resign his rectorship, which Razumovskii thought was irretrievably compromised by Śniadecki's cooperation with Napoleon during the French occupation. In 1814, as soon as the military situation permitted, Razumovskii appointed Professor Jan Lobenwein rector and sent him to Vilna.[14] Razumovskii knew that rectors were not appointed by the minister but elected by the faculty. He took illegal steps to get rid of Śniadecki. Since Śniadecki could not call on the still-absent Czartoryski for support, he decided it best for the university that he step aside, letting Lobenwein assume the rectorship with as little conflict as possible.

Śniadecki naturally resented Razumovskii. He also thought the Bible Society an affront. "One sends missionaries to barbarians," he wrote, "not to a great Catholic nation such as Poland." Czartoryski, however, seeing no reason not to cooperate with an organization that interested both Razumovskii and Golitsyn, took the lead in founding a chapter in Vilna. The Bible Society in Vilna amounted to little. It was all but stillborn in a society that felt little need for missionaries. Nonetheless, the move probably helped persuade Golitsyn to keep Czartoryski as Vilna's curator. Paradoxically, this made possible the election of Śniadecki's candidate for rector. Śniadecki and Lobenwein cooperated in arranging faculty elections in November, when Szymon Malewski, an old friend and supporter of Śniadecki, easily outpolled Frank—Czartoryski's choice—as well as Lobenwein, who finished a distant third.[15]

Czartoryski returned to Vilna in June 1817, his first appearance in the city in more than six years. He no longer had the confidence of the faculty, after his failure to help the university during the crisis of the war. Also, his marriage in 1817 to a beautiful teenager made him seem somewhat ridiculous, the butt of jokes among the faculty. Czartoryski, for his part, condemned the "low morale" and "careerism" he said he found among professors and students. Thus, although the university enjoyed record enrollments, several times

14. Beauvois, *L'Université de Vilna*, 65–66. Lobenwein fled the university at the approach of the French in 1812, spending the war years in St. Petersburg.
15. *Ibid.*, 67–68, 165 (quotation).

that of other universities, and its facilities (for example, a library now over 30,000 volumes) were the envy of others, Czartoryski's reports painted a bleak picture. In September 1819, while the struggle between Magnitskii and Uvarov occupied the ministry, Golitsyn decided to sent to Vilna a special inspector, I. S. Laval. Laval, like Magnitskii and others, owed his post in the ministry and on the Academic Committee to his work with the Bible Society. His report on Vilna, however, showed no trace of the Sturdza or Magnitskii cast of mind. He reported weaknesses, chief among them the lengthy absences of the curator. However, he found Vilna "rich" in able teacher-scholars, able and hard-working students, and excellent facilities. In sum, the Bible Society inspector at Vilna was no Magnitskii. He concluded, moreover, that the faculty was probably well advised to follow rector Malewski in moving slowly to accept Czartoryski's recommendations for making faculty appointments and other changes, for the university was generally successful.[16]

In May 1821 the faculty finally took up one of Czartoryski's recommendations, the appointment of a new professor of philosophy, but did not accept the candidate he proposed. Instead, the faculty committee that evaluated the candidates chose Józef Gołuchowski, a native of Galicia who began his university work in Vienna and completed his doctorate at Heidelberg. His dissertation showed him an accomplished interpreter of Kant and Schelling. Magnitskii's Instruction, apparently, held no terror for the Vilna faculty. Both Golitsyn and Czartoryski seemed concerned, however. Golitsyn sent an inquiry to the Imperial Commissioner in Warsaw, Novosiltsev, who promptly reported that Gołochowski was "highly praise-worthy in morals, assiduousness, and learning." Czartoryski, fearing, he said, that Gołochowski might be excessively "Germanized," suggested sending him to England for two years of study before he took up his professorship.[17]

Having postponed Gołochowski's arrival, Czartoryski in November 1821 warned the faculty that "great caution is required."[18] The danger he saw arose, not in Vilna, but in Cracow and Warsaw,

16. *Ibid.*, 43–44; Beauvois, "Czartoryski jako kurator," *Przegląd Historyczny*, 68–74.

17. Mark O'Connor, "Czartoryski and the Golochowski Affair at Vilna University," *Jahrbücher für Geschichte Osteuropas*, 31 (1983), 229–243, is the most thorough account.

18. *Sbornik istoricheskikh materialov, izvlechennykh iz arkhiva*, 8 (St. Petersburg, 1896), 263–265 (Czartoryski to rector, 3 November 1821).

where he followed with mounting alarm the career of his erstwhile friend Novosiltsev. After leaving his post as curator of the St. Petersburg district, Novosiltsev had some difficult days. Not least among his troubles was a serious problem with drink. Grievously unhappy as well as disgraced, he left St. Petersburg, spending the year 1811–1812 in Vienna. Czartoryski stayed in touch with him, and in 1814 encouraged him to accept Alexander's offer to return to service as a Russian minister in Warsaw. He served there as "Imperial Commissioner," a post whose duties were not well defined but that made him an influential figure. In 1820 a disturbance broke out among students in Cracow. Novosiltsev, Metternich, and Antoni Radziwill (appointed to represent the Prussian share in the partitions) had been named "conservateurs" of the University of Cracow. The president of Cracow's Senate, Count Stanisław Wodzicki, a bitter foe of university autonomy, called for an investigation of the student disorder. Novosiltsev, with his background in educational administration as well as in Polish affairs, was an obvious choice to chair the investigatory commission.[19]

Cracow's rector was elected by and from among the faculty, and the university governed itself through council and committees, the pattern of university governance that, as Novosiltsev well knew, the reformers in 1802–1804 found the model for Russian universtities. This pattern Novosiltsev now called the "republican form of government." He argued that the pattern naturally caused trouble, for it fostered a spirit of independence among faculty and students alike. Independence, when it conflicted with government policy, became insubordination. Thus, the cure was obvious: end the pattern of governance that inescapably promoted a spirit of independence leading to insubordination. Novosiltsev, therefore, recommended reorganizing the university so that the rector would be appointed and authority clearly run from the top down. Moreover, instruction had to include courses in religion taught by clergymen appointed for the purpose. Novosiltsev, clearly, had not changed his mind about the proper organization of academic institutions or their goals. His recommendations at Cracow in 1821 reproduced the regulations he wrote in 1804 for St. Petersburg Pedagogical Institute.

In September 1821 Novosiltsev received Tsar Alexander's permis-

19. For discussion of Czartoryski's relationship with Novosiltsev, see Zhukovich, "Pervyi russkii popechitel' vilenskago uchebnago okruga," *Khristianskoe chtenie,* 1892 (part one), 362–366, 380–381.

sion to investigate the schools in Warsaw, particularly the university, to search out the cause of "secret societies" that in the 1820s frightened authorities from Spain to St. Petersburg. Novosiltsev promptly reported that the problems at Warsaw stemmed from the same cause as at Cracow, or at the universities of Germany: the pattern of governance that made them little "academic republics." The problem was not Polish nationalism, but the institutional arrangements that encouraged autonomy. The self-governing university, far from the last word in modernity, he found a "survival from the middle ages" that was "not adapted to modern conditions of life."[20]

Czartoryski tried to ward off a similar investigation at Vilna by conducting his own. In March 1822 he appointed a faculty committee chaired by Professor Bojanus, whose competence and prestige were undoubted, particulary in St. Petersburg, where he spent the war years with Lobenwein. The Bojanus committee's investigation dismayed Czartoryski by revealing the existence of a secret student society called the "Radiants," an offshoot of an earlier and larger group called the "Philomaths." Bojanus, largely by bad luck, did not discover the Philomaths and concluded that the Radiants were harmless. The Radiants were devoted to encouraging study and religious devotion. The rector noted that under their influence, student attendance at religious services improved markedly. The society was well known to the rector, Malewski, whose son was one of its leaders. Acting on Czartoryski's advice to be "cautious," moreover, in the previous November, the rector had ordered the society to cease meeting. Students testified not only that the meetings had ceased but that since their group had met openly, if unofficially, and was well known to the rector, it could hardly be called "secret." The

20. Peter Brock, "The Struggle for Academic Freedom at the University of Cracow in the Early 1820s," *The Polish Review*, IX (No. 2, 1964), 30–52, makes clear that Wodzicki and other conservative Poles used Novosiltsev to attain their goals as much as he used them. Wodzicki described university autonomy as "bizarre proof of some kind of mental disorder" and urged Novosiltsev to end it at Cracow. For summary of Novosiltsev's work at Cracow and Warsaw in 1820–1821, see Beauvois, *L'Université de Vilna*, I, 50–52. Detailed discussion is in Frank W. Thackeray, *Antecedents of Revolution: Alexander I and the Polish Kingdom, 1815–1825* (Boulder, 1980). See especially *ibid.*, 67–70, 107–108, on Warsaw University. Founded by Alexander in 1816, its internal organization closely resembled that of the Russian universities founded in 1802–1804. Szymon Askenazy, *Tsarstvo pol'skoe 1815–1830 gg.* (Moscow, 1915), 66–105, provides extensive quotations from Novosiltsev's reports on his work in 1820–1821.

Bojanus committee concluded that there was "absolutely nothing" to sustain "the slightest suspicion."[21]

Czartoryski concluded that Malewski had mishandled the Radiants, by not keeping him informed about them, and he soon convinced many faculty members that a threatening situation was developing, making it useful to replace Malewski. The faculty agreed to accept Czartoryski's candidate and to elect him rector in September 1822, though he had not yet arrived in Vilna. Józef Twardowski, the new rector, took a doctorate in mathematics in Vilna in 1807 and served well as administrator of district schools for more than a decade. Because he was a rich noble, he had the status that Czartoryski thought necessary in a rector and lacking in an ordinary competent academic. With his candidate installed, Czartoryski called for "prudence" in the strict supervision of students, who should wear their uniforms, tend strictly to their religious duties, and carefully carry out all "printed instrucitons." Czartoryski specifically forbade "any many-membered meeting" that "could give the appearance of secretiveness."[22] Czartoryski's efforts to ward off trouble were in vain. In May 1823 a gymnasium student wrote on a blackboard a patriotic slogan: "Long live the constitution of 3 May!" Rector Twardowski assured the governor-general that the academic authorities had matters under control, but three days later Grand Duke Constantine ordered the rector's arrest. In July the tsar agreed to Constantine's suggestion to send Novosiltsev to conduct an investigation at Vilna.[23]

Novosiltsev's investigation, diligent though it was, produced nothing for many weeks. In October 1823 Tsar Alexander visited Vilna, passing through on a trip to the West. Czartoryski used the opportunity to present to him a memorandum on the Vilna schools. He found it "impossible to respond with precision to accusations" against the schools, for "no precise accusations have been made."

21. The best discussion of the Bojanus committee, and the whole question of "secret societies" at Vilna is Mark F. O'Connor, "Cultures in Conflict: A Case Study in Russian-Polish Relations: The University at Wilno" (Ph.D., Boston College, 1977), 256–266. Quotation 262.

22. *Sbornik istoricheskikh materialov*, v. 8, 257–262 (Czartoryski to rector, 9 November 1822). Quotation 261.

23. This investigation, unlike Magnitskii's at Kazan, or Laval's at Vilna, was not a ministry of education matter, but a special enterprise authorized by the tsar. The best discussion is O'Connor, "Cultures," 268–285.

The system of education was precisely the one that "with very little change [the tsar] confirmed" some twenty years ago. The system, Czartoryski declared, had proved remarkably successful, providing able graduates who served the district and empire as lawyers, civil servants, physicians, soldiers, teachers, and clergymen. "The principles of the education of such men are not erroneous, and their conduct does not merit blame."[24] This was the same defense that Uvarov made of St. Petersburg in 1821. Alexander made no reply to Uvarov then, and in 1823 made no reply to Czartoryski. Czartoryski guessed, however, that his curatorship would soon end, for shortly after his interview with the tsar, Novosiltsev reported the existence of the Philomaths. Since neither Czartoryski nor Bojanus had mentioned that group, Novosiltsev argued, with plausibility, that the Bojanus committee and Czartoryski had conducted, not an investigation, but a coverup.

The university community naturally resented Novosiltsev's investigation. His sharp questioning of Bojanus so angered the professor that he resigned in protest against treatment he thought contemptuous of the dignity due to senior scholar. Twardowski found that the investigator deliberately distorted what he found. The evidence made it clear that the Philomaths, no less than the Radiants, were devoted to encouraging learning and religion. They had conducted a "secret" society initially out of fear of the derision of their less-well-motivated peers, not to escape the government's notice. When investigators found evidence that indicated loyalty to the empire or religious devotion, it was "hidden or burned." But, Twardowski pointed out, when the investigators found "Polish writings," they "collected them diligently."[25] Clearly, Twardowski protested, the investigation was not an effort to learn the truth.

In October 1823, in the middle of the investigation, Gołuchowski returned from England to begin his lectures in philosophy. Rumor had it that Gołuchowski had been kept away for two years because the Russian government feared him. Such rumors helped to produce a crowd of six hundred for Gołuchowski's first lecture. The governor-general became alarmed and angry when Twardowski refused to obey his command to cancel Gołuchowski's course. Novosiltsev found Twardowski's insistence on the right of the university to de-

24. *Sbornik istoricheskikh materialov*, v. 8, 253–257 (Mémoire sur l'esprit des écoles de l'arrondissement de Vilna, 18 October 1823). Quotation 256.
25. O'Connor, "Cultures," 275.

cide what courses should be given, and who should be allowed to attend them, a clear illustration of how university autonomy naturally led directly to insubordination. No one could tell, he argued, where such insubordination might lead.[26]

It was August 1824 before Novosiltsev's investigation concluded with the dismissal of four professors, including Gołochowski, and exile for several students, some sentenced to complete their studies at Kazan University.[27] Some gymnasium pupils were treated very harshly, sentenced to the army as private soldiers. The severity of such punishment, together with the imprecise nature of the charges, angered more than it cowed the university community. The university had followed Czartoryski in trying everything possible to be cooperative, by stressing religion, tightening control over students, and adding Russian language, literature, law, and history to the curriculum. The policy of cooperation had proved a failure.

In his report of 11 June 1824 Novosiltsev explained why cooperation was not enough. Vilna's "weakness in university authority and police power" permitted "wide distribution of propaganda of the principles of the deceitful revolutionaries of the 18th century," whose "spirit of reform" had long "ruled in most German universities and in Warsaw and Cracow as well." Thus, "education comes to focus on developing republicanism in youth, and the hope for restoration of the former Poland." The intent to cooperate, then, was not enough, for the system of governance at Vilna was wrong on principle and thus, regardless of intent, ended in encouraging false, indeed destructive, hopes.[28]

Novosiltsev firmly rejected advice from Magnitskii to change the program of instruction, both the courses and the faculty teaching

26. Bielinski, *Uniwersytet Wileński*, II, 407; Beauvois, *L'Université de Vilna*, I, 271. Though the university refused to cancel Gołochowski's course, or admit that any but the university itself was responsible for deciding who was allowed to attend its lectures, for second term, starting in January 1824, Golochowski was assigned a new hour for his course—7:00 a.m.

27. Barkhattsev, "Iz Istorii," *RA*, 1216–1219, provides details on all the sentences. Golochowski was exiled to his "native land," Habsburg Galicia. Lelewel in exile published his famous *Novosiltsev a Vilna, ou Guerre imperiale avec les enfants et l'instruction* (Brussells, 1844), an account that gave the western world a picture in which Russian authorities in Poland appeared ridiculous as well as reactionary. Professor Bobrowski was cleared of all charges in 1826 and returned to the Vilna faculty. Professor Danilovich moved to Kharkov University, where he made a distinguished career.

28. Rozhdestvenskii, *Istoricheskii obzor*, 153–154; Barkhattsev, "Iz istorii," *RA*, 1220–1222.

them, in Vilna University. Instead, in March 1824 he saw through the Main School Administration of the ministry a reorganization proposed by Czartoryski, who had made the by-now-familiar complaint that the 1803–1804 statutes assigned to the rector and deans an impossibly difficult task. He recommended dividing the administrative work into smaller parcels for assignment to others. In August 1824, on the same day as the dismissals, Novosiltsev recommended "steps for improvement" that included requirements that students attend church, pay attention to their teachers, not join "secret societies," and avoid books that attacked religion or the government. Nothing in Novosiltsev's recommendations had not been recommended by Czartoryski and long since adopted by the faculty. Novosiltsev's reform at Vilna owed nothing to Bible Society religious concerns and, though he exploited the anti-Polish fears of conservatives such as Grand Duke Constantine, owed little to the sense of Russian nationalism that men like Magnitskii or Sturdza brought to the Bible Society. When he became curator of Vilna in September 1824, the program Novosiltsev undertook faithfully followed the model he had worked out for St. Petersburg Pedagogical Institute in 1804, and included neither changes in religious instruction nor Russification. The Bible Society reform was not attempted at Vilna.[29]

In 1822–1823 the university enrollment was 822 students, growing to 882 the next year, and to 893 the year after that. In short, the Novosiltsev investigation and purge did not even temporarily stop the steady growth of Vilna's student body. Faculty members bitterly condemned the dismissal of professors but soon filled the vacancies, with no apparent loss in quality. In many respects the university achieved the sort of success the reformers of 1802–1804 planned. Even instruction in the Russian language prospered. In 1822 I. N. Loboiko, warmly endorsed by Golitsyn and Czartoryski, joined the faculty to strengthen instruction in Russian and to provide a na-

---

29. *Sbornik postanovlenii*, I, 1756–1758 (O razdalenii pravleniia, 29 March 1824); 1778–1780 (O merakh prinatykh, 14 August 1824). For the exchange with Magnitskii, see Bielinski, *Uniwersytet Wileński*, II, 526; Bagalei, *Opyt istorii*, II, 153–155. In April 1824 Golitsyn nominated Laval, his Bible Society colleague, to be Vilna curator, but Novosiltsev was appointed, after Golitsyn's resignation. Pogodin, "Vilenskii uchebnyi okrug," *Sbornik materialov*, xxxvi–xxxvii, says that Laval was passed over for the curatorship because he asked for an additional 2000 rubles in salary. Laval requested the money, for which the ministry had ample precedent, but it seems clear that it was the end of the Golitsyn ministry that cost Laval the curatorship.

tive Russian on the faculty. Loboiko proved a hard-working, able teacher whose courses soon came to enroll more than a hundred students each term. He was particularly helpful to two able young scholars, Mickiewicz and Lelewel, and he made important contributions as a member of the Bojanus committee.[30]

The death of Czacki in 1813 and the expulsion of the Jesuits from the empire in 1820 made little difference to Vilna, for the Krzemieniec lycee continued to offer a program markedly more humanistic than Vilna's and to direct a practically autonomous district of its own, while the Jesuits' schools were turned over to another Catholic order, no more under Vilna's direction than the Jesuits. The character of the student body changed little. In many years the univesity failed to collect data on the social origins of the students. Nonetheless, it seems clear that the overwhelming majority continued to come from gentry of the three northwestern provinces of the Vilna district. Social mobility as promoted by Vilna meant improvement in the situation of poor gentry far more often than it did a change of class for those born in low estates. While faculty members continued to teach and write about the virtues of free labor, their impact on society was minimal. Indeed, to the dismay of Czartoryski and Śniadecki, the faculty assembly could not agree on a program to end serfdom on properties owned by the university.[31]

The lower schools remained open to all, however, and continued to grow. By 1822 they enrolled more than 22,000 pupils, more than sixty percent greater than the number enrolled in schools of the Moscow district, the second largest. Enrollment in the *uezd* schools of Vilna province came up to nearly 4,000 by 1822. Most schools were operated by religious orders. Eleven of seventeen *uezd* schools in Vilna province were sponsored by religious groups, including two Uniate and one Lutheran. The university's teacher-training program graduated but twenty men annually, most of whom became gymnasium science and mathematics teachers. That fact meant that the university contributed most where it was

30. Beauvois, *L'Université de Vilna*, I, 314–366, is a very thorough discussion of Vilna's students and provides the only accurate presentation of enrollment figures in print. On Loboiko, see *ibid.*, 284–285.

31. Beauvois, *L'Université de Vilna*, I, 130–134, is an incisive discussion of the university's handling of the serf question, concluding that in the end "the university accommodated itself very well to traditional servitude. . . ." On students and social mobility, see *ibid.*, 314–324, particularly on the students' perception of the difference between "panicze" and "szlachta," though both were "noble."

strongest and where the religious sponsors tended to be weakest. The university's annual reports on the lower schools often listed areas in need of improvement, particularly competent instruction in the Polish language. Not surprisingly, however, they usually concluded with a note of satisfaction that things went well.[32]

Even the seminary prospered. Though its building was destroyed during the war by French vandals, not by military action, by 1817 it was in full operation, soon graduating twenty men annually. Seventeen of fifty state student stipends were reserved for Uniates. The Roman Catholic and Uniate students lived and studied together. They met separately for a course on liturgy, though many of the Romans sat in on that course too, but for all other courses and for morning mass they came together. They formed two lines at communion time, each taking the sacrament according to the rite of his church. Since the mass and communion were naturally at the heart of the religious life of the institution, this mutually respectful witness of unity in diverse forms of worship was important for both. The seminary provided men well placed in both churches who had experience in mutually supportive cooperation. The Vilna seminary, against the expectations of the Catholic and Uniate bishops, and perhaps its founders too, produced, not "Josephinists" to run a state church for the purposes of the state, but men gaining experience at meeting the difficult task of improving relations between peoples who followed different ways of worship and whose differences had marked, if not made, generations of bitter hostility.[33]

That such a success might harbor "danger" for the Russian Empire was a consideration that never came up in the Bible Society era. When Novosiltsev became curator in September 1824 he cautioned against making additional changes, for he considered his university already successful. He was quite right about that. Nonetheless,

32. Beauvois, *L'Université de Vilna*, I, 343–349, II, 687–711; Pogodin, "Vilenskii uchebnyi okrug," *Sbornik materialov*, lxix–lxxxii. Nicholas Hans, who defined "enlightenment" in education as the development of a "secular, state-controlled, national system" ("Educational Reform in Poland in the Eighteenth Century," *Journal of Central European Affairs*, XIV (1954), 301), was not much impressed with the achievements of the Vilna district, which he summarized in "Polish Schools in Russia 1772–1832," *SEER*, XXXVIII (1960), 410–414.

33. P N. Zhukovich, "Ob osnovanii i ustroistve glavnoi dukhovnoi seminarii pri Vilenskom universitete (1803–1832 gg.), *Khristianskoe chtennie*, 1887 (No. 3–4), 237–286, provides detail particularly valuable on the religious life of the institution. See also Beauvois, *L'Universite de Vilna*, I, 330–338.

within a decade he was dismissed and the university closed, for the
1830 Warsaw revolt, when it was extended into the Vilna district,
convinced many that Novosiltsev was wrong not to find "Polonism"
a pressing threat. Novosiltsev's foes were quite wrong about that.
The danger at Vilna was neither Polonism nor Novisiltsev's *bête
noire*, "republicanism." The danger was frustration. The university
at Vilna tried hard to achieve the reform goals, and at every stage
cooperated fully with the ministry. The purges followed nonetheless. Bitter frustration was the natural legacy.

3. Mixed Results: Dorpat, Moscow, and Kharkov

The Bible Society curators of other universities did not contend
with turmoil comparable to that which destroyed the curatorships
of Uvarov and Czartoryski. All three—Lieven for Dorpat, Obolenskii for Moscow, and Karneev at Kharkov—instead found that the
problems they encountered responded well enough to the remedial
steps they took. Karneev was mistaken about the degree of success
he achieved. But that did not invalidate the more important point
that, though the Bible Society program in practice proved too
ephemeral to provide guidlines, the work of Bible Society curators
sometimes strengthened their universities.

The Dorpat area suffered unusually severe inflation during the
war years. Prices quadrupled, reducing university faculty members
to near poverty. None of Curator Klinger's recommendations to
help, which included free firewood from government stocks as well
as pay raises, interested Razumovskii enough to get action. In 1816
rumors spread that some Dorpat faculty members were helping
themselves by selling degrees. Klinger's investigation found that two
law professors were in fact arranging doctorates in exchange for
cash. Newly appointed minister, Golitsyn found this corruption evidence of the need for the Bible Society reform at Dorpat. Golitsyn
knew well that Klinger was not likely to prove helpful. In 1813, as
Procurator of the Holy Synod, Golitsyn condemned the work of one
of Dorpat's theologians and was astonished to have Klinger's response, that the work of the university's scholars was to be judged
only by the university. Klinger, on another occasion, refused to consider the appointment of a historian warmly recommended by Golitsyn, because the man was a "mystic," the very reason that Golitsyn

recommended him. As soon as he became minister, Golitsyn arranged to replace Klinger with a Baltic German noble who was also a fervent member of the Bible Society.[34]

Count Karl Lieven was a well-known member of the St. Petersburg chapter of the Bible Society, which he served as a "director" from its inception. Born in 1767, he served in the army for twelve years, and saw combat against both Turks and Poles before returning to his family estates in 1801. The following sixteen years were spent for the most part in Kurland, where he devoted himself to management of his family properties and became well known both for his wealth and for his knowledge of agriculture. Lieven had the rich and well-motivated amateur's interest in things "scientific" as well as genuine piety, although upon appointment as Dorpat's curator he described himself as "an old soldier with no pretense to intellectual or academic attainments."[35]

Addressing the faculty at the opening of the academic year in September 1817, Lieven called for not only "academic training, but also the moral formation which can prepare [students] to be responsible servitors of tsar, state, and mankind." Lieven soon showed he could be counted on to meet faculty needs as well as those of the Bible Society. By the spring of 1818 he successfully obtained a completely new budget for his university that nearly tripled the total, and more than doubled the income of professors. Shortly, he began work on a new statute.[36] He visited the university at least twice a year, worked out the statute in consultation with the rector, and had a faculty member join him in St. Petersburg to work full time on the statute proposal.

In January 1820 Lieven submitted to the Main School Administration of the ministry his proposed new statute. At the same time that the statute proposals made by Uvarov for St. Petersburg were subjected to vicious criticism, and never did gain adoption, Lieven's very similar proposal easily passed, confirmed into law by the tsar

34. Petukhov, *Derptskii universitet*, 314–319, discusses the inflation problem; *ibid.*, 270–275, the fraudulent doctorates. *Sbornik postanovlenii*, I 907–908, 1050–1052, are the reports by Klinger and Golitsyn. Sawatsky, "Golitsyn," 312–314, provides the details.

35. Petukhov, *Derptskii universitet*, 327. A useful summary of Lieven's career is in *RBS*, v. 10 (SPB, 1914), 424.

36. The new statute is printed in *Sbornik postanovlenii*, I, 1382–1439. For discussions of its provisions and path to enactment, see Petukhov, *Derptskii universitet*, 359–368; Rozhdestvenskii, *Istoricheskii obzor*, 154–156. Petukhov, *Derptskii universitet*, 319–322, discusses Lieven's handling of the budget matter.

in June 1820. Lieven took no part in the discussions regarding Magnitskii's inspection of Kazan or Uvarov's proposed statute for St. Petersburg. His prudence, keeping clear of the Magnitskii-Uvarov struggle, seemed fruitful for Dorpat if not for the university system.

The new statute statement of goals was copied word for word from that of 1803: Dorpat university was founded "for the common good," and "therefore the university accepts as students people of every class of natives of Russia and foreigners." The election of rector and deans, the independence of the university court, the censorship committee, the right to select faculty members, freedom from the regular police or indeed "all personal obligation" for all members of the university (faculty, staff, and students) and their families—all those elements of the 1803 statute were restated and affirmed. The only significant change was the budget, increased from 130,000 to 370,000 rubles.

No Bible Society statements of goals, certainly no Magnitskii-like warnings of peril, appeared in Dorpat's statute. Lieven was a deeply religious man, who shared the hopes of many well-motivated colleagues who served the Bible Society. "What the professors of other faculties in Dorpat believe is not my concern," he candidly observed, "but the professors of theology I choose myself." As he explained to Parrot, "Religion is not a matter of knowledge alone. . . . It is first of all a matter of heart and belief."[37] Lieven meant to improve his university's ability to train "responsible servitors of tsar, state, and mankind," by replacing "rationalists" in the theology faculty with evangelicals. At this he was successful, for by 1824 no member of the theology faculty remained who was in service when Lieven became curator. There was neither "purge," nor charge of "evil." All the "rationalists" left by retiring in the normal way, on full pension, two not until the sixth year of Lieven's curatorship. Lieven demonstrated that the Bible Society reform required no surrender of elements essential to the original reform, and clearly did not require the turmoil of a "purge." On the contrary, Lieven warded off a serious effort to limit the academic freedom of the university by the provincial governor, Paulucci.

In 1818, the university engaged J. W. Snell to come from Ger-

37. Quotations from "Erinnerungen des bibliothekars Emil Anders," *Baltische Monatsschrift*, xxxix (1892), 217; Friedrich Bienemann, ed., "Briefe des Fürsten Karl Lieven," *Baltische Monatsschrift*, xlii (1895), 272.

many to serve as professor of law. Paulucci took it upon himself to bar Snell's entrance to Dorpat. Dorpat students protested with a violent, rock-throwing, demonstration in the city that brought several of them jail terms (imposed by the university court) and convinced Paulucci that he had been right to intercept a dangerous agitator. In December 1820 the governor sent a long report to the tsar, denouncing "the academic republic" at Dorpat, recommending strong steps to prevent further contaminating contacts with German universities.[38]

Golitsyn directed the Academic Committee of the ministry to implement Paulucci's recommendation. The Committee concluded that a prohibition of study in all German universities was impossibly extreme. Paulucci contributed a list of universities that should be proscribed, though he made no explanation of his principles of selection. It was July 1822 before it was finally agreed that Russian students no longer would be allowed to take up studies at Heidelberg, Ghent, Giessen, or Würzburg universities (later all Jesuit institutions were similarly proscribed), and all students currently enrolled in those institutions were to be given the option of returning home or transferring to schools located in either Hanover or Prussia. Though the rationale of forbidding study in Germany while granting almost wholesale exceptions was not made clear, this arrangement finally became law in February 1823. Lieven, who found excessive even this much recognition of "danger" in study in German universities, obtained a postponement, giving his university additional time to accept transfer students from the four proscribed universities.[39]

Moscow was as much a "national" university as Dorpat or Vilna, and Curator Kutuzov himself expressed well the spirit of Great Russian patriotism that animated the life of Moscow University. Indeed, he went to some lengths to cultivate it. He seldom missed an oppor-

---

38. For the Snell affair, see Petukhov, *Derptskii universitet*, 343–344. On Paulucci's views of the university, see Marquis Filippe "Paulucci und seine Verfolgung geheimer Gesellschaften in den Ostseeprovinzen," *Baltische Monatsschrift*, xliv (1897), 501–513. Paulucci had served with great distinction, even heroism, in several armies that fought those of revolutionary France. Appointed governor of Livland in 1812, he did a remarkable job in organizing the defenses of the provinces. For a useful summary of his career, see *RBS*, v. 13 (SPB, 1902), 402–403.

39. *Sbornik postanovlenii*, I, 1605–1611, 1674–1681. See also Petukhov, *Derptskii universitet*, 549–551. In all discussions of the "danger" of "German" universities, Ghent was regularly included.

tunity to organize a ceremonial occasion to which he could invite the governor and other notables. He sent appeals to the ministry, urging the award of medals to local notables who had made contributions to the university. To some the curator seemed a comic figure, for nearly every day the ministry received from him letters full of praise for himself. Nonetheless, since he cultivated Rostopchin, Shishkov, and other members of Moscow's social and economic elite, he not only secured gifts of support for the university but also the confidence of people whose interest and support could be important. Kutuzov was willing to go far to ingratiate himself with local notables. In the spring of 1816, for example, he proposed to the faculty council the award of a doctorate to a wealthy young man named Vinogradov, who had boarded in the home of one of the language professors in 1815–1816 and had taken various lecture courses. In the spring of 1816 Vinogradov joined his family in St. Petersburg. The curator recommended waiving the "formality" of a thesis defense (and thus also the course work, examinations, and *kandidat* degree required for a doctorate) to award a doctorate to Vinogradov. The faculty council, without demurrer, approved the curator's recommendation.[40]

Despite Kutuzov's successes, Golitsyn replaced him with A. P. Obolenskii, a charter member of the Bible Society. Appointed curator in January 1817, months before the official formation of the dual ministry, Obolenskii could be expected to foster Bible Society aims while yielding nothing to Kutuzov in patriotism. Moscow-born, he had a creditable military career, which he left in 1799, returning to Moscow, where he actively participated in the social-cultural life of the city. Two excellent marriages enabled him to capitalize on the prestige of his family name. His first wife brought him more than four thousand serfs and much productive property. His second wife, a Gagarin, brought him into contact with those who had serious religious-moral interests, which in time brought Obolenskii and Golitsyn together.[41] Obolenskii insisted on regular office hours as well as efficient management. This contrast with Kutuzov's

40. On Vinogradov's degree, see the memoirs of Kutuzov's secretary, "Universitet v vospominnaiiakh Tret'iakova," *RS*, 1892 (August), 331–332; Shevyrev, *Istoriia*, 460.

41. *RBS*, v. 12 (SPB, 1905), 23–24. Except as otherwise noted, the account of Obolenskii's curatorship is based upon Tret'iakov's memoir in *RS*, 1892 (August), 334–344; *ibid.*, (September), 533–540, and Shevyrev, *Istoriia*, 425–440.

exceedingly irregular work habits was at first perceived by the office staff as an unfortunate turn of events. But the new curator also pleased the staff by finding ways to raise salaries. The university secretary received a 50 percent raise, up to 1,500 rubles. Obolenskii became acquainted personally with the faculty members, who were invited to his home for dinner, two at a time. This practice, continued over the years, provided Obolenskii with the opportunity to gauge well his faculty's views and needs. Though he seldom made use of the formal sessions of the faculty council, most faculty and staff members soon came to regard the curator as a friend to be trusted, as did the students.

Early in his curatorship, Obolenskii also made a contribution to the reform of the whole system. One of the problems encountered in the first decade was confusion over degree standards, or the meaning of an *attestat*. The original reform legislation made no mention of the "student" diploma, yet that had proved the degree most often sought. Learning of the cases of the fraudulent Dorpat doctorates, and of a similar problem at Kharkov, Alexander in 1816 suggested that perhaps all recently awarded doctorates should be reexamined and, meanwhile, ordered a moratorium on granting degrees until the ministry could assure him that proper standards were maintained.[42] In December 1817 Obolenskii formally protested the moratorium, for it unfairly punished, he argued, men who in good faith had already proceeded far in their studies. He secured from the ministry the right to award degrees to those who had begun study before the announcement of the moratorium. This right was extended also to the other universities.

In January 1819 the ministry responded to Obolenskii's urging with a regulation intended to make clear the degree requirements of Russian universities. The original statutes of 1803–1804 had listed three degrees, *kandidat, magister,* and doctorate. The new regulation recognized a fourth, that of "student," explaining that the "title of actual student applies to those who have completed the whole course of study in their faculty and have received therefore an appropriate *attestat*." To this description, the decree added a clarifying note: "Although those who are studying in universities are

42. The order for the moratorium is printed in *Sbornik rasporiazhenii*, I, 288. For Obolenskii's response, see *Sbornik postanovlenii*, I, 1108–1109. The text of the new regulation "on the awarding of academic degrees" is in *ibid.*, 1247–1258. Quotations 1250–1251.

already called students, they do not yet have the diploma of student." The *kandidat* degree was defined as requiring "outstanding success" in the end-of-course examinations and the submission of a scholarly paper. The paper could be accepted, and the degree awarded, no earlier than one year after the receipt of the "student" *attestat*. Similarly, the *magister* could be taken no earlier than two years after completion of the *kandidat*, while the doctorate required three years from the date of the *magister*, and both required completion and defense of the appropriate theses. This new regulation was, thus, a description of the best practices that had developed since the inauguration of the university reform in 1803–1804, together with rules clearly designed to proscribe the abuses that had also developed.

Obolenskii secured a major increase in funding for the medical faculty, and a splendid new university chapel, gained by securing the transfer of a well-endowed center-city church to the university over the strenuous objections of the local clergy. The new medical facilities occasioned a struggle within the faculty, since several members of the faculty had relatives and friends whom they thought deserved appointments. These disputes among faculty factions were limited to arguments over who should benefit most from the new appropriations, rather than over some issue of principle, and had little significance for Moscow's future.[43] In July 1819 the university opened a new main building, for which Alexander in January 1817 had authorized the expenditure of half a million rubles. The occasion was marked by appropriately impressive ceremonies. The new main building focused the attention of the city and the university, reminding all of how much had been accomplished in the seven years since the nearly complete devastation of 1812.

Another turning point was in 1819, the introduction of theology into the curriculum. In May Golitsyn sent a directive that theology, the subject "most needed for life," should be required of every student. The faculty, as elsewhere, was to find a teacher for this chair among the local clergy. In October Father Grigorii Levitskii began giving courses in church history and dogmatic theology. Levitskii's reading lists were made up entirely of books published abroad in French or German. Thus, 1819–1820, the year of Magnitskii's in-

43. Tret'iakov, *RS*, 1892 (August), 344, says that this "factionalism" was limited to the medical faculty. For the expanded medical program, see *Sbornik postanovlenii*, I, 1280–1282.

spection and "purge" at Kazan, saw at Moscow the introduction of religion on terms that doubtless would have occasioned a hostile "investigation" if Curator Obolenskii had chosen to report "danger," not success.[44]

Karneev, Kharkov's Bible Society curator, was well intentioned and wanted the best for his university, but Kharkov was a weak institution and Karneev not nearly so able an administrator as Lieven or Obolenskii. Kharkov's weakness was well illustrated in the case of Professor Schad's dismissal. Schad was one of the academic stars recruited by Potocki from Germany. He gave many courses that drew upon Kant and Schelling, and one on Roman law that was especially important for students intending a career in civil service. One of the few members of the Kharkov faculty who attracted students to stay long enough to write doctoral theses, Schad was, thus, an important and highly visible member of the faculty. There was no doubt also that he had a serious problem with drink, although this did not make him unique among foreign professors. Schad also often attributed the rise of "freedom" in the modern world to German influence and of "slavery" to that of the French. He was not only a prominent teacher of "idealistic" phiosophy, but one whose personal habits and lack of moderation, or of ordinary prudence, made him obnoxious to many of his faculty colleagues.

In December 1815 two of Schad's students presented theses for the doctorate.[45] Professor Degurov (formerly Dugour), the subject of denunciations himself at earlier faculty meetings, used the theses defense to attack Schad and idealistic philosophy, which he said was a "danger to youth," necessarily producing "errors" in conceptions of "political rights" and, since the teaching was anti-Christian, it led naturally to immorality and thus was a clear threat to the moral life of Russian students. Schad made no secret of his lack of regard for Christianity, for he had abandoned not only the Roman Catho-

---

44. *Sbornik rasporiazhenii*, I, 384–385, 395, for the Golitsyn-Obolenskii correspondence regarding the introduction of religion into the curriculum. The introduction of religion into the curriculum at Moscow is often wrongly presented as an example of "reaction" in the Magnitskii-Runich mold. See, e.g., Tikhomirov, *Istoriia*, I, 100.

45. For discussions of the affair of Schad's dismissal, see Bagalei, *Opyt istorii*, II, 41–46, 653–655 (Quotation 654); Lavrovskii, "Episod," *Chteniia*, 38–58; N. A. Lavrovskii, "Pedagog proshlago vremeni (Diugurov)," *RA*, 1869 (No. 9), 1550–1552; G. S. Chirikov, "Timofei Fedorovich Osipovskii," *RS*, 1876 (November), 468–470. Schad's 1815 manuscript is summarized and quoted in Bagalei, *Opyt istorii*, II, 700–702.

lic faith of his fathers but the practice of all formal religion. In 1815 he submitted a manuscript for a book that he wanted the ministry to publish (*Illustrious Men of Rome, from Romulus to Augustus*), in which he denounced "the moral plague which rules in Christianity."

Degurov charged also that Schad's students' theses were so close, in language as well as conception, to Schad's own works that they were hardly more than plagiarism. The faculty committee, appointed by the council to look into this charge, found that the theses did in fact follow very closely some of Schad's works, reproducing whole sections word for word. Degurov sent his charges also to Razumovskii, urging the minister to intervene by removing Schad.

Schad defended his students' work. "Students of philosophy," he said, "have no other sources and materials except my manuscripts and books. It is not possible to require from students that they compose their own system of philosophy. It is enough that they put down in good form the matter of my manuscripts and books and successfully defend them in public." He also charged that Degurov was a "demagogue" who had never satisfactorily explained his career in revolutionary France, or refuted charges that he sympathized with French war aims, even those of the "monster" Napoleon. The tactic of making such countercharges was an old practice in the Kharkov faculty council, and might have been effective had not Degurov found an important ally. Osipovskii, the leader among the Russians on the faculty, also joined the attack on Schad. Osipovskii had long maintained that idealistic philosophy had no contact with anything "real" and was worse than a waste of time in the education of young men who were expected to make careers in the public services. He ridiculed the work of Schad's students and of Schad himself. He wrote to Razumovskii, and encouraged others to do the same, attacking Schad's work and urging his dismissal.

Razumovskii, though he arranged to have the ministry ban the book that Schad had submitted for publication in 1815, hesitated to discharge the professor. When Golitsyn became minister, he had no such scruple, for he saw his duty clearly. He ordered Curator Potocki to discharge Schad. Potocki refused, for there had been no "trial," nor had Schad been convicted of violating any laws. Golitsyn began casting about for a replacement for Potocki and, in December 1816, sent a directive to the provincial military governor ordering Schad's removal. A detachment from the local garrison appeared at Schad's door, and within twenty-four hours he was under military escort to the frontier, for he was not only discharged from the university but expelled from the empire as well.[46] The authority to take such a step was not included in the legislation that founded the ministry. Nonetheless, arbitrary though it was, the step was taken. Potocki soon submitted his resignation. Alexander's reply made no mention of Schad or of his dismissal, but warmly thanked Potocki for his many years of able service.

Golitsyn was well prepared for Potocki's departure. In November 1816 he wrote to Z. Ia. Karneev, one of the founding members of the St. Petersburg Bible Society, asking him to accept the curatorship of Kharkov since none "could better serve the cause of true enlightenment than you." He added also: "Please keep this letter secret, for Count Potocki should not know of this yet."[47]

Karneev, from a poor gentry family of the Kharkov region, spent nearly twenty years in the army before transferring to the civil service in 1785. He had no formal education (there was "neither time nor money" for that, he said), but rose to the post of provincial vice-governor. In 1808 he reached the peak of his career with his appointment to the Senate. He was one of the earliest adherents of the Bible Society and thus came to Golitsyn's attention. Appointed Kharkov curator, Karneev promised to foster "education based on true enlightenment, in order to prepare the best possible citizens of this earthly fatherland and true sons of the fatherland in heaven."[48]

Before launching this effort, Karneev requested an additional pension of 3,600 rubles a year and the purchase of a house for his use in Kharkov. Well provided for the remainder of his stay on the earthly fatherland, Karneev made an inspection of his university in

46. So sudden was Schad's removal that he was forced to leave behind his wife and daughter, to follow when and as they could. In Germany, Schad resumed an academic career and published uncomplimentary accounts of the state of higher learning in the Russian empire. In 1819 he had an apparently cordial meeting with Tsar Alexander in Weimar, at which Schad presented the tsar with an autoraphed copy of the book that the Razumovskii ministry had banned in Russia. Schad kept up a correspondence with the ministry, protesting his dismissal and demanding reinstatement. In 1827, at the same time that Nicholas I declared closed the affair of the professors at St. Petersburg, he also approved payment to Schad of full pension and all back pay. Schad was not, however, to return to Russia. Bagalei, *Opyt istorii*, II, 47–51.

47. "Perepiska Kniazia A. N. Golitsyna s Z. Ia. Karneevym," *RA*, 1893 (No. 5), 129–130 (Golitsyn to Karneev, 6 November 1816, and reply, n.d.).

48. For accounts of Karneev's career to 1817, see Bagalei, *Opyt istorii*, II, 60–62; I. P. Shchelkov, "Iz istorii khar'kovsago universiteta," *ZhMNP*, 1890 (No. 10), 359–368. Quotation 368.

May 1817. He was puzzled to find that theology was not taught in the university, and he declared to the faculty that it would have to be introduced soon. He ordered that all members of the university, students and staff alike, attend church on Sundays. He repeatedly told the faculty that all teaching should be done in the "spirit of Christ," and encouraged them to read the Bible. Karneev made few changes in the staff and curriculum. He counted himself successful because the Bible Society achieved what he regarded as considerable success. In 1820, for example, the professor of botany, Deliavin, prepared French language translations of much Bible Society material that he proposed the university press should publish for the benefit of those members of local society who could not read Russian. Karneev thought that a wonderful idea, and the university council voted unanimously to support Deliavin's venture.[49] The impact of Professor Deliavin's work on the spiritual development of local society was not easy to detect, but his work was evidence of the easy cooperation Karneev received from his faculty.

Karneev's frequent reports of success received from both the minister and the tsar warm thanks and congratulations. Nonetheless, even Karneev's determined optimism could not entirely eliminate the intra-faculty struggles that had so long distinguished life at Kharkov. On the departure of most of the foreigners, much of the friction that produced struggles in the past also departed. However, the outstanding scholar and elected rector was Osipovskii, who did not distinguish between what he regarded as second-raters among foreigners and natives. He treated both with equal scorn. Almost routinely Osipovskii questioned the scholarly competence of his colleagues, especially during the public defense of student theses. When Karneev invited him to join the Bible Society, Osipovskii replied that he never got on with those who try to "explain the unplainable." On the evening of 14 November 1820 there gathered a faculty meeting of which the rector had not been informed, which voted to dismiss Osipovskii from the rectorship and to replace him with professor Dzhunkovskii. Osipovskii at once resigned and applied for his pension. His faculty colleagues were happy to vote support for his pension, and indeed to elect him distinguished professor emeritus, apparently on condition, however, that he leave town.[50]

49. Bagalei, *Opyt istorii*, II, 82–83, 92–98.
50. Osipovskii moved to Moscow, though he returned to Kharkov in 1823 for an

Satisfied that his goals were achieved, Karneev in the fall of 1821 requested retirement and at the same time recommended the appointment of his nephew, E. V. Karneev, as his successor. Golitsyn was at that time engrossed in the Runich investigation at St. Petersburg, which he described in great detail to Karneev. Genuinely sorry that Runich had uncovered "evil teaching" in St. Petersburg University, he sadly described the meetings with the St. Petersburg faculty. He was deeply grateful to have Karneev's reports of success. "I rejoice that you have seen the fruits of your efforts for Christianity in your university . . . for which you can thank the Lord."[51] Golitsyn was, thus, both surprised and distressed to receive the younger Karneev's first report, for it described serious deficiencies not only in the administrative-economic aspects, but also in academic work and in student discipline.[52]

The younger Karneev was a native of Kharkov and a graduate of Moscow University. After brief army service he transferred to the ministry of finance. In time he made a useful career as a financial administrator in several agencies and also in technical education with the Mining Institute. There was no doubt that his Bible Society connections, on which his uncle's recommendation capitalized, led to his appointment at Kharkov. But he made no effort to persuade the ministry that changes were necessary to foster a "good spirit" or to ward off "evil doctrines." "The first and most important thing," he said, was to "improve the situation and the support given to state students, among whom live also a number of self-supporting students who pay the fees required." Also, the library and the laborato-

---

extended visit with his children. Delays in the paperwork kept Osipovskii from actually receiving his pension for nearly eighteen months. Sukhomlinov, *Izsledovaniia*, I, 86, says that Osipovskii's dismissal resulted from Karneev's distress that Osipovskii advised a student to say that "God exists" rather than that "God lives." Bagalei, *Opyt istorii*, II, 113, doubts this story but concludes (*ibid.*, 138) that final "responsibility" for the dismissal of Osipovskii "belongs exclusively to the curator." Shchelkov, "Iz istorii," *ZhMNP*, 384–385, argues that Karneev knew rather little of what was taught in his university and would have been content to let things alone, if only Osipovskii would go along. Sukhomlinov, *Izsledovaniia*, I, 222–223, concluding his discussion of the impact of the "reforms" of Magnitskii, Runich, and Karneev, says that "In its internal administration and its relationship with society, the university acquired the form of a clerical, even medieval Catholic, monastery, and the reformers (i.e., Magnitskii, Runich, and Karneev) tried to destroy all aspects of secular education." Sukhomlinov's conclusion is clearly mistaken.

51. "Perepiska Golitsyna s Karneevym," *RA*, 131–132 (9 November 1821).
52. Bagalei, *Opyt istorii*, II, 143–145.

ries needed work. They were poorly managed because the professors responsible for building and keeping up the collections simply were not doing it. Moreover, Karneev reported that students spent too much time in classes, listening to lectures from early morn to evening, which allowed little or no time for reading, review, or study. Most students were busy copying lecture notes much of the time. Though many tried hard, and produced voluminous notes, they achieved little real learning.

The cures for these and other problems the curator had already worked out with the faculty council. He reported that the faculty agreed that all courses would have at least one examination annually. The faculty also agreed that in each class the professor should briefly review the material of the preceding lecture, and provide time for student questions. Then he should "explain the new material." He should also keep class lists and note attendance. The professor should use his own "notes" only in those subjects for which no textbook existed. The faculty agreed that if it was impossible to keep a scheduled class, due to illness or whatever, the rector should be informed and, if possible, arrangements made for a substitute. Finally, all candidates for admission would be required to take an examination, "no matter what *attestat* from any gymnasium" they might have. Clearly Karneev found his university lacking in ordinary academic competence. It seemed possible after all that Osipovskii was right, if impolitic, to imply that he was an academic giant among so many pygmies. Worse, it seemed possible that the development of a faculty of "very honorable Christian men," as the elder Karneev had described them, also meant the development of a faculty that needed quite elementary guidelines on what to do with each class hour.

In May and June 1824 the Academic Committee of the ministry, made up of Fuss, Laval, and Runich, turned down most of Karneev's requests for additional funding, while giving lengthy consideration to his proposals for changes in the university statute. Karneev wanted the ministry to appoint the rector "from among the professors or other educated officials, well versed in the sciences and experienced in service." The rector would do no teaching, for the point of the change was to provide a full-time administration that would have "both the time and the means" to do the job. Laval and Fuss heatedly rejected Karneev's proposal. Laval pointed out that the experience of most universities had made it clear that the rector needed assistance. Thus, others had appointed "directors" to manage non-academic functions. There was no need, therefore, to abolish the elective rectorship, which Laval did not find an improvement but the "destruction of one of the fundamental principles of organization of all our universities." Fuss agreed, declaring it especially important that the rector be "a scholar and teacher, chosen from the faculty he serves." Runich had little to say. The most interesting aspect of the discussion was, in fact, what was not said. No one mentioned the Bible Society or any of its concerns. Golitsyn made no comment on the conclusion of the discussion, for in the spring of 1824 even its leaders found the Bible Society prescriptions irrelevant to the problems they faced.

4. Faculty

Russian reformers, from the great Peter on, could always turn to the West to recruit some able professionals for any enterprise that Russia needed. Alexander's reformers realized the need to move beyond that by developing a native, self-replicating academic community, able to perform as teachers and scholars at a level seriously comparable with that of Western academics. Progress toward this goal was achieved in the first decade. In the decade of the Bible Society much progress was undone. The faculties of Kazan and St. Petersburg universities were less able to meet the reform goals, including those formulated by the Bible Society, in 1824 than in 1815, the replacement of foreigners with natives notwithstanding. Vilna's faculty remained strong, but the question had been raised whether that was good for Russia. The faculties of the other universities raised important questions too. Kharkov's faculty development undercut the reform as much as it fulfilled it. Dorpat grew stronger, though the place of a German Protestant university in Russia had yet to be worked out. Moscow met all the goals, for it produced a faculty of competent academics, natives who were at home with Russian values and mores. In faculty development, then, one of the six universities was unambiguously a success.

Kharkov's example well illustrated the nature of the problem. V. Ia. Dzhunkovskii, Osipovskii's successor as rector, was a gentry-born graduate of St. Petersburg. He took up service in a military hospital before securing appointment in 1790 as a language teacher at the

Medical-Surgical Academy. Within a few years he had also become librarian and archivist of the same institution as well as a member of the Free Economic Society. Over the years he published a good deal, including translations in medical history, especially of ancient Greece. He wrote essays on poetry, religion, and other topics. In 1818, on the recommendation of the curator and minister, he was elected by the faculty council at Kharkov to be professor of Greek. He had no university training, and his participation in the Bible Society was the chief reason for his appointment.[53]

Capitalizing on his Bible Society connections made Dzhunkovskii unique at Kharkov, for no other faculty member had any particular connection with the Bible Society. Dzhunkovskii joined the literature faculty (*slovestnost'*, which held the chairs of Russian and world history as well as those of languages and literatures), whose chair of Greek had never before been filled. In 1815 this faculty had but four members, one of whom, Degurov, left within a year. Two others died before 1820. Seven men, in addition to Dzhunkovskii, were added to this staff by 1824. All but one came from the clergy. The highest degree of all but one was a *magister* from Kharkov University. All were appointed initially in the rank of teacher or adjunct (those appointed as teachers were soon promoted to adjunct) in one or another language, though some, sooner or later, took on other subjects as well.

The physics-mathematics faculty numbered eight men in 1815, but half were gone before the year 1820 was out. Five men joined the faculty by 1825. Unlike their colleagues in literature, all came from the gentry. Like their colleagues, however, the highest degree of all but one was a *magister* from Kharkov. The other faculties, moral-political sciences and medicine, made appointments of men similar in background and training. Each added one man who had completed a doctorate at Moscow.

The teaching done by this staff was largely the presentation of the contents of textbook surveys of their fields in lecture courses that met four hours weekly. About a third of the courses were given on the basis of books written by members, or former members, of the

53. Bagalei, *Opyt istorii*, II, 486–501, provides discussion of the staffing of each faculty and brief biographical sketches of the members. The biographical dictionaries provide more extended accounts for all members except those of the medical faculty. Khalanskii and Bagalei, *Istoriko-filogicheskii fakul'tet*; Osipov and Bagalei, *Fiziko-matematicheskii fakul'tet*; Zagurskii, *Iuridicheskii fakul'tet*.

Kharkov faculty, including Rizhkii's work on rhetoric, Jakob's on political economy, Rommel's editions of Cicero, and Osipovskii's work on mathematics. Nearly another third of the courses were presentations of the "notes" of the professor, a practice Fuss and the Academic Committee of the ministry found most unproductive. Often enough, this practice degenerated into little more than dictation of lessons that the student was supposed to learn later. Even after the departure of some professors, the courses were taught by adjuncts who continued to present the "notes" of the departed professor.[54]

In the first decade of the university, the faculty's main scholarly activity was publication of textbooks. There was less textbook work in the second decade. Professor of Latin, I. E. Sreznevskii, a holdover from the first decade, published a number of studies of Horace as well as translations. Before his death in 1819, he also produced a number of articles of local interest, including one on the time of Khmelnitskii.

The fate of the university's learned society underscored how difficult it was to keep up scholarly work. In 1815 the *Obshchestvo nauk* held seven meetings. There was one meeting in 1818, and none thereafter. When the younger Karneev in 1823 tried to encourage the faculty to resuscitate the organization, the faculty council replied that there was "too little free time for the pursuit of the goals of the society," i.e., scholarship. The society published but one issue of its journal. The society expired, then, not because Bible Society curators tried to frustrate scholarship, but because the faculty could not keep it going.

In 1815 some adjuncts, a local gymnasium teacher, and a leader among the local gentry decided to take up the task of making the university journal a regular enterprise, with formal sections systematically devoted to each of the major disciplines. This journal, *Ukrainskii vestnik,* began to appear regularly in 1816. Its success owed much to the work of Sreznevskii, who took upon himself much of the editorial work, as well as the recruitment of contributions. Sreznevskii published in an early issue his own essay, "On love of country," which he had delivered as an address in 1805 at the

54. Bagalei, *Opyt istorii,* II, 583–590, discusses the faculty's teaching; *ibid.,* 676–722, their scholar work; *ibid.,* 752–759, describes the career of *Ukrainskii vestnik.* For details on the *Obshchestvo nauk,* see Bagalei, *Uchenye obshchestva,* 209–231; Bagalei, *Opyt istorii,* II, 740–745. Quotation 744.

opening of a gymnasium. Many other pieces also were somewhat reworked versions of addresses, usually by newly appointed faculty members, at the annual ceremony marking the opening of the academic year. *Ukrainskii vestnik* in time attracted Golitsyn's anxious interest, for in November 1819 he noted unhappily that in the last issue Schad was mentioned, if only in passing. Golitsyn's concern was soon mooted, for on the death of its most active worker, Sreznevskii, the journal too expired.[55]

The most important contributor, after Sreznevskii, was P. P. Artemovskii-Gulak. Gentry-born in 1791, Gulak completed his studies at Kiev Academy before entering Kharkov University in 1817 as an "auditor." Within the year he was named "teacher" of Polish language. In 1820 he was named "temporary teacher" of Russian history, and in the same year was awarded his *kandidat* degree. He completed the *magister* in 1821 and two years later was promoted to adjunct. He shared with Sreznevskii an interest in the Ukrainian language as well as in local history, and published a number of pieces in *Ukrainskii vestnik* in Ukrainian or dealing with topics in local history. It is easy to overestimate the significance of this writing for the future development of an Ukrainian language. But the importance of the journal to the university faculty is clear. The St. Petersburg faculty, to cite an obvious comparison, was nearly next door to the Academy of Sciences, which at this time supported six journals that published the work of many St. Petersburg faculty, as well as a press that published books by Balugianskii, Gräfe, and others. Such opportunities and stimulus were almost entirely lacking in Kharkov.[56]

Though Dorpat University did not operate its own press, or support any regular publications, the faculty found ample scope for scholarly work in the German academic world, in which some achieved considerable status. Hezel, for example, was a well-known

55. Bagalei, *Opyt istorii*, II, 760–761.
56. Estimates of the significance of Artemovskii-Gulak's work vary a good deal. See Khalanskii and Bagalei, *Istoriko-filogicheskii fakul'tet*, 319–326; George S. N. Luckyj, *Between Gogol and Sevcenko: Polarity in the Literary Ukraine 1798–1847* (Munich, 1971), 43–45; Pelech, "Ukrainian Ideologues," 59–62. On the St. Petersburg faculty and Academy of Sciences publications, see Ostrovitianov, *Akademiia Nauk*, II, 230–234, 244–251. In addition, there were some twenty-six presses active in St. Petersburg, nearly half in private hands, while in Kharkov the university operated the only press. See A. A. Sidorov, ed., *400 let russkogo knigopechataniia: russkoe knigopechatanie do 1917 goda* (Moscow, 1964), 267–268, 305–306.

and highly respected scholar of Scripture, most of whose many works were published in Leipzig. Thus, while Dorpat regarded itself as a first-class academic institution, its scholarship did not affect the local public in any particularly direct way. The scholarship and teaching of the Dorpat faculty had minimal impact on the Russian services too, for Dorpat gave little attention to things Russian. Kaisarov, the professor of Russian from 1810, made himself a popular and valued member of the faculty by his ability and hard work as well as by his attractive personality.[57] His death in combat during the war was a major loss, particularly since his replacement proved to have none of his virtues. On Klinger's recommendation, the faculty in March 1814 elected A. F. Voeikov, a rich (owning over two thousand serfs) and well-known member of Moscow literary circles. He was also a chronic complainer who constantly badgered friends and colleagues for help. Voeikov's friends solved one of their problems, and Klinger satisfied himself that he had made a useful gesture to those in high places by posting Voeikov to Dorpat. Students came to like him very much, for he entertained frequently, giving "receptions" that became the highlights of the university's social life. But Voeikov did not work at all.

The faculty council made no objection until Lieven in the spring of 1820, belatedly realizing the character of Voekov's contribution, demanded his removal. The vacancy was soon filled by the election of Perevoshchikov from Kazan. Perevoshchikov proved everything that Voeikov was not: hard-working, able, interested in his subject and his students. Nonetheless, Perevoshchikov had rather few students. Neumann, on his arrival in Dorpat from Kazan, proposed that Russian should be a degree requirement, at least for medical students, since the language was a necessary tool for any who entered state service. A long debate in the faculty council concluded that, while Russian should be offered, it could not be required, since requirements violate "academic freedom."

Gustav Ewers, the annually reelected rector, was primarily responsible for the absence of Russian history. Educated at Göttingen, he came to Livland as a teacher in a noble house near Dorpat in

57. For discussion of Russian studies at Dorpat, see Petukhov, *Kafedra russkago iazyka*, 40–48, 88; Petukhov, *Derptskii universitet*, 238–244; N. I. Grech, "A. F. Voeikov," *RS*, 1875 (No. 9), 625–628; "Erinnerungen Anders," *BM*, 286–287. The article in *RBS*, v. 13 (*SPB*, 1912), 497–499, stresses Perevoshchikov's publications and contacts in the literary circles of St. Petersburg.

1803. In 1808 he brought out a well-received book on the origins of the Russian state. This book earned him the praise of Karamzin, election to membership in the Society of History at Moscow University, and appointment to the Dorpat faculty in 1810 as professor of Russian history, statistics, and geography. Between 1812 and 1816 he published three more books on Russian history. But, after 1814, despite his preparation and writing in the field, he gave no course on Russian history.[58]

The theology faculty paid no attention to Orthodoxy. Russian history was not given after 1814. Few students appeared for courses in the Russian language. Thus the Imperial university at Dorpat gave remarkably little notice to things Russian. In consequence, Neumann and Perevoshchikov now and again made complaints in the faculty council that more should be done. But, though the two former Kazan professors were valued members of the Dorpat staff, their advice went unheeded. In addition to Perevoshchikov and Neumann, Dorpat added two others who fled the Magnitskii regime at Kazan: Erdmann in medicine and Bartels in mathematics. The medical faculty, after the appointment of Erdmann, saw no departures and made but one more addition, the appointment of Parrot's son Friedrich as professor of physiology in 1821. The law faculty, shaken by the scandal of the purchased doctorates, remained understaffed even after the promulgation of the new statute of 1820, but no other faculty had similar difficulties.

Even the replacement of "rationalists" with "evangelicals" in the theology faculty seemed to make little change. For example, the theologian whose work had troubled Golitsyn in 1813 was Hezel, whose many publications over many years made him well known thoughout the German-speaking scholarly world. Born in Franconia in 1754, with a doctorate from Ghent, he came to Dorpat in 1801, already a well-known scholar of scripture. His hard work, and prodigious output, added to his reputation, until he came to Golitsyn's attention in 1813. Hezel, under attack by Golitsyn, accepted a suggestion by his colleagues that he give up his Scripture course, teaching only the Eastern language courses until 1820, when he reached retirement age. His replacement was S. G. R. Henzi, a Swiss who had a recent Tübingen doctorate as well as a

58. For Ewer's career and work in Russian history see Levitskii, *Biograficheskii slovar' derptskago universiteta*, II, 510–536.

year studying history at Göttingen and a year in Paris studying Eastern languages. Elected to the chair of Scripture and Eastern languages, he seemed fully capable of growing in scholarship and making himself a suitable replacement for Hezel. Upon arrival in Dorpat, he joined the local chapter of the Bible Society, becoming its president within a year. While Lieven could not help but appreciate that gesture, it came after Henzi had demonstrated academic merit to qualify for his post.[59]

Lieven maintained close personal relationships with many faculty members. He was especially close to two, Gustav Ewers and Parrot, who, despite his status as the original and most unregenerate "rationalist" on the faculty, not only kept his post as professor of physics but became Lieven's close friend. Ewers too had great moral authority, even with those who disagreed with him. His annual reelection as rector, and his close cooperation with Lieven, helped to explain the orderly development of the university as well as its success.[60] Dorpat remained, thus, a sound German Protestant university that continued to offer competent instruction in the areas of learning that seemed appropriate for the usual German four-faculty university.

The contrast with the fate of the other "national" university in the western provinces of the empire was striking, but not difficult to explain. Polish armies had made enthusiastic allies of the French invaders. No German force had to be taken so seriously. Lutheranism was the state religion of a dependably dependant ally, Prussia. Poles were Roman Catholic, part of a world-wide movement that had powerful and intractably independent components, including the Pope at Rome, who had rejected the tsar's call to participate in his "Holy Alliance." Catholicism was hard to measure, or even explain coherently, as a danger to Russia. But it was felt a peril, and the emotional impact on the policy-makers in St. Petersburg was considerable.[61] Vilna gave instruction in Russian, as well as in Rus-

59. Discussion of the faculty, unless otherwise stated, is based upon the biographies of individuals in Levitskii, *Biograficheskii slovar' derptskago universiteta*, and the discussion of the faculties in Petukhov, *Derptskii universitet*, 392–421.

60. For discussion of Lieven's relationship with Ewers and Parrot, see Petukhov, *Derptskii universitet*, 329–334.

61. Pope Pius VII contributed to this feeling in St. Petersburg by issuing two briefs in 1816 (*Nimio et Acerbo* and *Magno et Acerbo*) that condemned the Bible Society in especially violent language. The policy of Pius VII (pontificate 1800–1823) was to avoid the extremes of ultramontanism as well as its opposite, Josephinism, i.e., dominance of the church by state authorities. The *zelanti* at Rome were a majority in the

sian history and law, tried to make available instruction in Orthodoxy, and provided many able and loyal servitors of the state not only in medicine and teaching but in the churches and law and administration as well. Dorpat's record in these matters was obviously weak. Vilna tightened discipline over its students, who had shown no tendency to disorder, while Dorpat students became well known for violent destructiveness and lack of discipline. Clearly, the perception of peril in St. Petersburg had little to do with what actually went on in the universities at Vilna and Dorpat.

The Moscow faculty changed no more significantly than the Dorpat or Vilna faculties over the decade of the dual ministry.[62] The moral-political science faculty, with the obvious exception of Father Levitskii, added no new men in the entire period. Each vacancy was filled by the promotion of adjuncts who had been trained in the university's first decade. Thus, the percentage of foreign scholars declined, and the university became more Russian, but without marking a significant change in the content of the courses offered. Schlözer, for example, continued to teach the courses of the chair of political economy, using texts he wrote himself, until his retirement in 1825. L. A. Tsvetsev, who graduated from Moscow University in

---

papal curia, however, and constantly pushed for vigorous, indeed extreme, assertion of the "rights"—i.e., independence—of the church on every front. The language of his briefs regarding the Bible Society was most untypical for Pius VII, and seems designed for internal, *zelanti*, consumption in Rome, rather than for its presumed audience in St. Petersburg. Not unexpectedly, the briefs were not promulgated in Russia, since the "Metropolitan" of the Catholic Church in Russia, Archbishop Siestrzencewicz-Bohusz, not only opposed the Jesuits and supported the Bible Society, but lied, claiming that he had never received the Pope's instructions. Nonetheless, Russian authorities, little aware of the politics within the papal court or elsewhere in Catholic circles, took the papal briefs at face value. For the contest between the styles as well as policies of the *zelanti* among the Cardinals in Rome and the Pope, see Alan J. Reinerman, "Metternich and Reform: The Case of the Papal State 1814–1848," *Journal of Modern History*, XLII (1970), 524–548; "Papacy and Papal State in the Restoration 1814–1846," *Catholic Historical Review*, LXIV (1978), 36–46; "Metternich and the Papal Condemnation of the Carbonari, 1821," *ibid.*, LIV (1968), 55–69.

62. The Moscow faculty of this period is described in Shevyrev, *Istoriia*, 441–450; Tikhomirov, *Istoriia*, I, 131–145. Biographical sketches of individuals in *Biograficheskii slovar' moskovskago universiteta* may be supplemented by Muzko, "Merzliakov," *RS*, 1879 (January), 115–119; Barsukov, "Kachenovskii," *RS*, 1889 (October), 199–202. On Dvigubskii, see also A. F. Kononkov, *Istoriia fiziki v moskovskom universitete 1755–1859* (Moscow, 1955), 80–93; D. I. Gordeev, *Istoriia geologicheskikh nauk v moskovskom universitete* (Moscow, 1962), 60–65. For the published scholarship of the faculty members, see also Shevyrev, *Istoriia*, 456–459; Tikhomirov, *Istoriia*, I, 146–181.

1798 and completed his doctorate at Göttingen under Murav'ev's and Schlözer's encouragement, continued to hold the chair of Roman law throughout the period. Thus, the Göttingen influence remained strong.

The career of I. I. Davydov, appointed adjunct in philosophy in 1821, well illustrated one of Moscow's characteristics. Moscow filled its staff with its own graduates, and often made teaching assignments without regard to statute listings, or even faculty divisions. Davydov, gentry born but from a very poor family, came to Murav'ev's attention during an inspection of district schools. Murav'ev invited Davydov to Moscow University in 1808, where Davydov took his *kandidat* (and a gold medal for excellence) in 1812. His *magister* thesis, completed in 1814, and his doctoral dissertation, completed in 1815, studied the scientific views of Francis Bacon and provided the basis for some later publications in the history of philosophy. His director was Professor Kachenovskii of the literature faculty. Davydov served as teacher of Latin in the *pansion* and as university librarian as well as adjunct in philosophy. In 1820, on the death of the professor of classics, Timkovskii, Davydov was appointed extraordinary professor in classics and began teaching the part of Timkovskii's offerings that concerned Latin literature. Another adjunct, Timkovskii's student Ivashkovskii, took over the Greek courses. Dividing Timkovskii's courses this way enabled Davydov to continue work in philosophy and to expand his offerings in that area too. Promoted to professor of Latin literature and language in 1822, Davydov nonetheless continued to teach courses in philosophy and during the years 1821–1824 published three books, one each on logic, Latin literature, and algebra (a translation of a German text), as well as many translations from classic authors. In 1821 Davydov turned over his course in logic to adjunct Malov, who continued to teach civil law, his subject as the late Professor Reinhard's adjunct. As Reinhard's replacement, Malov continued to use the texts written by Reinhard and published by the university press in the prewar decade.

There can be little doubt that the Moscow faculty could have recruited the new faculty members had that been desired. The swapping of course assignments, even over departmental lines, was not a desperate expedient but rather the Moscow faculty's choice. Filling vacancies with young Russian adjuncts not only helped to "Russify" the university, but helped to reward one's supporters and

friends as much as did the practice of using new budget authorizations to bring in friends as assistants in the medical institute or
pansion. It marked the continuation of one of the more important
patterns of Russian life: the reliance on personal, often family, connections rather than legal or professional qualifications, for social
security as well as advancement.[63] This pattern of faculty appointments showed neither the interests of the Bible Society nor any fall-
ing off in academic quality. Latin, for example, important in the
early years that were dominated by foreign-trained men, remained
very important both as a subject of study and as a teaching language. All theses were written and defended in Latin. Three members of the physics-mathematics faculty, of a total of nine in professorial ranks, taught at least part of their courses in Latin. Thus,
while the more career-minded St. Petersburg faculty criticized
Uvarov's plain to hold on to Latin as the language of learning, the
Moscow faculty, though increasingly "Russified," continued to
honor the place of Latin in the world of academic achievement.

The outstanding member of the physics-mathematics faculty was
I. A. Dvigubskii. The star student as well as adjunct of Professor
Strakhov, Dvigubskii became professor of physics on the death of
his mentor. He became the professor most respected, if sometimes
feared, by the undergraduates, as well as a prolific publishing
scholar who took a leading part in the university's learned societies
and edited the journal of physics and chemistry. The medical faculty,
which granted more doctorates than the other three faculties combined, saw only one member, Richter, professor of obstetrics, leave
the staff in the decade of the dual ministry, and he was replaced by
his son.

Instruction offered in the faculty of literature was particularly important, for it had more students than the others, especially among
the self-supporting. This faculty was perhaps not a match for the
others in the quality of its work, but few doubted that its members
were hard-working and competent. Its leader became Kachenovskii,
who took his doctorate in literature at Moscow in 1806 and held
many administrative posts (including the directorship of the univer-

63. G. L. Yaney, "Law, Society and the Domestic Regime in Russia in Historical
Perspective," *The American Political Science Review*, LIX (1965), 379–390, provides an insightful analysis of the persistence, as well as importance, of the "family-
type institutions of Russian society . . . where personal bonds have furnished the
only available guarantee of unity and solidarity. . . . "

sity press) before his appointment as professor of Russian history in 1821. Kachenovskii's teaching was highly regarded by students, and he published a good deal, including edited document collections focussed on pre-Petrine Russia. He was a sincere patriot who wanted to establish the importance of native Russian roots in the development of Russian polity and culture. He was also a careful scholar who did much to establish accurate texts of pre-Petrine legislation, and he was less willing than others to undervalue the importance of cultural borrowing for Russia's development.[64] His work supported that of Sandurov (and his adjunct Smirnov) in Russian law, and Tsvetsev in Roman law, all of whom stressed the importance of the autocracy in Russia's development and the worth of strong government in general. As appealing in patriotic and religious terms as it was professionally competent, the Moscow faculty's teaching nourished sympathetic interest in the university by the local elites so carefully cultivated for years by both Kutuzov and Obolenskii.

5. Students

The response to this teaching by Moscow's students was often less than gratifying to the faculty. The Moscow student body grew to more than eight hundred in 1824, nearly quadruple its best prewar enrollment. Increase in the number of degrees awarded did not keep pace, though after 1815 it was a rare year when fewer than twenty *kandidats* were awarded. Gentry were never a majority, nor were students from the clergy, though these two groups together usually made up nearly eighty percent of the total enrollment. Clergy, of course, tended to predominate among state-supported students, gentry among the self-supporting.

The contrast in the living arrangements of the two was often striking. Some gentry families took apartments within easy walking distance of the university, so that the young scholars had not only the benefit of parental supervision but the support of comfortable bed and board. Some state students lived in quarters so cold that "water froze on the walls." Both state and self-supporting students,

64. On Kachenovskii's work, see J. L. Black, *Nicholas Karamzin and Russian Society in the Nineteenth Century* (Toronto, 1975), 137–145. Kachenovskii drew the ire of some "conservatives" of the Arzamas group, since he failed to praise Karamzin's major work, the history of Russia published in 1818.

whether gentry or clergy, shared a deep interest in state service and continued to leave study as soon as possible, under conditions that often undercut the goals of the reformers. In 1817 many students, fearful of rumored more stringent examination and/or service requirements, scrambled to get *attestats* from the university as soon as possible. Many professors were easily persuaded to sign *attestats* testifying to "great success" in their courses. Dvigubskii was not one. He regularly refused to see the student's point of view in such cases. In one case, indeed, he not only refused to sign but replied to the student's request: "My dear young man, I have never seen you before." Many Moscow faculty found Dvigubskii's attitude unnecessarily severe. The rector was persuaded to sign an *attestat* giving the student credit for Dvigubskii's course. In 1820 a number of students tried to take advantage of an 1806 law that permitted university students to enter a six-month officer-candidate course in the army. In this case, the ministry intervened, ruling that state-supported students were required to fulfill an obligation of six years' service in institutions under the Ministry of Education and so were not eligible to apply for other programs.[65] Since the needs of the services remained great, and many Moscow students came from families with good connections, most students still left the university before finishing any of the faculty's programs. Many came seriously unprepared for university study. Gentry students seldom knew enough Latin, while clergy often knew too little French. Many found the lecture courses, the heart of the university's instruction, ineffective. "The professors read," one reported, "but we listened only out of obligation."

Still, gentry students, while they enjoyed the life of young "aristocrats," testified to the hard work of most of the "seminarians," as they called students from the clerical estate. Moreover, many also acquired serious interests. A. K. Koshelev thought he learned little in course work with professors. Nonetheless, during his years at Moscow University he read German philosophers, Schelling in particular, on his own and acquired an enduring interest in serious

65. The most detailed student memoir is D. N. Sverbeev, *Zapiski*, Sofia Sverbeeva, ed., 2 v. (Moscow, 1899), I, 82–187. Quotation 186. See also Koshelev, "Kruzhok," *Literaturnye salony* (Brodskii, ed.), 134–138. Quotations 135, 137. The state students' quarters acquired the nickname of "Siberia" in testimony to their usual cold temperatures. N. N. Murzakevich, "V Moskovskom universitete, 1825," *Moskovskii universitet* (Kovnator, ed.), 33. On the state students attempts to transfer to the army, see *Sbornik rasporiazhenii*, I, 433–435 (12 October 1820).

questions of life in society. Students in this decade easily passed the 1809 examinations. An almost impossible feat in 1809, by 1824 passing those exams had become routine. The level of competence that could be expected from Moscow University students, in sum, seemed to improve markedly. Some, particularly among the state students, became eager in their pursuit of learning, while many young gentry developed, if not first acquired, both sympathy and admiration for their "seminarian" colleagues, as well as a taste for notions of political and social freedom.[66]

On some occasions, those notions became very clear. The professor of Russian law, Sandurov, once closed a thesis defense because he found the student audience too "liberal." The thesis had concluded that monarchy was the best form of government, but many students in the audience protested that the history of the Greek republics and the Roman republic indicated the superiority of the republican form of government. Sandurov interrupted to point out that the Roman republic had "more than once degenerated into despotism."[67] When this observation seemed to change few minds, Sandurov noted, with perhaps a touch of regret, that he could not call the police, for the university was off-limits to them, but could call a halt to the discussion, which he did.

Both Dorpat and Kharkov continued to grow in student enrollment (Dorpat to more than 350, Kharkov to over 200), though Moscow had more students than both together. The Bible Society decade saw no significant change in the students' social origins, faculty of study, or lack of interest in a career in teaching in schools

66. S. S. Landa, *Dukh revoliutsionnykh preobrazovanii; iz istorii formirovaniia ideologii i politicheskoi organizatsii dekabristov 1816–1825* (Moscow, 1975), argues that for the most part future Decembrists acquired their ideas from life and from reading. See, for example, the discussion of N. I. Turgenev, *ibid.,* 75–76. Granted the wisdom of this view, nonetheless it seems unlikely that the schools had no role, although that role is obviously impossible to document in individual cases. University courses, if nothing else, often encouraged the reading and study of Montesquieu and others whose work must have had something to do with the development of ideas of moral and political freedom in some students. Other, weak, discussions of this topic, include I. Ia. Shchipanov, *Moskovskii universitet i razvitii filosofskoi i obschchestvenno-politicheskoi mysli v Rossii* (Moscow, 1957), 105–120; V. I. Orlov, *Studencheskoe dvizhenie moskovskogo universiteta v xix veke* (Moscow, 1934), 49–54. Shevyrev, *Istoriia,* dedicated at publication to Nicholas I, omits any mention of the Decembrists.

67. Sverbeev, *Zapiski,* I, 107–08. At least one student involved in this episode, S. M. Semenov, later became an active participant in the Decembrist revolt. Landa, *Dukh revoliutsionnykh preobrazovanii,* 327–328, note 107.

lower than in the gymnasium. Thus, the social reform, which some
of the original planners thought would be a consequence of the educational reform, came no nearer. Nonetheless, more students stayed
long enough to complete the student *attestat,* having "finished the
whole course." Despite the turmoil of some student rebelliousness,
which troubled Golitsyn and some others deeply, the Bible Society
decade saw some progress, albeit not the sort that was particularly
interesting to the Bible Society.

At Dorpat, the character and academic preparation of the student
body changed little from that of the first decade. More than half
came from the province of Livland, while never more than twenty
were Russians. The medical faculty became the most popular, enrolling 105 of the total of 309 in 1821. The student body remained
overwhelmingly noble, though the sons of Lutheran clergymen and
merchants were also important.[68] There were signs of increasing se-
riousness in attitudes toward study. Many faculty members, especially those in literatures, conducted "circles" that drew together
students who wished to deepen their learning, as well as to find an
outlet for good talk and fellowship. The number of degrees, while
still awarded to a minority of those who enrolled, began to climb,
especially after 1820. The new examination regulations issued by
the ministry in January 1819, at least in part as a response to the
scandal about degrees in the Dorpat law faculty, seemed to succeed
in fostering some confidence among both faculty and students that
the degree would be meaningful, in the long run worth the effort to
obtain it. The new statute too, which provided forty state stipends
in medicine at 750 a year (nearly double the old rate), also had
something to do with the greater rate of measurable success in study
at Dorpat. Moreover, the placement records of the students, whether
they took degrees or not, seemed remarkably good, for Dorpat men
continued to enter the provincial services, though rather rarely the
Imperial services, as well as to take up careers in medicine, teaching, the church, and in management of family enterprises.

This generally progressive record notwithstanding, the ministry
in St. Petersburg found the record of many Dorpat students deplor-
able. Their propensity to violence too often resulted in badly beaten
young men as well as in many broken windows and other damage

---

68. Petukhov, *Derptskii universitet,* 505–509; Petukhov, *Statisticheskiia tablitsy,*
4–5, 13–19, provides breakdowns of the enrollment figures.

in the city. In February 1816 Alexander sent a directive to the university, expressing his "great disappointment" in the "unworthy" conduct of Dorpat students. In 1817, distressed at hearing "again" of "disorders" among the Dorpat students, the tsar ordered that they be forbidden to carry "swords or any other weapon." The faculty council repeated the long-standing warnings against drunkenness, fighting, or going into town in disguises, and particularly ordered that students stay out of the city artisans' club. In March 1820 the faculty council requested the permission of the tsar to turn over to local authorities for trial a student who had compiled a record as a troublemaker, which was unusual even for a Dorpat student.[69]

The "disorders" among Dorpat students were not manifestations of a "revolutionary" current. They were entirely apolitical reflections of the ethos of local society. Governor Paulucci's dire warning that student rock-throwing indicated the influx of foreign revolutionary doctrines was not taken seriously by the faculty. Since the faculty and the curator maintained close, mutually respectful, relations, the curator's reports to the minister supported the faculty view.

The teachers' institute (at Dorpat called a "seminary") was directed by one of the most dedicated members of the faculty, Morgenstern, with the assistance of Perevoshchikov, who was particularly interested in the work and made a major contribution. Despite their work, the teacher-training program failed completely. Most of its students went to great lengths to avoid placement as teachers. Since most students did course work in the regular faculties, they often managed to transfer out of the institute and into a regular faculty. To avoid the six-year commitment in teaching that went with accepting the stipend for the teachers' seminary, some went so far as deliberately to fail their examinations. In March 1823 Lieven passed on to the ministry Morgenstern's recommendation for a system of fines (up to twenty-five rubles) for students whose interest in

---

69. The faculty must have expected Alexander to approve of this procedure, for he himself had threatened to deny student malfactors the benefit of university trial on earlier occasions when he expressed his dismay at the "unworthy" behavior of Dorpat students. *Sbornik postanovlenii*, I, 557 (October 1808), (17 February 1816), 981 (5 April 1817). On troubles in the artisans' club (the local police urged the university to forbid students to go there), see *ibid.*, I, 1313–1314, 1343 (8 March 1820).

qualifying for a teacher's post in the lower schools of the provinces was so low that they deliberately attempted to fail the course.[70]

Nonetheless, the gymnasia of the district, and even the *uezd* schools, were not badly off, since they were state-supported and could still be staffed by clergy. Primary schools suffered a sharp decline. The abolition of serfdom in the provinces, completed finally by 1819, did little for the economic security of the former serfs, for the lands they worked remained the property of the nobles. The village schools, moreover, had never been covered by a state budget, but were supported by local leadership, whether noble landlords or parish clergy. The end of the lords' "responsibility" for the peasants saw many of them abandon the village schools, which the peasants were neither willing nor able to sustain themselves. The governor of Estland in 1817 reported a drop in the number of village schools in the province from over two hundred to fewer than twenty. Lieven declared that the state would have to intervene, by assuming the responsibility of tax-supporting the schools, and making primary school education compulsory. But Lieven could not suggest a reliable source of teachers. Testimony to the university's lack of success in this area, neither Lieven nor anyone else in the university or ministry thought that the university could produce teachers for the village schools.[71]

At Kharkov the moral-political science faculty (i.e., the law faculty) remained the most popular, and physics-mathematics the least, but the least popular had more students in this decade than the most popular in the prewar years. Enrollment not only grew but changed in one other important way. Testimony to a degree of acceptance by local society, gentry, and "officer's" children came to provide a clear majority of the students, usually about seventy percent, with clergy and "others" each supplying about fifteen percent of the remainder.[72]

Most entering students were required to spend a year, sometimes two, in a "preparatory" course, remedial work designed to facilitate work in one of the regular faculties. The "full course" in the faculties, as in the other universities, required the student to take all the courses given in his faculty, which was a three-year program

70. Petukhov, *Derptskii universitet,* 469–480.
71. *Ibid.,* 480–493.
72. Bagalei, *Opyt istorii,* II, 856–883.

(four in the medical faculty), and to pass annual exams, usually given by an examination committee in each faculty in the spring. In 1815 Kharkov gave twenty-three degrees of all kinds, including the "actual student" *attestat*. In 1825 fifty-six were awarded. In between those years however, few degrees were given, in part because the unhappy episode of Schad's doctoral students seemed to call into question Kharkov's degrees. But, while arguments over degree standards and the rigor of Kharkov's examinations continued in faculty council meetings, they became less frequent and acrimonious, especially after the departure of Osipovskii. Instead, attention focussed on other aspects of the life of the students.

Concern for student behavior was not new. In 1812 the faculty council promulgated detailed rules for student behavior that, as in other universities, seemed more a catalog of problems encountered than a solution to them. The new "general rule for students" promised "severe punishment" for those who became "inebriated" or who showed "bodily uncleanliness or criminal spirit whether in public or private." The rule also stated that students should not only attend church but should be "reverent while in church," thus avoiding "scandal." Moreover, since they were students, they should have books and notebooks, which they should take to class and use.[73]

The state students lived together, and had a faculty-elected "inspector" assigned to monitor their behavior. The state students at Kharkov, however, had developed a measure of self-government, for they elected from among themselves leaders who collected from the university administration the state student stipends and managed the "economic" affairs of their colleagues. The students also supported one another by pooling clothing, since not many of them could afford to own a complete outfit. They were authorized to wear a uniform, as befitted their "rank" as students, but the uniform was seldom worn, as at other universities, because it was the student's financial responsibility to furnish it himself. Pooling therefore helped outfit at least some on those occasions when it seemed appropriate to appear formally dressed. The self-supporting students had no "inspector" and usually lived in various quarters

73. This "general rule" is printed in *Sbornik rasporiazhenii*, I 212–214 (28 April 1812).

around the town. The requirement to report their addresses to the administration was honored in the breach as often as not.[74]

These generally unsupervised living arrangements did not seem to trouble Potocki, or even catch his notice, until 1817, when the first of a number of "theater incidents" took place. Students (between thirty and sixty took part) in the local theater broke up a performance by jumping up on the stage, shouting, and generally enjoying themselves. Some began demanding a refund of the admission price, since the performance had stopped. Defending themselves before the university court, some students claimed that the police chief actually had "started it" by shouting at them. State students were forbidden to enter the theater again, for Potocki thought it inappropriate that state students should use part of their stipends to attend theater at all. Self-supporting students would be allowed in the theater only with prior authorization from the inspector of students.[75]

The elder Karneev, concerned as he was for the moral welfare of his students, over ninety of whom enrolled in his Bible Society chapter, asked for a more effective code of student conduct. The faculty council cooperated gladly by framing a new regulation, issued in 1820, which warned students to "show respect" for the faculty and told them not to walk out of a class without an "important reason." The new regulation required students to attend church on Sundays and prayer services on other days. They were also to go to classes faithfully, to take notes in class, and to study. In the evenings, they were reminded to be quiet so that others could study. The regulation naturally also contained the familiar prohibitions against drunkenness, leaving the university at night without permission, visiting the local theater without permission, fighting, gambling, and so on.[76]

The younger Karneev faced a new "theater incident" in October 1823. Some students, clearly familiar with the goings on of the local theater despite the continued ban on student attendance, threatened an actor who displeased them, extracting a promise from him that he would not again appear on the stage. When the actor failed to

74. Bagalei, *Opyt istorii*, II, 930–940, quotes at length memoirs of former students on these matters.

75. *Ibid.*, 959–993, details the 1817 "theater incident" and many other examples of ill behavior.

76. *Ibid.*, 933–936; *Sbornik rasporiazhenii*, I, 436 (8 December 1820).

live up to his "promise," the students were ready, greeting his appearance with a salvo of apples and other missiles and shouting demands for his immediate departure. The ensuing melee made this incident a difficult "case" to try, for there were a great many witnesses and much contradictory testimony. The university's file on the case finally came to nearly 500 pages. Those students who could be identified were finally given sentences, ranging from expulsion to jail for a month or more. Some faculty, while not quite defending the students, protested what they thought was an unnecessarily enthusiastic reponse by the police. Karneev's reports to the ministry led Golitsyn to conclude that the cause of the affair was the persistence of the "spirit of self-will" among students, the same judgment he had pronounced on the 1817 theater incident.[77]

Golitsyn brought this case to the Committee of Ministers, where it was decided that the university had done all that could be done and needed no further authority to punish student evildoers. As the ministers seemed to realize, Golitsyn overstated the significance of even this most dramatic of the theater incidents. Most students most of the time, as one recalled in his memoirs, "lived quietly, at home, rarely going into the town," in large part because they had no money.[78] The excitement, and sheer fun, of the theater incidents was doubtless a welcome if not inevitable break in the students' dreary everyday life in Kharkov (even though the long-range costs were high for some individuals) and needed no deeper, let alone "spiritual," explanation. Discouraging though it was to Golitsyn and others, the "disorders" among the students—routine drunkenness, fighting, and stealing—did not connote moral retrogression, but were only commonplaces of life in the provinces. On balance, indeed, even Kharkov University saw clear improvement. In 1824 enrollment, temporarily reduced by the events of 1823, regained its upward growth. The faculty school committee, while still complaining of overwork, nonetheless in 1824 reported some solid progress. Though there were not many more schools in 1824 than in 1815 (in fact there was one gymnasium fewer), the number of students in gymnasia increased by nearly a quarter, up to 1,200, and in lower schools up to over 8,000. In sum, in 1824–1825, the Kharkov dis-

77. *Ibid.*, 995–1013, provides details on the incident and samples of the contradictory testimony.
78. *Ibid.*, 932. This memoir was written in 1875. For the Committee of Ministers' consideration of the matter, see Seredonin, *Komitet ministrov*, 576–578.

trict had grown to nearly the point that Moscow had reached a decade earlier.[79] Not all of this growth could be attributed directly to the influence of the university, and in many ways, given the area and population of the district, it remained no more than a beginning. Nonetheless, the university in Kharkov had more than survived, and its influence was beginning to be more widely felt.

In the spring of 1822 a rumor circulated among Moscow's students that Magnitskii planned to launch an investigation of the university. Another rumor had it that Magnitskii intended to replace the lower schools of the district with Lancaster schools.[80] Whatever Magnitskii's intent, Moscow students openly planned to protest. That Moscow students could express such views underscored the importance of the curator in the development of the university. Obolenskii had made it his business to foster the development of his university. Not only did he capitalize on his connections in Moscow society, important though that was; he also managed to secure more than Moscow's share of the ministry's budget allocations. He spent much, perhaps most, of his time in Moscow and tended daily (including Sundays and Holydays, to his secretary's chagrin) to university business. After 1819, indeed, he carried out inspection tours of the lower schools of the district himself, as well as paying attention to the reports of the faculty, who continued to send out two-man teams to each province of the district each year. Most important, Obolenskii simply saw no danger lurking in his university in the form of "free-thought" or any of the other evils of the age that Magnitskii decried elsewhere. The reading lists, the courses, in many cases the men themselves, remained much the same in the dual ministry decade as in the first decade of the university's existence. In May 1823 Magnitskii proposed to the Main School Administration that instruction in philosophy, among other things, should be curtailed, since the subject of its nature led to "danger." He held up as an example of the political-moral "danger" to youth inherent in philosophy the recently published book on principles of logic by Davydov.[81] Magnitskii's proposal did not get far in the min-

---

79. For the schools of the district, see Bagalei, *Opyt istorii*, II, 1019–1049. Tkachenko, *Rol' Khar'kovskogo universiteta*, 9, says that "incomplete records" show that faculty members made not fewer than eighty-two inspection trips throughout the district.

80. N. P. Barsukov, ed., *Zhizn' i trudy M. P. Pogodina*, 22 v. (SPB, 1888–1910), I, 164.

81. On Magnitskii's recommendation, and analysis of Davydov's book, see Feok-

istry. More important, at Moscow University nothing happened. Davydov went on teaching, and publishing, as a respected member of the faculty. Throughout the decade of the dual ministry, no member of the Moscow faculty was censured, "warned," or in any way threatened on account of any views expressed in any way. In truth, of course, the Moscow faculty did nothing to merit censure, for even the "liberals" among them were more than willing to work within the possibilities provided by the autocratic system. In this they were not different from the faculties at Kazan, St. Petersburg, or Vilna. The difference lay in the curators.

Moscow's success consisted in more than mere absence of mindless repression, or hypocritical careerism, in its administration. It had developed a largely Russian faculty that not only managed a national press but published a steadily increasing number of studies, from belles lettres to handbooks on soil properties for the farmer. The learned societies sponsored by the university continued to sustain the work not only of faculty members but of the practitioners of medicine and nearly every professional enterprise in the district. The numbers of schools at the local level grew but slowly, but the number of students in them nearly doubled in the decade, from barely over 7,000 to more than 14,000.

Given this much success, it was noteworthy that the faculty council at Moscow was often not consulted on important questions. The Moscow faculty perhaps lacked confidence in its organs of self-government and certainly preferred to rely upon individual relationships with the curator, who had access to those in real power. Compared with the Göttingen model, the view of the reformers who in 1803–1804 planned the organization of "autonomous" self-governing universities, the pattern of government that had developed at Moscow fell far short of success. Moscow's governance instead followed models characteristic of the Russian polity, in both state and society. This congruence with Russian society helped to nourish not only the faculty's sense of security but the sense of Moscow society that the university was "theirs," not some exotic transplant that threatened unwelcome change in the conditions of

---

tistov, "Magnitskii: materialy," *RV*, v. 52 (1864), 407–415; "Dva mneniia popechitelia kazanskago uchebnago okruga, N. M. Magnitskago," *RA*, 1864 (No. 3), 325–330. In his attack on Davydov, Magnitskii used the same approach and language he had turned on Kunitsyn at St. Petersburg, and explicitly compared Kunitsyn and Davydov as examples of the same sort of evil.

Russian life. In short, the atrophy of the role of a faculty council, inconceivable at Vilna or Dorpat, at Moscow probably strengthened the university's ability to strike ever deeper roots in its society during the Bible Society decade.

Among the good things the curator supplied his faculty, in addition to shielding them from Magnitskii or his like, were Obolenskii's nearly annual recommendations to the tsar that several faculty members deserved to be honored with medals and other awards in recognition of their outstanding service to the nation. It was a rare year that did not see four or five members so honored. In the fall of 1823, therefore, the curator's secretary was somewhat startled to see that the curator's list of recommendations for honors was not accepted but instead, apparently at the behest of Arakcheev, passed to a committee for study.[82] Shortly thereafter, the curator informed his secretary that a new minister had been chosen. Though he did not say it, it was clear that Obolenskii expected that his curatorship also would soon end. The era of the dual ministry was finished.

82. Tret'iakov, "Universitet v vospominaniiakh," *RS,* 1892 (September), 539.

CHAPTER V

REFORMING THE REFORM, 1824-1834

"MY DEAR PRINCE," said Tsar Alexander to Golitsyn, "for some time I have wanted to have a serious discussion with you. The fact of the matter is that the ministry entrusted to you just has not worked out for us. I plan to release you from the ministerial post and to divide the dual ministry."[1] Golitsyn agreed completely. Indeed, he went to see the tsar on that day in April 1824, determined to resign, for he had long since come to the conclusion that the dual ministry had not worked out. Golitsyn's resignation marked the end of the Bible Society's reform of the universities and the beginning of a new search for answers to the problems that troubled the universities. Since the reforms inspired by the Bible Society were themselves among the chief problems, reversing many of them was itself a worthwhile first step. Ending Bible Society repression was not enough to answer problems encountered since the foundations in 1803–1804. The decade of 1824–1834 saw the continued, and in the end largely successful, pursuit of adequate answers. The university reform of Alexander I, thus, was completed nearly a decade after the death of the tsar who launched it.

The failure of the Golitsyn administration itself created serious problems. Golitsyn had taken upon himself a subtle and difficult task, that of infusing the spirit of religion into the whole educational enterprise. Aside from Schad, and a few other holdovers who continued to cling to the radically rationalist version of the En-

1. "O sud'be Pravoslavnoi Tserkvi Russkoi v Tsarstvovanie Imperatora Aleksandra I-go; iz zapisok A. S. Sturdzy," *RS*, 1876 (February), 285. These notes, edited

lightenment, few in Russia, or in the West, for that matter, in the decade after the defeat of Napoleon opposed turning to religion. But Golitsyn baffled friend and foe alike. The "instructions" of Sturdza or Magnitskii made clear some of the general aspirations of Bible Society reformers, but contradicted others, while the actions of the ministry befogged the issues even more. Kunitsyn's book was condemned as evidence of "evil" at work at St. Petersburg University, because Runich said it was. Davydov's very similar book was not evidence of evil at Moscow, despite Magnitskii's dire warnings to the contrary, because Obolenskii said it was not.

The contradictions and vacillations became more obvious the longer and harder Golitsyn worked at his task. By the spring of 1823 Golitsyn had come near despair of the possibility of success. The excellent beginning of 1817–1818 was followed, not by more success, but by ever-increasing, apparently endless, turmoil and trouble, beginning with Magnitskii's investigation of Kazan in 1819.

The problem was not fundamentally that Gotlitsyn, and other "reactionaries," meant to defend the established social-economic-political order, while "liberals" attacked it. There was, to be sure, an element of that. Sturdza, for example, clearly preferred to preserve the existing arrangements, while Kunitsyn found much to deplore in them. Moreover, in 1818 it was clear that Uvarov and many others looked forward to, indeed confidently expected, a "constitution" in Russia's future, while Shishkov and many others were appalled at the idea. Nonetheless, it is too narrow a reading to see in Golitsyn's work no more than a "reactionary" defense of the existing order. Golitsyn had difficulty describing with clarity what sort of earthly society he would regard as good, except that it would not resemble contemporary France. The secularism of the Western world, with its intense interest in solutions, constitutional as well as technical, to this world's problems, Golitsyn found fundamentally wrong, for it stressed satisfaction of the "self-will" of the individual. Unfortunately, the West was the home not only of a multifaceted Enlightenment but of pietism and indeed of the Bible Society itself, among other things that Golitsyn cherished. This made consistent anti-Westernism impossibly difficult, a fact that finally made Golitsyn and his fellow-thinkers seem arbitrary, inconsistent, even erratic

---

by N. I. Barsov, were written during the winter of 1848–1849. Sturdza here recalls what Golitsyn had told him, in a conversation that took place in 1828.

in what they chose to support or condemn. Their practice indeed was arbitrary, inconsistent, and erratic because their beliefs were just that, if often deeply held.[2]

The Bible Society's difficulties were complicated by other factors. The mocking comment of Grand Duke Nicholas to Runich ("Throw out more such men from the university . . .") was not an isolated incident.[3] A ministry whose foes ranged from Uvarov and Balugianskii, on one side, to Shishkov and Zhukovskii, on the other, had formidable enemies. Moreover, the murder of Kotzebue in 1819 and the Semenovskii revolt in 1820 frightened Alexander, while his increasingly severe health problems obviously distracted him. On the day he was told of his dismissal, indeed, Golitsyn found the tsar suffering great pain in his legs, "as was usual for him in those days," he noted. Alexander's failure to respond to the pleas of Uvarov, Czartoryski, and others associated with the original reform owed much to these circumstances. Golitsyn too, in 1822, was depressed and distracted by a brush with death, for he broke through the ice on the Neva in an accident that easily could have killed him. In addition, he found himself in conflict after 1821 with Lieven over organization of a "consistory" for the management of the Protestant confessions in the empire, with Speranskii over proposed changes in the civil laws on marriage, and with Orthodox hierarchs, who came to regard many of his policies as detrimental to Orthodoxy. Finally, against him formed a conspiracy, whose chief members were Arakcheev and Magnitskii.[4] Arakcheev and Magnitskii hoped to further their own careers by convincing the tsar that Golitsyn was a "danger" to the welfare of the empire and should be removed. At this they failed, for Alexander not only continued to value Golitsyn's personal friendship but kept him as a member of the

2. The notion that the Bible Society's attempt at reform was really no more than reactionary defense of the existing elites' privileged position is most clearly argued in Soviet scholarship. For a particularly able example, see Kosachevskaia, *Balugianskii*, 164–191, especially 174–175.

3. Among the more telling critiques of the Golitsyn ministry, and Magnitskii in particular, were those of the editor of *Syn otechestva*, N. I. Grech. See his *Zapiski o moei zhizni* (SPB, 1886), 289–311. Gordon Cook, "Petr S. Chaadaev and the Rise of Russian Criticism 1800–1830" (unpublished Ph.D. dissertation, Duke University, 1972), 169–180, describes well the contempt for the Golitsyn ministry that united many men who otherwise disagreed on many important matters.

4. Sawatsky, "Golitsyn" 404–430. For details on the Arakcheev-Magnitskii conspiracy, see also K. R. Whiting, "Aleksei Andreevich Arakcheev" (unpublished Ph.D.

government, as director of the postal service and, with ministerial rank, as member of the Committee of Ministers.

The tsar's continued high regard for Golitsyn notwithstanding, it was clear that the reform of the dual ministry had not worked and had to be replaced. But neither Alexander nor Golitsyn had any idea about what to do next. The tsar took perhaps the only step possible. He appointed as minister a distinguished old patriot who could preside over the ministry with some dignity, but not actually do very much, while a study committee worked up a plan for new reform. The essential goal did not change. The university system was to provide high-level academic training to produce able, loyal, well-motivated servicemen, including teachers. The question was, then, not what to do but how to do it. The "rationalism" of the Enlightenment had been tried in the first decade, with mixed results. The answer proposed for the problems that stemmed from "rationalism," i.e., "pietism," had been tried in the next decade, with results that led the tsar and minister to agree that something else had to be tried. Shishkov was appointed minister in May 1824 to preside over, if not quite lead, the search for that something else.

1. The Shishkov and Lieven Ministries

Shishkov promised to "slowly, carefully" draw up a plan, showing "good will" to all, and in "close consultation" with all the individuals and agencies whose work would be affected. He promised, thus, just what Alexander wanted. Yet, Shishkov had never hidden his opinion that the young men who formed the Secret Committee, and LaHarpe, were completely mistaken on fundamentals when they helped launch the original reform. He was equally outspoken in his opposition to the Bible Society. Shishkov thought Russia should cease borrowing from the West and instead rely on development of its own values and traditions. Thus, he thought it a mistake to adopt either French Enlightenment or German Pietism as models for Russia. In 1824, however, at seventy years of age, and willing to promise the tsar that he would go about his work "slowly and

dissertation, Harvard, 1951), 209–215, 259–270; Joseph L. Wieczynski, "Apostle of Obscuratism: The Archimandrite Photius of Russia (1792–1838)," *Journal of Ecclesiastical History*, XXII (1971), 319–331.

quietly," Shishkov seemed unlikely to push very hard to get his views enacted into policy. Shishkov, thus, had qualities nearly ideal for a caretaker minister.[5]

Popov, Turgenev, and other members of the ministry staff were soon dismissed and Shishkov brought in a number of new men. Still, Shishkov did not want to clean house. The university curators, clearly the key men in both formation and execution of policy, were changed but slowly, and then not at Shishkov's initiative. In February 1825 Obolenskii submitted his resignation, though Shishkov would have been happy to see him stay on. Indeed, upon receiving his resignation, Shishkov asked Obolenskii to continue in office until the following September. In March 1825 Shishkov accepted the resignation of Karneev from the Kharkov curatorship, and recommended in his stead a "well-educated patriot," A. A. Perovskii, who had a doctorate from Moscow as well as family connections. He was the son (albeit illegitimate) of the former minister, Razumovskii. Lieven and Novosiltsev remained curators throughout Shishkov's term as minister. Most striking, it took two years more to replace Runich and Magnitskii, whose dismissals Shishkov apparently had not expected, let alone desired, upon taking office.

In December 1824 Shishkov appointed some committees to make studies of various aspects of the ministry's work. The most important might have been the "temporary committee on statutes" for universities and lower schools. The only holdover member of the ministry appointed to this committee was Magnitskii. Yet, Magnitskii's position in the ministry was far from secure. His proposal, in 1823, to cut or abolish altogether instruction in subjects such as philosophy, as inherently "dangerous," attracted much criticism in the ministry. Novosiltsev rejected Magnitskii's critique of the work in religion done at Vilna, and Laval, Lieven, and Perovskii all submitted papers to the Main School Administration condemning Magnitskii's proposal. In Feburary 1825 Parrot wrote a long letter to Alexander, condemning "that cruel man," Magnitskii.[6] Magnitskii had abandoned Golitsyn in time to escape dismissal at the

5. For Shishkov's acceptance, and promise, see N. I. Kiselev, Iu. Samarin, eds., *Zapiski, mneniia i perepiska Admirala A. S. Shishkova*, 2 v. (SPB, 1870), II, 163–164.

6. Magnitskii's proposal and the responses of Laval, Lieven, and Perovskii are reproduced in Feoktistov, "Magnitskii: materialy," *RV*, v. 52, 407–428. Parrot's letter is in Petukhov, *Derptskii universitet*, 344–345, and Shil'der, *Aleksandr*, IV, 298–299. Magnitskii's response to the attacks on his proposals came to stress the

demise of the dual ministry, scheming with Arakcheev against Golitsyn in the hope of securing for himself the appointment as minister. He was passed over for minister, and even his place in the ministry was in jeopardy, for his proposals were attracting unusually sharp rejoinders from many sides.

In February 1825 Magnitskii signaled his colleagues that he was prepared to change course again. He abandoned Runich, his long-term supporter in the ministry. At a meeting of the new committee on statutes, he pointed out that he had "noticed" that Runich's reports from St. Petersburg University called the newly "reformed" university a great success. Magnitskii expressed doubt about that. "I think it necessary," he said, "that the minister obtain from the curator [Runich] detailed information" making clear "just what he has done to improve the university." This signal was a bit too subtle for Shishkov, who simply forwarded a request for the information to Runich. In the committee's March meeting, Magnitskii tried again. He said that he had "noticed" that his instruction to Kazan had been adopted in 1821 for St. Petersburg University. "But," he went on, "that instruction says that the curator at the end of each year must submit a report to the minister concerning the fulfillment of the instruction's requirements." Asserting that he had "looked for these reports in the files" but found none, Magnitskii asked that the minister look into the matter.[7] Had Magnitskii really wanted to inquire about such reports, he could have walked down the hall and asked about them, for he and Runich had offices in the same building. It better suited his purposes to ask about reports for which he knew Runich was legally responsible but had never completed. Magnitskii realized that the tide had turned against those who valued pure hearts more than correct legal form, and hoped to go with that tide. Magnitskii's maneuver, turning against Runich, failed. It ended in his own disgrace and dismissal, a turn of events that could prove important for the committee's consideration of statute reform.

---

danger of "foreign" influence more than its "godless" character, a marked shift in emphasis from his positions of 1819–1820. See, e.g., his retort to Lieven, printed in *Chtenie v Imperatorskom obshchestve istorii i drevnostei rossiiskikh pri moskovskom universitete*, v. 75 (1870), *smes*, 208–210.

7. Rozhdestvenskii, *Materialy*, 378–380 (Journal of temporary committee on statutes, 12 February 1825); TsGIAL, f. 733, op. 20, d. 219, list 68 (Journal of temporary committee on statutes, 5 March 1825).

Shishkov was slow to conclude that Magnitskii should be dismissed. But Magnitskii had no defenders in the ministry after he turned on Runich, and a large if indeterminate number of ministry officials of all ranks and capacities by the spring of 1825 had formed an anti-Magnitskii cabal whose object was to persuade the minister to drop him. Shishkov disappointed them several times when he failed to take seriously—or to see the point of—charges made against Magnitskii. Moreover, the conspirators were uneasy, for some feared Magnitskii's ability to turn the tables on them somehow. By mid-May 1825 Shishkov came to realize that since Magnitskii had not visited Kazan since 1819 but had several times withdrawn ministry funds for expenses for trips to Kazan, he was guilty of "illegal" behavior. In early August Magnitskii decided that his university and district needed inspecting after all, and he went to Kazan for six weeks of careful scrutiny. Meanwhile, the Academic Committee of the Main School Administration in September met to consider the annual reports submitted by the curators for the academic year 1824–1825. Fuss, taking up the report on Kazan, said that he "always read with great pleasure the annual reports submitted [by Magnitskii] on the condition and successes of the university and district" entrusted to him.[8] However, he concluded that "it is not possible to accept this report," since its contents were clearly untrue. Fuss's colleagues agreed and, in Magnitskii's absence, voted to reject the report.

The blow fell on 1 December 1825. Magnitskii was visited in the middle of the night by a police detachment with orders from "the highest authority" that he should proceed at once to Kazan. Magnitskii had received a similar visit from police years before when, as Speranskii's assistant, he was banished to the east. Now he tried to delay the proceedings by assuring the police that he had just returned from Kazan and that as a member of the ministry his duties required that he stay in St. Petersburg. Shishkov, however, had that very day informed the city chief of police that "it has become known that Magnitskii has on his own volition arrived here without permission to do so from central authority." He requested that the

8. TsGIAL, f. 733, op. 40, d. 157, listy 17–20 (Journal, Academic Committee, 12 September 1825). Except where otherwise noted, this account of the cabal in the ministry against Magnitskii is based on that of one of the participants, Panaev, "Vospominaniia," VE, 1867 (No. 4), 78–113. For Magnitskii's inspection trip to Kazan, see Zagoskin, Istoriia, IV, 489–514.

police "explain to Mr. Magnitskii that it would be best if he had departed for his post by tomorrow." Magnitskii sent an appeal to Shishkov on the morning of 2 December, arguing that "you know that by *ukaz* I serve as a member of the Main School Administration, and thus my duty post is here." Shishkov replied, to the chief of police rather than to Magnitskii, that "there is no clear rule as to where the curators of educational districts should maintain their residences" and went on to note that the Moscow curator lived in Moscow. He made a number of other points too, including the fact that 400 rubles from the ministry travel funds had been taken by Magnitskii as long ago as 1822. Thus, Shishkov asked that the police carry out his original request to see that Magnitskii departed for Kazan at once.[9]

In mid-December 1825 Russia was shaken by the news of the mysterious death of Tsar Alexander, by the confusion regarding the succession that followed, and by the tragedy of the Decembrist revolt. The Decembrist rising indeed marked one of the most significant turning points in Russian history, raising in stark dramatic terms the most penetrating questions of freedom and unfreedom, indeed of the legitimacy of Russia's whole public order. Though it changed much in the perceptions of most members of the government and of educated society, in the proceedings at Kazan, and in the ministry in St. Petersburg, the December Revolt made no difference. On the day, 14 December, that tragedy unfolded on Senate Square, when Russian soldiers offered, and gave, their lives for noble causes, Magnitskii was in Kazan, unhappily preparing for an "inspection" of his university whose conclusion was all but foregone. Shishkov informed army general P. Th. Zheltukhin in mid-January 1826 that Tsar Nicholas wanted him to conduct an investigation of Kazan University, "paying particular attention to the behavior and actions of curator Magnitskii himself."[10]

9. Panaev seemed especially pleased to note that the police called at Magnitskii's door "in the middle of the night." Panaev, "Vospominaniia," *VE*, 111. The correspondence between Shishkov, the police (Military Governor-General A. S. Miloradovich) and Magnitskii, 1–2 December 1825, is printed in Zagoskin, *Istoriia*, IV, 527–530.

10. Zagoskin, *Istoriia*, IV, 536–537 (Shishkov to Zheltukhin, 12 January 1826). The files on the Zheltukhin investigation and the dismissal of Magnitskii comprise two unusually large delo in TsGIAL, f. 733, op. 40, d. 204 and 205, each containing over 400 pages of materials. A generous selection from them is printed in Zagoskin, *Istoriia*, IV, 537–584. A well-chosen selection hostile to Magnitskii is in Feoktistov, "Magnitskii," *RV*, v. 52, 435–449. Except where noted otherwise, the account

Zheltukhin submitted a detailed report, dated 10 March, which recommended the dismissal of Magnitskii, turning over management of the district to Rector Fuchs for the time being, and abolishing the office of director as "unnecessary." The main charges against Magnitskii were that he had not followed the statute in faculty appointments and that Kazan's finances were in disorder. It could not be determined how much money was missing, but several accounts seemed to show substantial deficiencies.

The Main School Administration met on 10 April 1826 to consider Zheltukhin's report. Runich excused himself from the discussion, explaining that his "recent unhappy personal relations with Magnitskii" were such that he "could not take part in the consideration of this matter."[11] No other member felt moved to pass up the chance to vote for the condemnation of the man whose name for long seemed to many members of educated society to represent what their work was about. On 6 May the tsar signed the order that dismissed Magnitskii from service, turned over to Rector Fuchs the management of Kazan University and the district, and suppressed the office of "director." In the fall, at Shishkov's request, the Kazan faculty discussed what needed to be done to repair the damage of the Magnitskii era. The faculty replied that "the goal of education of students is the training of true sons of the church, true servants of the tsar, and good and enlightened citizens of the fatherland."[12] Magnitskii himself could not have said it any better.

The dismissal of Magnitskii, and that of Runich, which was not long delayed, signaled that something important had happened but did not make clear what it was. The charges against Magnitskii and the methods used against him were in good measure nearly as fraudulent and underhanded as those he himself had used so masterfully to advance his career. To be sure, it was literally true that there was no "clear" rule that a curator should reside in St. Petersburg, but Shishkov could hardly doubt that twenty-odd years of experience as well as the text of the 1804 legislation made it ob-

---

given here is based on materials in Zagoskin. General Zheltukhin was a native of Kazan who had recently requested that his next duty assignment take him to the Kazan area.

11. TsGIAL, f. 733, op. 40, d. 204, list 172 (Journal, Main School Administration, 10 April 1826).

12. *Ibid.*, list 431 (Fuchs to Shishkov, 8 November 1826). The order for Magnitskii's dismissal is printed in *Sbornik postanovlenii*, II, 24.

vious that curators were expected to live and work in the capital. Shishkov was not the first Minister of Education to shade the truth, or violate the law, for Zavadovskii, Razumovskii, and Golitsyn had all done so, apparently in good conscience, at various times in pursuit of one or another laudable aim. Use of such methods against Magnitskii, then, while it may have had the flavor of poetic justice, was not precedent-making and carried no promise of improvement in the conduct of ministry business. Appeals to religious values, too, helped little to establish what the end of the Magnitskii era might bring, for such appeals had been his own stock in trade for too long. Thus, though few doubted that the dismissal of Magnitskii was a worthwhile step, none could say yet what it signified. The path ahead remained to be decided.

Shishkov, in September 1824, sketched out his idea of the path. Addressing a meeting of the Main School Administration, he said: "To us is entrusted an important matter: supervision of the education and upbringing of Russian youth. We must answer to God and to the Fatherland. . . . Deep appreciation or righteous censure will be ours . . . before the court of the future, depending upon the happy or ill results of our work." What that could mean Shishkov tried to make clear by inviting his audience to look some distance "into the future and take thought about the results of our labors. We will see a very large number of citizens throughout the vast expanse of Russia. . . ." working at all sorts of occupations. But, he went on, we should see them "well formed in love of God and in loyalty to Tsar and Fatherland, in love of truth, in honor and in charity toward all mankind." On the other hand, one should not see men "infected with sophist thought, . . . puffed up pride, or evil self-love."

Naturally, the good results that Shishkov envisioned stemmed from a well-balanced educational program. "Learning which is cultivated by the mind does not deserve public confidence if it is not grounded in faith and good morals." Moreover, he went on: "Learning is useful only when, like salt, it is applied in the measure appropriate to the needs of the people and to the needs which each rank has. Too much, as well as too little, is the enemy of true enlightenment. To teach reading to the whole nation, or a disproportionate number of people, is to do more harm than good." Nonetheless, "instruction in the law and truth of Christianity and in good morals are necessities for everyone." Shishkov concluded his remarks with a heartful wish. "I am confident," he said, "that these thoughts of mine concerning the nature of true enlightenment are no different from your own, and I hope that on their basis we may give thanks to God, honor to the monarch, and greater service to the Fatherland."[13] Shishkov doubtless was completely earnest in his desire to do good while avoiding evil, to give to all the knowledge each would need, without giving "too much" to a "disproportionate number." At the conclusion of his speech, nonetheless, it remained to be decided how much was too much, how the right amounts could be delivered, or even what was required.

In December 1824 Shishkov appointed a number of study committees, including one to draw up a "detailed report on the present condition of our academic institutions" and a "projected general statute for the universities and schools."[14] The committee met regularly from January 1825, but had achieved little when, a few days after Magnitskii's dismissal, Tsar Nicholas called on the ministry to work out a plan to "strengthen and correct the statutes" of all academic institutions and appointed a new, much enlarged and strengthened comittee to take up the work. This "Committee on the organization of academic institutions" was the first example of what became a characteristic feature of the reign of Nicholas I: the formation of special, *ad hoc,* agencies whose members held the trust of the tsar and who were appointed to work out reform in particular areas of activity. Such committees could, and often did, complicate rather than solve problems, for they easily worked at cross-purposes with the ministries. This committee on the educational problem did not meet such difficulties, however, for its chairman was the Minister of Education and the man who became its most important member, S. S. Uvarov was not only informed and interested in educational matters, but a skilled veteran of work in the Russian bureaucracy.

This committee took over the files accumulated by the "temporary" committee on statutes appointed by Shishkov and, in effect, became an agency of the ministry.[15] Its membership gave little in-

13. Shishkov's speech is printed in *Sbornik rasporiazhenii,* I, 527–530 (11 September 1824).

14. The work of the "temporary committee on statutes," January 1825 to May 1826, is well summarized in Rozhdestvenskii, *Istoricheskii obzor,* 176–178.

15. The "reskript" for the Committee on the organization of academic institutions is in *Sbornik postanovlenii,* II, 25–26 (Ob uchrezhdenii Komiteta . . .) and in

dication of the direction the work should take. Shishkov and Uvarov were well known for holding widely varying views. They were joined by Lieven and Speranskii, who continued a deep interest in evangelical religion, and by Heinrich Storch of the Academy of Sciences, who remained a most prolific exponent of Enlightened "rationalism." These men were joined by a number of career military officers and others who had no prior connections with academic concerns. To the first meeting of the new committee Shishkov outlined an eight-point program. Three were particularly important. First, Shishkov thought the statutes should promote the goal of "providing education which is directly related to the needs of the various classes." Second, there were a number of problems to be solved in order that young nobles would study in "Russian" schools, rather than in "foreign" or "private" schools. He noted that "private schools were often the enterprises of the "foreigners." He also proposed, finally, that the autonomy of the universities had to be curbed, in particular by having rectors appointed by the government, not elected by the faculty.[16]

Shishkov also proposed that the censorship function should be exercised by a special agency, not by committees of professors. Nicholas soon enacted Shishkov's proposal into what became known as the "cast-iron" statute, not only severe but unworkable. This development was less important to the academic institutions than at first seemed likely. Transferring the censorship function (though many of the censors continued to be chosen from among academics) was but part of Shishkov's plan to remove from the control of faculty councils all functions that were not strictly academic. Thus, police, maintenance, and all "economic" matters, he thought, should be handled by an administration chosen for that purpose. None of

---

RS, 1901 (December), 681–682, titled "O preobrazovanii uchebnykh zavedenni: Reskript imperatora Nikolaia—A. S. Shishkova, 14 go Maia 1826 g." For detailed presentations of the work of this committee, see Rozhdestvenskii, *Istoricheskii obzor,* 179–219; Steven H. Allister, "The Reform of Higher Education in Russia during the Reign of Nicholas I, 1825–1855" (unpublished Ph.D. dissertation, Princeton University, 1974), 20–107; Constantin Galskoy, "The Ministry of Education under Nicholas I: 1826–1836" (unpublished Ph.D. dissertation, Stanford University, 1977), 166–193. All show thorough knowledge of the committee's files and "journal," in TsGIAL, f. 737. Unless otherwise noted, the discussion of the work of this committee is based on these works.

16. Rozhdestvenskii, *Istoricheskii obzor,* 179–181; Allister, 25–30; Galskoy, 176–178.

his ideas, therefore, were original, for all had been heard many times before.

General Sievers and Count Lambert made lengthy presentations in support of Shishkov. Both seemed especially interested in seeing the schools reorganized on lines that would both facilitate the path of gentry into state service and also provide education for other classes that more clearly "met the needs" of those classes, not the open and academically orientated system founded in 1804. Lieven and Storch made equally detailed presentations that forcefully argued the opposite case. Both agreed that it was important to encourage young gentry to come into the public system. But that meant to satisfy the standards of competence required for genuine public service by meeting the requirements of the 1803–1804 and 1809 legislation. Storch rejected Shishkov's explanations for the deficiencies of the system, i.e., "foreign" influence, lack of good "spirit," and such. Storch thought the chief deficiency was inadequate funding, which kept the teachers' salaries, to cite the obvious example, too low for the requirements of the task.

Lieven agreed with much of Storch's view, but also thought it important to note that the original 1803–1804 legislation was not wrong in taking so little notice of class differences. "In states where the lines between classes are clear and where passing from one class to another, especially from the middle class to the nobility, is very difficult and it is rare to reward long and distinguished service with a grant of nobility—in such states," said Lieven; "it is easy to organize education the way" Shishkov had proposed. "But," he went on, "in Russia, where no middle or citizen class exists, where only the merchant class (*kupecheskoe soslovie*) in some ways resembles one . . . where the nobility extends from the foot of the throne at one end and nearly merges into the peasantry at the other, where every year many from the citizen and peasant classes enter the ranks of the nobility by achieving the required rank in military or civil service—in Russia it is very difficult to organize schools" on the basis of hereditary class.[17] Lieven suggested, and Storch vigorously agreed, that the chief obstacle to the enrollment of nobles in the schools was not the question of class exclusivity, but the poverty of most nobles, which often matched that of members of other classes.

Throughout the academic year 1826–1827 and well into the

17. Rozhdestvenskii, *Istoricheskii obzor*, 197–198.

next summer, the committee labored industriously, discussing every conceivable aspect of the development of the schools at every level, and supplied answers to some particular questions. In October 1824 Runich had requested permission to appoint a new rector for St. Petersburg University. He repeated his request several times, the last in July 1826, shortly before his dismissal. The committee reviewed his requests at length and each time denied permission to have an appointed rector.[18] On the other hand, Novosiltsev in the same month, July 1826, requested permission to appoint the rector at Vilna University and was granted his request almost at once. Novosiltsev, in fact, had already appointed his choice, Professor Pelikan of the medical faculty. Nonetheless, Novosiltsev requested permission to do what he had already done, warmly praising Pelikan and arguing that it seemed useful to harmonize the procedure at Vilna with the other Polish universities, Warsaw and Cracow, where rectors were appointed, not elected. There was no doubt, however, that for Novosiltsev the main reason to institute the appointment of rectors by the curator or ministry was the same he held in 1803–1804. "Election of rectors was characteristic of the ancient German universities," he argued, but not appropriate for modern Russia. The "republican form of governance . . . works against the goals for which our universities were founded" and was moreover "out of harmony with the general pattern of governance" of the Russian empire.[19]

In the summer of 1826, thus, the committee had settled the question of the election of university rectors by and from the faculty in both ways, upholding the procedure at St. Petersburg while abolishing it at Vilna. Since most matters before the committee seemed to make similar progress, it was not surprising that Nicholas began to feel discontented with the committee's work. He was kept informed, since the committee sent him the minutes of its meetings. He replied by making penciled remarks on the margins of the minutes and returning them to the committee.

18. TsGIAL, f. 733, op. 209, d. 219, list 158 (Runich to Shishkov, 14 October 1824), list 182 (Runich to Shishkov, 17 June 1825), listy 260–264 (Runich to Shishkov, 3 July 1826).

19. Sbornik postanovlenii, II, 31–33 (Ob opredelenii rektorov . . . 28 July 1826). Pelikan, Czech by birth, received his higher education at the St. Petersburg Medical-Surgical Academy (1809–1813). He was elected dean by his colleagues in the medical faculty. Beauvois, L'Université de Vilna, 70–72; Pogodin, "Vilenskii okrug," Sbornik materialov, IV, xxxvii.

In August 1827 he intervened more directly. Following the debates in the committee, he could see that the committee was completely divided on the question of the usefulness of limiting access to the schools on the basis of social class. Hence, the tsar made a decision. He wanted education, he said, that met the "true needs" of both the student and the state, "neither below nor above the condition in life in which the student will most likely stay in the ordinary course of things." But, he went on, "it has come to my attention" that "often serfs (*krepostnye liudi*) from both towns and villages study in gymnasia and other higher educational institutions." Therefore, the tsar concluded, "I now find it necessary to order that admission to universities and gymnasia is restricted only to those of the free classes, not excluding also the emancipated . . . though they may not have enrolled yet [in a new class] or have any kind of rank." Since the tsar's order in reality did no more than describe the policy that had been in effect for more than a decade, it did not meet the committee's questions, but simply ended its discussion.[20]

If Shishkov concluded from this that the tsar wished to replace him as minister, he was not mistaken. Shishkov was retired on grounds of his "advanced age and very poor health." During his tenure, the committee brought to conclusion three important projects: the foundation of a "Professor's Institute" at Dorpat University to train future faculty members, the reorganization of a Main Pedagogical Institute in St. Petersburg to train teachers for the lower schools of the whole empire, and, finally, the drafting of a new statute for all schools in the empire below university level. Though this last was not promulgated until December 1828, the work was completed in all essentials in January of that year. None of these steps were a turning away from the original 1802–1804 reform. In-

20. Rozhdestvenskii, *Istoricheskii obzor,* 182. The tsar's order regarding access to the schools is printed in *Sbornik postanovlenni,* II, 71–73 (Reskript . . . 19 August 1827). Nicholas had ordered Kochubei, Chairman of the State Council, to have the Council issue a law forbidding the admission of serf children to public schools. Kochubei, pointing out that a law issued from the State Council "would become known throughout Europe," persuaded the tsar to settle for a *reskript* to the Minister of Education, which presumably would cause less embarrassment since it would be less likely to become widely known. Clearly, the tsar was not proud to defend serfdom, and able officials knew that. D. N. Bludov, newly appointed to the Committee on Schools, wrote the *reskript* that the tsar signed, describing the existing system instead of introducing the change that the tsar seemed to want. For details, see Shilder, *Nikolas,* II, 32–34.

stead, all three projects continued, and strengthened, that reform.[21]

One of the soldiers Nicholas appointed to the committee, General Sievers, in July 1826 urged steps to revive the Pedagogical Institute at St. Petersburg. He suggested particularly that the Institute recruit as students sons of clergy who could be trained to serve as teachers in the gymnasia, or in the lower schools too, of all the empire. Sievers clearly meant to advance not only the development of the schools, but also education that both further strengthened and took advantage of traditional class interest in certain vocations, much the same recommendation counseled by Kochubei in 1814 and by Pnin, Martynov, and others in 1804. Sievers thought seminarians likely to prove especially suitable as teachers because they were morally reliable. Uvarov, who warmly seconded Siever's proposal, accepted the task of preparing a draft of a statute for the Institute. His work was completed and finally approved by the tsar in September 1828, though its main outlines had been clear more than a year before. The final document looked remarkably like, indeed in places copied word for word, the legislation that Uvarov had completed, and seen to enactment, for the Main Pedagogical Institute in 1816 and for its "second course" in 1817. It cited the "experience of the Teacher's College of the time of Catherine II," as had Uvarov in 1817, and concluded that "*mainly* graduates of seminaries should be admitted to the Pedagogical Institute." The school was to prepare teachers for the schools of all levels, from gymnasium down, in all parts of the empire. The students were to be state-supported, recruited "mainly," but not exclusively, from the clergy. In sum, Uvarov's draft continued and expanded the work of the institute.[22]

A Professors' Institute at Dorpat University was recommended by

21. There were some other matters on which decisions had been reached, largely on an ad hoc basis by the tsar himself. In September 1826 the uniforms for university students were redesigned. Henceforth students were expected to wear them as routinely as military personnel wore theirs, at least at St. Petersburg and Moscow Universities. Permission was granted to the curator at Kharkov, at his request in 1827, to make additions to the faculty without the participation of the faculty council. Also in 1827, Nicholas agreed to a proposal from Moscow's curator that self-supporting students who lived off campus at Moscow University should be subject to the city police authority. *Sbornik postanovlenni*, II, 1–3, 38–43 (on uniforms), 33 (on Kharkov), 73 (on Moscow students).

22. *Sbornik postanovlenii*, II, 175–189 (30 September 1828). Underscoring Uvarov's.

Parrot, the recently retired professor of physics who had come St. Petersburg to work in the Academy of Science, of which Uvarov remained president. In September 1827 Bludov, Uvarov's colleague since the days when both were founding members of the Arzamas society, presented Parrot's plan to the committee. The plan called for the complete renewal of the faculties of the "Russian" universities, by replacing the entire faculty of Moscow, Kazan, and Kharkov universities with newly trained men, chosen from graduates of those schools, sent to Dorpat for advanced work in their fields and then to Berlin and/or Paris to complete their studies. St. Petersburg University was not to have the benefit of this program, for Parrot thought it so weak that it was beyond hope of improvement. He assumed that although other universities in the empire needed drastic renovation of their faculties, Dorpat was so strong that it could provide the training needed for the others' *kandidats* to become scholarly professionals. His recommendation also called for full-time directors of the program at Dorpat, Berlin, and Paris, who would be salaried at 10,000 a year each. The total annual budget for the program Parrot estimated at nearly a quarter million rubles. Shishkov and Speranskii thought Parrot's plan so outlandish that it was not worthy of discussion. Lieven, Uvarov, and Storch, however, thought it merited invesigation.

Uvarov drew up a draft that made substantial changes in Parrot's plan. The number of candidates from each university was set at twenty, not fifty-two; the course at Dorpat was scheduled for two years, not five; and St. Petersburg University was included after all. By offering a compromise, Uvarov secured the support of men who earlier found the proposal unacceptably extreme. At the end of November, when Nicholas approved the final draft of the legislation, he added one more note; "I agree to this on condition that without fail the candidates chosen must be native Russians."[23]

Uvarov's notion of what was both proper and possible thus was enacted in the cases of the new Main Pedagogical Institute and the Professors' Institute. He was also particularly important in deciding the final shape of the statute for the schools below university level,

23. *Sbornik postanovlenni*, II, 107–111 (Ob izbranii . . . 27 November 1827). Parrot's plan is in *ibid.*, 95–101, together with the committee's decision to send it up to Nicholas. See also Rozhdestvenskii, *Istoricheskii obzor*, 186–187, 250–251; Allister, "Reform," 59–60; Petukhov, *Derptskii universitet*, 486–489. On Bludov, see Galskoy, "Ministry," 145–154.

enacted in December 1828. In its final form, the new statute retained the main features, and most of the details, of the 1804 law.[24] The gymnasium curriculum was much simplified, so that it resembled very closely the revised curriculum that Uvarov had introduced into the St. Petersburg district in 1819. In essence, it remained an academic, not vocational, system of three levels: village, *uezd*, and gymnasium. Each level prepared its graduates for the one above, concluding finally in the seven-year gymnasium course that prepared its graduates for university admission. The gymnasium curriculum was designed for a "double purpose: to provide . . . education for youth who have no wish or are unable to pursue university study" and also "to provide the preparation necessary" for university work. Shishkov and others quite correctly pointed out that the majority of gymnasium students did not proceed to a university. Nonetheless, Uvarov argued for, and won, a classical bias in the curriculum. Though he much preferred offering Greek in all gymnasia, he settled for requiring it only in schools located in university towns, since it was not possible to provide adequate teachers of the subject elsewhere. But Latin was to be required in every gymnasium in the empire, despite the vigorous opposition of those who thought that training for state service, the prime goal of the system, was a vocational matter that needed "science," not ancient languages. Even in the matter of modern languages, Uvarov won his point. Alone of the committee members, he thought that both French and German should be required of all gymnasia. Shishkov was particularly unhappy with keeping French—the language of the enemy—in the curriculum. Most members thought German would be enough. Uvarov persuaded Nicholas to intervene, with another of his decisive marginal notes, requiring the inclusion of both French and German.[25]

Most striking was the outcome of the class question. The debates in the committee seemed to assume that the public system should restrict private education, eventually supplanting it altogether in

24. This point is made by Rozhdestvenskii, *Istoricheskii obzor*, 195.

25. Shishkov, and the committee majority, recommended that Greek replace Latin and French in the gymnasium, making it possible for Uvarov to assume the posture of the moderate, prudently recommending Latin and French in all gymnasia, Greek only in university towns. See "K istorii klassitsizma v Rossi: Mnenie (grafa) S. S. Uvarov (1826)," *RA*, 1899 (No. 11–12), 465–466. Shishkov responded with an attack on the teaching of French, which he thought led to many evils, among them that students of French soon "think they know everything." *Ibid.*, 467–468.

order to bring gentry into a public system designed to prepare them for state service. Together with this clearly went restructuring education on class lines, particularly after the tsar showed his sentiments on the subject, if not his grasp of the law, in August 1827. It seemed that all that remained was to decide the degree of class exclusivity needed and to make clear the limits. Uvarov made gestures in this direction, proposing that the *uezd* gentry assembly elect an "honorary curator" who could meet with the district supervisor of schools and make suggestions to him. Intended to interest gentry in the local schools, this proposal, perhaps too clearly, gave the gentry no authority over the schools, even in their own localities. The final text of the 1828 statute stated that its "general goal" was to make available to youth the means to acquire "the knowledge most necessary for each class." But in subsequent chapters the village schools were to "accept children of all classes," while the "*uezd* school is open for people of all classes, and especially for children of merchants, craftsmen, and other urban dwellers." The admission requirements for the gymnasium were stated entirely in terms of academic preparation, making no mention of class or even of the "liberation" papers that had been required of those from "obligated" classes since 1814. Thus, the 1828 statute preserved the ambiguity on class matters that had characterized the 1804 statute, despite the volume of discussion, and distress, that had arisen about it over the past quarter century as well as within the committee itself.[26]

26. The text of the statute is in *Sbornik postanovlenii*, II, 200–257. Quotations 203, 205, 211. The statute included one important distinction on class lines. Those who finished the "whole" seven-year gymnasium course received rank fourteen in state service, "born nobles after one year, personal nobles after three years, and others after five years of active service." *Ibid.*, 241. Thus, a "born noble" who went to the university and obtained after three or more, usually four, years a "student" diploma, would achieve rank fourteen in service at least two years later than he could expect had he entered service directly from the gymnasium. On the other hand, a student from the "others" category who obtained a "student" diploma and thereby rank fourteen, saved himself at least two years of service time to acquire that rank. This arrangement, clearly, was unlikely to advantage "born" nobles. Those who studied Greek in gymnasium, however, went directly to rank fourteen, with no time delay or discrimination by class. Given the enthusiasm in the committee for both class-orientated and vocational education, it is extraordinary that Uvarov managed to get those provisions included in the law. The provision that stated the statute's goals in class-orientated terms was in the introduction. The provisions that nullified the class distinctions were buried deep in the log document. It has been asserted often that one of the main features of the 1828 statute was to replace the all-class "ladder" system of 1804 with one that broke the connection between the various levels in the

The Shishkov ministry had not been barren, for the 1828 statute, the Pedagogical Institute, and the Professors Institute proved worthwhile accomplishments. Nonetheless, it was striking how few of Shishkov's recommendations were brought into practice. He called repeatedly for education limited to that which each class "needs," for the end of "foreign" influence, and for limiting university autonomy by abolishing faculty election of rectors. His views were shared by many, including the tsar. Yet, none of these steps was taken. Uvarov's ideas, not Shishkov's, survived to enactment. Nonetheless, when Nicholas sought a new Minister of Education in the spring of 1828, he turned to Lieven, not to Uvarov. Uvarov's role had been important, but not ostentatious. He offered neither programatic statements about the goals of the system, nor propositions of his own. Instead, he took up others' propositions, compromising them until they resembled those he had presented a decade earlier. This technique was effective at getting results but seemed to attract little attention from the tsar or from many others.

Lieven began his ministry by calling upon the committee to turn its attention to the work of drafting a general statute for the universities. He pointed out, in May 1828, that the statute for the lower schools was in final form and that the statutes for the universities at both Dorpat and Vilna had been reformed recently enough to suffice. The plan for a statute for the "Russian" universities he outlined preserved in all essentials the 1804 legislation, as had his 1820 statute revision at Dorpat. The main differences were in much increased budget allocations and in changing some of the arrangement of chairs by faculty, in the interest of academic efficiency.[27]

Many other members of the committee had not changed their minds either. Thus, the discussions were long and detailed, but produced few conclusions. A particularly important issue, since it repeatedly came up, was the election of the rector by and from

---

schools so that each was devoted to providing vocational training according to social class. Most such treatments follow, directly or indirectly, Miliukov, *Ocherki*, II, 344–346. A recent sophisticated elaboration of this view, based on the sources rather than on Miliukov, is in Edwards, "Maistre and Educational Policy," *SR*, 72–75. This view is based on the assumption that Shishkov's various pronouncements may be taken as statements of policy. That assumption proved unwarranted, however. Neither this law nor the practice of the schools changed in essentials in regard to the class character of the system.

27. This account of the Lieven ministry follows, except where otherwise noted, Rozhdestvenskii, *Istoricheskii obzor*, 183–192; Allister, "Reform," 74–104.

among the faculty. Those who wanted this feature of the 1804 legislation to be continued, whatever other changes they might propose, in general wanted to keep and build upon the 1804 system. Those who wanted to do away with the elective character of the university rectorship also wanted in some measure to halt or reverse the work of the 1804 system. By late 1829 those who wanted to continue the basic thrust of the 1804 legislation, strengthened by the support of organized religion and by the more efficient curriculum and administration, seemed to be gaining the upper hand, for Lieven appointed a subcommittee, made up largely of men sympathetic to that view, to draft the university statute. Perhaps warned of the direction the draft was taking, Nicholas in July 1830 sent the committee a message, which declared simply that "university rectors in the future are not to be chosen from among the professors by election of the university council, but are to be named by the government, and named to a term not limited in time."[28] The importance of such a clear, direct order from the tsar to the committee could hardly be doubted.

The Lieven ministry, and the minister himself, also had to take up many issues not directly related to the work on the statute, but that doubtless affected its progress. The Polish revolt of 1830 had many consequences, not the least of which was to call into question the "success" that Novosiltsev had been reporting from Vilna, and that led to the redrawing of the boundaries of the districts in the western provinces. But the most complicated question remained that of the reorganization of the lines of authority in the university. After some time, the subcommittee on the draft statute produced a compromise, recommmending that the university faculty choose from among themselves three candidates for rector. The curator would report the faculty choices to the tsar, together with the faculty vote, and add his own recommendation. Then the tsar would choose (or have the minister choose) from among the three candidates a rector for a three-year term.

Golitsyn, curator of Moscow, protested this compromise so vigorously that the discussion went back to the full committee. The discussion was probably useful, for it provided the occasion when nearly every member heard, if not read and studied, the recommendations submitted from the various universities as well as from

28. Rozhdestvenskii, *Istoricheskii obzor*, 191.

those in the ministry. The discussions eventually made it clear that nearly everyone agreed on the need to separate as cleanly as possible the academic functions from the non-academic and to turn over to some sort of body of specialists the economic, police, and administrative functions. In turn, this led to general agreement that administration of the huge school districts by small "school committees" chosen from the faculty was not effective and distracted the faculty members from tasks—teaching and scholarship—they might be able to handle if not overburdened.[29]

Finally, in August 1832, the subcommittee members agreed on a draft text for the general statute for the four Russian universities. In October the draft was sent to the Senate, together with the approval of the ministry and with several explanatory appendices. The draft moved from the Senate through the State Council to the Law Department, where in May 1833 Uvarov requested its return to the ministry for reconsideration.

Uvarov was named "acting minister" in March 1833, to replace Lieven, who retired at once for "reasons of health." On 11 April Uvarov informed the statute committee that he thought much remained to be done before the statute was ready for promulgation, and he requested the formation of a committee of professors, chaired by Balugianskii, to begin work on a revision of the university program in legal studies.

Differences between Uvarov and Lieven were not the reason for the change in ministers. Lieven sent Uvarov in the fall of 1832 to make a detailed inspection of Moscow University. The report that Uvarov filed was a lucid statement of the situation in Russian higher education, and was well tuned to the problems that troubled the tsar. At nearly the same time, Lieven made a serious mistake. It was probably not politic to circumvent a direct order of the tsar, who had forbidden the participation of the faculty in electing the university rector, by a compromise that had the faculty put up three candidates among whom the tsar would have to choose. Worse, Lieven recommended to the tsar in December 1832 the creation of a new academic district composed of the provinces of what had been the

29. Storch and Kruzenstern to the end could not be persuaded to accept this view and as late as May 1832 continued to argue that, in Kruzenstern's words, "the health of the schools requires that there be a close organizational connection between the university and all the schools in its district." Rozhdestvenskii, *Istoricheskii obzor*, 192.

"New Russia" of Catherine the Great, on the grounds that those provinces could be safely withdrawn from the Kharkov district since their mixed populations did not make them Russian provinces anyway. Nicholas not only refused to accept Lieven's proposal; he denounced it. "I know this district very well," he wrote. "*It is Russian.*" [30] As the tsar lost confidence in Lieven, Uvarov, well regarded by all in the ministry and with the recent inspection of Moscow to his credit, seemed an easy choice for the tsar to make. In April 1834 Uvarov was confirmed as minister. His confirmation brought into office one who had not changed his mind about the proper path for Russia's educational establishment, remaining committed to positions he had marked out long before. In that, at least, Uvarov well exemplified a striking characteristic of the Shishkov and Lieven ministries. Shishkov was not alone in restating at length old positions. Few new proposals were heard from any side, for most offered positions little different in essentials from those of 1802–1804 or 1815–1817. Whatever else it showed, the continued restatement of old positions indicated that the experience of the universities had relatively little influence on the views and judgments of many in the ministry. Nonetheless, while opinion in the ministry seemed constant, the experience of the universities saw a good deal of important change.

2. The Experience of the Universities

The Uvarov ministry, which lasted to 1849, proved particularly important for the history of the Russian universities, for its successes and failures did much to influence, if not indeed decide, the future of the university system. No contribution of the Uvarov ministry was more important than the statute of 1835. The statute concluded a decade's work, a decade in the universities that saw the continuation of some old problems, but also some successes in overcoming them. During their first two decades the universities were prevented from achieving the goals of the original reformers—the

---

30. Rozhdestvenskii, *Istoricheskii obzor,* 184. Underlining Nicholas'. Lieven had provoked the ire of Count Benckendorf too, in 1830, when he resisted pressure from the tsar's special police chief to pass on to the police, the Third Section, the records of the ministry's censors. Lieven, with some anger, told Benckendorf that what the police chief wanted was "contrary to law" which "no one has the right to demand." Sidney Monas, *The Third Section: Police and Society in Russia under Nicholas I* (Cambridge, 1961), 146–150.

meaning of "success" in this context—by a number of factors and factions. First, the professors able and willing to meet those goals proved difficult to obtain in adequate numbers. Second, it was even more difficult to recruit adequately prepared and motivated students. Few professors were up to the multi-faceted task of scholarship and teaching while also running the empire's censorship services and all the lower schools of the vast country, as well as managing the financial and police administration of the universities. Students often enough, naturally, brought with them the mores of the society that nurtured them, a fact resulting in behavior that featured more drunken violence, not to mention fraud and deceit, than the original reformers had anticipated. Third, the physical facilities—the capital investment in plant, libraries, laboratories, and all the necessary auxiliary enterprises, even to include adequate facilities for housing and feeding students well enough so that they could get on with the work—were developed but slowly. There was also the resistance of various factions or groups who tried to prevent the achievement of "success" because they sought instead to substitute class-professional, vocational, education, while minimizing the universities' potential for change in Russian society. They fostered such "reforms" as removing philosophy, political economy, or even Latin, from the curriculum and abolishing the election by faculty of the rector as well as the professors' role in selecting their faculty colleagues. These problems and issues remained in the life of the universities in the decade 1824–1834, and were much of what the discussions in the ministry were about. The statute of 1835, the final product of the perceptions of those problems as worked out by Uvarov and the many who joined in the reform effort, was perhaps as close as Russia could come to meeting those problems and still cling to the main elements of the original reform of 1803–1804.

There were important new developments that complicated the work. For reasons that owed nothing to the work of the ministry, or to the universities, Vilna University was destroyed and replaced by St. Vladimir at Kiev. The progress of the universities, particularly of Moscow, was retarded by a natural disaster, the cholera outbreak of 1830–1831. The "renewal" of the faculties of all the universities, and one of its instruments, the Professors' Institute at Dorpat, by contrast, owed everything to the ministry. The "renewal" of the faculties helped the development of the universities, for the general level of professional competence rose perceptibly at the end of the decade. The renewal of the faculties, moreover, was matched by steady growth in numbers of students and in academic quality, insofar as degrees awarded and publications issued can attest. By the mid-1830's, the universities were ready to train ever-increasing numbers of candidates who were better equipped for service in terms of motivation and cultural sophistication as well as in technical competence. Thus the success in developing the 1835 statute was matched by the universities' success by 1835 in meeting some of the problems that no statute reform of any dimension could help.

For these reasons, the Professors' Institute at Dorpat was important far beyond the relatively small numbers of men whom it trained. After Nicholas gave his approval for the program in November 1827, the ministry immediately sent out a call to the universities to provide candidates. The universities were to nominate the twenty best candidates from among their "students," though they might also nominate *kandidats* and *magisters* from among both the state-supported and self-supporting. The universities were asked to distribute their nominations among fields of learning so as to promote the development of all faculties, but the prime consideration was to be the "talent for scholarship" and "moral soundness" of those chosen. The program at Dorpat was scheduled to open in September 1828. The response was less than what Uvarov, who wrote the circular, had hoped. Moscow, St. Petersburg, and Kazan each sent in seven nominations, Kharkov none. "It certainly is shameful," the tsar noted on Uvarov's report, "that Kharkov University could not find a single candidate for this useful service. Pick a few students from Vilna University on the same conditions as the others."

Kharkov was not the only school to have difficulty finding candidates. St. Petersburg's curator, Borozdin, reported that the faculty had agreed on eight candidates. Only two were "students," for the others were all first-year men. He reported also that the university had thirteen *kandidats* but that they all declined to be considered for "assignment" to Dorpat. Moscow offered this "assignment" to thirty-nine young men, but only seven were willing to go to Dorpat. Kharkov in fact had chosen twenty-three *kandidats* and "students" (and considered several second- and third-year men whose ability suggested they would succeed at Dorpat) but could persuade none to accept the appointment. As one of the Kharkov *kandidats* candidly explained, his "family situation" required that he "enter service as soon as possible." Doubtless there were other reasons, but the most important single reason that young men declined to go to Dorpat was simply poverty, for most continued to need to get into regular "service" as soon as possible.[31]

The candidates, who were to receive 1,200 rubles as an annual stipend and for travel expenses, assembled in St. Petersburg in late June 1828 for examinations conducted at the Academy of Sciences. They did not number twenty-one, for of those nominated there appeared but six from St. Petersburg, five from Moscow, two from Kazan, and three from Vilna. At the conclusion of the examinations, the professors-to-be joined in a solemn liturgy in the university church, and set out for Dorpat. In October 1828 there arrived in Dorpat four additions from Kharkov, whose faculty council had been stung by Nicholas' comment, and one from Moscow. Moreover, a Russian student at Dorpat was accepted into the program too. Two Vilna men were kept in St. Petersburg, enrolled as doctoral students in the university there. The others were joined in Dorpat by another addition from Moscow, a medical graduate named Pirogov, who had not been included in the faculty's original selection but who volunteered to go, though he was too late to take part in the examinations at St. Petersburg. Pirogov in time not only became one of Russia's leaders in medical education and administration, but received world renown for his contributions to medical science. In achieving success he was not alone. One of the members of this first group died during his first student year at Dorpat. Two dropped out, though one finished his degree at St. Petersburg University and made an academic career. All the others completed the program and began long, in may cases distinguished, service as professors in one or another of the four "Russian" universities.

At Dorpat, Professor Perevoshchikov, long the supporter of Russian students there, was named director of the institute and served it well. Some of the students thought he paid too much attention to providing "moral" leadership, but all recognized his dedication to the success of the students. Perevoshchikov was not alone in his view that the point of the program was to train loyal servants of the

31. Rozhdestvenskii, *Materialy*, 478–481, lists the St. Petersburg students willing to go to Dorpat. For Uvarov's report, and Nicholas' comment, see *Sbornik postanovlennii*, II, 131–135 (20 February 1828). Petukhov, *Derptskii universitet*, 489–490, lists all those who came to Dorpat. L. I. Nasonkina, *Moskovskii universitet posle vosstaniia dekabristov* (Moscow, 1972), 88, and Bagalei, *Opyt istorii*, II, 670–671, discuss also all those who were considered but who declined the appointment.

tsar—the meaning of "morality" in this context—as well as professionally capable scholar-teachers.[32] Perevoshchikov secured the ministry's agreement to lengthen the course. In the end, the students spent four years at Dorpat in course work, not the two originally called for, and an additional six months preparing for examinations. None of the students were sent to Paris; instead, they went to Berlin or Vienna. This first class, known as the "First Professors' Institute," departed Dorpat in the spring of 1833. In March of that year the ministry called for a "Second Professors' Institute," which proved to be the last. The call this time produced only nine candidates willing and able to do the work, four of them from Kharkov. Of this group, one died soon after arrival in Dorpat, two others dropped out. Of those who remained, none were sent abroad but all finished doctorates at Dorpat by 1838 and were placed in Russian universities.

In 1828 and 1829 also, under Speranskii's direction, twelve students were recruited from the theological academies at St. Petersburg and Moscow for training in the Second Section of the tsar's chancellery, the special agency Nicholas had appointed to work at legal reform. Speranskii, the chief of the section, supervised the work, which culminated in the Digest of Laws, and tried to improve legal education for the future service men who would be responsible for the execution of the law. This, he thought, required much improved legal training in the universities.

The students recruited for the Second Section program undertook a program designed to foster the development of legal educators. They studied the law and legal procedure under the guidance of Balugianskii, Kunitsyn, and Plisov, faculty colleagues at St. Petersburg in the days of the Runich "purge" who now served together in the Second Section. The students were enrolled also at St. Petersburg University for part of their training, and in time joined the Dorpat Institute men in study abroad, principally at Berlin.

32. Curator Borozdin encouraged the St. Petersburg contingent at Dorpat to "pursue tirelessly the great goal which Providence and the tsar have placed before you. Enrich your minds with new learning to carry back with you to the fatherland. But return also with pure hearts, return loyal sons of the Orthodox Greek-Russian Church, with unflagging faith in the tsar, with deep love for the fatherland, in a word—return Russians." Grigor'ev, S. Peterburgskii universitet, appendices, 28, note 165 (8 August 1828). Petukhov, Derptskii universitet, 488–498, is the best discussion of the institute's work. See also "O litsakh komandirovannykh za granitsu," ZhMNP, 339–341.

They, and some of the Dorpat men, returned to St. Petersburg, where they defended doctoral theses and were awarded the degree under a committee composed of Balugianskii, Plisov, and Kunitsyn, none of whom were current members of the St. Petersburg faculty. Speranskii's Second Section law students brought to nearly three dozen the number of able young Russians trained for professorial appointments in less than seven years. Their development marked an important success, training the nucleus of Russian faculty members prepared specifically to focus on replication of their own number, contributing to the education of future cadres against the day when university faculty would not be numbered merely in dozens.[33]

The importance of success in a program of faculty development was underscored by developments in the universities in the western provinces, Vilna, Kiev, and Kharkov. Vilna's faculty remained stable in the period after 1824, with no more than ordinary coming and going. The four men dismissed as a consequence of Novosiltsev's "investigation" in 1824 were replaced by men whose training, background, and teaching marked no significant change. Bobrowski returned to fill his own slot, cleared of all charges. Danilovich was replaced by Jozef Jaroszewicz, from the Krzemieniec lycée, who was not only Polish but a first-rate academic. Gołuchowski's replacement was Aniol Dowgird, a Catholic priest who was also Polish and a competent scholar, though students found his lectures almost unbearably dull. Lelewel was replaced by P. V. Kukolnik, who was regarded by the students as incompetent as well as dull.[34]

Novosiltsev, however, was pleased with Kukolnik and with the progress of his university. He resisted strenuously all recommendations to remove parts of his district from Vilna's jurisdiction, particularly the recommendations made by the governor-general of Belorussia, Prince Khovanskii, who wanted not only to withdraw

33. This point is made by Petukhov, *Derptskii universitet,* 497. On the Second Section men, and the award to them of St. Petersburg degrees, see Grigor'ev, S. *Peterburgskii universitet,* 112–113.
34. O'Connor, "Cultures," 304–306. Kukolnik was the son of one of the "Carpathio-Russians" who were recruited with Balugianskii for the Pedagogical Institute in St. Petersburg by Novosiltsev. After passing the 1809 law examinations in St. Petersburg, Kukolnik entered the Jesuit college at Polotsk, where in 1815 he defended a thesis on the influence of Roman law in Russia. In 1818–1820 he published a five-volume "Abbreviated" survey of world history. He taught history in several schools until called to Vilna by Novosiltsev in 1824. A dedicated convert to Orthodoxy, Kukolnik served in a number of capacities in Vilna until his death in 1884. See *RBS,* v. 9 (SPB, 1903), 537–53.

provinces from Vilna to form a separate Belorussian district but to require that all schools of the district use Russian as the language of instruction. Novosiltsev argued that "the youth of the Belorussian provinces are in descent, mores, custom and language significantly closer to local society than to native Russian society and therefore their education should be conducted according to the local arrangements." He concluded that "the return of the Belorussian provinces and of the Kiev province to the Vilna district would be best for their welfare and equally advantageous for the government." [35]

Pelikan, Novosiltsev's rector, also prided himself on how well things were going, in particular that his rigorous enforcement of new rules for student discipline (which were very similar to those promulgated by Czartoryski years before) guaranteed good order. He was startled in 1827 to receive a report from one of his "spies" among the students that a "secret society" had formed to keep up the Philomath cause. Investigation of this group revealed that a handful of students, calling themselves the "Sarmatian tribes," had held a meeting and drawn up a single "proclamation." One of the students implicated Professor Onacewicz, professor of Russian diplomatics and statistics, as an instigator. Pelikan at once ordered the faculty council to remove Onacewicz, thus demonstrating that the university could police itself as well as keep the investigation brief and limited. Novosiltsev, angry that the case had arisen at all, approved of Pelikan's work. Unfortunately for them, Onacewicz refused to go. Though the faculty council voted to expel him, he protested that he was being libeled, and charged that the members of the medical faculty were conspiring against him, if not against the whole faculty of politics. He appealed his case to Constantine and to the ministry and, worst of all, sued in the courts. Pelikan tried to quiet things by offering Onacewicz reinstatement, on condition that he drop his suit, but Onacewicz would not accept. In 1832 he finally won vindication in court. But by that time the university had been closed. The Onacewicz-Sarmatian tribes case was unsettling since the professor's public denunciations of his foes gave the matter more visibility than Novosiltsev, or Pelikan, wanted. [36] But it told little, if

35. Quoted in O'Connor, "Cultures," 305. See also Barkhattsev, "Iz istorii," RA, 1224–1225.
36. O'Connor, "Cultures," 308–311, well summarizes the extensive Polish literature devoted to this case.

anything, of the "moral health" of the university, i.e., its ability to produce competent service men and loyal citizens.

The Polish Kingdom revolt broke in Warsaw in November 1830. It was not surprising that in the end several hundred of Vilna's students took part, for, once the shooting began, as in 1812, it was difficult for Poles not to take the side of a Polish government against the Russians. Nonetheless, a month after the "insurrection" in Warsaw, Novosiltsev reported that Vilna University "maintains perfect institutional order and complete calm." He described the recent visit of General Dibich, commander of Russian forces in Poland, and the address he made to the students, who "listened quietly and in good order." So confident was Novosiltsev that things went well in Vilna that he left shortly thereafter on vacation, taking the waters in Karlsbad. The spread of the revolt to the "Lithuanian" provinces in March 1831 spelled the doom of the university. But Novosiltsev had not been mistaken in reporting that all went well in his university. On the contrary, his report was quite correct, if irrelevant in the end, for Vilna University fell victim to forces that it could hardly influence, let alone control.[37]

Despite its academic excellence, and its record in providing numbers of well-trained, loyal service men, the Vilna faculty could not be used as a pool from which to staff other universities. The tsar, who ordered the closing of the university in May 1832, after all, believed sincerely that he was blocking the influence of men who were Russia's natural enemies. Thus, Vilna's replacement in the system, the new university in Kiev, could not make appointments from among the Vilna faculty. In January 1834, faced with the need to recruit a faculty in time for the opening of his university in the following July, Curator Von Bradke recommended the use of the Krzemieniec staff. He also made other recommendations, including the appointment as professor of history V. F. Tsykh of Kharkov University. The curator admitted that Tsykh did not have a doctorate,

---

37. For Novosiltsev's report, 26 December 1830, see Zhukovich, "Pervyi russkii popechitel'," *Khristianskoe chtenie*, 398; Beauvois, *L'Universite de Vilna*, I, 56. For the students' (who numbered nearly 1,500 in 1830) participation in the revolt, see Pogodin, "Vilenskii okrug," *Sbornik materialov*, IV, xl. The university was closed in May 1832, but much of it continued to operate: the medical faculty as the Vilna Medical-Surgical Academy, the "Main" seminary as a Roman Catholic seminary (the Uniates transferred to their own institution at Polotsk), much of the arts and sciences taken over by a new "Noble Institute." Novosiltsev from 1834 to his death in 1838 served as president of the State Council.

which the statute required for the rank of professor. Indeed, Tsykh had only the year before completed his *magister* at Kharkov. However, Von Bradke pointed out, the new university would badly need "a Russian especially in a rank which gives him the right to participate in the council meetings," which adjuncts could not do. Not incidentally, Tsykh would not come to Kiev unless he were given a professorship, for Kharkov had already offered him that rank, degree or not. Uvarov, if reluctantly, agreed to the appointment of Tsykh.[38]

The faculty whom Tsykh joined at Kiev for the academic year 1834–1835 numbered eighteen. Twelve were appointed from the staff of the now closed Krzemieniec lycée. Seven held degrees from Vilna University. The Catholic theologian, Chodkiewicz, was a graduate of the Jesuit college at Polotsk. Two members, Skovortsev in Orthodox theology and Novitskii in philosophy, were appointed from the Kiev Ecclesiastical Academy. The professor of technology was a Prussian-born and educated Lutheran. In 1835 the law faculty made three important additions, Danilovich, expelled from Vilna in 1824 in the Novosiltsev "purge" and since assigned to Kharkov University, and two young men with new doctorates from St. Petersburg who had completed the Second Section law course and had spent two years at Berlin. Both Nevolin and Ornatskii had long, productive careers ahead of them.[39]

The most important single addition was M. A. Maksimovich, elected rector almost upon arrival. Maksimovich, a native of the Ukraine, had made a career at Moscow University. First trained in biology, he developed an ever-deepening interest in language and literature. In 1833 he made an extended trip through the Caucasus, partly for reasons of health, gathering specimens for the Moscow University botany collection. His real interests were made clear in

38. TsGIAL, f. 733, op. 69 d. 166, list 7 (Von Bradke to Uvarov, 19 January 1834). On the margin of this letter, in which Von Bradke gives his reasons for appointing Tsykh, there is a note that "The minister explained orally to the curator why he cannot agree to this appointment." Nonetheless, on 10 February, Tsykh was appointed full professor.

39. V. S. Ikonnikov, ed., *Biograficheskii slovar' professorov i prepodavatelei imperatorskago universiteta Sv. Vladimira 1834–1884* (Kiev, 1884) is the most convenient source on the early faculty at Kiev. See also Shul'gin, *Universitet Sv. Vladimira,* 51–54; M. F. Vladimirskii-Budanov, *Istoriia Imperatorskago Universiteta Sv. Vladimira* (Kiev, 1884), 60–70, 90–95. Vladimirskii-Budanov concluded (p. 62) that "St. Vladimir University was without doubt simply the Krzemieniec lycée transferred to Kiev," a judgment that much exaggerated the influence of the Polish professors.

1830 in an address to the faculty at Moscow, soon published in one of the burgeoning new journals, *Russkii zritel'*. He praised the "role of Moscow University in the enlightenment of Russia." He traced the work of Lomonosov and Shuvalov, the university leaders in the eighteenth century who set the tone for its whole history, carrying out the work begun by Peter the Great. The history of the university ever since was the training of "teachers who taught in Russian" and gradually providing "Russian educated men" to all parts of the empire. Thus, Moscow was successfully producing what the tsar wanted: "patriotic youth who have received a Russian education."[40]

In 1832 Maksimovich made another major address to the faculty assembly at Moscow, soon published in *Teleskop*. Maksimovich's article, "On Russian Enlightenment," began with praise for Peter the Great, specifically for his creative borrowing from the West, but pointed out that the "Russian spirit, full of health and youth" had "completed the learning needed" from the West and so was ready to assume "independence." He pointed out that "not everything done in Europe is useful also for Russia." The task of the university was clear, for "our tsar . . . wants education which is patriotic," producing students who are "true Russians." Moreover, in the Petrine tradition both "*enlightenment* and *service* are the constant requirements of the hereditary nobility." Education aimed at "the elevation of our nationality requires also our *love for the fatherland*." Naturally, "true enlightenment . . . requires also religious-moral formation of the heart and will." The schools also had to take care to offer a "many-sided, complete education, avoiding the dangers of the half-done." Finally, Maksimovich found Moscow University especially important for all this, since "Moscow is the heart of Russia."[41]

In March 1834 Maksimovich wrote to both Uvarov and Von Bradke, seeking an appointment in the new university in Kiev. Both were very happy to accept him as professor of Russian literature. Von Bradke wanted to appoint him also dean of his faculty, but instead Maksimovich became the first rector of the new university. Maksimovich's highest degree was a *magister* from Moscow. But the views he expressed in 1830 and 1832 recommended him for his

40. M. A. Maksimovich, "Ob uchastii Moskovskago universiteta v prosveshchenii Rossii," *Russkii zritel'*, No. XXI–XXII (1830), 3–19. Quotation 18.
41. M. A. Maksimovich, "O russkom prosveshchenii," *Teleskop*, 1832 (No. 2), 169–190. Quotations 173, 176, 178, 179, 182, 184, 187.

new position. They explained well the views that in the version Uvarov gave them in 1833 later became known as "Official Nationality." Maksimovich, thus, had well stated the goals of the new university at Kiev, even before its foundation was planned.[42]

Maksimovich took his responsibilities very seriously. The first rector of the new university not only taught a full schedule, and kept up his writing, but called meetings of the faculty council three times a week. He met also with the directorate three times weekly and almost weekly invited all members of the faculty to gatherings in his home. Maksimovich's schedule was nearly matched by Von Bradke, who spent much of his time visiting classes, talking with students and faculty, encouraging all he could. He also kept up a stream of correspondence to the ministry, requesting budget increases, particularly for the support of state students. Maksimovich and Von Bradke were supported by the orthodox bishop for Kiev, Innokentii, who became a warm personal friend of both as well as a valuable ally in the development of the new institution.[43]

42. TsGIAL, f. 733, op. 69, d. 166, list 34 (Maksimovich to Uvarov, 14 March 1834), 41 (Von Bradke to Uvarov, 27 March 1834). In September Von Bradke reported to Uvarov the election of Maksimovich as rector (ibid., 131–135) but mentioned no other candidate or any vote. It seems likely, therefore, that Maksimovich was simply presented as rector, his colleagues' silence being taken as consent. Uvarov vetoed many of Von Bradke's suggestions for faculty members, usually on the grounds that they lacked adequate academic training, arguing that those who "lack the doctorate" should not be appointed professors. For Von Bradke's recommendation to use former Krzemieniec faculty members, and his request to have a four-year term for rector, see ibid., 1–2 (Von Bradke to Uvarov, 17 January 1834). The term "Official Nationality" was not used by either Uvarov or Maksimovich. That name was given to their views late in the century by liberal historians. Whittaker, Uvarov, 95–110, is the most judicious discussion of "Official Nationality" extant in any language.

43. Both Maksimovich and Von Bradke are treated at length in Shul'gin, Istoriia, and Vladimirskii-Budanov, Istoriia. Useful summaries on each are in Entskilopedicheskii slovar', IV (SPB, 1891), 535–536; ibid., XVIII (1896), 442–443. Maksimovich became best known perhaps as the ethnographer whose work played a role in the develoment of the modern Ukrainian national consciousness. The best brief introduction to his career remains Ikonnikov, Biograficheskii slovar', 379–397. For recent accounts of his role as faculty member at St. Vladimir see D. F. Ostrianin, Svitogliad M. O. Makisimovicha (Kiev, 1960), 10–13; P. G. Markov, M. O. Maksimovich: vidatnii istorik XIX st. (Kiev, 1973), 27–35. An extremely interesting essay on Maksimovich and Uvarov in the development of the university is in Pelech, "Ukrainian Ideologues," 92–118. Unfortunately, for this analysis of Uvarov's goals at Kiev, Pelech relies much on Uvarov's Desiatiletie Ministerstva narodnago prosveshcheniia 1833–1843 (SPB, 1864), a report Uvarov submitted to Nicholas in 1843 to celebrate the successes of his ten years as minister and to assure the tsar that all went well on the academic front. Pelech is not alone in using the Desiatiletie as a

Uvarov made an extended visit to Kiev in 1837, and pronounced himself well satisfied with all he saw in the university. He had reason for satisfaction. Addressing the students, Uvarov said that he was especially interested in the progress of the university, which he called his "creation," but warned that he would not hesitate to discipline it should it fail in its task, which he said was to "spread Russian education and Russian national consciousness (*narodnost'*) in the Polonized region of western Russia." He saw no sign that the university was not making progress, and was especially pleased with a brilliant address Maksimovich made to the assembled students and faculty, which lucidly applied the doctrine of "Official Nationality" to Kiev's history and the university's goals.[44] None of this meant that the professors recruited from Krzemieniec were about to be dismissed. Instead, they were congratulated on their able contribution to the joint effort. Von Bradke, on more than one occasion, said that he "knew neither Russians, nor Poles, nor Germans, but only good men or bad."[45] The university opened in 1834 with 62 students. Enrollment doubled in 1835, and more than doubled again, to 263 in 1836. The faculty grew to 30 (including twenty from Krzemieniec) in 1835. The praise of Uvarov, Maksimovich, Von Bradke, and others was not misdirected, therefore. In less than

---

source for discussion of the events of the 1830s (see e.g., Allister, "Reform," 210–220). It should be noted, however, that much of the *Desiatiletie* was *post hoc* rationalization rather than reliable guide to the work. Pelech well uses archival sources to show that, regardless of the motives, the lower schools of Kiev's district were no more, perhaps less, effective in spreading education to non-Polish speaking villagers than were those schools in the days of Czacki and Kołłątaj. Pelech, "Ukrainian Ideologues," 95–105. For discussion of the university's early years, see Vladimirskii-Budanov, *Istoriia*, 96–140; *Kiev i universitet sv. Vladimira pri imperatore Nikolae I 1825–1855* (Kiev, 1896), 57–68; E. V. Spektorskii, *Stoletie Kievskago universiteta Sv. Vladimira* (Belgrade, 1935), 9–57. The account of the foundation and early development of the university in Zhmuds'kii, *Istoriia*, 16–21 follows that given in Rozhdestvenskii, *Istoricheskii obzor*, 296–308.

44. Accounts of Uvarov's visit in Ikonnikov, *Biograficheskii slovar'*, 383–386, and S. Ponomarev, "Mikhail Aleksandrovich Maksimovich," *ZhMNP*, 1871 (October), 216–217, stress the harmony of views between Uvarov and Maksimovich. Maksimovich's address, which obviously pleased Uvarov, is in "Ob uchastie i znachenii Kieva v obshchei zhizni Rossii: rech . . . 2 Oktiabriia 1837 goda," *ZhMNP*, 1837 (October), otdel' ii, 1–29. Maksimovich identified Poles, Jesuits, and Uniates as enemies of the historic development of Kiev and Russia (pp. 18–25), but in his conclusion, though he urged Kiev's students (more than half of whom were Polish Catholics) to serve loyally the tsar and fatherland, he omitted any mention of Orthodoxy or religion.

45. Shul'gin, *Istoriia*, 66.

two years, the new university at Kiev had made more measurable progress than the "new" Russian universities at St. Petersburg, Kharkov, and Kazan had made in their first ten, or twenty, years.

Part of this progress resulted, to be sure, from the admixture of the Polish element and was thus in some measure a repetition of the experience of Vilna, and not really comparable, therefore, with backward Kharkov or Kazan. But the differences from the Vilna experience were perhaps more important than the similarities. Unlike Vilna in 1804, or at any other time, St. Vladimir was led by a vigorous, interested, and informed minister, Uvarov, who had the whole-hearted cooperation of the curator and rector. The language of instruction was Russian, and there could be no room for doubt that the goal of the university was to integrate into the Russian service the young Poles who came to the university at Kiev for their higher educations. Moreover, while Poles of necessity would for some years remain a majority, assuming the administration remained committed to appointment of the best faculty it could find and the admission of the most qualified students, the "Russian" element promised to grow steadily. While the university offered instruction in Polish, and made mandatory study of Catholic doctrine for the Polish students, the Poles who came to Kiev knew well that they were expected to cooperate in the development of the Russian empire, though they were not asked to pretend that they were becoming "Russians."[46]

For reasons that had nothing to do with the university, but much to do with Nicholas' fear of subversion, the tsar ordered the closing of St. Vladimir in 1838. Four students were tried for treason by a military court, found guilty of subversive activity (one had kept a book by the poet Mickiewicz in his room and the other knew of it), and sentenced to duty in the Russian army garrison at Orenburg. Von Bradke bitterly protested that the evidence showed that the university was in no way guilty of evil behavior, as did Innokentii and Maksimovich, who pointed out that the "Polish professors have been very careful and prudent in their teaching." Uvarov tried to

46. Jan Tabiś, *Polacy na uniwersytecie kijowskim* (Cracow, 1974), 30–47, provides details on the students, showing that until at least the early 1860s, Polish nobles from "Right bank" Ukraine made up a clear majority of Kiev's students. The Polish students were divided almost equally between law and science, with fewer than ten percent in the literature-history section, a nearly complete reversal of the pattern at Krzemieniec under Czacki.

minimize the blow, arguing that since "the *majority* of students did not take part in the activities of a *small number*," it was reasonable "to soften as much as possible the severity of the measures" taken against the university. He managed to persuade Nicholas to continue the faculty on full salary, while they occupied themselves with the production of texts and other instructional materials, and also to allow the students to transfer to any other university in the empire or to return to Kiev without penalty, and finally to limit the closing of the university to but a few weeks.[47] This episode was an important turning point for Uvarov. The meaning and importance of "nationality" in the 1840s became increasingly significant in Uvarov's management of the schools in the western provinces. But in 1835 its significance was yet to be realized, for the university that Uvarov helped to found at Kiev in 1834 was a trial of the 1835 statute, the solution proposed to the problems encountered by the Russian universities in their first decades. It was not remarkable that the tsar overreacted to irresponsible police reports, though Von Bradke denounced the police chief in Kiev as "stupid" and "drunk." It was remarkable that the university in Kiev, in both faculty and students, developed as quickly and well as it did.

To be sure, neither Vilna nor St. Vladimir could be taken as measures of the success of the university system, precisely because they involved so clearly the participation of Poles, both as faculty and students. While the excellence of the contribution made by Poles cannot be doubted, nonetheless participation by Poles complicated and distorted the issues to be met in building a high-quality university capable of providing able, loyal state servicemen, for the Poles themselves were a "problem." The "Polish question" in various guises had troubled many Russian governments for generations and would continue to pose dilemmas long after the demise of the Uvarov ministry. As the experience of Vilna in 1824 and 1830–1831 and of St. Vladimir in 1838 showed, there was little, if indeed anything, a university could do to help or hinder the problems. Uvarov in the decade of the 1840s expended much energy in an

47. Among the many accounts of this episode, the most detailed is Vladimirskii-Budanov, *Istoriia*, 161–210. Von Bradke's candid account (he wrote it for his children, not for publication) is in "Avtobiograficheskiia zapiski," *RA*, 1875 (No. 3), 278–288. Quotation 286. See also M. A. Maksimovich, *Mysli ob universitete Sv. Vladimira v kontse 1838 goda* (Kiev, 1865), 2–7. Quotation 3. Uvarov's report to Nicholas is in TsGIAL, f. 733, op. 69, d. 444, *listy* 1–6 (Uvarov to Nicholas, 6 January 1839). Quotation 1 (underscoring in original).

effort to smooth over, if not solve, these problems. His achievements were not inconsiderable, as indeed were those of the university at Vilna and then at Kiev. But the persistence of the "Polish problem" made difficult, and in some senses irrelevant, solution of the problems that were within the sphere of the university's influence.[48]

Kharkov, though "Ukrainian," did not face ethnic-national problems comparable to those of Vilna-Kiev, and it thus provided a clearer index of the degree of success achieved in meeting the goals of the educational reformers. Kharkov's record left much to be desired. Uvarov in March 1834 reported to Nicholas that "of all our universities, Kharkov has made less progress than any other towards achieving its goals and at present lags far behind the others in implementing the new directions prepared for their renewal and which are already taking effect to one degree or another in our institutions of higher learning."[49] Uvarov was correct in his evaluation. Nonetheless, the problem at Kharkov was much simpler than those at Vilna or Kiev. The faculty at Kharkov remained weak, in both numbers and quality. Redesigning the faculty workload, the point of much of the 1835 statute, and "renewing" the faculty by additions and replacements, went far to correct the problem.

Successive curators seemed to agree on the need for this solution, though getting it implemented in practice was another matter. In 1825 Shishkov replaced the "Bible Society" curator, the younger Karneev, with A. A. Perovskii, a member of the Razumovskii family who had completed a doctorate in literature at Moscow and was fluent in both French and German. Perovskii, who had compiled an excellent record in the army during the Napoleonic wars, was an active and valued member of the literary circles of the two capitals. He volunteered to "serve society" by taking on the curatorship at Kharkov, where he found himself much less at home. Shishkov cautioned him to see that the professors fostered "good morals" among the students and that the Gospels were read "by the Slavonic texts."[50]

---

48. For a more extended discussion of these issues, see J. T. Flynn, "Uvarov and the 'Western Provinces': A Study of Russia's Polish Problem," *SEER*, 64 (1986), 212–236.

49. Uvarov to Nicholas, 14 March 1834, quoted in Bagalei, *Opyt istorii*, II, 244–245.

50. On Perevoskii, see Bagalei, *Opyt istorii*, II, 168–176.

At Kharkov, Perovskii found that student morals were not his problem. Instead, he spent much of his curatorship berating faculty members for failure to do their jobs and reporting to the ministry on the continuous decline in the faculty. In 1827, for example, he reported that thirteen of the twenty-eight chairs called for by the statute remained vacant. They were covered "temporarily" by adjuncts and/or "teachers," except for the chair of theology, which was not filled at all. Perovskii recommended, among other things, that the university censorship committee be abolished, since it had so little work to do in view of the minimal publication activity going on in the district. The few professors who published wanted to publish in Moscow anyway. More serious, the curator thought the council was simply not doing its job. Covering chairs by "temporarily" appointing adjuncts, he thought, showed that the faculty was either unable or unwilling to choose faculty members. Moreover, appalled at the "politics" of choosing adjuncts and other officers, such as "inspectors," Perovskii made a speech to the council in which he tried to persuade the professors that they "should help each other," not continually undercut each other. Unable to convince many, or to achieve results that he could measure, Perovskii resigned in 1830.[51] He was replaced by exactly the wrong sort of "civil servant."

Though he had the confidence of the tsar, V. I. Filat'ev had no experience in education. His own education was entirely of the old gentry "home" variety. After a long military career, he served for some years as marshal of the nobility in his home province, Iaroslav. Upon arrival in Kharkov, the new curator complained that his faculty was badly understaffed. There were but two professors teaching in the moral-political science staff, for example. Professor Danilovich, though "assigned" to Kharkov, really spent his time in St. Petersburg, leaving his courses to be taught by adjunct Spasskii, whose poor health unfortunately kept him out of the classroom too.[52] Filat'ev's contribution to strengthening the faculty was to appoint, over the protests of the council, as professor of philosophy Th. Th. Chanev, a former gymnasium teacher from Iaroslav. Chanev had a long career in education behind him, as well as a long-

51. For some of the high points of Perovskii's dealings with his faculty, see Bagalei, *Opyt istorii*, II, 30–35, 359–373.
52. Bagalei, *Opyt istorii*, II, 200.

standing friendship with Filat'ev, for he had taught languages, history, mathematics, literature, philosophy, physics, and several other subjects in several schools for nearly thirty years. But he had no higher education, let alone degrees. The Kharkov faculty's complaints at the appointment of Chanev might have seemed a bit disingenuous, since the new curator was doing no more than the faculty had been doing for years, i.e., using the university budget to reward his friends, and perhaps punish enemies, on grounds more personal than academic-professional.[53]

The problem of the Kharkov faculty came to a climax of sorts in the case of a member of the medical faculty, A. S. Venediktov. Gentry-born in Kharkov province, Venediktov took a *kandidat* at Kharkov and went on to the St. Petersburg Medical-Surgical Academy, returning to Kharkov as an adjunct in medicine in 1821. In 1833 and 1834 Venediktov sent a series of reports to the Third Section, motivated, he said, by "love for the fatherland" and "devotion to the tsar." He reported that many students, including relatives of the rector, were admitted to the university without proper credentials or knowledge. He suggested that many of those students were really recruits for some underhanded plot against the security of the autocracy. The rector made unexplained trips to Moscow. One of those trips, Venediktov pointed out, came at the same time that a relative of one of the Decembrists made a trip to Moscow. This same relative, "as I heard in Kharkov, burned some sort of a green book at the time of the police investigation" of the December revolt. Moreover, the rector and several others were partial to Poles, who were admitted as students despite the obvious dangers. A Third Section investigator spent some weeks in Kharkov, checking into Venediktov's charges. He apologized for his inability to get an informer "within his family," but nonetheless was confident that he had learned enough about Venediktov. In the continual "politics" of the Kharkov faculty, Venediktov had been a frequent loser. For many years he had been making increasingly sharp denunciations of his colleague-foes, charging them with malfeasance, if not with probably treasonous relationships with Poles, and sometimes with Decembrists. The investigator, however, could find no reason to believe him, for there was no evidence for anything except that Venediktov

53. See *ibid.*, 490–491, for a discussion of Chanev's appointment.

"does not belong to the rector's party" and thus had shared little in the rewards the Kharkov faculty council had to distribute.[54]

Uvarov concluded, in his report to Nicholas on the matter, that the weakness of the Kharkov faculty showed the need for changes. Unfortunately, Uvarov noted, Venediktov had several children, owned a home in Kharkov, and had an excellent medical practice in the city. Thus, dismissal from Kharkov for him would be a heavy penalty indeed. Nicholas was keenly interested in Moscow University, and in Poles, but was not similarly taken up with Kharkov. "Decide it yourself," he wrote on Uvarov's margin.[55]

Uvarov decided to keep Venediktov in Kharkov, out of purely personal humanitarian concern, and to replace Filat'ev with Count Iu. A. Golovkin, a member of the State Council with many years in financial administration behind him. Golovkin remained curator to his death in 1846, ably carrying out the policies Uvarov wanted. Golovkin made many recommendations for improvement, including the "complete separation" of the academic from the economic administration, and the transfer of as much as possible from the Vilna University library to build up Kharkov's collections. Golovkin made one recommendation that must have startled Uvarov, however. He pointed out that all students began study of Latin in the first year of the gymnasium course. He suggested that it would be better to begin Latin in the *uezd* school, and to reform a number of *uezd* schools into "Gentry *Uezd* Schools" in which would study "for the most part the children of gentry and of active duty service men." Thus, such students would not only be better equipped to use the gymnasium to prepare for admission to the university but Latin could be used to screen out non-gentry from the path to the university by making it an entrance requirement for the gymnasium. Uvarov rejected Golovkin's recommendation, noting that the Committee on the organization of schools had considered such recommendations and found them "out of harmony with the goals of the

54. Venediktov's most detailed report to Benckendorf is printed in *ibid.*, 237–242 (Quotation 238); Major Paniutin's report on the professor in *ibid.*, 242–244.

55. Uvarov's report in *ibid.*, 244–247. Quotation 247. Uvarov noted (p. 245) that "the spirit of parties and continual struggles among the professors and officials have always existed in [Kharkov] University." He might have added that the demise of the "foreigners" party after 1815 had not resulted in any diminution of the struggles, nor had the end of the dominance of the Bible Society, for the struggles seldom concerned issues of principle, but rather the much more traditional concerns of jobs and stipends for friends and relations.

schools." He agreed that there were gentry *uezd* schools in the Belorussian district (the former eastern provinces of the Vilna district), but that was due to "local conditions." [56]

Uvarov accepted Golovkin's recommendation that something be
done to augment and improve the faculty. The new curator reported
that the university lacked both numbers and quality in its staff. For
example, the moral-political science faculty had but one full professor, not the seven called for by the statute. All but the chair of
religion were covered by adjuncts. Since the faculty seemed unwilling or unable to appoint candidates who held a doctorate, the statutory requirement for the rank of professor, the ministry would have
to assume responsibility for it. In July 1835 Uvarov sent a letter to
the curators of all the universities, excepting Dorpat and St. Vladimir. His letter informed each that the Committee on academic institutions had completed its "many years of work" on a new statute
for the universities. He requested that each curator propose a list
"of the professors in your university who in ability, knowledge, and
effort are worthy to be kept in the new university staff, and . . .
those who in your judgement should be released." He asked also for
a list of the "chairs for which new professors will need to be appointed." Before Golovkin had time to compose a reply, Uvarov
began Kharkov's "renewal," appointing a new professor of history,
A. O. Valitskii. Valitskii was a graduate of Vilna University. When
Kharkov could not provide willing candidates for the first "Professors Institute" and the tsar ordered that substitutes be chosen
from Vilna, Valitskii was one of those chosen. He spent five years in
study at Dorpat, completing his doctorate with a dissertation in
ancient history, and then spent two years in study in Berlin. Appointed to the faculty in August 1835, he began a fruitful career in
Kharkov, where he remained a prolific teacher and publishing
scholar and, from 1837, director of the Pedagogical Institute until
his death in 1856. [57]

Valitskii was the first of many new appointments. By the early

56. TsGIAL, f. 733, op. 49, d. 944, *listy* 1–65 (Golovkin to Uvarov, 11 November 1834). Quotations 3, 5. *ibid.*, list 69 (Uvarov to Golovkin, 23 March 1835).

57. TsGIAL, f. 733, op. 22, d. 142, list 1 (Uvarov to curators, 21 July 1835). The
biographical sketch on Valitskii in Khalanskii and Bagalei, *Istoriko-filogicheskii
fakul'tet*, 175–183, includes a bibliography of his many works, which he published
in Polish, German, and French as well as Russian.

1840s the Kharkov faculty had been quite successfully "renewed," benefitting in part from the ministry's need to place Polish professors in institutions other than Vilna or St. Vladimir. The new faculty appointments were particularly effective because the university had also solved much of its problem in recruiting students. In 1827 enrollment topped three hundred, never again to fall below that number. The character of the student body changed little, either in class origins or academic preparation, from what it had been in the previous decade, for gentry and officers' sons, graduated from the district gymnasia or *pansions,* usually made up something more than sixty percent of the students. By 1840 the number enrolled topped four hundred and continued to increase, if modestly, thereafter. The number of students in the lower schools of the district steadily grew over the decade 1824–1834, from something over 8,000 in 1824 to nearly 14,000 in 1834.[58] In short, the days when Potocki had to worry seriously whether there would be a student body at all were far, and permanently, behind.

The development of Kazan University in the decade after 1824 was similar to that of Kharkov. Kazan too had difficulty building up a faculty that was competent as well as loyal, but under able leadership kept working at the problem until, by the early 1840s at least, that problem had been overcome. Meanwhile, as at Kharkov, student enrollment increased steadily if slowly, as did the number of *kandidats* and student diplomas awarded, while the library, laboratories, and other facilities improved too. Kharkov opened a new, handsome university church in 1831, began a program of "public lectures" quite successfully in 1832, and used a gift of 3,000 library volumes (from Vilna University's collection) to begin a second undergraduate library. While these achievements were not matched at Kazan, nonetheless, Kazan University benefitted from steady leadership. In 1827 Lobachevskii replaced Fuchs as rector, and M. N. Musin-Pushkin was appointed curator. The two remained in office, and worked hand-in-glove to 1845. Lobachevskii not only served well as rector, but in some years also taught all the courses of two chairs, while keeping up the scholarship that won him world

58. The accuracy, and detail, of reports on the lower schools of the district, and of the university's enrollment, improved markedly after 1834. It is possible, therefore, that the growth in enrollments is overstated, reflecting more complete reporting as well as true increase in student numbers. See Bagalei, *Opyt istorii,* II, 1049–1056.

renown. He also had the ability, including concern for detail as well as familiarity with local circumstances, to provide excellent administration.

Lobachevskii was fortunate to have Lieven and Uvarov to work with. In December 1830, for example, Lobachevskii included in the annual report for the academic year 1829–1830 the observation that "the students throughout the year behaved very well. The few incidents that occurred were due to the youth and inexperience of the students, and deserved no important punishment."[59] This was the same argument Uvarov made, most unsuccessfully, to Golitsyn in 1821. Its easy acceptance in the ministry gave an indication of the difference the change in ministers made. Kazan faced serious trouble in 1830, when an outbreak of cholera forced the closing of the university. Lobachevskii was naturally happy to report that the closing had worked, for not one member of the university, student, staff, or faculty was infected with the disease. Lobachevskii seemed well enough pleased with the student body, which reached 113 before the forced closing in the spring of 1830, recovered to nearly 190 by 1836, and went over 350 by 1840. The military governor of the district in 1832 recommended, through the Committee of Ministers, that the self-supporting students at Kazan, who lived in "private apartments" around the city "without close supervision," should be housed in a university building under the direct control of an inspector of students. Lobachevskii politely but firmly rejected this advice, arguing that neither the university nor the students could stand the added expense, which was unnecessary anyway, since the "moral welfare of the self-supporting students has always been considered an important part of the responsibilities of the administration of the university. The behavior of the students to this time has been sufficiently good to make unnecessary new arrangements."[60]

Lobachevskii was not so well pleased with the faculty. In 1833, indeed, he sent a formal complaint to the ministry that the faculty

59. TsGIAL, f. 733, op. 40, d. 406, *list* 1 (Lobachevskii to ministry, 28 December 1830).

60. TsGIAL, f. 733, op. 41, d. 57, *listy* 1–11, contains excerpts of the journal of the Committee of Ministers, as well as Lieven's responses to the committee, relaying the judgment of Lobachevskii and Mushin-Pushkin, 27 September 1832 to 9 November 1832. Quotation 8–9. Enrollment in the lower schools of the district grew also, to something over 8,500 in 1836. Not surprisingly, the enrollment of gentry and "officers'" children grew at a faster rater than that of others. Shurtakova, *Rukovodstvo Kazanskogo Universiteta*, 32.

was not living up to its responsibilities, specifically by not taking part in the deliberations of the council. Some members of the faculty said that they "did not have the time to read all the materials required," let alone come to decisions about them. Lobachevskii wanted a ruling from the ministry that made it clear that faculty members had no choice but were "required" to participate.[61] When, in July 1835, Uvarov sent his letter, requesting a list from Kazan of those faculty members who should be dropped in order to "renew" the university, Lobachevskii replied almost at once. His list included most of the men appointed under Magnitskii in the early 1820s. In August 1835 Uvarov appointed to the Kazan faculty two of the graduates of the Dorpat Professors' Institute program, Kotel'nikov in philology and Skandovskii in medicine. But finding replacements for all the men to be dropped, and candidates for the expansion called for, was difficult. It was 1837 before enough progress had been made for Lobachevskii and Mushin-Pushkin to consider the new statute in effect.[62]

Lobachevskii and Uvarov, then, seemed to agree not only on the nature of Kazan's problems but on their solutions as well. It was not surprising, therefore, that both came to think the university was on the right track. Lobachevskii was especially interested in making Kazan a center of "eastern studies." He suggested, in 1833, that if necessary Kazan might drop Greek language studies, which were well done elsewhere in the empire, substituting Tartar, Arabic, Persian, or Turkic, thus capitalizing on the university's location in "Kazan, where European Russia is united with the Asiatic." Although Uvarov was loath to give up Greek, the two cooperated for years in

61. TsGIAL, f. 733, op. 41, d. 84, list 1–2 (Mushin-Pushkin to Uvarov, 21 January 1833).
62. TsGIAL, f. 733, op. 41, d. 183, *listy* 1–178. Correspondence 21 July 1835 to 13 September 1837. Lobachevskii's requests included shifting some men from one faculty to another within the university, as well as the replacement of others. The *formuliarnie spiski* (service records) of those retired for reasons of health are in *ibid.*, 77–93. Some of the men "released" had served the university well, all things considered. One indeed, V. Ia. Bulygin, was awarded a special purse of 800 rubles in April 1835 in recognition of his excellent service. Upon his retirement in 1837, he was granted the Order of St. Vladimir, as well as 2,000 a year pension. Bulygin, a gentry-born native of Kazan, had served as history professor since 1822, and served on every committee, inspection team, and administrative assignment possible since that time. His highest academic degree was a *magister* from Kazan (1811). See N. P. Zagoskin, *Materialy dlia istorii kafedr i uchrezhdenii imperatorskago kazanskago universiteta 1804–1826 gg.* (Kazan, 1899), 9; Zagoskin, *Biograficheskii slovar'*, I, 47–49.

developing a first-rate program in eastern studies, especially languages, at Kazan.[63]

Until December 1835, when he suggested some changes to bring
Dorpat "closer" to the model of the Russian universities, principally
by stress on improved instruction in Russian, Uvarov paid little attention to Dorpat. He was not alone in that. The curator from 1828
to 1835 was Karl M. Pahlen, who from 1830 was also military
governor of Riga and governor-general of the three "Ostsee" provinces. He rarely visited the university and seemed to know little
about it. He visited Dorpat in June 1830 in the company of the tsar,
who, though he spoke Russian with Pahlen, seemed to find it not
out of the ordinary to speak German with staff members. The Professors' Institute contributed to Dorpat's reputation for academic
excellence as much as it helped develop faculty members for other
schools. The response of the student body to the Polish revolt of
1830—more than two hundred volunteered for military duty to
fight the Poles—also doubtless added to Dorpat's positive image,
certainly with the tsar. Dorpat continued to elect its rector annually,
to fill its faculty ranks in the main with natives of the provinces who
had higher degrees from German universities, and to experience
slow but steady growth in its student body (fluctuating a few over
400 in the early 1830s, then growing steadily to over 600 by the late
1840s) without changing its class or social character, or making
much impact on the lower schools of the district.[64] There could be
little doubt that Dorpat had become indeed the self-governing au-

63. TsGIAL, f. 733, op. 41, d. 86, *listy* 1–14. Correspondence 14 April 1833 to
14 September 1835. Quotation 2.

64. Petukhov, *Derptskii universitet*, 422–426, prints Uvarov's plans for "reform"
at Dorpat, December 1835 and December 1836. On students, see *ibid.*, 507–511;
on faculty, 394–411; on Nicholas' visit, 598; on student volunteers against the
Poles, 602. In May 1841 Uvarov recommended that the Dorpat faculty council consider making some appointments from among those whose doctorates came from
Russian universities (*ibid.*, 400), but without apparent success. Uvarov was quick to
report success to the tsar, however. In August 1839, for example, he informed Nicholas that the inhabitants of the Baltic provinces were becoming "more and more
convinced that steps taken to spread the knowledge of the Russian language every-
where are for them a great boon, and they for their part eagerly prepare to unite
themselves by all means with the Government." TsGIAL, f. 735, op. 10, d. 293b, list
750 (Uvarov to Nicholas, 6 August 1839). In 1843, in his *Desiatiletie*, Uvarov reported at length (and included copies of earlier reports in an appendix) that the
"spread" of the Russian language was eagerly welcomed not only in the Baltic provinces but in Vilna, Kiev, and throughout the western provinces of the empire, where
the Poles, he said, (*ibid.*, 46), were particularly enthusiastic about learning the tsar's
language.

tonomous university Parrot had planned three decades before, though the difference that development made in the life of the provinces had turned out to be more limited than Parrot or his foes would have dreamed possible. Nonetheless, the Dorpat faculty was understandably pleased with itself.

Though it seems unlikely that many Dorpat faculty members would have believed it, the development of Moscow and St. Petersburg universities at least matched that of Dorpat, not only in numbers but also in the quality of students and faculty. But the path was not smooth. The horror and devastation of the cholera epidemics of 1830 and 1831 were widely distributed, but the two capitals suffered especially, each with populations over a quarter million, a fact that made them vulnerable to the disease. The impact was heightened by the terror and panic, intensified by the quarantines enforced by the police and army. The universities were closed, though the personnel, especially the Moscow medical faculty, were engaged in the struggle against the epidemic, which hit Moscow especially hard in the fall of 1830. Thousands fled the city, thousands more were prevented from doing so by the quarantine. The university itself was quarantined, and no students allowed in or out for months. Many, perhaps most, of the students and faculty volunteered for service, many giving themselves freely, working in hospitals throughout the emergency. In the spring of 1831 the university decided against attempting to hold the end-of-year examinations. Instead, all students were required to repeat the year, which had already been hopelessly lost. Enrollment, which fluctuated between a reported 614 and 714 in the years 1825–1830, reached 734 in 1831, doubtless due to the number of students who were held over for an extra year to complete their work. Moscow's economy had been crippled by the cholera; all normal lines of trade and communication were disrupted. In the immediate post cholera-years, Moscow's population dropped, if temporarily. So too did the university enrollment, down to 435 by 1834–1835. Growth was resumed in 1835–1836, reaching 865 by 1840. Thus, desperate though the cholera crisis was, its impact on the university was relatively short-lived.[65]

65. Nasonkina, *Moskovskii universitet*, 26–38, provides a detailed study on all aspects of Moscow's student enrollments, 1824–1834. Nasonkina's work, based on study of the students' "personal fonds" rather than the university reports, makes obsolete all earlier studies of Moscow's students. Nasonkina (*ibid.*, 189–196) also provides an informative discussion of the life of the university. Nonetheless, Nason-

The crisis was no less terrifying in St. Petersburg. The horror of the disease was matched there by the furious struggle of much of the population to escape what it feared was the death-dealing, not saving, ministrations of the medical services, as well as the quarantine enforced—sometimes bloodily—by police and soldiers. Yet, St. Petersburg University, unlike the city, was hurt relatively little by the cholera epidemic because it was so small and weak that it presented but a tiny target. Enrollment, depressed to fewer than 50 in the Runich days, grew to more than 130 in the fall of 1830. Though the next two years, the plague years, saw no growth, thereafter the student body grew quickly, to more than 300 in the fall of 1835. Perhaps more important than the growth in numbers was a change in the social composition of the student body. There had always been numbers of "officers" about, but in the past they were usually special students of one sort or another, active duty civil or military personnel who pursued professional, or sometimes personal, advancement, but seldom as fulltime matriculated students. By the mid 1830s, the gentry made up a clear majority of St. Petersburg's students, with the sons of "officers" a distant second, while the numbers from the clergy actually declined.

Many, perhaps most, of the gentry were poor.[66] By the mid 1830s, however, the influx of students from families not only noble but often enough the most prestigious "aristocratic" families, became noticeable. It was important to the health of the development of both the services and the universities to persuade the gentry—or, better, the "aristocratic" elements of the nobility—to take university education as well as service seriously, and to see them linked. At St. Petersburg in the 1830s, this process gathered strength. At Moscow too gentry enrollment steadily gained, though gentry and "officers," i.e., personal nobles, men promoted to ennobling ranks in the services, even taken together never made up a majority. It was noteworthy too that at Moscow the gentry never made up a major-

kina attributes the drop in enrollment after 1831 to government policy. "The figures on enrollment show the very slow growth rate and limited possibilities for the development of higher education, the result of the government's desire not to increase the number of students in the university, in spite of the extreme need for teachers and especially for doctors." *Ibid.*, 30. No mention is made of the growth in enrollment after 1835. On the cholera crisis, see Roderick E. McGrew, *Russia and the Cholera 1823–1832* (Madison, 1965), especially 75–128 on Moscow and St. Petersburg.

66. Mavrodin, *Istoriia Leningradskogo universiteta*, 59.

ity of the students in any single faculty, including that of moral-political sciences (i.e., law), which attracted gentry more than any other.[67] But Moscow had long enjoyed strong community support. The enrollment of the sons of the aristocracy promised that St. Petersburg would soon gain similar standing in its community. For an institution that had been limited to a teachers' college for much of its existence, and of interest to the capital's society thereafter principally as the locus of a scandalous "purge" of professors, the change in the character of its student body was a healthy sign. Perhaps equally important, by the middle 1830s, nearly three-quarters of Moscow's students stayed long enough to qualify for the student diploma. At St. Petersburg, about half of the students admitted finished the course and were awarded the diploma. There was no comparable growth in the number, or percentage, of graduate degrees, *magister* or doctorate. But the growth in the production of diploma students augured well for institutions whose main task was the preparation of graduates to staff the civil services with educated, perhaps even cultivated, men.[68]

The leadership given the universities in the two capitals by their curators, taken together with the work of other curators, to be sure, showed the acceleration of a development well launched even before Uvarov became minister: the decline in the importance of the curator. Uvarov reorganized the ministry and, probably more important, gave the minister's job the sort of intense interest and full-time commitment impossible to imagine from a Zavadovskii or Razumovskii, and outdid even Golitsyn and Lieven. After 1833, and even more after 1835, there was much less committee work in the ministry than had been the usual practice since its beginning, and much more staff work, reports submitted to the minister not for discussion by a commission or committee but for the minister's de-

67. Nasonkina, *Moskovskii universitet,* 35.

68. For St. Petersburg's enrollment and degrees awarded, see Rozhdestvenskii, "Obrazovanie," *Materialy,* xciv–xcv; Steinger, "St. Petersburg University," 130–131. A. A. Chumikov, "Studencheskiia korporatsii v Peterburgskom universitete v 1830–1840 gg.," *RS,* 1881 (February), 367–369, recalled that during his student years (he entered in 1833) students wore their uniforms "proudly," as a sign that they prepared for an honored career in public service, and that during those years the number of students from aristocratic families (Dolgorukov, Golitsyn, Kochubei, and others) grew noticeably. To this development Chumikov attributed a marked improvement in student "morals and manners." See also Grigor'ev, *S. Peterburgskii universitet,* 100–105; Th. Fortunatov, "Vospominaniia o S. Peterburgskom universitete za 1830–1833 goda," *RA* 1869 (No. 2), 309.

cision. The curators after 1835 expected to live and work in the city of their university, and no longer functioned as effective members of the ministry governing board, the Main School Administration. Without their participation on a reasonably regular basis, that committee soon lost its importance, as did the views of the curators, who became in effect assistant ministers of education for their districts, subordinate commanders in a bureaucratic chain of command, rather than participants in policy formation. Assuming, of course, the quality of ministerial leadership, this development promised improved efficiency in the work of overcoming obstacles to the success of the reform, for the near autonomy of the curators, like that of the faculty councils, had not proved an unmixed blessing.

Moscow's curator of the Shishkov era, General A. A. Pisarev, who served from 1825 to 1830, had no part in the development of this pattern, or much else. He worked at seeing to it that the students wore their uniforms, but otherwise knew little about his university and had little impact on it. His replacement in 1830, S. M. Golitsyn, was appalled to find that the Moscow faculty expected to cooperate rather than obey. Both he and the university were much distracted for some years by the cholera crisis, but in time Golitsyn became the most vigorous opponent in the ministry of the election of the rector by the university faculty. When that feature of the 1804 legislation was retained in the 1835 statute, Golitsyn resigned. His replacement, S. G. Stroganov, also knew a good deal about Moscow, since at the tsar's direction he had conducted a special inspection of it in 1826. As a member of the committee on the organization of the schools since that time, he had become one of Speranskii's stoutest supporters. He and Uvarov shared many goals, and assumptions, and so had no difficulty cooperating for many years.[69]

St. Petersburg was spared a curator of the Pisarev type. Runich was replaced as curator by K. M. Borozdin, who served from 1826 to 1833. A career soldier who had served on Novosiltsev's staff in Poland, Borozdin travelled much in the West, whose intellectual and social trends much interested him. He proved an honest, hardworking bureaucrat who looked on his curatorship as a chance to serve society. His replacement, A. M. Dondukov-Korasakov, served for a

69. On Pisarev and Golitsyn, see Nasonkina, *Moskovskii universitet*, 22–23; Tret'iakov, "Universitetv vospominaniiakh," *RS*, 1892 (September), 540–553; N. N. Murzakevich, "Zapiski 1806–1883," *RS*, 1887 (February), 269–270.

decade, loyally cooperating with the ministry in the implementation of the new statute and the "renewal" of the faculty.[70] Curators were probably even less important at St. Petersburg than they became elsewhere, for the renewal of the faculty there brought about the appointments of men who were personally as well as professionally close to Uvarov. The university became Uvarov's in ways beyond the powers of even the most loyal curator to deliver.

The "renewal" began at St. Petersburg in 1832 when three of the men who were Runich's mainstays, led by Tolmachev, were dropped. P. A. Pletnev proved the model Uvarov appointee. Clergy-born, educated in a seminary, he came to the Main Pedagogical Institute at St. Petersburg for his higher education. An excellent student, he not only finished the course with distinction, but came to the attention of the curator, Uvarov. With Uvarov's support, Pletnev gained many teaching assignments, in and around the capital, including in the end a tutor's post to the future Alexander II. A prodigiously hard worker, Pletnev also made himself a valued member of the city's literary circles, well acquainted with, if not personally close to, Pushkin. He had no higher academic degree, however. Yet, despite his insistence on the doctorate for professors, Uvarov saw no difficulty in arranging Pletnev's appointment to a chair in the university.[71]

Nikolai Gogol received an appointment, as adjunct in history, in 1834, but his academic career proved short-lived. To his surprise and disappointment, his teaching performance was almost wonderfully bad. When Uvarov sent the curator, Dondukov-Korsakov, his letter of July 1835, requesting a list of the faculty members who should be released in order to strengthen the university, Gogol's name was on the first list the curator returned.[72] Soon thereafter,

70. Borozdin in 1833 became a senator and began several studies in pre-Petrine history. Dondukov-Korsakov in 1835 became vice-president of the Academy of Sciences. Neither man had a university education, for both came from 'aristocratic" families that provided home education and early admission to a cadet corps. See RBS, v. 6 (SPB, 1905), 591–592; Entsiklopedicheskii slovar', IV (SPB, 1891), 444.

71. On Pletnev, see RBS, v. 14 (SPB, 1905), 79–91. Uvarov made many exceptions for friends. When his old friend and colleague, Gräfe, professor of classics, wanted to secure a teaching job in a gymnasium for one of his students, who did not meet the legal requirements, Curator Dondukov-Korsakov candidly suggested that Gräfe should see Uvarov, since "with Sergei Semenovich (Uvarov) for you there are no laws." Th. Fortunatov, "Vospominaniia o S. Peterburgskom universitete za 1830–1833 gody," RA, 1869 (No. 2), 319.

72. TsGIAL, f. 733, op. 22, d. 142, list 30 (Dondukov-Korsakov to Uvarov, 11

Uvarov appointed Th. N. Ustrialov professor of history. The son of a retired non-commissioned officer who worked as an estate manager for an absentee noble landlord, Ustrialov, though poor, had unusual advantages. The third of thirteen children, he lived in the lord's house, not in a village *izba*. Naturally bright, he learned to read early, and benefitted from the instruction of an itinerant French tutor. At the age of ten, he entered the local *uezd* school, which was fifty versts away, requiring therefore that the young scholar live away from home for the remainder of his school years. He completed the course at St. Petersburg University during the Runich years and entered service in the Ministry of Finance. He maintained an interest in the intellectual life, completed and published translations that in time brought him to the attention of the president of the Academy of Sciences, Uvarov. He served as lecturer from 1828 but when in 1835 Ustrialov took up his new career as history professor he lacked a doctorate. Within less than a year, however, the curator was happy to report that Ustrialov had completed all requirements for the degree, the thesis defense having been conducted "brilliantly" on 21 November 1836.[73]

Pletnev, Ustrialov, and several others brought the university no new point of view, for none seriously gave thought to challenging the concepts of "Official Nationality." Ustrialov, indeed, wrote history that assumed, and in some cases was meant to demonstrate, the suitability of that sort of "patriotic" loyalty to Russia's needs. This was not a change in fundamentals from the views of Balugianskii or Speranskii. The change lay in the competent professionalism that Ustrialov and others brought, which was not possible for a Tolma-

---

December 1835). The curator pointed out (*ibid.*, 32) that Gogol had failed to pass the examination for a higher degree.

73. Ustrialov, "Vospominaniia," 26–30; TsGIAL, f. 733, op. 22, d. 142, list 254 (Dondukov-Korsakov to Uvarov, 12 December 1836). Grigor'ev, S. *Peterburgskii universitet*, 90, notes that students appreciated Pletnev not for his scholarship but for his warm, open personality and his interest in them. *Ibid.*, 88–94, is a good short discussion of the change in the university faculty. See also Steinger, "Government Policy and the University," 125–129. N. K. Piksanov, N. I. Sokolov, "Izuchenie russkoi literatury v Peterburgskom-Leningradskom universitete (1919–1969)," *Vestnik Leningradskogo Universiteta*, No. 2 (1969), 69–70, described Pletnev as the first "important" professor in the university's history, since he "started the cult of Pushkin." Throughout the year 1969, *Vestnik Leningradskogo Universiteta* published a series of articles on the history of the various *kafedra* (chairs). Unfortunately, few of them provide much more than the materials available in Grigor'ev and Pletnev.

chev or many of the men of the Runich era.[74] Ignatii Iakinthovich, for example, brought professionalism to the study of diplomatics. A native of Minsk who took his first degree at Vilna, he was one of those chosen for the Professors' Institute at Dorpat, where he completed his doctorate in 1832. He spent the next years in study in Berlin, and contributed to the journal of the ministry in 1835 an article on the nature of the "science of diplomatics." He joined the St. Petersburg faculty in 1836 and to his death in 1886 proved a prolific and hard-working teacher-scholar.

Not all able faculty members were newcomers. Gräfe and Chizov, elected dean of the mathematics-science section in 1836, were among the holdovers who gave excellent service for many years. Nor were all the departures involuntary. Osip Senkovski, a Vilna-trained professor of eastern languages, was well known as an able scholar and brilliant lecturer. It was also well known that he held his colleagues and students in nearly complete contempt, for he thought their abilities so far below his level that he felt he wasted time and talent working with them. Nonetheless, despite his marriage to a rich banker's daughter, which appeared to solve any financial worries he might have had, in 1833 Senkovski resigned to devote himself full time to the publication of a new journal, *Library for Readers,* which aimed at developing a popular audience. He edited this journal for the successful bookseller A. F. Smirdin, and, with Grech, Bulgarian, and several others, helped to launch genuinely popular, commercially successful, publishing in Russia. Senkovski's success was the very antithesis of what Uvarov had in mind, for aiming low, or the popular level, was not what he had ever meant by serious work that would benefit the nation. Uvarov's disdain for Senkovski's work, and that of all those who worked with Smirdin's enterprises, was matched by the contempt in which Belinskii and others of the rising intelligentsia held Senkovski and his colleagues, whom they found to represent the "reptile" press.[75]

74. Rozhdestvenskii, "Obrazovanie," *Materialy,* lxxxvii, makes this point in regard to Pletnev. *Ibid.,* lxxxv–xciii, provides an insightful discussion of the "renewal" of the faculty. Among the vacancies to be filled, one of those most keenly felt was that left by Chizov's adjunct and putative successor, Shchelgov, who died in the cholera epidemic in 1831. On Iakinthovich, see *Biograficheskii slovar' professorov i prepodavateli imperatorskago S. Peterburgskago universiteta 1869–1894* (SPB, 1896), 269–270.

75. On Senkovski, see Rozhdestvenskii, "Obrazovanie," *Materialy,* xc–xci; a

Nearly all those who were offered retirement or reassignment to some other, lower, school, were sons of clergy who had received their higher educations in the Main Pedagogical Institute. Their replacements did not always have the legally required doctorates. Nonetheless, though the replacements too often enough were sons of clergy trained in St. Petersburg, they usually were an improvement in academic quality over the staff they replaced. By 1836–1837 the new St. Petersburg faculty more than met the statute requirements in numbers and in quality were a clear advance over what had gone before. When in 1837 St. Petersburg University was moved back to its former river-bank location on Vasilevskii, it marked the return of a university so much strengthened and improved that it was finally up to the task that the reformers of 1803–1804 had envisioned some thirty-odd years before.[76]

Moscow's faculty problem was different. In 1826–1827 Moscow had fifty-four teaching members of the faculty, far more than the statute required at the time.[77] But the renewal of the Moscow fac-

---

useful introduction is in *Entsiklopedicheskii slovar'*, XXIX (SPB, 1900), 531–532. Nikitenko in his diary in 1828 recorded a common evaluation of Senkovski: "He is an outstanding orientalist, but it must be said that he is a bad man." *Zapiski i dnevnik*, I (SPB, 1904), 164–165. For Belinskii's views, see T. Grits, others, *Slovestnost' i kommertsiia (Knizhnaia lavka A. F. Smirdina)*, V. B. Shlovskii, B. M. Eikhenbaum, eds. (Moscow, 1929), 310–311. Senkovski scorned Belinskii and other "serious" journalists as much as they did him, for he thought their achievements well below his own. Consistent with their aim to achieve popularity, which included cultivating the emperor's taste, to be sure, Senkovski, Grech, and Bulgarin all came to espouse vociferously the sort of primitive patriotism that later came to be called "jingoism." Some excellent examples are the reviews the three published of Gogol's *Inspector General*, conveniently collected in E. L. Voitolovskaia, *Komediia N. V. Gogolia 'Revizor': kommentarii* (Leningrad, 1971), 43–58. The best introduction to the careers of all three remains N. V. Riasanovsky, *Nicholas I and Official Nationality in Russia 1825–1855* (Berkeley, 1959), 59–70.

76. TsGIAL, f. 733, op. 22, d. 142, *listy* 50–114, contains the service records of all those involved. Uvarov vetoed many suggestions, and delayed the appointments of others, on the grounds that they lacked the doctorate. It does not appear that anyone pointed out that his support for Pletnev and Ustrialov was, on that ground at least, inconsistent. St. Petersburg's facilities were much improved also, not only by the return to Vasilevskii but by the acquisition of the library of the former Jesuit college at Polotsk, and much else. The Pedagogical Institute, legally separate from the university since 1828, was left in center city, its physical separation from the rest of the university marking, and making effective in practice, the division between the two institutions.

77. For discussion of the renewal of the Moscow faculty, see Nasonkina, *Moskovskii universitet*, 42–72. Nasonkina finds ideological-political motives for Uvarov's

ulty presented some difficulties, since all those to be released, and nearly all the replacements, were Moscow-trained. The adjunct of Professor Davydov, responsible for the philosophy chair, was S. P. Shevyrev, a very able and active young graduate of the university whom his colleagues put forward as professor for 1835–1836. Uvarov vetoed the promotion, on the grounds that Shevyrev lacked the doctorate. The case became complicated, since the new curator, Stroganov, argued that, degree or not, Shevyrev was very able and well suited for the job. Before long, the faculty solved the problem by getting Shevyrev through a doctoral program in time to qualify for a professorship in 1837.[78]

On balance, such difficulties proved minimal, however, and did not seriously delay the work. Pogodin, already well launched on his long career, described his own promotion, and all the other changes, to his friend Maksimovich at Kiev in terms that must have excited the envy of an administrator at St. Vladimir, for Moscow had no difficulty in finding more than adequate replacements for the newly departed.[79] The ever-growing student body too was more than

---

dismissal of several. See, for example, the discussion of the case of I. E. Diad'kovskii of the medical faculty. Uvarov consulted the faculty of the St. Petersburg Medical-Surgical Academy regarding the scientific competence of Diad'kovskii's work, which was controversial, but Nasonkina is sure that Uvarov wanted him removed because he was a "materialist." *Ibid.,* 56–57. The discussions of Moscow's faculty in Tikhomirov, *Istoriia Moskovskogo universiteta,* I, 103–133, and Shevyrev, *Istoriia moskovskogo universiteta,* 544–554, have useful information on the teaching and publishing of some of the better-known individuals.

78. TsGIAL, f. 733, op. 30, d. 185, list 48 (Stroganov to Uvarov, 29 November 1835). The Uvarov-Stroganov correspondence on Shevyrev is in *ibid.,* list 10 (Stroganov to Uvarov, 25 September 1835), 27 (Uvarov to Stroganov, 11 October 1835), 34–35 (Stroganov to Uvarov, 5 November 1835). In addition to his lack of a doctorate, it was more than inconvenient, as Uvarov pointed out, that the faculty had elected Shevyrev to a chair (theory of art) that did not exist in either the old or new statute. Shevyrev's service record (*ibid.,* 11–26) showed that he was an unusual academic, since he was gentry-born and owned eighty serfs. Many of Moscow's faculty, both new and old, were from the gentry, but very few owned property, especially serfs. For Stroganov's reports of the Moscow faculty's program to get Shevyrev his doctorate, see *ibid.,* list 77 (Stroganov to Uvarov, 17 December 1835), list 164 (Stroganov to Uvarov, 19 May 1837). Davydov remains best known as the philosopher denounced as "dangerous" by Magnitskii, Shevyrev as a prolific promoter of "Official Nationality."

79. S. I. Ponomarev, ed., *Pis'ma M. P. Pogodina k M. A. Maksimovichu* (SPB, 1882), 9 (Pogodin to Maksimovich, 16 November 1835). The memoirs of Herzen, brilliantly presented in Martin Malia, *Alexander Herzen and the Birth of Russian Socialism* (Cambridge, 1961), 57–93, *passim,* are too well known to need repeti-

pleased with what they found in the Moscow faculty. The physicists Pavlov and Perevoshchikov, Nadezhdin in literature as well as Pogodin in history—all products of Moscow University itself—were among those whose lectures a generation of students remembered as particularly valuable.

Of all the Moscow faculty, Pogodin had good reason to be pleased. His work had been well received by students for years and continued to find a receptive audience throughout his long career. Uvarov heard him lecture in 1832 and was favorably impressed with both his style and substance. As Pogodin well knew, from that time on he had a supporter in the minister, who gave him effective aid, such as the time and funds for several extended study trips abroad. This support, of course, could be crucial. In 1831, under the impact of the bitter news from Poland, Pogodin wrote a piece justifying Russia's position in "Lithuania." He sent it to Count Benckendorf, chief of the Third Section, who liked it very much. Soon published in *Teleskop*, Pogodin's article attracted warm praise from Nicholas, who even suggested a "reward" for the young scholar. Somewhat taken back by the suggestion that he should be paid for expressing patriotic sentiments, Pogodin was even more taken back in 1833, when he found that Nicholas could not remember him, confusing him vaguely with Polevoi.[80] His contact with the nearly Gogolesque buffoonery of the court of Nicholas notwithstanding, Pogodin was an accomplished teacher-scholar, whatever one made of his conclusions. Though he and Kachenovskii carried on what both called a "thirty-years war" over what should be regarded as the "fundamen-

---

tion, but may be supplemented, and corrected, by the collection of memoirs presented in Kovnator, *Moskovskii universitet v vospominaniakh*, and Ia. I. Kostenetskii, "Vospominaniia iz moi studencheskoi zhizni, 1828–1833," *RA*, 1887 (No. 1), 99–117, (No. 2), 229–244. Most studies of the intellectual formation of the Moscow students who became founders of the "intelligentsia" include discussions of the student circles at Moscow in the 1830s and the influence of professors, particularly Pavlov and Nadezhdin. For example, in addition to Malia, see Herbert E. Bowman, *Vissarion Belinskii 1811–1848* (Cambridge, 1954), 35–45; Edward J. Brown, *Stankevich and His Moscow Circle 1830–1840* (Stanford, 1966), 7–14.

80. Ulrich Picht, *M. P. Pogodin und die Slavische Frage* (Stuttgart, 1969), 207–208. For Pogodin's relationship with Uvarov, see *ibid.*, 217–223. Picht's account of Pogodin's dealings with Kachenovskii, *ibid.*, 10–24 *passim*, is based on Pogodin's autobiography. Pogodin was named to the chair of "general history" in 1835, Kachenovskii to the chair of the history and literature of Slavic languages, though both continued to work in Russian history.

tal" characteristics of Russian history, Kachenovskii did not find Pogodin another Karamzin, i.e., a gifted patriotic amateur, but a scholarly professional who held different views.

Not all those whose lectures pleased the students found Uvarov's favor. Professor of physics M. G. Pavlov's lucid explanations of the doctrines of Schelling not only captivated students but provided fundamental categories of thought for Stankevich, Herzen, Belinskii, and a number of others. Unfortunately, he also published a text in his field, *Basic Physics* (1833), which contained so many errors of fact and doubtful judgments that it became something of a scandal. "He lectures better than he writes," remarked Uvarov.[81] Pavlov, an early case of publish and perish, joined in early retirement Ivashkovskii and Snegirev, whose teaching Uvarov in 1832 had reported as deficient in command of their subjects. Ivashkovskii and Snegirev in 1831 voted against the promotion of Nadezhdin, on the grounds that he taught the doctrines of Schelling, which the two classicists found "morally dangerous" for the students. Their support for the ideologically safe side did not keep their positions safe.

Nadezhdin too had a much shortened career, though his name was not on any of the lists of faculty proposed for weeding out in order to strengthen Moscow's academic competence. Clergy-born, Nadezhdin studied in the Moscow seminary until he was assigned in 1824 to teach in the seminary in his native Riazan. Two years later he was back in Moscow, released from the clergy for "reasons of health." He worked closely with Kachenovskii, who taught classics, literature, and history and edited *Vestnik Evropy* as well. Kachenovskii, clearly impressed with the young scholar's ability, spon-

---

81. N. K. Kozmin, "N. K. Nadezhdin—professor moskovksago universiteta," *ZhMNP*, 1907 (May), 128. Despite the title, this work provides an excellent acount of Pavlov's career. See also *Biograficheskii slovar' moskovskogo universiteta*, II, 183–199. Pavlov was clergy-born and spent a year at Kharkov University before entering the Moscow Medical-Surgical Academy. He came to Moscow University as a teacher in 1820, having spent a year in western Europe in studying agricultural techniques. Perevoshchikov was gentry-born and finished his *kandidat* at Kazan University in 1809. He served as gymnasium teacher before joining the Moscow faculty in 1826 as teacher in mathematics. He was promoted to adjunct, extraordinary professor, and finally to professor, all during the year 1826. See *ibid.*, 209–216. Though their lectures much impressed students, it proved not difficult for graduates of the Dorpat Professors' program to match Pavlov and Perevoshchikov in training and scholarship.

sored his *magister* and doctoral work. Nadezhdin's rapid rise, therefore, owed much to his journalistic prowess, the basis for his connection with Kachenovskii and others. Nadezhdin's scholarly career came to an abrupt halt in 1836, when he published in his journal, *Teleskop,* Chaadaev's "First Philosophical Letter." Nadezhdin, whose lectures students found as enthralling as those of Pavlov, had earlier published his own article, "The Question of Russian National Consciousness (*Narodnost'*)" in the same journal, in which he argued that "Russia has no past . . . but only the present," which Peter founded and which was still being developed. Perhaps Nadezhdin thought that Chaadaev's views only extended the same idea. If so, his expectation proved unfounded, for Chaadaev's piece caught the tsar's anxious attention. Academic competence was the most important criterion for appointment and advancement at Moscow, as the 1835 statute was introduced. However, Nadezhdin's dismissal showed that it was not always the only criterion. As Uvarov remarked to Pirogov, the young medical scholar returned from Dorpat and Berlin, "Never forget, the tsar is the real minister of education, not I."[82]

Though Nadezhdin might have accepted that assessment, Uvarov exaggerated a good bit. The tsar was his own minister only on those occasions when something or someone somehow got his attention, provoking a decisive margin note. While Nicholas was courageous, honest, and hard-working, he lacked the sophistication to understand much of the important business that went on about him. His interventions in the ministry's work were random and episodic. Given patience, and perhaps a bit of craft, it was quite possible for a minister to work around even Nicholas' direct orders. The universities whose experience contributed to the making of the 1835 statute had made remarkable progress toward meeting the goals set forth by the reformers who founded the universities early in the reign of Alexander I. It was clear enough that Nicholas I's concept of what would be best for Russia was not likely to include a set of

82. N. I. Pirogov, *Izbrannye pedagogicheskie sochineniia,* V. Z. Smirnov, ed. (Moscow, 1952), 357. Pirogov, writing in 1862, recalled a conversation with Uvarov. Unfortunately he did not indicate the date of the conversation, but, judging from context, it probably took place in 1833 or 1841. For Nadezhdin's career, see Kozmin, "Nadezhdin," *ZhMNP,* 1905 (September), 1–14; 1907 (July), 62–71. The account in *Biograficheskii slovar' moskovskago universiteta,* II, 153–155, gives details on Nadezhidin's doctoral thesis and courses taught, but makes no mention of Chaadaev.

universities that continued institutional and faculty autonomy in many important respects, continued fundamentally liberal arts education for most, regardless of putative vocation, or continued a "ladder" system open to all classes. But that was the system that developed and that provided the foundation for much of the definitive statute of 1835.

CHAPTER VI

SUCCESS AND ITS CONSEQUENCES

MANY IN THE RUSSIA of Nicholas I did not find it a success that the universities continued to have significant autonomy in self-government and teaching. Many since, moreover, have argued that to have such universities in autocratic Russia was to confront Russia with the dilemma that came to be called the "University Question." One could have either the autonomous university or autocracy, not both. The free university and the tsarist state were fundamentally contradictions. The attempt to have both inescapably produced conflict that harmed both university and state and, more important, the society both were presumed to serve.[1]

Uvarov, and a good many others, did not accept the dilemma. Indeed, those who played the key roles in developing the statute of 1835 believed, rather, that for many years to come Russia would need to preserve as much as possible of university autonomy together with the autocracy of the Petrine state, balancing the ambiguities and contradictions for as long as necessary to make possible the long-range success of the reform. At bottom, then, the statute of 1835 was founded on the conviction that the reformers of 1802–1804 had not been mistaken in attempting to use the power of the autocratic state to launch a liberal reform. Assuming their essential soundness, the main features of the 1802–1804 legislation were kept, to be strengthened by the support of organized religion. Thus

---

1. For a well-informed discussion, see Klaus Meyer, "Die Entstehung der 'Universitätsfrage' in Russland. Zum Verhältnis von Universität, Staat und Gesellschaft zu Beginn des Neunzehnten Jahrhunderts," *Forschungen zur Osteuropäischen Geschichte*, Bd. 25 (1978), 229–238.

the new statute signaled the rejection of the belief, shared in effect by Enlightened rationalists and Bible Society pietists, that obscurantism and religion were the same thing. In the end, therefore, the statute of 1835 was the plan for the future sought since the time when Alexander and Golitsyn realized that the Bible Society ideology had not worked out as the guideline for the schools. It was a plan that did not represent the development of yet another ideological blueprint, but was rather a set of basically pragmatic solutions to particular problems. It summed up the goals of the Alexandrine university reform, the problems faced and their solutions, or their intractability, and showed how far Russia had come in some three decades of effort to develop universities, institutions devoted to higher learning and capable of providing high-level professional training for men who could transform the government as public servants or who could bring enlightenment to the whole nation as teachers.

1. Uvarov and the Statute of 1835

In early November 1832 Uvarov reported his inspection of Moscow University. His report was less revealing in some ways than his 1818 speech, for in 1832 he discussed long-range goals only in the rather general terms that became known as "Official Nationality." Nonetheless, Uvarov made clear enough the path he wanted to take. First, he proposed to describe the "morality, scholarship, and general spirit of the university." Second, he recommended "steps for the improvement of Moscow university." While calling for improvement, Uvarov's reports, to the day of his dismissal in 1849, constantly praised the achievements of the schools and especially lauded their loyalty to tsar and fatherland. He began this report with praise for the "earnest support and work of assistant curator Golokhvastov," and for the "complete calm among the students." The severity of the examinations, both for admission and for the student "diploma," were all that could be asked. Moreover, "the steps needed for the proper support of the state students . . . and for supervision over them, has been assigned to Professor Shchepkin, an able and effective Inspector." Uvarov concluded that "in close and detailed observation, in lectures which I attended nearly every day, in private meetings and in group meetings with professors, I noted not the slightest deviation from good spirit or from sound principles. I am completely confident that . . . Moscow University merits no censure of any kind."

There was another side, however. "The influence of sound principles and good morals has complete force over minds, especially of the young, when it is joined to fundamental education, in the well-expressed thought and writing of learned professors." The argument that even the most superior education is only as good as the goodness of its morality, or the morality of the teachers, had been made by Shishkov and others so often that it approached the status of truism. Uvarov reversed the argument, pointing out that good morals could be effective only if united with and supported by sound learning. Since good morals required academic excellence, therefore, Uvarov went on to estimate the excellence of the faculty from that point of view. Perevoshchikov ("well educated and intelligent . . . in all respects deserves the respect of the government") and adjuncts Pogodin and Maksimovich were among those lauded. The professor of theology, Father Ternovskii, not only was learned but impressed Uvarov "with the completeness and clarity of his lectures, his use of language and his methods of teaching." Lamentably, however, there were many faculty members whose advanced age limited if not curtailed their effectiveness, among them Dvigubskii, the oft re-elected rector.

"It is difficult, of course," Uvarov modestly noted, "in such a short time" to be sure of these matters, but he concluded: "nonetheless, in these judgments about personnel, I do not think that I can be very far from the truth." Fortunately, Uvarov could point out that the rather limited problem of inadequate faculty could be solved easily. One need but replace the inadequate professors with those who could do the job. In fact, several months before, in the previous May, Uvarov had outlined this very problem and its solution in a talk with a recent graduate of St. Petersburg University who was serving in the ministry. Uvarov offered him the opportunity to become professor of literature at his alma mater. Tolmachev and several others were already on his list for removal, to be replaced with men not only younger, but able by training and talent to fill the professor's role. Clearly, Uvarov, long before he made his inspection of Moscow, had no intention of simply waiting for the natural course of the years to improve the faculties. While he had not supported all of Parrot's plan to completely restaff the "Russian" universities, Uvarov encouraged the Professors' Institute at Dorpat, for it answered well one of the system's needs as he saw it.[2]

The university, said Uvarov, faced "one of the most difficult problems of our time, providing true education, a fundamental necessity of our century, with deep reverence and warm faith in the truly-Russian conservative principles of orthodoxy, autocracy, and nationality." Uvarov was happy to note that chances of success at this "most difficult problem" were remarkably good. "During my whole stay in Moscow," he said, "I visited freely not only with teachers but also with students. I had conversations with them nearly every day . . . and could see on their faces and hear from all sides . . . love for the monarch and the fatherland." Clearly, all well understood and accepted their "obligations to the throne and church, and the necessity to be Russians in the spirit of old while striving for European education, the necessity to unite true faith with higher learning, and with that enlightenment which belongs to all people and all ages." Uvarov "rejoiced" at his good fortune in being able to bring this good news to the attention of the tsar.[3]

However, there was a problem. The faculty and students were not alone in having influence on the "mental calm or even the spirit of the university." Uvarov warned that "the student, who has no contacts with society, the poor, lonely student reads eagerly the journals, seeking there food for mind and heart. What does he find in them? Ignorance of the rules of logic and language, sharp and narrow-minded judgment, offered up by the same people from whom he is supposed to receive his education. What can a student think when he looks up at a professor he saw just yesterday splashing about in the journalistic mud?"[4] All was not beyond hope,

2. For a discussion of Uvarov's inspection, see Nasonkina, *Moskovskii universitet,* 110–120. For Uvarov's offer to Nikitenko on 14 May 1832, repeated on 6 June, as well as his plan to improve the university by replacing Tolmachev and others, see A. V. Nikitenko, *Dnevnik, v trekh tomakh* (Leningrad, 1955), I, 222. For a misleading abridgement, see *The Diary of a Russian Censor, Aleksandr Nikitenko,* abr., ed., trans. H. S. Jacobson (Amherst, 1975), 38. The text of Uvarov's report, dated 4 December 1832, is printed in *Sbornik postanovlenii,* II, 502–529. Quotations 504, 505, 507, 508–509. The tsar read this report on 4 December. Uvarov submitted it nearly a month earlier. TsGIAL, f. 735, op. 1, d. 491, *list* 8 (Uvarov to Lieven, 9 November 1832), the cover letter for the report (which is in *ibid., listy* 12–45). The tsar responded in his usual fashion, making comments in pencil on the margins.

3. *Sbornik postanovlenii,* II, 511–512.

4. *Ibid.,* 513–514. Uvarov knew the tsar's contemptuous fear of the "evil intent"

Uvarov was pleased to say, for he had warned the censorship committee of the difficulties ahead. "In general," he went on, "with advice and counsel, it is possible to lead the periodical press step by step to come to agree with the government's views. This, I think, is a much better procedure than any sort of forced closings, particularly of journals which have many followers and eager readers among the middle and even lower classes. I must add also that the publisher of *Telegraf*, Polevoi, more quickly than others accepted my advice and that even the Moscow public noticed the change in the tone of his journal, though they did not know the reason for it."[5] Advice and counsel behind the scenes was not the only solution to this problem. Indeed, "it is not enough. Direct, effective influence, particularly on the minds of university students, whom I have always especially in mind, can be achieved only by the provision of a new pure source of learning and news." In short, Uvarov wanted to sponsor a journal himself.[6]

Replacing incompetent professors and founding a serious journal were meant as important reforms. But Uvarov found most important his third proposal, a major increase in funding. Though he said that "there is no need to expand on this subject," he went on for several pages, describing some of the outstanding needs before the university. For example, the gentry *pansion* had been "reformed,"

---

of Moscow journalists, a fear fed, and exploited, by the Third Section, the special political police. The Third Section usually recommended "repressive measures," while Uvarov recommended "persuasion" as the best response. Nonetheless, Uvarov's repeated use of journalists as scapegoat did nothing to allay the tsar's fears and in the long run proved dangerous for both the universities and Uvarov himself. See Monas, *The Third Section*, 79–82, 154–155; Whittaker, *Uvarov*, 220–235.

5. *Sbornik postanovlenni*, II, 515. In March 1834 Polevoi embarrassed Uvarov, publishing in *Telegraf* a review of a recent patriotic play, poking fun at those whose tastes were vulgar enough to applaud it. Since the tsar was among those who liked the play very much, he ordered Uvarov to find out how such an evil-minded review managed to appear in the public press. Polevoi, realizing his "error," made desperate efforts to retrieve that issue, but he was too late. Furious that Polevoi had embarrassed him, Uvarov ordered the closing of the journal and, after delivering a severe tongue-lashing to the unfortunate editor, forbade Polevoi from writing anything under his own name (though he could publish anonymously!) in the future. Nikitenko's diary entries from 5 and 9 April 1834 (*Dnevnik*, I, 141, well translated in Jacobson, *Diary Nikitenko*, 47–48), are the often-cited source for most accounts of the closing of *Telegraf*. An exception is Monas, *Third Section*, 160–164, which is based on Benckendorf's version of the affair. There is nothing in either source to indicate that the author knew that Uvarov had recently boasted to the tsar of his influence over Polevoi's journal.

6. *Sbornik postanovlenii*, II, 516–517.

i.e., made into "gymnasium No. 1." Its enrollment dropped, presumably as a result of that change. Uvarov recommended that it be
reformed again, into a special "gentry institute," whose program
would attract gentry because it would go beyond that of the gymnasium. This proposal, he argued, not only recognized the special
role of the gentry in state services, but also necessitated a much
augmented budget and the formation of an additional, third, gymnasium to meet the needs of the city. Moreover, the university badly
needed additional dormitory space for nearly 350 self-supporting
students who lived in the city, "in various apartments, where they
are surrounded by bad people, even though in small numbers."
Alert to Nicholas' particular concerns, Uvarov noted that among
such students were "natives" of the Polish provinces, in Moscow to
finish the courses they began at Vilna. "Who can answer for the
spirit they bring with them? Perhaps they will be influenced by the
Russian spirit, or perhaps they will spread the spirit of their own
tribe." While "to such questions one can hardly propose definite
answers at this time," Uvarov concluded that all would be safer if
such students were housed in university buildings under supervision. The building would cost about 250,000 rubles, a modest
enough part of a budget request that totalled some 1,440,000
rubles.[7] Uvarov concluded with assurances that he had seen in
Moscow "not the least sign of disorder or lack of discipline." In
fact, "all seem ready to become instruments of Your August will,
dedicated completely to the common good."[8]

The journal Uvarov wanted, the *Journal of the Ministry of Public
Education,* began publication in January 1834. The first issue carried a circular addressed to the district curators (dated 21 March
1833), which announced Uvarov's assumption of office as minister.
He promised his "best efforts to further the work of the universities
and other schools" and expressed his hope "to find in their work
that earnest and active striving for the common good which ani-
mates our service. Please inform the university councils and others
in the universities," he went on, "of my sincere wish to see in them

    7. *Ibid.,* 526, 527.
    8. Uvarov sent similar assurances to Benckendorf, reporting "with pleasure that
the most perfect tranquility continues to reign among the students of [Moscow]
university . . . and all the other universities too." "Dva pis'ma ministra prosveshcheniia grafa S. S. Uvarova k shefu zhandarov grafu A.Kh. Benkendorfu," *RA,*
1885 (No. 3), 366 (14 October 1832).

that degree of excellence which must characterize institutions of our fatherland. Our main responsibility is that public education, in agreement with the highest intentions of the august monarch, is completely unified in the spirit of Orthodoxy, Autocracy, and Nationality. I am confident that every professor and teacher, imbued with one and same sense of dedication to Throne and Fatherland, will exert every effort as befits a worthy instrument of the Government and will serve it with complete faithfulness." He hoped also that each would bring "the teaching of his science to the desired level of perfection, with dedicated constant effort and unremitting diligence in the education of the youth entrusted to each." Uvarov concluded his message with a request that the curators report on the students "so that I may not neglect to give proper attention to those whose academic success, good morals, prudence, and obedience to authority marks them as especially worthy."[9] It is easy to overestimate the significance of this announcement. Brief and bland, it did little more than repeat the "God, tsar, and fatherland" slogan that for years had been used by all Uvarov's predecessors as minister, as well as Magnitskii, Speranskii, the faculty councils of the universities, and many others.

At the same time, January 1834, Uvarov had to come to some specific conclusions about the details of a university statute. The tsar had decided that, as the constitution of Congress Kingdom Poland was abolished in consequence of the 1830 revolt, so too the Poles in the "western provinces" had forfeited their right to the university at Vilna. Instead, education in the western provinces was reorganized and the university at Vilna replaced by a new institution at Kiev, to direct a new district made up of the southern provinces of the old Vilna district. Neither Uvarov nor any other member of the Ministry of Education was involved in these decisions, but they naturally had to deal with their consequences.

The new Kiev district was founded in December 1832. Appointed curator was an able and loyal soldier, Egor von Bradke, a

9. ZhMNP, 1834 (January) xlix–l, printed also in Sbornik rasporiazhenii, I, 837–839. This circular, in particular the line that "public education . . . is completely unified in the spirit of Orthodoxy, Autocracy, and Nationality," is often quoted as the foundation of the doctrine of "Official Nationality." To this tripartite formula Uvarov, and many others, returned often, for it neatly touched all the bases, particularly on ceremonial occasions. Nonetheless, in this circular it received no particular stress, less than that placed on academic excellence, and seemed in usage nearly synonymous with hoary if not routine "dedication to throne and fatherland."

Baltic German who had the confidence of the tsar but no experience in educational matters. The plans for the new district included the organization of a lycée at Kiev, presumably to replace Vilna University, which had been closed in the spring of 1832, as the supervising center for education in these provinces. Most schools in these provinces, especially those above village level, had been closed after 1830, the famed lycee at Krzemieniec shut down in August 1832. Thus, the new district needed much work to get it launched. Von Bradke, after making an inspection tour of the schools of the St. Petersburg district in order to familiarize himself with what a school district should look like, made an extended tour of his new district. He was especially pleased with what he found in Krzemieniec, for it was not the "fortress of Polish fanaticism" he feared but a school whose excellent facilities and personnel could be transferred to Kiev, founding the new lycée required there with relatively little trouble and expense.[10]

In May 1833 von Bradke reported to the newly installed Minister Uvarov, recommending the transfer of the Krzemieniec lycée to Kiev. Uvarov, seconding the curator's views, passed them on to the tsar, who gave his approval almost at once. Another proposal came from General Count V. V. Levashev, military governor of Kiev, and after 1833 of Volhynia and Podolia too. In May 1833 he recommended, to the "western provinces committee," the organization of an Institute for Law named for St. Vladimir, a school of gymnasium-lycée level to train state-supported young gentry in law, as preparation for entry to state service. In the fall Uvarov made a new proposal, accepting neither von Bradke's nor Levashev's suggestion. Instead, he said, "In Kiev there should be *university,* for Kiev is the center of southern Russia." By closing "the lycée at Krzemieniec, the government took upon itself an obligation to replace it with

10. The decree closing Vilna is dated 1 May 1832 (*Sbornik postanovlenii,* II, 476), that founding the Kiev district 14 December 1832 (in *ibid.,* 533–535). Benckendorf, in his memoirs described the foundation of Kiev as a consequence of the Polish revolt of 1830, without mentioning Uvarov. Von Bradke in his memoirs recounts his appointment, without mention of Uvarov. Von Bradke at first did not wish to accept the curatorship of the new district, since he had no experience or knowledge of education, but was persuaded by Count Bludov that it would be best not to "disappoint" the tsar. "Avtobiograficheskiia zapiski Egora Fedorovicha Fon-Bradke," *RA,* 1875 (No. 3), 268–273, Quotation 273. Benckendorf's memoir of the years 1832–1837 is printed with the title "Zapiski" in an appendix to Nikolai Shil'der, *Imperator Nikolai Pervyi, ego zhizn' i tsarstvovaniia,* 2 v. (SPB, 1903), II, 647–664. For the selection of Kiev for the new district, see p. 680.

another institution." Moreover, "only a university can meet all the requirements." Uvarov granted that Kiev could have neither a theology nor a medical faculty, at least for the present. The tsar at once gave his approval, "but on condition that there be only two faculties, philosophy and law."[11]

Uvarov lost no time. Within a week he dispatched to the tsar, with copies to the Committee on the organization of schools, the Senate, and the Committee of Ministers, a draft for an *ukaz*, signed into law by the tsar on 8 November, which announced the foundation in Kiev of St. Vladimir University. At the end of the month Uvarov called a special joint meeting of the Committee on the organization of schools with the Main School Administration of the ministry, to which General Levashev was invited. Uvarov presented to the meeting a draft statute and proposed budget for the new university. No one else came to the meeting so well prepared or even ready to comment. Speranskii wanted the record to show that the committee was working on a general statute for all the universities, to which the Kiev statute would have to conform, "saving only local differences." To the report on this meeting, which accepted Uvarov's recommendation for a "temporary" statute for a two-faculty university, the tsar replied in December that "If the work on the general statute is nearing completion, perhaps it would be better to issue them all at the same time."

Uvarov ignored the tsar's suggestion, but in his reply, on 13 December, he promised that the new university's statute would "differ from the former university statutes. For example, the university court . . . will be abolished." Moreover, the "authority" of the curator and the "influence of the minister" would be strengthened. The university would give "strict examinations" both for admission and for degrees. Law would be taught according to the arrangement of the recently completed law code that Speranskii had finally brought to completion. Finally, the "internal police" of the university and its

11. *Sbornik postanovlenii*, II, 564–565 (O zakrytii . . . 14 May 1833), 574–578 (O peremeshchenii . . . 23 May 1833); TsGIAL, f. 733, op. 69, d. 111, *list* 4 (Taneev to Uvarov, 31 October 1833), *listy* 5–10 (Uvarov to Nicholas, 30 October 1833). With the exception of Uvarov's recommendation of 30 October cited here, the important documents relating to the foundation of Kiev are printed in *Sbornik postanovlenii*, II, 647–666, and are quoted or summarized in Allister, "Reform," 117–120; Rozhdestvenskii, *Istoricheskii obzor*, 242–243; Shul'gin, *Istoriia Universiteta Sv. Vladimira*, 35–40; M. F. Vladimirskii-Budanov, *Istoriia Imperatorskago Universiteta Sv. Vladimira* (Kiev, 1884), 60–65.

"economic" administration would be entrusted to officials specially chosen, not let to committees of academics.[12] Uvarov's promises appealed to some of what the tsar wanted to hear, such as the prospect of really "strict" examinations. It also outlined the solutions Uvarov thought best for many of the problems that had been reported from the universities for years.

The draft statute for Kiev delivered on Uvarov's promises.[13] It contained no statement of "goals" in terms of "Official Nationality" or any other "principles," though it took note of "local conditions" by providing for a chair in Roman Catholic theology and for instruction in Polish. The two senior officials remained the rector, elected from and by the professors for a two-year term, and the curator, appointed by the tsar on the minister's recommendation and required to "maintain his permanent residence in Kiev." The university council elected the rector and the faculty members, though both remained subject to confirmation by the ministry. The council was also responsible for all academic affairs of the university. The faculties, as promised, were two. The philosophy faculty, however, was divided into two sections. The first had five "chairs," of philosophy, of Greek, Roman, and Russian literature, and of world and Russian history and statistics. The second section had eight "chairs," in mathematics and the usual divisions of the natural sciences, with the eighth a chair of applied "technology, agriculture, forest-management, and architecture," obviously designed to provide instruction useful for those who would manage agricultural estates. The law faculty had seven chairs, one of "general or so called encyclopedic law," five that followed the section divisions of the *Svod zakonov,* and a seventh of Roman law.

Outside the two faculties were two chairs of theology (which included church history and scripture, as well as dogmatic and moral theology), one Roman Catholic, one Orthodox. These were to be filled in the usual way by the faculty council, but also required the consent of the local bishop of each communion. In addition, there were to be four language teachers, French, German, Italian, and Polish. Comparison with the "former statute" illustrated the direction of the changes Uvarov thought needed. Of the literature faculty, Russian, Greek, and Roman literature were kept. Russian and world

12. *Sbornik postanovlenii,* II, 655–656.
13. Text of the statute is printed in *Sbornik postanovlenii,* II, 667–683.

history, however, were combined into a single chair, as at Dorpat since 1820. Eastern languages and the chair of art and archeology disappeared. Of the old moral-political science faculty, theology and church history-scripture were combined into a single chair, though, due to "local conditions," two chairs were still required at Kiev. Of the chairs of law, made into a separate faculty, the former chair of legal history became what it usually had been in practice, devoted to Roman law, while the old "general" chair remained much the same. The former single chair devoted to Russian law was expanded into five. The chair of philosophy was kept, as were all the mathematics-science chairs, though pure and applied mathematics were combined into one, and two technology chairs were also combined. Political economy, however, seemed a conspicuous exception, for it disappeared from the curriculum.

The new course distribution agreed with the often-repeated view that the training of state service men required a more practical, even technical, education than that offered by the academic program of the 1804 reform and that, though it was not exactly pre-professional training, formal instruction in religion was a useful part of the preparation of all who expected to work for the common good. Nonetheless, Uvarov remained convinced that a basically liberal arts education had an important contribution to make, for even in the law faculty, the one most clearly aimed at the professional training of civil servants, instruction on the nature and concept of law and on Roman law was clearly not mere vocational training for high-level clerks. The original reformers had counted on liberal arts and sciences as the best preparation for "youth in training for the various state services," as the 1804 statute put it. Others had argued that more pragmatic, even vocational, training was needed. Uvarov, though he continued to value high-level academic work, especially in the classics, which he sometimes called simply "serious" work, saw to the introduction of much more professionally orientated training into the curriculum. The result was a compromise that continued liberal arts education, if simplified from the heady days when Parrot proposed a chair for nearly everything, augmented with professional as well as religious training.

There were other compromises that needed to be made. The council remained responsible for the academic affairs of the university, but the "directorate" received complete authority over police and "economic" matters. In the 1804 arrangements, the "directorate" was primarily the steering committee of the faculty council, in which the elected rector and deans managed the day-to-day operations. The new directorate was chaired by the rector, or by the curator if he chose to attend, and included the elected deans, but it also included two appointed officials, a "councilor" chosen by the curator for economic administration and a legal officer, the "sindik," chosen to oversee the university chancellery and general administration. The directorate reported to the ministry through the curator, not to the faculty council. The university's police function thus was managed by a body that was chaired by an elected rector, and had a majority of elected members. This body, the directorate, was responsible for drafting the police regulations it was to administer. But the university court, like political economy in the curriculum, had disappeared.

Nonetheless, a "school committee, elected by the council" remained, charged with the responsibility of inspecting the district's schools. The point of this arrangement was not entirely clear. In the Kiev district in 1833–1834, most schools remained closed or operated under the auspices of agencies not subordinate to the Ministry of Education. Even the remains of the university at Vilna, where the medical faculty of the closed university continued to operate as the Vilna Medical-Surgical Academy, was under the control of the Ministry of the Interior, since Nicholas remained convinced that education in Vilna was still largely a police, not academic, affair. Moreover, the Committee on the organization of schools had held many discussions in which it seemed agreed that the curator's office should have strengthened control over the schools of each district. The university curators and faculties long contended that the task of inspecting, let alone actually supervising, the schools of the districts was more work than could be handled by men who also were responsible for the academic work of the university. Yet, in 1828, at the promulgation of the new statute on the lower schools of the empire, the role of the curator and of the universities in the administration of the districts had been left unclear. The Kiev statute offered no solution but left the matter as ambiguous as had the 1828 law.

Upon promulgation of the new Kiev statute, Uvarov asked for the reactions of the curators and the faculty councils of the universities. In short order, the responses showed that the curators and faculties had received what they wanted. They made suggestions for improving the language and other details to make clear the separation of the academic from economic and police administrative matters and, predictably, suggestions for increases in the budget. But none lamented the passing of direct faculty responsibility for governance in economic and police matters. Even the end of the university court went unmourned. The rector and deans continued to be elected by and from the faculty, whose council controlled academic matters, such as admission of students, courses, degrees, examinations, and faculty appointments and promotions, and the elected rector and deans also served with the curator on the "directorate." The new statute thus maintained university autonomy in the areas most meaningful to the faculty, while shedding it in those areas where it had proved more burden than boon.[14]

The next step, the conclusion of the general statute for the other universities, extending throughout the system the changes agreed upon for the Kiev statute, took more than a year and a half. Uvarov first worked to "renew" the university faculties, as he had promised, to launch his journal, and thereby to argue his case for the changes to be made, especially in the curriculum, to argue before the tsar the importance and need for new support for eastern studies, for medical education, and for substantial budget increases for all faculties, and to complete, at Nicholas' express direction, yet another detailed inspection of the "spirit" prevailing at Moscow University.

The move to renew the faculties was simple enough. It began in March 1833, when the newly appointed minister sent a message, marked "secret," to the assistant curator for Moscow, Count Golokhvastov. Uvarov asked that Golokhvastov submit a list of suggestions, naming "the professors and teachers whom you find it necessary to release from the university upon the introduction of the new statute." Uvarov went on to order that "this measure must be carried out without any abuse or harm to the faculty members or even any public exposure." All would be pensioned off, retired for "reasons of health." The list returned by Golokhvastov was, not surprisingly, a faithful copy of the list Uvarov drew up the previous fall.[15] It took months, in some cases years, to effect the changes, for some faculty resisted retirement while in other cases finding better re-

14. Allister, "Reform," 119–120, summarizes the responses Uvarov received.
15. TsGIAL, f. 735, op. 1, d. 491, listy 56, 57 (Uvarov to Golokhvastov and reply, 23 March 1833, 18 May 1833).

placements proved quite difficult. But once under way, Uvarov's "renewal" of the faculties proceeded remarkably well.

The *Journal of the Ministry of Education* also proceeded remarkably well. The first issue (January 1834) carried an untitled introduction, unsigned but doubtless Uvarov's work, which spelled out, if in general terms, what the work of the ministry should be.[16] "In our time," Uvarov began, "there seems no need to argue the usefulness of education . . . for all seek enlightenment." Indeed, enlightenment is such a natural part of "civil societies" that "if only it does not meet invincible obstacles, it may and must spread itself among peoples by itself. But wise governments, in view of the vital importance it has for the fate of the state, make education a subject of special concern." For that reason, "the immortal Enlightener of Russia, the reformer of our Fatherland, not only gave her new glory, not only secured her from external danger, but also opened to her the path to make perfect internally all the paths of civil life." Uvarov emphasized the role of the state, and pointed out that its requirements changed over time. "When Russia . . . trailed behind Europe in successful education," Tsar Peter naturally led in the direction of learning from Europe. "But this is a different time. Russia stands at the height of glory and influence and has clear awareness of her own merits. She sees on the throne a *Tsar* sent by Providence, a tsar who is the Defender of her *Faith* and *nationality*. Having left behind the period of mere imitation, Russia better than her foreign teachers knows what is required in order to adjust the fruits of education to her own needs." Naturally, Russia would accomplish this by holding on to the "unity-giving third element, the Autocracy."

This introduction to the journal, and work, of Uvarov's ministry perhaps masked as much as it revealed, for it was a mixture of rhetoric appropriate for ceremonial occasions and sincere faith, in proportions difficult to measure. Clearly much of it would appeal to the tsar, not only because it stressed the primacy of the autocracy, but because of the comparisons with Peter the Great, Nicholas' own hero. Whatever the merit of a brief statement of general goals, the

---

16. *ZhMNP,* 1834 (No. 1), iii–vii. The views Uvarov expressed in his 1818 speech remained in most important respects his beliefs for the remainder of his life, though naturally their expression changed with differing circumstances over the years, as for example in this statement. This point is especially well made in Cynthia H. Whittaker, "The Ideology of Sergei Uvarov: An Interpretive Essay," *The Russian Review,* v. 37 (1978), 158–176.

remainder of the journal was designed to provide information and guidance useful to all who worked in education. The first issue featured five "parts." The first section of Part I printed all laws relating to education, 18 March to 1 September 1833, starting with the *ukaz* that made Uvarov minister. The second section printed ministerial rulings, starting with Uvarov's circular on his appointment, dated 21 March 1833. This section carried notice of staff changes throughout the empire, including in this issue the release of Degurov at St. Petersburg and Dvigubskii at Moscow, as well as the promotion of Perevoshchikov and Pogodin at Moscow. The second "part" also had two "sections," one for "literature," the other for "science." The "literature" section of the first issue was an article by Professor Pletnev of St. Petersburg, stressing the importance of "nationality" as a factor in literature. Pletnev's article defended the notion that literature should be a part of the education offered to all, regardless of vocational aims, since literatures are expressions of each nation's concept of self, a vital ingredient in the upbringing of all who love and serve their fatherlands. The "science" section was an article by the newly promoted Professor Pogodin of Moscow University, devoted to the teaching of "world history." Pogodin defended teaching general history, not just Russian, as part of the education necessary for all who hoped to understand the development of all modern society, one's own included. He outlined a sketch of mankind's history, which proceeded along a path marked out by Providence "with the same immutable laws which govern the physical world." Thus, Pogodin outlined the same "historicist" understanding of the nature of human development sketched in Uvarov's 1818 speech. Naturally, since it was the path followed by all mankind, this pattern of development deserved an important place in the Russian universities' curriculum.

Throughout 1834 and 1835, each issue of the journal contained in Part II carefully crafted explanations of the contents and approach of one or another major discipline and a defense of its importance in the course of studies offered in the Russian university. Some subjects were not treated. Mathematics, for example, seemed to need no defense. But history, philosophy, and classics (the subject of three major pieces within a year) received particular support. These subjects had been attacked at various times as either "dangerous" or unnecessary for the training of Russian civil servants, by critics as varied as Magnitskii, Shishkov, and Balugianskii. Uvarov made no reference to these views. In the ministry's journal, space was given only to positive evaluations of the importance of history, philosophy, and classics in the education offered to all at the university level.

The other sections of the journal were just as carefully crafted to foster developments that Uvarov wanted to sponsor. Section III was devoted to "News of academic institutions in Russia." The first issue contained an interestingly detailed article on the organization and progress of St. Petersburg University and its district, though no mention was made of the students' social classes, and a short history of the university made no mention of Runich. The fourth section was "News of foreign academic institutions." Thus, though he had argued that Russia had left behind dependence on foreign learning, nonetheless Uvarov's journal devoted a whole section to what foreigners were doing. The first issue's article described public education in Prussia, making clear that the Prussian system was an admirable one that achieved the goals set for it. Though no special point was made to underscore the fact, it was also clear that Prussian universities, though they maintained "autonomy," did not run the lower schools of their districts. The lower schools, including the gymnasia, were supervised by directors appointed for each of the kingdom's eight districts by the ministry in Berlin. Uvarov's journal, then, was important not only for the information and assistance it offered teachers, though that was not inconsiderable, but as an explanation-defense of what he thought was the universities' task and of the features he planned to include in the general statute.

Despite the aura of success in educational matters that the ministry's journal projected, Tsar Nicholas worried a good deal about Moscow University. His friend Count Benckendorf directed the most important of all the "special committees" Nicholas appointed, the Third Section, the political police. Benckendorf repeatedly probed the background of Moscow students. Third Section operatives sometimes questioned university faculty members about students who had left the university more than a decade before. The number of "cases" developed, by itself, seemed to generate anxiety. The "dangers" uncovered were miniscule, but a number of students paid dearly for running afoul of one or another of these "investigations." In the Kritskii brothers "affair" in 1827, several students were expelled, some sent into the army. The evidence for their participation in "anti-government" conspiracy was astonishingly thin.

In 1831 similar punishments were meted out to the "Sungurov group." In this case the Third Section established that some sort of "group" existed and that some of its members knew socially some Poles. Other individuals were sentenced to exile, or to the army, for expressing any sort of sympathy with the Decembrists. The work of the Third Section told little or nothing about the university. But the time, attention, and sheer psychic energy that Nicholas and his police expended in "keeping watch" over the students at Moscow testified to the depth and strength of the fear that the Decembrist experience made a permanent feature of Nicholas' character.[17]

In the summer and fall of 1834, while Uvarov tried to persuade the tsar of the need for increases in the university budgets, a series of fires of unknown origin caused considerable panic in Moscow. Characteristically, Nicholas appointed a Special Commission to investigate. Meanwhile, the Third Section developed "information" that suggested a link between the fires and certain, but unknown, subversive elements in the university. Uvarov repeatedly postponed action, but finally agreed with Nicholas that it was "very useful" for him to inspect the university in the fall of 1834. Uvarov's report, completed in late November, assured the tsar that all was well. "Not speaking about the events which are currently the subject of investigation by a Special Commission," he wrote, "I found nothing whatever in the spirit of the university to merit criticism." There was a problem in Moscow, for some "inexperienced youth" were led astray by the periodical press. Thus the "danger" that existed was "outside the university." Even so, things were improving. The "step by step" replacement of those faculty members who "are completing their term of service" with "teachers who are more talented and better prepared to carry out the government's views" augered well. Finally, Uvarov said that he had spent "several days observing

17. An introduction to the "conspiracies" among the students and the government's response is in Martin Malia, *Alexander Herzen and the Birth of Russian Socialism* (Cambridge, 1961), 134–137. Nasonkina, *Moskovskii universitet*, provides a very detailed discussion of this topic. See especially pp. 169–185 on the Kritskii brothers, pp. 222–266 on the Sungurov group. In 1876 the Third Section drew up a report concluding that the Kritskii brothers made "an insignificant attempt to form a secret society in Moscow" and that the Kritskii and Sungurov cases "were quickly proved to be isolated instances of no political importance." P. S. Squire, *The Third Department: The Political Police in the Russia of Nicholas I* (Cambridge, 1968), 200, note 2. This "Jubilee Report" did not point out that one of the Kritskii brothers died in prison, where he and others were held for years without trial, and that many others' lives were ruined, wasted in prison or exile.

the severe examinations" being given in each faculty. "The results were in general excellent."[18]

Uvarov had much his own way with the journal of the ministry and doubtless was pleased to report that "results" were "excellent" at Moscow. He was not successful, however, in all his dealings with the tsar. In June 1835 he admitted an important failure, for it was clear that the budget increases he had been working for would not be forthcoming.[19] Waiting for them no longer, he asked Speranskii to take on the task of drawing up the final draft for the general statute for the universities.

Nearly ready, in June 1835, to forward the draft of a general statute for the universities, Uvarov first decided what role the universities should have in supervising the schools of their districts. The article published in his journal on the Prussian system already indicated the decision that Uvarov had come to favor. On 16 June he sent the tsar the Committee's recommendation to remove supervision of the lower schools from the responsibility of the universities and to turn it over to the curators. "The Committee on the organizations of schools," he wrote, concluded that "thirty years of experience has shown the inadequacy of the present system of supervising the lower schools through the universities. First, the professors . . . have neither the time nor the means to provide in practice direction for the gymnasia and schools. Second, if in other states the supervision of the schools is not entrusted to the universities, how much less convenient it is for our universities to direct schools which are spread over distances of three and four thousand versts." Uvarov reported that the committee unanimously endorsed Speranskii's recommendation to assign supervision of the schools to the curators. Assigning supervision of the lower schools to the curators removed that function from men who were paid to serve as university teachers and thus sacrificed one of the chief advantages of the previous

18. TsGIAL, f. 735, op. 10, d. 103, *listy* 1–3 (Nicholas-Uvarov correspondence, 31 August and 2 September 1834), *listy* 4–12 (Uvarov to Nicholas, 28 November 1834).

19. Allister, "Reform," 120–122, summarizes Uvarov's requests to the tsar and Kankrin, the Minister of Finance. In 1831 Kankrin sponsored the foundation of a Practical Technological Institute in St. Petersburg, under the auspices of the Ministry of Finance, which indicated his views of the sort of education most suitable for Russia at that time. The school remained small and not particularly successful, in part at least because Kankrin was loath to fund it adequately. See W. M. Pintner, *Russian Economic Police under Nicholas I* (Ithaca, 1967), 94–96.

arrangements, its low cost. The new arrangement required the appointment of a new set of assistants to the curators, at a projected expense of 122,300 rubles a year.[20]

With the lower schools question out of the way, the committee turned its attention to Speranskii's draft of the general university statute. Uvarov added to the draft the right for the minister to make appointments to the university faculties. He had, in fact, been doing just that in staffing St. Vladimir University during the previous year. Nonetheless, Speranskii objected and suggested instead that the minister have the right to make recommendations to the faculty council, which would proceed then in the normal way. Speranskii was supported on this point by Balugianskii and Stroganov. Uvarov seemed ready to agree, but at this point came an intervention from a member of the committee who previously had been all but invisible, Count N. A. Protasov. A rich noble whose own education was entirely with private tutors, Protasov had reached the peak of a military career in combat against Polish revolutionaries in 1831. Having thus earned the tsar's esteem, he was appointed to the committee on the organization of schools. Protasov denounced "the opinion of several members of this committee that persons who are engaged in academic work must be exempted from the general rules of service." Protasov found it simply outrageous that academics should vote on the selection of their peers, for that sort of "independence is not given even to the most important officers of the civil administration." He thought the right to select faculty members should belong to an "authority which is free from the spirit of parties and intrigue which has so often disoriented the activities of the scholarly class." Moreover, this would "tend to harmonize our universities, up to now following irrelevant foreign examples, with the spirit of other state institutions of our fatherland." Nicholas' comment was brief: "I agree completely with Count Protasov." The draft for the new statute, consequently, provided the minister with the right to make faculty appointments.[21]

20. *Sbornik postanovlenii*, II, 955–960, prints Uvarov's report and the *ukaz* to the Senate. Quotations 955, 958. Speranskii's recommendation, which Uvarov summarized in his report, is printed in A. A. Kochubinskii, "Graf Speranskii i universitetskii ustav 1835 g.," *VE*, 1894 (May), 29–31. This matter is usually mistakenly described as a major diminution of university autonomy. See, e.g., Alston, *Education in Tsarist Russia*, 34.

21. Rozhdestvenskii, *Istoricheskii obzor*, 243–244. On Protasov, see Galskoy, "Ministry," 154–158.

The statute of 1835, signed into law on 26 July, was designed, said its introduction, to "complete the organization of the higher academic institutions and to bring them to the appropriate level."[22] Completing this work apparently called for no other statement of goals, for the new statute made none, not even a repetition of the old. Nonetheless, the goal remained clear: the formation of able service men for all the branches of the public services. Those elements which in the experience of thirty years seemed to distract from that goal were altered or dropped altogether. Directing the lower schools of the district, management of the censorship function, and maintaining its own court for its own members had proved time-consuming burdens, rather than the cherished rights that LaHarpe, Parrot, and others among the early reformers had projected, at least for Russian-born and trained members of the faculties. All three elements disappeared from this statute. All three of these functions remained in Lieven's draft of 1832, which Uvarov sent back to committee upon his appointment as minister. All three remained in effect in the Dorpat district, to which the 1835 statute did not apply. But the experience of the "Russian" universities, to which the new statute did apply, made dropping all three seem a useful reform.

The faculties were three: medicine, law, and philosophy, though philosophy was divided into two sections, each with its own dean. Thus, four deans were to be elected from among and by the faculties of each unit. The council of the university was composed of the professors and extraordinary (i.e., associate) professors, under the chairmanship of the rector. The "directorate" consisted of the rector, the deans, and the "sindik." The sindik was the official appointed by the curator to take charge of the administration of the university chancellery. He was also required to observe all council meetings. In the event that, in the sindik's judgment, a decision of the council was contrary to law, he was to so inform the council, with a written statement of his opinion. The council could appeal this judgment to the ministry through the curator.

The council was obligated, first, to meet "according to a regular

22. The statute is printed in *Sbornik postanovlenii*, II, 969–995. Quotations 969, 973, 974, 976. For summaries, see Rozhdestvenskii, *Istoricheskii obzor*, 244–249; Allister, "Reform," 120–134. Most histories of individual universities also provide summaries of the 1835 statute, e.g., Tikhomirov, *Istoriia moskovskogo universiteta*, I, 114–117; Grigor'ev, *S. Petersburgskii universitet*, 108–110.

schedule, in hours free from teaching." All members were required to take part. In the event that a faculty member could not attend a council meeting, he was required to submit a statement of his reason in writing to the rector, who would enter the statement in the minutes of the meeting. If having a clear "rule" was a solution, then this part of the statute met the many complaints made over the years regarding faculty members who shirked their responsibilities in the council. Moreover, no decision made by the council would be valid if the meeting was not attended by at least two thirds of the members eligible, testimony to the framers' fear that many faculty members might continue to avoid participation in council affairs.

The council's responsibilities were to elect the rector and to elect the professors and adjuncts, though the minister had the right to make appointments too. The council was also to "judge the recommendations of the faculties concerning measures to improve the teaching of all subjects in the university" and to "supervise the distribution of courses and schedules." In fact, everything relating to courses, degrees, examinations, and all other academic matters were the responsibility of the council. The council was also obliged to provide the curator with a monthly report of its work and an annual report that described its "most important activities and decisions" for transmission through the curator to the ministry.

The "directorate" of the rector, deans, and sindik was also required to meet "regularly in hours free from teaching." The sindik, the legal officer chosen by the curator, not from among the teaching faculty, was to take part as an equal with the other members. The directorate was charged with the "economic and police administration" of the university. Under the first charge, the directorate was required "to keep the treasury in a safe palce, under the rector's key." The directorate was responsible for the payment of all accounts, including the distribution of the state students' stipends. The directorate had the right to make changes in any given item, up to 500 rubles. A shift of 500 or more required the authorization of the curator, of more than 1,000 the concurrence of the minister.

In "police" matters, the directorate was to preserve "decent good order among the persons who belong to the university, to maintain the cleanliness of the buildings, and to safeguard them from the danger of fire." Criminal matters were to be turned over to the "local courts, to which must be referred also all matters at issue between university members, without any kind of participation of

the university." The value of the university court in such matters
clearly had not impressed the framers of the statute. The chief university police official would no longer be an elected faculty member
but an officer appointed by the directorate. In addition to seeing to
the cleanliness and security from' fires of the buildings, this officer
also was to see that "no one who does not belong to the family of a
member of the university takes up permanent residence in a university building without the permission of the directorate." Finally,
"the promulgation of detailed internal police regulations is the duty
of the directorate, with the confirmation of the curator."

Overall supervision of the university was entrusted to the curator,
now required to live in the city of his university, though he remained
a member of the ministry Main School administration. He could, if
he so chose, preside over both council and directorate meetings. He
could also appoint his assistant curator, with the approval of the
tsar. The rector, elected by and from among the full professors for a
four-year term, also required the confirmation of the tsar. The rector
was required to see to it that all members of the university carried out
"in detail the obligations assigned to them" and that "university
teaching is carried out successfully." The rector could "warn" and
report to higher authority any who failed to meet their obligations.
He also could preside at the meeting of any faculty he chose and was
to "safeguard" the university press. The rector, thus, was responsible for the "papers of those who enter the university."

Another official, appointed by the curator, was the "inspector."
The inspector was to maintain "special and close observation over
the morality of all who study in the university." Just what he was to
look for was left to the curator, who was charged with providing
the inspector with "detailed regulations, which take into account
local conditions." The inspector reported, not to the directorate,
but to the curator, though he could be invited to participate in
meetings of the directorate, on which occasion he would have a vote
equal to that of any other member. The separation of the academic
and financial-police administration of the university, called for so
often by so many in both the universities and ministry, appeared to
be accomplished at last. Nonetheless, the chief agency, the directorate, was composed of but six men, five of whom not only were
elected by the professors but continued to serve as professors. Since
the faculty group that would elect them, and with whom they
would continue to serve, usually would number not many more

than thirty-five and often enough formed a closed, tightly knit community, it remained to be seen whether the separation between academic and purely administrative-police matters would be as clear in practice as in law.

The "chairs," the fields of study, in the medical faculty, the law faculty, and the second section (mathematics-physics) of the philosophy faculty, were different from the old medical faculty and the law and science divisions of the Kiev statute in no important respect. The chair of theology, apart from any faculty, introduced in the Kiev statute, was maintained. The first section of the philosophy faculty was in essence the old moral-political science and literature faculties, merged but with the law courses removed. There were differences from the Kiev statute. Russian and world history again became two separate chairs, and the chair of eastern languages, included in the 1804 statute if not often taught, was reinstated. A new chair was added in Slavic languages and literatures, thereby extending to the others the chair successfully introduced at Moscow in 1811. Finally, political economy, missing from the Kiev statute, was reinstated.

Some important matters were not taken up. The statute gave no directions regarding the contents of instruction in any subject. No mention was made of the social class of students or of the suitability of various sorts of instruction for any particular "condition" in life. These were not oversights. These were matters that had received much attention in the deliberations of the various committees since 1824. In May 1830 Balugianskii submitted a draft for a university statute that made very detailed, specific recommendations for each.[23] His draft began with a word-for-word copy of the 1804 statute's statement of goals (and a footnote reference to that document) that the "university is the highest learned organization, founded for the dissemination of learning. In it youth prepare for entrance to the various branches of state service." Balugianskii proposed a four-faculty university, of (1) law and politics, (2) medicine, (3) physics-mathematics, (4) philosophy-literature, whose graduates would be

---

23. TsGIAL, f. 1260, op. 1, d. 341, *listy* 12–14, 61–62, 74. This draft, dated "May 1830," circulated among members of the committee. Balugianskii also wrote a "short explanation" of his draft for the information of the Commission on the composition of the laws. *Ibid.,* d. 342. Balugianskii (d. 341, *list* 95) recommended turning over the management of the lower schools to the directorate, but also (d. 342, *listy,* 43–44) pointed out that the lower schools could be managed by the curators or the universities, with advantages and disadvantages either way.

trained with specific service requirements in mind. The law and politics faculty, for example, would "train youth primarily for the civil services in which are required basic knowledge of law and political science . . . the ministry of justice, of foreign affairs, of finance, of internal affairs, and of public education," though the faculty of philosophy-literature was suggested for those planning a career as "academics." Students in the physics-math faculty were to be "trained primarily for military and naval service."

Balugianskii recommended a very detailed statement of the admission requirements, including an explanation of the significance of Tsar Alexander's November 1811 *ukaz* and the procedure for admission for students from "obligated" classes. He also gave a list that, in addition to gentry and officers, said that admission was open to "students from the clergy, raznochintsy, merchants, townsmen, state peasants, and other free classes. . . . " Balugianskii also proposed some detailed suggestions for the faculty's teaching, including the note that "all must realize that the citizen's first obligation before God is to give true faith to his Lord. In teaching, in conversations, in all ways, it must be made clear that in truth there is *no authority which does not come from God.*" Balugianskii had not changed his mind about some positions that he took during Runich's "investigation." His draft gave the council the right to appeal to the ministry when it disagreed with any step taken by the curator. Students too would have received detailed instructions, had Balugianskii's recommendation been taken. Among other things, he warned against "making noise during class or in the library." Moreover, "all students must attend church on Sundays and holydays and during the time of the liturgy they must obey the rules of the church. Those who make noise during the services will be brought to the dean, or on repetition to the rector, who may have them arrested for several hours or several days, depending on the degree of guilt." [24]

This sort of detail, on matters great and small, Uvarov thought best omitted, leaving it to the faculty council to manage the contents and schedules of the courses and to the curator, rector, deans, and inspectors to work out the detailed rules that they would administer in their schools. It was unlikely that this demonstrated Uvarov's great confidence in the prudent wisdom of the university

24. *Ibid.*, d. 341, *listy* 35–36, 75, 95, 173, 180.

faculties, which he was still trying to "renew" by pressuring many individuals to accept early retirement. It was more likely that he found it useful to leave many things unsaid, particularly detailed statements of the goals and methods of education or any mention of social class, because the tsar had demonstrated a propensity to re-act in unfortunate ways to matters placed before him, issuing spur-of-the-moment orders, literally in margin comments. Indeed, the statute of 1835 ignored some of the questions in which Nicholas had expressed interest, as well as his specific order forbidding the retention of an elected rectorship. It also marked significant modi-fication from the Balugianskii drafts, or the Lieven draft of 1832. Most important, while pruning away the faculty members' involve-ment in running the lower schools, courts, and even the administra-tion and discipline of their own universities, the Uvarov statute re-tained the heart of the 1804 reform. As in the 1804 statute, the new one proposed to give civil servants-in-training, and future gym-nasium teachers too, an education that was in fundamentals classi-cally orientated liberal arts and sciences, whose academic degrees continued to be linked to ranks in the Table of Ranks provided by Peter.

The medical faculty was the obvious exception, in Russia as else-where, for the medical student took a five-year program, compared with four in the other faculties, which was not only technical-scientific but entirely vocational. The medical faculty also added chairs, from six in the 1804 statute to ten in the new. This, in com-bination with the additions to the law and philosophy faculties, raised the total number from twenty-eight to thirty-nine. Professors' salaries were increased from 3,000 to 4,000 at Kazan and Kharkov, to 5,000 in the two capitals. Increases in the salary and number of professors accounted for part of the budget increase for each uni-versity, from 130,000 in the 1804 statute (though in fact the uni-versities had secured increases meanwhile, Moscow up to 220,000) to 450,000 for Moscow, 370,000 for Kazan and Kharkov, and 270,000 for St. Petersburg, the one of the four universities that con-tinued to lack a medical faculty. Balugianskii's plan had called for a medical faculty for St. Petersburg and a total budget for the univer-sity of 540,000. The final numbers, thus, while providing substan-tial increases, were much short of what many members of the minis-try and the committee had worked to obtain.

Censorship was a state function assigned to the universities in

1803–1804 primarily to get this function away from the police and into the hands of men whose learning and judgment the reformers thought could be counted on to promote the national welfare. The management given this function by Golitsyn and Shishkov had not achieved the original reformers' goals, for they yielded little to any police agency in either arbitrariness or severity. Count Lieven resisted with courage the increasing intrusion of the police, but by 1830, though many of the primary censorship functions were still carried out by ministry and university personnel, the Third Section's "review" of the work in fact amounted to shifting the function to the police in most important respects. The statute of 1835 recognized what had happened. The university censor committee lost its responsibility to serve as the primary censorship agency for its district. Though the ministry continued to have overall responsibility, and university personnel often served as censors, the university as an institution remained charged only with censorship of materials published by the university press itself, and for materials imported or otherwise obtained for the use of members of the university. Put another way, though it was not underscored in the text that Uvarov presented to Nicholas for ratification, the university remained in this matter autonomous, for it, alone among state or private institutions, had the right of self-censorship.

Thus, the statute of 1835 not only kept the main thrust of the 1804 statute in academic matters, offering liberal arts education as the best way to prepare state servitors, it also kept much of the "autonomy" of the universities themselves. The election of the rector was important symbolically as well as in practice, for it had been long discussed and contested in the committees that worked at this reform for more than a decade. The university also wrote its own internal police rules, and managed its own censorship. Count Protasov would have been quite correct to point out that such rights in Russia were seldom given to even the most important officers of the civil administration.

2. The Questions Behind

The statute of 1835, and the thirty years of experience that lay behind it, provided answers to many of the questions raised in 1802–1804. But, often enough, the answers remained difficult to grasp, even when repeatedly given. Confusion and ambiguity continued to cloud the issues. For example, questions still arose regarding the promotion of students from lower classes upon completion of the university course. In August 1840 St. Petersburg University forwarded to the ministry, for transmission to the Senate, the list of those from "obligated" classes who had completed successfully examinations for the student diploma that year, requesting certification of their "release from obligated class." But one was the son of a Finnish carpenter employed by the Evangelical Church in St. Petersburg. Since Finnish carpenters did not constitute a guild or commune, *obshchestvo*, or "owner," there was no one to provide legally the required "liberation certificate." The award of the student's degree was delayed until October 1841, when Uvarov obtained, in place of a certificate, the testimony of the State Secretary for the Grand Duchy of Finland, Count Armfelt, that "all natives of Finland of all classes have the same right to choose their futures according to their own wishes, and even persons of the low classes may, equally with persons of all other classes, open to themselves the path to state service by study in a university." [25]

There were yet few Russians in a position to "open to themselves the path to state service," or any other. That generous hope of the early reformers had not worked out; in fact, it was all but impossible. That hope was founded on an assumption not uncommon among the enlightened that Russia was held back by forces and institutions that stifled the naturally fruitful creativity in people. That assumption proved wrong. Opening paths to free the forces of society, removing the obstacles to social change, had not worked out because such forces barely existed. Given an opportunity to choose, few members of Russian society chose to embark on the arduous task of social reformation that would begin by accepting the unpredictable consequence of drastic change in their own lives. That they were prevented from voluntarily taking up such change mainly by the autocracy's chains, which kept them locked in their status and places, was deeply believed by many intellectuals, whether enlightened rationalists or their romantic successors. But the experience of the schools made that view difficult to credit, for those who had expected, in hope or fear, significant social change to follow the reforms in 1802–1804, had been proved mistaken.

25. TsGIAL, f. 733, op. 23, d. 150, *listy* 1–2 (Curator St. Petersburg, to ministry, 22 August 1840), 16 (Count Armfelt to Uvarov, 14 October 1841), 17 (Uvarov to curator, 23 October 1841).

The absence of significant social change was important not only because three decades of experience made clear that the hopes of a Parrot and the fears of a Zavadovskii were equally unrealistic, but also because it required altering some of the terms of the original reform. Removing responsibility for the lower schools from the university was a benefit for the universities. It was also a confession that guiding and stimulating the development of a national network of primary schools was beyond the capacity of the only institutions in Russia likely to take this responsibility as a serioius, desirable, enterprise. While the universities grew and strengthened themselves, the village and even *uezd* schools remained weak and undernourished. Though the universities continued to maintain Pedagogical Institutes of state-supported students who trained for assignment to teaching in lower schools, the plans of a LaHarpe, or of Alexander I himself, to bring light and learning to the villages of Russia remained but plans. Worse, it had been realized that the task was beyond the capacities of the universities and so it was assigned to the curators, who had no more, perhaps fewer, resources than had the universities' school committee.

Uvarov more than once praised this step as wonderfully successful, but that he knew that in reality he was accepting defeat is suggested by two articles he published in 1834 in his journal, one on the public schools of Prussia, another on those of the St. Petersburg district. The total enrollment in the St. Petersburg district was reported as 8,778, of which 2,326 were in private schools. In the smallest of the eight school districts of Prussia, Posen, the enrollment figure was 96,812.[26] Posen, Prussia's Poland, was small and poor. Yet, the difference between Russia and even this nearest neighbor to the West was made clear by such numbers. They indicated that there was little another government-sponsored reform could do for schools for the masses.

Uvarov did not make explicit the comparisons. He seemed to realize that it was not often helpful to compare Russia with nineteenth-century advanced great powers, such as Great Britain or France, for with such states Russia could compete only militarily. Instead, in the early 1840s he simply reported, accurately enough, great progress in the development of the lower schools, noting that enrollment in village schools had grown to nearly 100,000 pupils, an increase

26. *ZhMNP*, 1834 (No. 1), 54, 80.

of almost forty percent in a decade.[27] Proud though Uvarov said he was to report such progress, the figures he gave helped to show why he had in reality given up on this aspect of the original reform. Uvarov in the 1830s and the reformers in 1802–1804 knew that the government could not finance village schools all over the vast Russian empire, and it made no effort to do so. Instead, they tried to encourage as much local initiative and effort as possible, to make effective use of state-sponsored teacher training and other forms of support, including occasional financial assistance for particular needs.

A similar policy was taken at the introduction of the Felbiger village schools in the Habsburg Empire under Maria Theresa. After a decade, the village schools of Austria and Bohemia enrolled over 200,000 pupils. After four decades the Russian village schools had not much more than half that number. Even Ireland, a poor peasant country run by absentee landlords, developed village schools. In 1831 the British government organized a National Board of Education for Ireland whose principal program was to offer matching funds to support schools in those localities which would provide schools for themselves. Within two years, nearly 800 "Board Schools" came into existence, enrolling more than 100,000 pupils. A decade later there were nearly 5,000 such schools, with more than half a million pupils. Rural Ireland, with less than one tenth Russia's population, provided schools for five times more pupils than Russia. Thus, other poor rural societies provided village schools, often but not always with the leadership of local clergy, on a scale that made it clear that Russia lacked something essential to make successful such a reform. Uvarov made no effort to explain why Russia could not match other poor rural societies in the local initiative necessary to make a success of village schools. Instead, he accepted the lesson of experience: that Russia still lacked the culture, wealth, and social development that made formal education seem desirable to many in other parts of the European world. He

27. S. S. Uvarov, *Desiatiletie Ministerstva narodnago prosveshcheniia 1833–1843* (St. Petersburg, 1863), 103–105. Accurate statistics were difficult to obtain from the schools and some computational, or perhaps typographical, errors mar Uvarov's report. Nonetheless, the rough magnitudes seem beyond reasonable doubt. The discussion of Uvarov's work with schools below university level in Whittaker, *Uvarov*, 128–151, makes obsolete all earlier treatments.

chose to concentrate on the areas in which he thought it possible to achieve success.[28]

Even there, in the universities, the lesson of the experience of thirty years showed that it was asking too much to hope that students would always take seriously their responsibilities to God, tsar, and fatherland and thus avoid cheating and fraud, let alone the drunken violence that life in a society much influenced if not dominated by the ethos of serfdom made almost second nature. The reform in the 1830s, thus, included the introduction in all the universities of yet another disciplinary code for students, as well as the reassignment of discipline functions to officials who were not teaching faculty. The generous hope that the self-motivation of faculty and students would suffice to promote good self-government, free from fraud or contention, had proved misplaced. Aside from the dismissal of some of the more egregious offenders, particularly those who made a career of masking their deeds in a verbal cloud of appeals to religion, patriotism, and any other noble value that came to mind, the reformers had few options if they meant to continue the heart of the original reform. Thus, they made changes in the administrative pattern of the universities in order to minimize the importance, if not the prevalence, of "intrigue" and the "spirit of parties" in the faculty and student bodies of the universities.[29]

28. The most detailed recent study, Mary Daly, "The Development of the National School System, 1831–40," *Studies in Irish History presented to R. Dudley Edwards,* A. Cosgrove and D. McCartney, eds. (Dublin, 1979), 156, points out a "high degree of continuity" since most schools that became board schools in the 1830s "were already in existence prior to 1831." In the Habsburg case, the government sometimes did assume financial responsibility in areas considered too poor to build and staff schools with local resources. These areas were confined to the southern border districts. O'Brien, "Maria Theresa's Attempt," *Paedagogica Historica,* v. 10, 542–65; Adler, "Habsburg School Reform," *SR,* V. 33, 23–45. Walker, "Popular Response," *History of Education Quarterly,* 1984, 527–543, has demonstrated that local initiative, founding and supporting village schools in the reign of Alexander I, was much more extensive than previously realized. Nonetheless, local, private activity was far less extensive, and depended much more completely on the central government's initiative, than developments in other poor rural societies.

29. Many scholars have pointed out that the tsarist state was not often willing to countenance seriously signs of independence in the schools. For examples, see P. L. Alston, "Recent Voices and Persistent Problems in Tsarist Education," *Paedagogica Historica,* XIV (1976), 203–215; W. L. Mathes, "The Process of Institutionalization of Education in Tsarist Russia, 1800–1917," *Russian and Slavic History,* D. K. Rowney, G. E. Orchard, eds. (Columbus, 1977), 26–48; Allen Sinel, "Review Essay: Problems in the Periodization of Russian Education: A Tentative Solution," *Slavic and European Education Review,* 1977 (No. 2), 54–61; Judith E. Zimmerman,

While it would be unwise to underestimate the importance of greed, willfull selfishness, or more passive failings such as simple laziness, among both faculty and students, there was a more important factor explaining the failures of the reform. Russia's poverty was so deep and so general that it distorted and conditioned every aspect of life. The ramifications for the schools were many, from the desperate poverty of students who walked many miles, living a hand-to-mouth existence in order to survive at all, to the state's inability to provide budget increases that might include livable salaries for many teachers. An important result of Russia's poverty was the condition of the village schools. Since the central government could not reach down into the villages to provide state-funded public education, little was provided at all. The contrast was striking even with Poland and Ireland, poor and conquered countries that nonetheless found the resources to maintain village schools on a scale far beyond the Russian. The poverty of the Russian villages not only conditioned the habits and thus limited the abilities of the students who came out of them and made unlikely local initiative in providing local schools; it also limited the impact of the universities. Students who left the village, who somehow managed to "open to themselves the path to their own happiness," to cite again the 1803 statement of the reformers' expectations, seldom could be persuaded that the path should lead them back to the village.

Perovskii, newly appointed curator at Kharkov, in 1825 sent in a report deploring the "evil behavior," the drunken disorderliness and so on, of too many students. He said their evil behavior kept them from "success in their studies." The new curator thought he could explain that behavior, for he pointed out that the state students realized that if they achieved success and were graduated, they would be sent out into the villages as teachers, a fate they viewed "as though it were a punishment."[30] That view was widely held. In 1831 the young Belinskii, a student at Moscow, wrote a play that he confidently expected would be a huge success, bringing him "at least around six thousand" rubles. He submitted his play to the

"The Uses and Misuses of Tsarist Educational Policy," *History of Education Quarterly*, v. 16 (1976), 487–494. The point to add here is that the attempt to rely on the independent self-motivation of both students and faculty, made in the universities' first period, produced results that the university faculties, as well as Uvarov, found not worth the cost.

30. Bagalei, *Opyt istorii*, II, 943.

university committee for censorship, having included in his work thanks to the "wise and solicitous government" that worked toward "completely wiping out" the evils the play portrayed. Nonetheless, the faculty committee judged his play very unfavorably. Shaken, Belinskii confided his worst fears to his roommate. "I'm dead and done for," he exclaimed, "they will send me to a forced labor camp." His roommate thought that unlikely. "The worst they can do," he replied, "is send you out as a village school teacher."[31]

The students were not wrong. The low intellectual and moral standards of the villages were matched by the low standards in food, housing, even elementary sanitation, and obviously in cultural life. The standard of life that appalled newly appointed foreign faculty members in Kazan or Kharkov were, compared to those in the villages, a marvelous step up. Naturally then, if the reform was to depend on the voluntary self-motivated action of those who took the path to their own happiness, then the village school would need to wait a long time before the impact of the university reform would reach down to it.

Nonetheless, the reform of 1803–1804 had achieved success by the mid-1830s. The main goal of the original reform was to develop universities, as distinct from professional-vocational schools of engineering, police, or military "science," or whatever. These universities had to be of sufficiently high quality that their work would make a palpable difference in the numbers and quality of men available to the state services, including the staffs of the *gymnasia* and universities themselves. By the mid-1830s, that work was accomplished, for the universities themselves were the chief fruit of the reform. They had developd faculties whose scholarship and competence as teachers was not only much improved over that available in the universities' first decade, but was sound and general enough to become self-replicating. Thus, the universities had developed sufficiently so that a new "reform" would not be needed every decade or so in order to keep up the necessary level of competence and work. In a society that, over the passage of more than a century, had seen launched many promising reforms only to see them falter, or disappear entirely, when the government turned its attention elsewhere, this was a development of much significance.

31. N. A. Argillanov, "Vissarion Grigor'evich Belinskii," *Moskovskii universitet* (Kovnator, ed.), 37, reprinted from *Russkaia Starina*, 1880 (May), 142. On Belinskii's play, see Bowman, *Belinskii*, 35–37.

It was clear, of course, that the professor in an autonomous Russian university was a civil servant. He cherished not only his state salary and pension benefits but also the opportunity to pursue a career in which he made an important contribution to the welfare of the nation, cooperating in conscience as well as in law with a state whose main goals, at least, he shared. Men whose educations were completed in the Dorpat Professors' Institute and Berlin University were not the majority of the faculties of the universities in the 1830s, but they and the force of their example proved important to the concept of the reform held by most university men. Humboldt's University of Berlin in the 1830s, while yielding to Göttingen nothing in academic excellence and regard for scholarly integrity, nonetheless recognized less ambiguously than had Göttingen at the turn of the century that the professor was a civil servant. His service and independent professional judgment were particularly prized because he conscientiously served not himself but society through the state. While Uvarov, characteristically, did not make explicit the comparison, the rise of Berlin as the model for Russian academics signalled an important shift in emphasis in the ideals to which Russian academics aspired.

The supply of students too was not so much improved as radically altered.[32] With the sole, but not too weighty, exception of Moscow, and the irrelevant-for-Russia experience of Vilna, the universities in their first decades could recruit students only by extraordinary means that did not promise well for the future. Since the reform was predicated in large measure on the usual Enlightenment concept of the nature of man, well stated by Brandes to the planners of the original reform, the autocratic state could not use the forceful techniques of a Peter the Great to produce a student body to educate for

32. The most successful effort at a survey of university enrollments is Iu. N. Egorov, "Reaktsionnaia politika tsarizma v voprosakh universitetskogo obrazovaniia v 30–50 kh gg. XIX v.," *Nauchnye doklady vyshei shkoly: istoricheskie nauki*, 1960 (No. 3), 60–75. The same data is presented, a bit more grossly, in the same author's "Studenchestvo Sankt-Peterburgskogo universiteta v 30–50 kh godakh XIX v.; ego sotsial'nyi sostav i raspredelenie po fakul'tetam," *Vestnik Leningradskogo Universiteta*, 1957 (No. 14), 7–19. Deficiencies in Egorov's work include doubtful choices, such as including clergy with *raznochintsy* while counting merchants separately, and giving results in tables and percentages, which conveys an impression of exactitude not possible to attain in view of the nature of the sources. Unfortunately, also, many of the conclusions presented do not flow from the evidence. With these caveats noted, Egorov's work may be as close to an accurate survey as the sources will permit.

"service." It was a remarkable success, thus, that by the mid-1830s the student bodies of the universities were coming to include volunteers from aristocratic families, not only poor gentry and clergy driven by need, and had become as steadily self-replicating as the faculties. Moreover, although deficiencies remained and every university annually sent in budget requests for more and better equipment, the gradual buildup of the necessary plant and tools was important too. Delayed, as with the development of faculty and student bodies, by limited resources complicated by fraud and incompetence, nonetheless by the mid-1830s libraries, laboratories, classrooms, and living quarters adequate to the task were in place.

At least as important as these successes in develoment in the faculty, student body, and physical facilities were the solutions worked out to some hard questions. The question of what should be taught, the curriculum, and to whom, the "class" question, were vexed and difficult for many reasons. The appropriate mix between liberal learning and professional training was not only a controverted matter in its own terms, as usual in most times and places, but in Russia in the early nineteenth century it was inextricably tangled with the even more vexed and difficult questions of class. Pnin and Balugianskii, who could hardly be counted among the "reactionaries," found it difficult to see wisdom in providing liberal education on an all-class basis. The statute of 1828 and 1835 made concessions to such views, and more sharply "reactionary" ones too, by backing off from the "encyclopedic" version of general liberal education, in which students were to take a course or two on nearly everything. Yet, pruning away many of the courses and chairs recommended by LaHarpe or Parrot, and adding vocational-professional training, as well as some formal instruction in religion, was not a retreat from the original reform. It was rather a prudent compromise to promote achievement of the goals of the original reform. Other compromises included in the statute of 1835 were the separation of the "economic" from the academic administration, and ending university responsibility for its court, for the lower schools, and for censorship. These steps were not designed as diminutions of university autonomy but as adjustments that time and experience showed were needed in order to facilitate achievement of the universities' main goals.

Though it would take time to realize it, the successful development of the universities meant that the state services came to receive ever better qualified candidates. Given the scope of the problem, and the continuation of serious needs, it was perhaps too easy to overlook how much was being accomplished. By mid-century, in some important respects the Russian civil service had changed, for the ever-increasing percentage of those in the middle and higher ranks, though not yet the lower, who had acquired a higher education was striking.[33] Other schools continued to train service personnel. Each ministry operated training programs, at least intermittently, and some were important enterprises. The Medical Academies of St. Petersburg and Moscow were operated by the military services and produced well-trained medical personnel, if in the class-vocational patterns familiar since Peter. The most important note regarding these schools, however, was their relatively small size. All the lycées together, for example, usually enrolled fewer students than the smallest university. The churches' seminaries were the most important alternative to universities as a source of trained civil servants, as distinct from military officers, but they operated for the most part at gymnasium level and by the 1830s their influence was clearly waning, the class-professional notion of the hereditary clergy being used as the nation's "learned class" giving way before the example, and success, of the university.

Russia remained undergoverned in most important respects, for the state could not deliver the range of services, including ordinary police protection, provided by the societies that the early and mid-nineteenth century regarded as modern.[34] Increase in the size of the bureaucracy was not among the high priorities of many who sought

33. Walter M. Pintner, "The Russian Higher Civil Service on the Eve of the "Great Reforms'," *Journal of Social History*, 1975 (spring), 55–68; W. M. Pintner, "The Social Characteristics of the Early Nineteenth Century Bureaucracy," *Slavic Review*, v. 29 (1979), 429–443. The seminaries, specifically as an alternative to the university system, are well described in Christopher B. Becker, "The Church School in Tsarist Social and Educational Policy from Peter to the Great Reforms," (unpublished Ph.D dissertation, Harvard, 1964), especially 90–199 on the Alexandrine era and its consequences. A convenient listing of basic information on all the other "higher" schools of the empire is provided in Erik Amburger, *Geschichte der Behördenorganisation Russlands von Peter dem Grossen bis 1917* (Leiden, 1966), 467–501.

34. S. Frederick Starr, *Decentralization and Self-Government in Russia 1830–1870* (Princeton, 1972), 3–50, is a lucid analysis of this problem. At mid-century the Russian civil service, despite rapid growth, numbered not more than 1.4 per 1,000 of the population, compared with Great Britain's 4.1. "Such figures suggest," Starr concludes, "that what the government was doing badly in the provinces was not as important as what it was not doing at all."

reform in Russia. Even *chinovniki* routinely blamed evils of the time on the gross excesses of the bureaucracy, denouncing the corruption and stupidity of the crude, miserable creatures who manned the tsar's service. The only thing worse than the expansion of the bureaucracy was any conceivable alternative. The increase in the number and improvement in the quality of the servicemen was of capital importance to the ability of the Russian state to meet the needs of its populace, despite the continuation of serious shortcomings within the services.[35]

Uvarov was neither the first nor the last to believe deeply that a liberal arts education, the cultivation of the mind and sensibilities, *Menschenbildung*, was in some important way more effective in the long run in the education of servicemen than more practical, job-related vocational training. Nor was he the first or last to have difficulty spelling out precisely what constituted the nature of the liberal arts, or the particular advantage of liberal education, especially in including Latin or ancient history. He had no doubts, however, that the universities' course should stress history and the language and literature of the ancient classics, rather than "cameral sciences" or accounting. The curriculum of the universities remained, thus, in this important if mundane sense, a liberal arts program. Consequently, the services as they grew in size in the late 1840s and 1850s increasingly came to be manned by men who had at least some part of a liberal education at a respectably high level.[36]

35. The deficiencies are well presented in up-to-date form in Hans-Joachim Torke, "Das russische Beamtentum in der ersten Hälfte des 19 Jahrhunderts," *Forschungen zur Osteuropäischen Geschichte*, v. 13 (Berlin, 1967). See especially pp. 224–241 for an able summary of the literature dealing with the corruption in the services, especially theft of state funds. *Ibid.*, 209–221, presents some doubts regarding the inflated numbers sometimes given for the size, and growth, of the bureaucracy, but no doubts regarding the entirely negative consequences of the growth, expressed in the main as increase in paper-work, a "Papierflut." Torke deftly summarized his argument in "Continuity and Change in the Relations between Bureaucracy and Society in Russia 1613–1861," *Canadian Slavic Studies*, V (1971), 457–476, concluding that "in summary, until the Great Reforms of the 1860's there was much continuity, and the changes were trivial, touching only formalities. A change in the nature of the Russian bureaucracy and of Russian society, and consequently of their mutual relations, came about only in the second half of the nineteenth century" (*ibid.*, 474). Still, noting the service's ability and willingness to cooperate in the Great Reforms, Torke suggests (p. 475) "that apparently something had happened to the bureaucracy as well. It is more difficult to determine what occurred, since there was no major reform of the civil service." It is hoped that the present study makes it easier to understand what had occurred.

36. James C. McClelland, *Autocrats and Academics: Education, Culture, and So-*

The development of sound universities that produced an ever-growing body of able, well-motivated candidates for the civil services, the main goal of the original reform, was, therefore, successfully achieved. This success was not obvious to the tsar and many of his closest coworkers in the court and in other high places, who often saw not success but peril in this development. They regarded the universities as perils because they threatened change. This was what the university had been founded to do, to provoke and promote change, as indeed was appropriate for institutions that cherished, or at least praised, the legacy of Peter the Great. Neither lip-service nor heartfelt devotion to Peter's memory, however, could mask something important. The Russian state had been the promoter of change, the very engine of progress, since Peter's time. The state, seldom pushed into reform by popular demand, usually had to overcome resistance, not only of the gentry but of the church, merchants, and of many other groups as well. During the long reign of Nicholas I that era in Russia's history ended. The state no longer unambiguously thought of itself as the dynamic engine of change, though it could hardly deny its Petrine legacy, but rather came to represent the defense of the status quo. In 1847, indeed, Nicholas and others seriously considered a proposal to abolish the Table of Ranks, and thereby to turn Russia's nobility into a closed, hereditary class. An ennobling slot in the Table of Ranks would not then be the normal result of successful academic work in the universities. Closing the path to social mobility through promotion in the state services, this step would defend the status quo, but at a price that Uvarov condemned. He warned Nicholas that this plan would deny to the state the advantage of the willing service of talented "sons of fathers of unknown merit." The strength of the system was, Uvarov

---

ciety in Tsarist Russia (Chicago, 1979) traces the continuation of the state's agreement with the "academic intelligentsia" on liberal arts education, rather than vocational training, in the preparation of servicemen, to the final days of the empire in 1917. McClelland argues that both state and "academic intelligentsia" made a serious mistake in so doing. The literature on the civil services has grown of late to include a number of important studies on the development of the reforming as well as loyal and competent civil service men under Nicholas I. Among the best are Wortman, *Development of Russian Legal Consciousness,* especially 52–88, and W. Bruce Lincoln, "The Genesis of an Enlightened Bureaucracy in Russia 1825–1856," *Jahrbücher für Geschichte Osteuropas,* v. 20 (No. 3, 1972), 321–330; "Russia's 'enlightened' Bureaucrats and the Problem of State Reform 1848–1856," *Cahiers du monde russe et soviétique,* v. 12 (1971), 410–421.

insisted, that "the son of a famous lord or the richest land-holder on entering state service has no legal advantage, but only the advantage of constant zeal, in which he may be well matched by the son of a poor father." [37] Worse, if the state blocked the path to advancement through the universities, this would not only retract one of the main promises of the reform begun in 1802–1804, it would close the path to fulfilling lives to many who would cooperate with the autocracy, forcing people to find their own path, "their own understanding, their own judgment and dreams, not concerned with the government's goals." In sum, Uvarov continued to believe in the promise of a system that combined the autocracy and its Table of Ranks and the universities open to able sons of the low-born, to mark the path for all to follow to a happier future.

Thus, ambiguity came to mark the state's attitude, for Benckendorf, Kankrin, and many others counseled not only caution but resistance to change, while for Uvarov it was enough that the system he led was staffed by prudent, loyal men who would not push Russia precepitously into uncalled-for, perhaps dangerous, extremes. He could not doubt that the university system "opened the path" to ever-increasing numbers of men from the "obligated classes" to enter service in ennobling ranks. In time, this process probably would have a significant effect on the relations of the social classes, as well as on the government's services. In December 1844 Uvarov responded to a request from Nicholas for recommendations on how to "moderate the influx" of new men into the universities. He replied that any such steps would need to be implemented "quietly and unofficially" in order to avoid "clearly destroying the basic principles on which the state has operated for a whole century." [38] Uvarov knew, clearly enough, that Nicholas I would not willingly destroy the Petrine inheritance he was sworn to uphold. In June 1845 Nicholas raised the question again, asking, "Are there no means of making it difficult for *raznochintsy* to enter *gymnasia?*" [39] He meant, clearly, to ask: were there no means of defending the

37. "Vsepoddanneishaia zapiska . . . Uvarovym v fevrale 1847 goda," Evreinov, ed., *Grazhdanskoe chinoproizvodstvo*, 83. Iu. B. Solov'ev, *Samoderzhavie i dvorianstvo v kontse XIX veka* (Leningrad, 1973), 67, note 231, cites the TsGIAL number for this document, rather than Evreinov's book, and mistakenly interprets it as reactionary defense of noble privilege.

38. Rozhdestvenskii, *Istoricheskii obzor*, 255.

39. *Sbornik postanovlenii*, II, otedel ii, 631.

existing social order without sacrifice of the legacy of Peter? Uvarov dodged the question, replying with a simple recitation of the regulations on the requirements for "liberation certificates." But such technicalities were not Nicholas' concern. His anxious disquiet went deeper than that, for he correctly sensed that the success of the university reform presented a dilemma for those who most cherished the existing order. The success of the universities, when they achieved the goals set for them, inescapably worked, if in the very long run, to undermine the institutions and mores Nicholas cherished.

Uvarov promised more than once that the universities would provide education not dangerous to the state, but would blend successfully both modern learning and unshakeable loyalty to Russia's traditional values. But swearing loyalty to Petrine principles was to swear loyalty to a system that fostered significant change. To be sure, the fear of the university developed by Nicholas, and maintained in varying degrees to the end of the tsarist regime by those who shared his belief in the essential justice and rightness of the existing order, was in great part an irrational, if deeply felt, response to a "foreign" transplant. But it was also a response to the success of the university reform that was not mistaken, given the principles and expectations that animated it. The growth of fear of the university, and the life of the mind it nourished, among important elements of the state, thus, was one of the results of the success of the university reform.

Another result was the rise of the intelligentsia, that grouping of educated Russians—not, of course, all intellectuals or even very well educated—who came to oppose the state. In the mid-1830s that development was yet in the future, and far from a forgone conclusion. *Intelligenty* came from all classes, backgrounds, and abilities. They shared with many of the servicemen whose state they most bitterly opposed a commitment to change for Russia, for the universities nourished the growth of the intelligentsia at the same time that they fostered the growth of a state bureaucracy willing and able to effect meaningful reform. Except in terms of the personal psychology of individuals, there was nothing to distinguish the *intelligent* minority from the majority of their classmates who spent lives at work in one or another ministry, for the intelligentsia was formed from a cross-section of the student bodies, not different, particularly in moral values, from the student bodies at large.

One of the founders of the intelligentsia, Belinskii, in 1839 gave a

hint as to what they were about. "In the word tsar there is marvelously blended the consciousness of the Russian people," he
wrote. "Our *freedom* is in the tsar because of our new civilization,
our enlightenment, comes from him, just as from him comes our
life. One great tsar freed Russia from the Mongols and united its
separate parts, another even greater one brought it into the sphere
of a broader life; and heirs of both completed the work of their
predecessors. And that is why every step forward of the Russian
people, every movement of development in its life has been an act of
the tsar's powers." [40] The intelligentsia came to mean opposition to
the tsarist state, indeed to be synonymous with conscious-dedicated
opposition to the regime. Yet, it was clear that the intelligentsia
shared with the reforming bureaucracy, and indeed with the men
who launched the university reform, a commitment to promoting
"progress," change to benefit the well being of all Russian society.

Men able and willing to pursue such goals in substantial numbers
were one product of the university reform. Some of them soon, a
few in the 1840s, many in the 1860s, concluded with increasingly
desperate hostility that the "heirs" of that "greater" tsar who had
"brought [Russia] into the sphere of a broader new life" were am-
bivalent, if not flatly opposed, toward further "steps forward." Not
all rejected their former allegiance with the angry vehemence of
Belinskii, but the development was clear enough. The university reform had been mainly responsible for the birth of an educated, ar-
ticulate, and highly motivated opposition that was completely unlike
the opposition of old. Until the mid-nineteenth century, opponents
of the Russian state—the cossacks, or Old Believers, or such gentry
figures as Shcherbatov, or indeed Pugachev—fought against mod-
ernizing change in defense of old Russian ways. The intelligentsia
was an opposition that did not fight change, but instead fought the
state, the former force for change, convinced that the state had
turned itself into a defender of the status quo. [41]

40. Riasanovsky, *Parting of the Ways,* 214.
41. The rise of the intelligentsia is among the most thoroughly studied developments in Russian history and hardly needs extended comment here. The literature on
the subject is immense. For those whose main interest is the universities, rather than
the intelligentsia itself, the following works are especially useful. Riasanovsky, *Parting of the Ways,* 148–245, is a richly nuanced discussion. See also Alain Besançon,
Éducation et société en Russie dans le second tiers du XIX siècle (Paris, 1974),
which, despite its title, is a brilliant, if somewhat impressionistic, essay on the rise of
the intelligentsia. Daniel R. Brower, *Training the Nihilists: Education and Radicalism in Tsarist Russia* (Ithaca, 1975), is a detailed study of some four hundred

One day in August 1835 Nikitenko, in his capacity as censor, visited Uvarov to show him a manuscript of an article submitted by Senkovski. The article, with the fearless straightforwardness of the sycophant, argued that Frederick the Great of Prussia had developed a marvelously successful form of government, the "military autocracy," that met all the needs of modern society. Such a form of government was just what Russia needed and, *mirabile dictu,* had wisely attained. Uvarov, long disgusted with Senkovski's prostitution of his talents in vulgar journalism, told Nikitenko to remove all references to Russia from the article, thereby robbing it of its self-serving point. Then he talked on. The man who had just successfully managed the promulgation of a new university statute that preserved the best of the reformers' achievement and that provided prudent solutions for the problems encountered, betrayed no hint of elation at his success. Instead, he seemed almost weary at the prospect of what remained to be done. "We people of the nineteenth century," he said, "are in a difficult position; we live among storms and political upheavals. Peoples are changing their whole mode of life, all are renewing, changing, pressing ahead. In this situation, it is difficult to be independent, to set one's own course. But Russia is young yet, still fresh and need not endure, at least not now, such bloodly struggles. Well, that's my political system. I know what our liberals want, our journalists and their crowd: Grech, Polevoi, Senkovski and the others. But they will not succeed . . . If it is given to me to hold back Russia for fifty years from what [their] theories propose, then I will have carried out my responsibility and will die a happy man."[42]

Nikitenko's recollection of what Uvarov had to say cannot be taken as considered statements of policy. They were off-the-cuff remarks, made at the end of a long August day in the office. Nonetheless, there was in his remarks a serious and revealing note. Though the university reform was a success in important ways, much remained to be done before its impact on either the state services or

---

members of the radical intelligentsia in St. Petersburg, demonstrating conclusively that the intelligentsia came from a representative cross-section of the student population. For a summary of Soviet scholarship on the question, see V. R. Leikina-Svirskaia, "Formirovanie raznochinskoi intelligentsia v Rossii v 40-kh godakh XIX v.," *Istoria SSSR,* 1958 (No. 1), 83–104. Leikina-Svirskaia assumes that the rise of non-gentry through the schools was the main element in the development of the intelligentsia.

42. Nikitenko, *Zapiski i dnevnik,* I, 267, the diary entry for 8 August 1835.

the village schools could be felt. But Uvarov continued to believe that Russia was "young" and full of promise, and could be spared the turmoil that wracked her neighbors and destroyed their chances for progress as he saw it. The generous hope of the original reformers, that once the path was opened, people would follow it to peaceful happiness, had not worked out. Now it was necessary for the Minister of Education to cling to the worthwhile essentials of the earlier reform, but not to its utopian extremes. Given enough time to work its way thoroughly into the fabric of the national life, the successful establishment of sound universities could effect healthy change in every aspect of the developing nation, promoting, indeed, making possible, a future better for all. In short, in order to build upon the success of the university reform and capitalize on its potential for the development of the nation, Uvarov hoped that the tsarist state would have time to work it all out.

In the long run, perhaps, Uvarov was only restating a generous hope of his own, which would prove as misplaced, perhaps utopian, as that of the original reformers of 1803. They expected that "opening the path" would be enough to lead people to take "the path to their own improvement." Thirty years of experience had convinced Uvarov, and many others, that merely opening paths was not enough, that autocracy, if not Petrine force, was yet required for success in achieving the main goals of the original reform. While Uvarov never expressly said as much, it was clear that the schools, and most clearly the universities, concerned but a tiny minority. Most members of the low classes paid little interest in the schools because they correctly judged that the schools had little that was relevant to their lives and goals. Those few who took the path to improvement provided by the schools took it, not as a way to improve life in the village, but as a one-way road away from village life. Uvarov could justly conclude that the reform he codified had successfully developed native institutions of higher learning and had begun, at least, the provision of a civil service staffed by men who had the basic elements of a good liberal education. Yet he had also to recognize that so much would need to change significantly in order to achieve the remaining goals of the reform, that the fifty years he called for might not be too much.

The system Uvarov had refined into the statute of 1835 long outlived him. In essentials, indeed, it remained to the end of the life of Imperial Russia in 1917. This durability is the more remarkable since throughout the life of Imperial Russia the educational system was repeatedly counted a failure that needed reforming. The recurring waves of reform and reaction that marked the history of Imperial Russia seldom failed to include attempts to change the educational system. Yet, in most essentials the 1835 system was retained, for it seemed, to those who had to choose, the best solution of which Tsarist Russia was capable. There were those, then and since, who thought that what was needed was to turn Tsarist Russia into something else, whether a parliamentary democracy, or a socialist commonwealth, or a pre-Petrine autocracy, or another of the visions of the future held among nineteenth-century Russians. For them, the Uvarov solution was one of the obstacles in the path of progress and thus a failure that needed change. Those who agreed with Uvarov that it was worthwhile to work at making Tsarist Russia a viable modern state by developing its own values thought that the Uvarov system, or something very much like it, was the best solution. That system seemed to some a threat to autocracy and to the class system with which it was almost symbiotically entwined. Some, including Uvarov, faced that threat with equanimity. Others found it a pressing problem whose solution required the abolition of university autonomy and all-class admissions, as Nicholas I, Shishkov, and many of their successors down to 1917 repeatedly insisted. Thus, the note of confusion and ambiguity in the university reform need not be ascribed to the "enigmatic" character of its founder, Alexander I, for it was inherent in the situation itself.

Had Uvarov made the clear choice favored by Nicholas I, he might have eliminated a good deal of ambiguity and confusion. But Uvarov refused to make that choice, and he refused also to make its opposite, the promotion of complete autonomy for the universities and the end of all class considerations. There were those who vigorously supported that choice. N. I. Pirogov, national hero as well as leading academic and educator, called for that solution in his 1863 essay, "The University Question," which practically defined the terms of the question in the debate that continued for the remainder of the life of Imperial Russia.[43]

Uvarov would make neither of these clear choices. He clung instead to a system that maintained the stability and unity of autocracy while also providing as much autonomy and social mobility

43. For the essay "The University Question," see N. I. Pirogov, *Izbrannye pedagogicheskie sochineniia* (V. Z. Smirnov, ed., Moscow, 1953), 324–393. Even Piro-

through education as he thought could be had without paying too high a price in the risk of precipitous change and its unpredictable consequences. In 1847 Uvarov expressed alarm, indeed, because he feared that the tsar might make a clear choice by abolishing the Table of Ranks and making the nobility a closed hereditary estate. Uvarov not only believed in the virtues of the western university's autonomy; he treasured also the autocracy and its historic goals of bringing enlightenment and modernity to Russia. Many of Uvarov's contemporaries, many of his successors, and many historians since have concluded that the attempt to use the western university, with its claims to autonomy in learning, teaching, and even self-government, as the means of achieving the ends of an autocratic state was to erect a dilemma impossible to resolve. One could have either an autonomous university or an autocratic state. Thus, the critics have found that Uvarov's trust, and that of those who agreed with him, in the promise of autocratic Russia was misplaced, and that continuation of the basic elements in the Alexandrine university reform signified, not prudence unwilling to attempt more than could be achieved, but rather obstinacy that made the tsarist bureaucracy incapable of solving its problems.[44] The Alexandrine university reform and its protagonists have not dominated most perceptions of their time. Indeed, reading Karamzin or Pushkin, the Decembrists or Belinskii, provides an entirely different picture of what was going on, and what was important, in Russia in the first three decades or so of the nineteenth century. Nonetheless, the importance of what the university reform achieved by 1835 deserves acknowledgment. The Alexandrine university reform as refined under Uvarov gave Russia a set of institutions that met world standards in scholarship and academic service and that continued to serve Russia as long as Russia was governed by men unwilling in the long run to answer the university question by choosing one of the extreme solutions and by pressing that choice on the universities by truly draconian means.

---

gov, however, granted that "in the contemporary centralized state" the best that could be achieved in practice was making "the university as little bureaucratic as possible." *Ibid.*, 397. Pirogov's views are cogently reviewed in William L. Mathes, "N. I. Pirogov and the Reform of University Government 1856–1866," *Slavic Review*, v 31 (1972), 29–51.

44. The literature on this, the "University Question," is extensive. "Obstinate" is the term used by Klaus Meyer, "L'histoire de la question universitaire au XIX siècle," *Cahiers du Monde Russe et Soviétique*, XIX (1978), 302.

BIBLIOGRAPHY

Unpublished papers for this study are in the Central State Historical Archives in Leningrad (designated TsGIAL in the footnotes), for the most part in fonds 733 and 735. In a Soviet archive, the researcher rarely is able to see the collection, or consult an index or catalog. Rather, an assigned worker brings to the reading room materials chosen for the researcher. An unusually able "sotrudnitsa," Agnessa Valietinova Muktan, provided materials well chosen to meet my needs. Nonetheless, much of the material brought to me I recognized as published in one place or another over the past century. In the present study, whenever it is known to me, the published document is cited, rather than the archive, since it is relatively easy for an interested reader to consult a printed document but quite difficult to get to the archive. For those who have the opportunity to consult the archive collections in Leningrad, the footnotes provide complete reference for each document cited.

This bibliography lists everything cited in footnotes in the following categories: primary sources, works dealing with Russia from mid-18th to mid-19th century, works dealing with education, whether in Russia or abroad. Cited in footnotes but omitted in this bibliography are a few well-known general studies (e.g., Blum in note 3, chapter II) and works not focussed on our subject (e.g., Stone in note 53, chapter III).

Abramov, Iakov Vasilevich, *V. N. Karazin, osnovatel' Khar'kovskago universiteta, ego zhizn' i obshchestvennaia deiatel'nost'*. SPB, 1891.

Adler, P. J., "Habsburg School Reform among the Orthodox Minorities, 1770–1780," *Slavic Review*, v. 33 (1974), 23–45.

Aksakov, S. T., "Vospominaniia," *Sobranie sochinenii*. S. Mashinskii, ed., 4 v., Moscow, 1955, II, 7–163.

Aleksandrov, I. V., *Problemy geografii v Kazanskom universitete*. Kazan, 1964.

Aleshintsev, I., *Istoriia gimnazicheskago obrazovaniia v Rossii XVIII i XIX vek.* SPB, 1912.

Allister, Steven H., "The Reform of Higher Education in Russia during the Reign of Nicholas I, 1825–1855." Ph.D., Princeton University, 1974.

Alston, P. L., *Education and the State in Tsarist Russia.* Stanford, 1969.

————, "Recent Voices and Persistent Problems in Tsarist Education," *Pedagogica Historica,* XVI (1976), 203–215.

Amburger, Erik, *Geschichte der Behordenorganisation Russlands von Peter dem Grossen bis 1917.* Leiden, 1966.

Askenazy, Szymon, *Tsarstvo pol'skoe 1815–1830 gg.* Moscow, 1915.

Bagalei, D. I., *Istoriia goroda Khar'kova za 250 let ego sushchestvovaniia.* Kharkov, 1905.

————, *Kratkii ocherk istorii Khar'kovskago universiteta za pervyia sto let ego sushchestvovaniia 1805–1905.* Kharkov, 1906.

————, *Opyt istorii Khar'kovskago universiteta 1802–1835.* 2 v., Kharkov, 1893–1904.

————, *Prosvetitel'naia deiatel'nost' Vasiliia Nazarovicha Karazina.* Kharkov, 1893.

————, *Uchenye obshchestva i uchebnovspomogatel'nye uchrezhdeniia khar'kovskogo universiteta 1805–1905 gg.* Kharkov, 1911.

Baitsura, Tamara, *Zakarpatoukrainskaia intelligentsiia v Rossii v pervoi polovine xix veka.* Bratislava, 1971.

Barkhattsev, Sergei, "Iz istorii Vilenskago okruga." *RA,* 1874 (No. 1) 1149–1262.

Barsukov, N. P., "Mikhail Trofimovich Kachenovskii, professor moskovskogo universiteta, 1775–1842," *RS,* 1889 (October), 199–202.

Beauvois, Daniel, "Adam Jerzy Czartoryski jako kurator wileńskiego okręgu naukowego" *Przeglad Historyczny,* LXV (1974), 61–85.

————, "École et societé en Ukraine occidentale 1800–1825," *Revue du Nord,* No. 225 (1975), 173–184.

————, "Les Jésuites dans l'Empire Russe 1772–1820," *Dix-Huitieme Siècle,* No. 8 (1976), 257–272.

————, *Lumières et Société en Europe de l'Est: l'Université de Vilna et les écoles polonaises de l'Empire russe (1803–1832),* 2v., Paris, 1977.

Becker, Christopher B., "The Church School in Tsarist Social and Educational Policy from Peter to the Great Reforms." Ph.D., Harvard University, 1964.

Beletskii, A., *Istoricheskii obzor deiatel'nosti Vilenskago uchebnago okruga za pervyi period ego sushchestvovaniia 1803–1832.* Vilna, 1908.

Beliavskii, M. T., "Shkola i sistema obrazovaniia v Rossii v kontse XVIII stoletiia," *VMU,* 1959 (No. 2), 105–120.

Bendzius, A., *Vilnianus universitetas.* Vilna, 1966.

Besançon, Alain, *Éducation et société en Russie dans le second tiers du xixe siècle*. Paris, 1974.

Bieliński, Józef, *Uniwersytet Wilenski 1579–1831*. 2 v., Cracow, 1899–1900.

Bienemann, Friedrich, *Der Dorpater Professor Georg Friedrich Parrot und Kaiser Alexander I*. Reval, 1902.

Biograficheskii slovar' professorov i prepodavatelei

———, *Imperatorskago iur'evskago, byvshago derptskago, universiteta*. G. V. Levitskii, ed., 2 v., Iurev, 1902–1903.

———, *Imperatorskago kazanskago universiteta 1804–1904*. N. P. Zagoskin, ed., 2 v., Kazan, 1904.

———, *Imperatorskogo moskovskago universiteta*. 2 v., Moscow, 1855.

———, *Imperatorskago S.Peterburgskago universiteta 1869–1894*. SPB, 1896.

———, *Imperatorskago universiteta Sv. Vladimira 1834–1884*. V. S. Ikonnikov, ed., Kiev, 1884.

Black, J. L., *Citizens for the Fatherland: Education, Educators, and Pedagogical Ideals in Eighteenth Century Russia*. Boulder, 1979.

———, *Nicholas Karamzin and Russian Society in the Nineteenth Century*. Toronto, 1975.

Boehlingk, Arthur, *Friedrich Caesar Laharpe*. 2 v., Bern, 1925.

Borozdin, I. N., "Universiteti v Rossii v pervoi polovine XIX veke," *Istoriia Rossii v XIX veke*. A. I. Granat izd., SPB, 1907–11, I, 349–368.

Bowman, Herbert E., *Vissarion Belinskii 1811–1848: A Study in the Origins of Social Criticism in Russia*. Cambridge, 1954.

Brock, Peter, "The Struggle for Academic Freedom at the University of Cracow in the Early 1820's," *Polish Review*, IX (1964), 30–52.

Brodskii, N. L., ed., *Literaturnye salony i kruzhki pervaia polovina xix veka*. Moscow-Leningrad, 1930.

Bronner, F. K., *Professor Frants Ksaverii Bronner ego dnevnik i perepiska*. D. Naguevskii, ed., Kazan, 1902.

Brower, Daniel R., *Training the Nihilists: Education and Radicalism in Tsarist Russia*. Ithaca, 1975.

Brown, Edward J., *Stankevich and His Moscow Circle 1830–1840*. Stanford, 1966.

Bulich, B. N., *Iz pervykh let Kazanskago Universiteta*. 2 v., SPB, 1904.

Chaev, N., "Mikhail Aleksandrovich Maksimovich," *RA*, 1874 (No. 2), 1055–1087.

Chamcówna, Mirosława, *Jan Śniadecki*. Cracow, 1963.

Cheshkhin, E., "Studencheskiia bezchinstve v Derpte 1804," *RA*, 1887 (No. 10), 265–281.

Chirikov, G. S., "Timofei Theorovich Osipovskii, rektor khar'kovskago universiteta, 1820 g.," *RA*, 1876 (November), 463–490.

Christian, David, "The Political Views of the Unofficial Committee in
1801: Some New Evidence," *Canadian-American Slavic Studies*, v. 12
(1978), 247–258.
Chumikov, A. A., "Studencheskiia korporatsii S. Peterburgskom universite
v 1830–1840 (iz vospominanii byvshago studenta," *RS*, 1881 (Febru
ary), 367–380.
Cook, Gordon S., "Peter Ia. Chaadaev and the Rise of Russian Cultural
Criticism 1800–1830." Ph.D., Duke University, 1972.
Czartoryski, A. A., *Memoirs of Prince Adam Czartoryski*, Adam Gielgud,
ed., 2 v., London, 1888.
———, "Pis'ma Kniazia A. A. Chartorizhskago k N. N. Novosil'tsevu (iz
semeinago arkhiva gr. V. N. Panina," *Sbornik Russkago Istoricheskago
Obshchestva*, v. 9 (SPB, 1872), 431–443.
Daly, Mary, "The Development of the National School System, 1831–40,"
Studies in Irish History Presented to R. Dudley Edwards, A. Cosgrove
and D. McCartney, eds., Dublin, 1979, 150–163.
Dmiterko, Ia., D., "O razvitii materialisticheskoi filosofii na Ukraine,"
Voprosy Filosofii. 1951 (3), 108–118.
Dubrovin, N., ed., *Sbornik istoricheskikh materialov, izvlechennykh iz
arkhiva sobstvennoi ego imperatorskago velichestva kantseliarii*. v. 7–8,
SPB, 1895–96.
Dudareva, L. N., "Pedagogicheskaia podgotovka uchitelei v Peterburg-
skom universitete v xix veke," *VLU*, 1969 (No. 5), 141–144.
———, *Podgotovka uchitelia i razvitie pedagogicheskoi nauki v Peter-
burgskom-Petrogradskom universitete v period s 1819–po 1917 god*.
Avtoreferat dissertatsii. Leningrad, 1969.
Edwards, David W., "Count Joseph Marie de Maistre and Russian Educational Policy, 1803–1828," *Slavic Review*, v. 36 (1977), 54–75.
Egorov, Iu. N., "Reaktsionnaia politika tsarizma v voprosakh universitetskogo obrazovanii v 30–50 kh gg. xix v.," *Nauchnye doklady vysshei
shkoly: istoricheskie nauki*, 1960 (No. 3), 60–75.
———, "Studenchestvo Sankt-Peterburgskogo universiteta v 30–50 kh
godax xix v., ego sotsial'nyi sostav i raspredelenie po fakul'tetam," *VLU*,
1957 (No. 14), 5–19.
Entsiklopedicheskii slovar'. F. A. Brokhaus, I. A. Efron, izd., 41 v., SPB,
1890–1904.
Fedosov, I. A., "Moskovskii Universitet v 1812 godu," *Voprosy Istorii*.
1954 (6), 106–117.
Ferliudin, P., *Istoricheskii obzor mere po vysshemu obrazovaniiu v Rossii*.
Saratov, 1893.
Flynn, James T., "The Affair of Kostomarov's Dissertation: A Case Study of
Official Nationalism in Practice," *SEER*, LII (1974), 188–196.
———, "Magnitskii's Purge of Kazan University: A Case Study in the Uses

of Reaction in Nineteenth-Century Russia," *Journal of Modern History*, v. 43 (1971) 598–614.

———, "The Role of the Jesuits in the Politics of Russian Education 1801–1820," *Catholic Historical Review*, LVI (1970), 249–265.

———, "S. S. Uvarov's 'Liberal' Years," *Jahrbücher für Geschichte Osteuropas*. v. 20 (1972), 481–491.

———, "Tuition and Social Class in the Russian Universities: S. S. Uvarov and 'Reaction' in the Russia of Nicholas I," *Slavic Review*, v. 35 (1976), 232–248.

———, "V. N. Karazin, the Gentry, and Kharkov University," *Slavic Review*, v. 28 (1969), 209–220.

———, "Uvarov and the 'Western Provinces': A Study of Russia's Polish Problem," *SEER*, v. 64 (1986), 212–236.

Foigt, Karl K., *Istoriko-statisticheskiia zapiski ob Imperatorskom Khar'kovskom universitete i ego zavedeniiakh ot osnovaniia universiteta do 1859 goda*. Kharkov, 1859.

Fortunatov, Th., "Vospominaniia o S.—Petersburgkam universitete za 1830–1833 gody," *RA*, 1869 (No. 2), 305–339.

Freeze, Gregory L., *The Russian Levites: Parish Clergy in the Eighteenth Century*. Cambridge, 1977.

Galkin, I. S., *Moskovskii Universitet za 200 let*. Moscow, 1955.

Galskoy, Constantin, "The Ministry of Education under Nicholas I: 1826–1836." Ph.D., Stanford University, 1977.

Giżycki, Marek Jan, ed., *Materialy do dziejow Akademii Polockiej i szkol od niej zalesnych*. Cracow, 1905.

Glinka-Mavrin, B. G., "Grigorii Andreevich Glinka," *RS*, 1876 (January), 75–105.

Goetze, Peter von, *Fürst Alexander Nikolajewitsch Galitzin und seine Zeit*. Leipzig, 1882.

Golitsyn, A. N., "Kniaz A. N. Golitsyn (v ego pis'makh)," *RA*, 1905 (No. 11), 360–455.

———, "Perepiska Kniazia A. N. Golitsyna s. Z. Ia. Karneevym," *RA*, 1893 (No. 5), 129–134.

———, "Razskazy Kniazia A. N. Golitsyna: iz zapisok Iu. N. Barteneva," *RA*, 1866 (No. 3), 129–166.

Gordeev, D. I., *Istoriia geologicheskikh nauk v moskovskom universitete*. Moscow, 1962.

Grech, N. I., "A. F. Voeikov," *RS*, 1875 (No. 9), 625–628.

Grech, N. N., *Zapiski o moei zhizni*. SPB, 1866.

Grigor'ev, V. V., *Imperatorskii S. Peterburgskii universitet v techenie pervykh piatidesiatilet ego sushchestvovaniia*. SPB, 1870.

Grigorievskii, A. I., *K istorii uchenago komiteta ministerstva narodnago prosveshcheniia*. SPB, 1902.

Grimsted, P. K., *The Foreign Ministers of Alexander I*. Berkeley, 1969.

Grits, T., *Slovestnost' i kommertsiia (knizhnaia lavka A. F. Smirdina)*, V. B. Shlovskii, B. M. Eikhenbaum, eds., Moscow, 1929.

Hans, Nicholas, "Educational Reform in Poland in the Eighteenth Century," *Journal of Central European Affairs*, xiv (1954), 301–310.

———, *History of Russian Educational Policy 1801–1917*. London, 1931.

———, "Polish Schools in Russia 1772–1831," *SEER*, xxxviii (1960), 394–414.

Hasselblatt, A., Otto, G., eds., *Album Academicum der Kaiserlichen Universität Dorpat*. Dorpat, 1889.

Haxthausen, August von, *Studies on the Interior of Russia*. S. Frederick Starr, ed., E. L. M. Schmidt, trans., Chicago, 1972.

Hollingsworth, Barry, "A. P. Kunitsyn and the Social Movement under Alexander I," *SEER*, XLIII (1964), 116–128.

Ikonnikov, V., "Kiev v 1654–1855 gg.," *Kievskaia Starina*, 1904 (September), 213–274; (October), 1–64.

———, "Russkie universitety v sviazi s khodom obshchestvennago obrazovaniia," *VE*, 1897 (No. 9), 161–206; (No. 10), 492–550; (No. 11), 73–132.

Imperatorskoe russkoe istoricheskoe obshchestvo. *Sbornik Imperatorskago russkago istoricheskago obshchestva*. 148 v. SPB, 1867–1917.

v. 74 (1891), *Zhurnaly Komiteta uchrezhdennago vysochaishim reskriptom 6 Dekabriia 1826 goda*.

v. 90 (1894), *Bumagi komiteta . . . 6 Dekabriia 1826 goda*.

v. 131 (1910), *Perepiska imperatora Nikolaia Pavlovicha s . . . Konstantinom Pavlovichem, 1825–1829*.

v. 132 (1911), *Perepiska imperatora Nikolaia . . . s Konstantinom, 1830–1831*.

Istoriia Moskvy v shesti tomakh: tom vtoroi: period feodalizma XVIII v. Moscow, 1953.

Janowski, Ludwik, "Uniwersytet Charkowski we początkach swego istnienia 1805–1820," *Rozprawy Akademii Umiejętności wydział filogiczny*. v. IV (Cracow 1911), 127–285.

Jobert, Ambrose, *La Commission d'éducation nationale en Pologne, 1773–94*. Paris, 1941.

Johnson, W. H. E., *Russia's Educational Heritage*. Pittsburgh, 1950.

Kalinin, N. F., *Kazan: istoricheskii ocherk*. Kazan, 1955.

Kalitkina, N. Iu., "A. P. Kunitsyn—Professor Peterburgskogo universiteta," *VLU*, 1969 (No. 5), 147–149.

Karamzin, N. M., *Memoir on Ancient and Modern Russia*, Richard Pipes, ed. and trans. New York, 1966.

——, *Pisma N. M. Karamzina k. I. I. Dmitrievu*, Ia. K. Grot, ed., SPB, 1866.

Karazin, V. N., *Sochineniia, pis'ma i bumagi*. D. I. Bagalei, ed., Kharkov, 1910.

——, "Vasilii Nazarovich Karazin, osnovatel' Khar'kovskago universiteta," [Karazin, F. V., ed.] *RA*, 1875 (February), 329–338; 1875 (May), 61–80; 1875 (September), 185–200; (October), 268–279; (December) 470–477.

——, "Zapiska predstavlenniia Imperatoru Aleksandru I chrez ministra vnutrennakh del gr. V. P. Kochubeia, 1820 8. *RA*, 1871 (January), 16–38.

——, "Pis'mo k doktoru Remanu, 1810," *RA*, 1875 (April), 750–758.

——, "Pis'mo k M. M. Speranskomu, 18 April 1810," *RA*, 1872 (January), 82–83.

——, "Pis'mo k Imperatoru Aleksandru I, 22 March 1801," *RA*, 1871 (July), 68–80.

——, "Pis'mo k Kniaziu Adamu Chartoryskomu, 21 November 1804," *RA*, 1871 (June), 700–718.

——, "Zametki i materialy po istorii khar'kovskago universiteta: novyia dannyia dlia biografii V. N. Karazina," D. I. Bagalei, ed. *Zapiski Imperatorskago Khar'kovskago universiteta*, 1905 (No. 1), 81–164.

Keep, John L. H., "The Russian Army's Response to the French Revolution," *Jahrbücher für Geschichte Osteuropas*, 28 (1980), 500–523.

Khalanskii, M. G., Bagalei, D. I., *Istoriko-filologicheskii fakul'tet khar'kovskago universiteta za pervyia 100 let ego sushchestvovania 1805–1905*. Kharkov, 1908.

Kiev i Universitet Sv. Vladimira pri imperatore Nikolae I 1825–1855. Kiev, 1896.

Kizevetter, A. A., *Istoricheskie ocherki*. Moscow, 1912.

Klier, John D., "The Origins of the Jewish Minority Problem in Russia 1772–1812." Ph.D., University of Illinois, 1975.

Klingenstein, Grete, "Despotismus und Wissenschaft: Zur Kritik norddeutscher Aufklärer an der österreichischen Universität 1750–1790," *Formen der europäischen Aufklärung*, Friedrich Engel-Janosi, others, eds., in *Wiener Beiträge zur Geschichte der Neuzeit*, Bd 3 (1976), 127–157.

Klostermann, R. A., "Speranskijs Sturz in L. H. Jakobs Denkwurdigkeiten," *Archiv für Kulturgeschichte*, XXIII (1932), 217–233.

Kobeko, Dmitrii, *Imperatorskii tsarskoselskii litsei: nastavniki i pitomtsy 1811–1843*. SPB, 1911.

Kochubinskii, A. A., "Graf Speranskii i universitetskii ustav 1835 g.," *VE*, 1894 (April), 655–683; (May), 5–43.

Kononkov, A. F., *Istoriia fiziki v moskovskom universiteta 1755–1859.* Moscow, 1955.
Konstantinov, N. A., "Prosveshchenie," *Ocheriki istorii SSSR: Rossiia vo vtoroi polovine XVIII v.* Moscow, 1956, 419–426.
Korbut, M. K., *Kazanskii gosudarstvennyi universitet za 125 let.* Kazan, 1930.
Korf, M (A.), *Zhizn' grafa Speranskogo.* 2 v. SPB, 1861. Korolivskii, S. M., *Khar'kovskii Gosudarstvennyi Universitet.* Kharkov, 1955.
Kosachevskaia, E. M., M. A. *Balugianskii i Peterburgskii universitet pervoi chetverti xix veka.* Leningrad, 1971.
———, "M. A. Balugianskii-pervyi rektor peterburgskogo universiteta," *VLU,* 1958 (14), 46–63.
Kosmin, N. K., "N. I. Nadezhdin-professor Moskovskago universiteta," *ZhMNP,* 1905 (September), 1–41; 1907 (May), 124–137; (June), 281–325; (July), 26–71.
Kostenetskii, Ia. I., "Vospominaniia iz moi studensheskoi zhizni, 1828–1833," *RA* 1887 (No. 1), 99–117, (No. 2), 229–244, (No. 3), 321–349, (No. 5), 73–81, (No. 6), 217–242.
Kovnator, R. A., ed., *Moskovskii universitet v vospominaniiakh sovremenikov.* Moscow, 1956.
Krachkovskii, Iu. Th., *Istoricheskii obzor deiatel'nosti Vilenskago uchebnago okruga za pervyi period ego sushchestvovaniia 1803–1832 g.* Vilna, 1903.
Krause, J. W., "Das Erste Jahrzehnt der Ehemaligen Universität Dorpat," *Baltische Monatsschrift,* LIII (1902), 229–250.
Kravets, I. N., "T. F. Osipovskii-vydaiushchiisia russkii filosof-materialist i estestvoispytatel'," *Voprosy filosofii.* 1951 (5), 111–120.
Kukiel, M[arian], *Czartoryski and European Unity 1770–1861.* Princeton, 1955.
———, "Lelewel, Mickiewicz, and the Underground Movements of European Revolution 1816–33," *The Polish Review,* V (1960), 59–76.
Landa, S. S., *Dukh revoliutsionnykh preobrazovanii: iz istorii formirovaniia ideologii i politicheskoi organizatsii dekabristov 1816–1825.* Moscow, 1975.
Lavrinenko, Iurii, *Vasil' Karazin: Arkhitekt Vidrodzhennia.* Munich, 1975.
Lavrovskii, N. A., "Vasilii Nazarevich Karazin i otkrytie Khar'kovskago universiteta," *ZhMNP,* 1872 (January), 57–106; (February), 197–247.
———, "Vospominanie o Vasilii Nazaroviche Karazine," *ZhMNP,* 1873 (March), 294–311.
———, "Pedagog Proshlago Vremeni (Diugurov)," *RA,* 1869 (No. 9), 1542–1553.
———, "Epizod iz istorii Khar'kovskago Universiteta," *Chteniia v Impera-*

torskom Obshchestve Istorii i Drevnostei Rossiiskikh pri Moskovskom Universitete, 1873 (No. 2), Smes, 1–58.

Lebedev, A. S., "Anton Antonovich Degurov: biograficheskii ocherk iz istorii khar'kovskago i peterburgskogo universitetov 1806–36 gg.," *VE,* 1876 (March), 135–176.

Leikin-Svirskaia, V. R., "Formirovanie raznochinskoi intelligentsii v Rossii v 40-kh godakh XIX v.," *Istoriia SSSR,* 1958 (No. 1), 83–104.

Lepskaia, L. A., "Sostav uchashchikhaia narodnykh uchilishch Moskvy v kontse XVIII v." *VMU,* 1973 (No. 5), 88–96.

Likin, N., "Moskovskii Universitet v Nizhnem-Novgorode v 1812 gody," *ZhMNP,* 1915 (June), 206–215.

Likowski, E., *Dzieje Kościoła unickiego na litwie i Rusi w XVIII i XIX w.,* 2 v., Warsaw, 1906. II.

Lincoln, W. B., *Nicholas I: Emperor and Autocrat of All The Russias.* Indiana, 1978.

———, "Russia's 'Enlightened' Bureaucrats and the Problem of State Reform, 1848–1856," *Cahiers du monde russe et soviétique,* v. 12 (1971), 410–421.

———, "The Genesis of an Enlightened Bureaucracy in Russia, 1825–1856," *Jahrbücher für Geschichte Osteuropas,* v. 20 (1972), 321–330.

Liphits, S. Iu., *Moskovskoe obshchestvo ispitatelei prirodi za 135 let suschestvovaniia 1805–1940.* Moscow, 1940.

Litak, Stanislaw, "Das Schulwesen der Jesuiten in Polen: Entwicklung und Verfall," *Wiener Beitrage zur Geschichte der Neuzeit,* Bd 5 (1978), 124–137.

Liubavskii, M. K., *Moskovskii Universitet v 1812 godu.* Moscow, 1913.

Luckyj, George, S. N., *Between Gogol' and Sevcenko: Polarity in the Literary Ukraine 1798–1847.* Munich, 1971.

Lysenko, V. I., *Nikolai Ivanovich Fuss 1755–1826.* Moscow, 1975.

Madariaga, Isabel de, "The Foundation of the Russian Educational System by Catherine II," *Slavonic and East European Review,* v. 57 (1979), 369–395.

Magnitskii, M. L., "Magnitskii, Materialy dlia istorii prosveshcheniia v Rossii," E. M. Feoktistov, ed. *Russkii Vestnik,* v. 51 (1864), 464–497; v. 52 (1864), 5–55, 407–449.

———, "Dva mneniia popechitelia kazanskago uchebnago okruga, M. L. Magnitskago," *RA,* 1864 (No. 3), 321–330.

Maikov, P. N., *Ivan Ivanovich Betskoi: opyt ego biografii.* SPB, 1904.

Maksimovich, M. A., *Mysli ob universitete sv. Vladimira v kontse 1838 goda.* Kiev, 1865.

———, "Ob uchasti i znachenii Kieva v obshchei zhizni Rossii," *ZhMNP,* 1837 (October), otdel' ii, 1–29.

———, "Ob uchastii Moskovskago universiteta v prosveshchenii Rossii," *Russkii zritel'*, No. XXI–XXII (1830), 3–19.

———, "O russkom prosveshchenii," *Teleskop*, 1832 (No. 2), 169–190.

Malia, Martin, *Alexander Herzen and the Birth of Russian Socialism*. Cambridge, 1961.

Markov, K. K., Sauskhin, Iu. G., *Geografiia v Moskovskom Universitete za 200 let*. Moscow, 1955.

Markov, P. T., *M. O. Maksimovich-vidatnii istorik xix st*. Kiev, 1973.

Martins, K., "Iz zapisok starago ofitsera," *RA*, 1902 (January), 87–114.

Martinson, E. E., *Istoriia osnovaniia tartuskogo (b. Derptskogo-iurevskogo) universiteta*. Leningrad, 1954.

Martynov, D. Ia., ed., *Istoriia Kazanskogo gosudarstvennogo universiteta imeni V. I. Ul'ianova-Lenina*. Kazan, 1954.

Mathes, William L., "The Process of Institutionalization of Education in Tsarist Russia, 1800–1917," *Russian and Slavic History*, D. K. Rowney, G. E. Orchard, eds., Columbus, 1977, 26–48.

Mavrodin, V. V., *Leningradskii Universitet: kratkii ocherk*. Leningrad, 1957.

———, *Istoriia Leningradskogo universiteta 1819–1969: ocherki*. Leningrad, 1969.

———, ed., *Leningradskii universitet v vospominaniiakh sovremenikov*. I; 1819–1895. Leningrad, 1963.

Mazitova, N. A., *Izuchenie blizhnego i srednego vostoka v kazanskom universitete*. Kazan, 1972.

McClelland, J. C., *Autocrats and Academics: Education, Culture, and Society in Tsarist Russia*. Chicago, 1979.

McConnell, Allen, "Alexander I's Hundred Days, The Politics of a Paternalistic Reformer," *Slavic Review*, v. 28 (1969), 373–393.

———, *Tsar Alexander I: Paternalistic Reformer*. New York, 1970.

McGrew, Roderick E., *Russia and the Cholera 1823–1832*. Madison, 1965.

Meshcherskii, N. A., Dmitriev, P. A., "Russkoe i slavianskoe iazykoznanie v Peterburgskom-Leningradskom universitete za 150 let," *VLU*, 1969 (No. 2), 80–91.

Mikhailovich, Nikolai, *Imperator Aleksandr I*. Petrograd, 1914.

———, *Graf Pavel Aleksandrovich Stroganov*. 3 v., SPB, 1903.

Mikhailovskii, A. I., *Prepodavateli, uchivshiesiia i sluzhivshie v kazanskom universitete 1804–1904*. 3 v., Kazan, 1901–1908, I.

Miliukov, P., *Ocherki po istorii russkoi kul'tury*, 3 v., 4th ed., SPB, 1905. II.

Miller, D. P., "Arest i ssylka V. N. Karazina," *Istoricheskii vestnik*, 1900 (March), 1047–1053.

Ministerstvo narodnago prosveshcheniia. *Opisanie del arkhiva Ministerstva narodnago prosveshcheniia*. S. F. Platonov, ed., Petrograd, 1917. I.

————, *Sbornik materialov dlia istorii prosveshcheniia v Rossii izvlechen-nykh iz arkhiva ministerstva narodnago prosveshcheniia*, 4 v., SPB, 1893–1902.

————, *Sbornik postanovlenii po ministerstvu narodnago prosveshcheniia*, 15 v., SPB, 1875–1902, I, II, IIii.

————, *Sbornik rasporiazhenii po ministerstvu narodnago prosveshche-niia*, 6 v., SPB, 1866–1901, I.

Modzalovskii, L. B., *Materialy dlia biografii N. I. Lobachevskogo*. Leningrad, 1948.

Monas, Sidney, *The Third Section: Police and Society in Russia under Nicholas I*. Cambridge, 1961.

Morley, Charles, "Czartoryski as a Polish Statesman," *Slavic Review*, v. 30 (1971), 606–614.

Moroshkin, Mikhail, *Iezuity v Rossii s Tsarstvovaniia Ekateriny II-i do nashego vremeni*, 2 v., SPB, 1867–1870.

"Moskovskii universitetskii blagorodnyi pansion, 1783–1883," *RS*, 1883 (April), 231–237.

Murzakevich, N. N., "Zapiski N. N. Murzakevicha," *RA*, 1887 (January), 1–46; (February), 263–298; (March), 651–666.

Muzko, Nikolai, "Aleksei Fedorovich Merzliakov 1778–1830 g.," *RS*, 1879 (January), 113–140.

Narkiewicz, O. A., "Alexander I and the Senate Reform," *SEER*, XLVII (1969), 115–136.

Nasonkina, L. I., *Moskovskii universitet posle vosstaniia dekabristov*. Moscow, 1972.

Nechkina, M. V., ed., *Ocherki istorii istoricheskoi nauki v SSSR*, III, IV, Moscow, 1963–1966.

Neupokoev, V. L., "Preobrazovnie bespomestnoi shliakhty v litve v podat-noe soslovie odnodvortsev i grazhdan (vtoraia tret' XIX v.)," *Revoliu-tsionnaia situatsiia v Rossii v 1859–1861 gg*. M. V. Nechkina, ed., v. 6 (Moscow, 1974), 3–22.

Nikitenko, A. V., "Aleksandr Ivanovich Galich, Byshii Professor S.-Peter-burgskago Universiteta," *ZhMNP*, 1869 (January), 1–100.

————, *Diary of a Russian Censor: Aleksandr Nikitenko*. H. S. Jacobson, ed. and trans. Amherst, 1975.

————, *Dnevnik v trekh tomakh*, Moscow, 1955. I.

————, *Zapiski i dnevnik*, 2 v., SPB, 1904–05. I.

"O litsakh, komandirovannykh ministerstvom narodnago prosveshcheniia za granitsu dlia prigotovleniia k zvaniiu professorov i prepodavatelei s 1808 po 1860 god," *ZhMNP*, 1864 (February), otdel' II, 335–354.

O'Brien, G. M., "Maria Theresa's Attempt to Educate an Empire," *Paeda-gogica Historica*, v. 10 (1970), 542–565.

O'Connor, Mark F., "Cultures in Conflict: A Case Study in Russian-Polish Relations: The University at Wilno." Ph.D., Boston College, 1977.

——, "Czartoryski and the Golochowski Affair at Vilna University," *Jahrbücher für Geschichte Osteuropas*, 31 (1983), 229–243.

Okenfuss, M. J., "Education and Empire: School Reform in Enlightened Russia," *Jahrbücher für Geschichte Osteuropas*, v. 27 (1979), 41–68.

——, "The Jesuit Origins of Petrine Education," *The Eighteenth Century in Russia*. John Garrard, ed. (Oxford, 1973), 106–130.

——, "Technical Training in Russia under Peter the Great," *History of Education Quarterly*, 13 (1973), 325–345.

Orlov, V. I., *Studencheskoe dvizhenie moskovskogo universiteta v xix veke*. Moscow, 1934.

Osipov. I. P., Bagalei, D. I., eds., *Fizikomatematicheskii fakul'tet Khar'kovskago universiteta za pervyia sto let ego sushchestvovaniia 1805–1905*. Kharkov, 1908.

Ostrianin, D. F., *Mirovozzrenie M. A. Maksimovicha*. Kiev, 1960.

Ostrovitianov, K. V., ed., *Istoriia akademii nauk SSSR v trekh tomakh*. Moscow, 1958–1964. II.

Panaev, V. I., "Vospominaniia V. I. Panaeva," *VE*, 1867 (September), 193–270; (December), 72–181.

Panin, A. N., "Pamiatnaia zapiska o professorakh Moskovskago universiteta, pomoshchnika popechitelia grafa A. N. Panina," *RA*, 1880 (August), 780–782.

Parrot, G. K., Mardarev, M., ed., "Pis'ma i Zapiski Georga Fridrikha Parrota k Imperatoram Aleksandru I i Nikolaiu I," *RA*, 1895 (May), 191–219.

Paulsen, Friedrich, *The German Universities: Their Character and Historical Development*. E. D. Perry, trans., New York, 1895.

Paulucci, [Filippe], "Marquis Paulucci und seine Verfolgung geheimer Gesellschaften in den Ostseeprovinzen," *Baltische Monatsschrift*, XLIV (1897), 491–514.

Pelech, Orest, "Toward a Historical Sociology of the Ukrainian Ideologues in the Russian Empire of the 1830's and 1840's." Ph.D., Princeton University, 1976.

Penchko, N. A., *Osnovanie moskovskogo universiteta*. Moscow, 1953.

Petukhov, E. V., *Imperatorskii Iurevskii, byvshii Derptskii, Universitet 1802–1865*. Iurev, 1902.

——, *Kafedra russkago iazyka i slovesnosti v Iur'evskom (Derptskom) universitete*. Iur'ev, 1900.

——, "Mikhail Nikitich Murav'ev," *ZhMNP*, 1894 (August), 265–296.

——, "Petr Tseplin, pervyi professor Kazanskogo universiteta 1772–1832," *ZhMNP*, 1906 (February), 344–366.

———, *Statisticheskiia tablitsy i lichnye spiski po imperatorskomu iur'evskomu byvshemu derptskomu universitet*. Iurev, 1902.

Picht, Ulrich, M. P. *Pogodin und die Slavische Frage*. Stuttgart, 1969.

Piksanov, N. K., Sokolov, N. I., "Izuchenie russkoi literatury v Peterburgskom-Leningradskom universitete 1819–1969," *VLU*, 1969 (No. 2), 69–79.

Pintner, Walter M., *Russian Economic Policy under Nicholas I*. Ithaca, 1967.

———, "The Russian Higher Civil Service on the Eve of the 'Great Reforms,'" *Journal of Social History*, 1975 (Spring), 55–68.

———, "The Social Characteristics of the Early Nineteenth Century Russian Bureaucracy," *Slavic Review*, v. 29 (1970), 429–443.

Pipes, Richard, *Russia under the Old Regime*. New York, 1974.

Pirogov, N. I., *Izbrannye pedagogicheskie sochineniia*. V. Z. Smirnov, ed., Moscow, 1952.

Plakans, Andrejs, "Peasants, Intellectuals, and Nationalism in the Baltic Provinces, 1820–90," *Journal of Modern History*, v. 46 (1974), 455–457.

Pletnev, P. A., *Pervoe dvadtsatipiatiletia Imperatorskago Sankpeterburgskago Universiteta*. SPB, 1844.

Pogodin, A. (L.), "Vilenskii uchebnyi okrug 1803–1831 g.," *Sbornik materialov dlia istorii prosveshcheniia v Rossii izvlechennykh iz arkhiva Ministerstva narodnago prosveshcheniia*. IV (SPB, 1902), i–cxxxiii.

Pogodin, M. P., *Pis'ma M. P. Pogodina k M. A. Maksimovichu*. S. I. Ponomarev, ed., SPB, 1882.

———, *Zhizn' i trudy M. P. Pogodina*. N. P. Barsukov, ed., 22 v., SPB, 1888–1910. I.

Polievktov, M., *Nikolai I: Biografiia i obzor tsarstvovaniia*. Moscow, 1918.

Polz, Peter, "Theodor Jankovic und die Schulreform in Russland," *Die Aufklärung in Ost- und Südosteuropa*. Erna Lesky, others, eds. (Koln, 1972), 119–174.

Popov, A. N., "Moskva v 1812 gody," *RA*, 1875 (No. 8), 369–402.

Popov, N., "Obshchestvo Liubitelei Otechestvennoi Slovesnosti i Periodicheskaia Literaturea v Kazani s 1805 po 1834 god," *Russkii Vestnik*, XXIII (1859), 52–98.

Popov, Nil, "Moskovskii universitet posle 1812 goda," *RA*, 1881 (No. 1), 386–421.

Potocki, S. O., "Mnenie o uchrechdenii universiteta v Sank-Peterburge," *Chteniia v Imperatorskom Obshchestve Istorii i Drevnostei rossiiskikh pri Moskovskom Universiteta*, 1860 (No. 4), smes', 308–313.

Predtechenskii, A. V., *Ocherki obshchestvenno-politicheskoi istorii Rossii v pervoi chetverti xix veka*. Moscow, 1957.

Pugachev, V. V., "K voprosu o politicheskikh vzgliadakh S. S. Uvarova v
1810e gody," *Uchenye zapiski gor'kovskogo gosudarstvennogo universiteta*, 1964 (No. 72), 125–131.

Pypin, A. N., *Die Geistigen Bewegungen in Russland in der ersten hälfte
des xix Jahrhunderts*. B. Minzes, trans., Berlin, 1894.

———, "Russkoe slavianovedenie v XIX stoletii," *VE*, 1889 (August),
683–728.

Raeff, Marc, "Le climat politique et les projects de réforme dans les pre-
mières années du règne d'Alexandre Ier," *Cahiers du Monde Russe et
Soviétique*, II (1961), 415–433.

———, *Comprendre l'ancien régime russe*. Paris, 1982.

———, "The Domestic Policies of Peter III and His Overthrow," *American
Historical Review*, 75 (1970), 1289–1310.

———, *Michael Speransky, Statesman of Imperial Russia*. The Hague,
1957.

———, *The Well-Ordered Police State: Social and Institutional Change
through Law in the Germanies and Russia 1600–1800*. New Haven,
1983.

Ransel, David L., *The Politics of Catherinian Russia: The Panin Party*. New
Haven, 1975.

Razumovskii, A. K., *Semeistvo Razumovskikh*. A. A. Vasil'chikov, ed.,
4 v., SPB, 1880–1887. II.

Reinerman, Alan J., "Metternich and Reform: The Case of the Papal State
1814–1848," *Journal of Modern History*, XLII (1970), 524–548.

———, "Papacy and Papal State in the Restoration 1814–1846," *Catholic
Historical Review*, LXIV (1978), 36–46.

Repsczuk, Helma, "Nicholas Mordvinov (1754–1845): Russia's Would-be
Reformer." Ph.D., Columbia University, 1962.

Riasanovsky, Nicholas V., *Nicholas I and Official Nationality in Russia
1825–1855*. Berkeley, 1959.

———, *A Parting of Ways: Government and the Educated Public in Russia
1801–1855*. Oxford, 1976.

———, "Russia and Asia: Two Nineteenth Century Russian Views," *Cali-
fornia Slavic Studies*, I (1960), 170–181.

Rieger, M(aximilian), *Fredrich Maximilian Klinger Sein Leben und Werke*.
2 v., Darmstadt, 1880–1896.

Roach, E. E., "The Origins of Alexander I's Unofficial Committee," *The
Russian Review*, v. 28 (1969), 315–326.

Roslavskii-Petrovskii, A., "Ob uchenoi deiatel'nosti Imperatorskago
khar'kovskago universiteta v pervoe desiatiletie ego sushchestvovaniia,"
ZhMNP, 1855 (July), 1–36.

Rouët de Journal, M. J., ed., *Nonciatures de Russie*. 4 v., Vatican City,
1952. III.

Rozhdestvenskii, S. V., *Istoricheskii obzor deiatel'nosti Ministerstva narodnago prosveshcheniia 1802–1902*. SPB, 1902.

———, "Iz istorii idei narodnago prosveshcheniia v Aleksandrovskuiu epokhu," *Sbornik stat'ei po russkoi istorii posviashchennykh S. F. Platonovu*, Petrograd, 1922, 382–396.

———, "Iz istorii uchebnykh reform imperatritsy Ekateriny II," *ZhMNP*, 1909 (March), 47–100; (June), 186–226.

———, "Komissiia ob uchrezhdenii narodnykh uchilishch 1782–803 g. i ministerstvo narodnago prosveshcheniia," *ZhMNP*, 1906 (May), 14–18.

———, "M. M. Speranskii i komitet 1837 goda o stepeni obucheniia krepostnykh liudei." *Sbornik stat'ei posviashchennykh S. F. Platonovu*, SPB, 1911, 254–279.

———, *Ocherki po istorii sistem narodnago prosveshcheniia v Rossii v XVIII–XIX vekakh*. SPB, 1912.

———, "Proekty uchebnykh reform v tsarstvovanie Imperatritsy Ekateriny II do uchrezhdeniia Komissii o narodnykh uchilishchakh," *ZhMNP*, 1907 (December), 173–228; 1908 (February), 160–182; (May), 43–70.

———, ed., *S. Peterburgskii universitet v pervoe stoletie ego deiatel'nosti 1819–1919: Materialy po istorii S. Peterburgskogo universiteta*. Petrograd, 1919.

———, "Soslovnii vopros v russkikh universitetakh v pervoi chertverti xix veka," *ZhMNP*, 1907 (May), 84–108.

———, "Universitetskii vopros v tsarstvovanie imp. Ekateriny IIoi i sistema narodnago prosveshcheniia po Ustavam 1804 goda," *VE*, 1907 (July), 5–46, (August), 437–457.

———, "Vopros o narodom obrazovanii i sotsial'naia problema v epokhu Aleksandra I." *Russkoe Proshloe*, v. 5 (1923), 37–49.

———, ed., *Materialy dlia istorii uchebnykh reform v Rossii v XVIII–XIX vekakh*. SPB, 1910.

Runich, D. P. "Iz Zapisok D. P. Runicha," V. V. Timoshchuk ed., *RS*, 1901 (February), 325–357; (March), 597–633; (April), 153–168; (May), 373–394.

Russkii biograficheskii slovar'. 25 v., SPB, 1896–1913.

Ruszczyc, Ferdynand, ed., *Księga Pamiątkowa Uniwersytetu Wileńskiego*. Vilna, 1929.

Sapunov, A., *Zametka o kollegii i akademii iezuitov v Polotski*. Vitebsk, 1890.

Savel'ev, P., "Predprolozheniia ob uchrezhdenii Vostochnoi Akademii v Peterburge 1733 i 1810 godov," *ZhMNP*, 1856 (February), 27–36.

Sawatsky, Walter William, "Prince Alexander N. Golitsyn (1773–1844): Tsarist Minister of Piety." Ph.D., University of Minnesota, 1976.

Schmid, Georg, "Zur russischen Gelehrten-geschichte: S. S. Uvarov und Chr. Fr. Gräfe," *Russische Revue*, v. 26 (1886), 77–108.

Schmidlin, Joseph, *Papstgeschichte der Neuesten Zeit: Papsttum und Päpste im Zeitalter der Restauration 1800–1846*. 2nd ed., Munich, 1933.

Semenov, V. F., *Ekonomicheskie idei v Kazanskom universitete v period razlozheniia i krizisa feodal'nogo khoziaistva 1804–1861 gg*. Avtoreferat dissertatsia, Kazan, 1961.

Semevskii, V. I., *Krest'ianskii vopros v Rossii v XVIII i pervoi polovine xix veka*. 2 v., SPB, 1888, I.

Seredonin, S. M., *Istoricheskii obzor deiatel'nosti Komiteta Ministrov 1802–1902*. 2 v., SPB, 1902, I.

Shabaeva, M. F., *Ocherki istorii shkoly i pedagogicheskoi mysli narodov SSSR: XVIII v.-pervaia polovina XIX v.*. Moscow, 1973.

Shchelkov, I. P., "Iz istorii Khar'kovskago universiteta," *ZhMNP*, 1890 (October), 358–385.

Shchepkin, D. S., ed., "K istorii moskovskago universiteta: pis'ma professorov vo vremia moskovskago razorenia," *RA*, 1904 (No. 1), 43–50.

Shchipanov, I. Ia., *Moskovskii universitet i razvitii filosofskoi i obshchestvenno-politicheskoi mysli v Rossii*. Moscow, 1957.

———, ed., *Russkie prosvetiteli: ot Radishcheva do dekabristov*. 2 v. Moscow, 1966.

Shevyrev, Stepan, *Istoriia Imperatorskago Moskovskago Universiteta*. Moscow, 1855.

Shil'der, N. K., *Imperator Aleksandr I: ego zhizn' i tsartvovanie*. 2 v., SPB, 1903.

Shilov, L. A., "Iz istorii iuridicheskogo fakul'teta Peterburgskogo universiteta 1819–1917 gg.," *VLU*, 1969 (No. 5), 107–119.

Shishkov, A. S., *Zapiski, mneniia i perepiska Admirala A. S. Shishkova*. N. Kiselev, Iu. Samarin, eds., 2 v., SPB, 1970.

———, "S. S. Uvarov i admiral Shishkov," N. P. Barsukov, ed., *RA*, 1882 (No. 6), 226–228.

Shugurov, M. T., ed., "Doklad o evreiakh imperatoru Aleksandru Pavlovichu. 1812," *RA*, 1903 (No. 2), 253–255.

Shul'gin, Vitalliia, *Istoriia Universiteta Sv. Vladimira*. SPB, 1860.

Shurtakova, T. B., "Rol kazanskogo universiteta v organizatsii i rukovodstve uchebnym protsessom v shkolakh uchebnogo okruga v 1805–1836 gg.," *Uchenye zapiski kazanskogo gosudarstvennogo universiteta imeni V. I. Ul'ianova-Lenina*, 1957 (No. 10), 183–228.

———, *Rukovodstvo Kazanskogo universiteta razvititiem nachal'nogo i srednego obrazovaniia v kazanskom uchebnom okruge v 1805–1836 gg*. Avtoreferat dissertatsia. Kazan, 1959.

Sidorov, A. A., ed., *400 let russkogo knigo-pechataniia: russkoe knigopechatanie do 1917 goda*. Moscow, 1964.

Sinel, Allen, "Review Essay: Problems in the Periodization of Russian Education: A Tentative Solution," *Slavic and European Education Review*, 1977 (No. 2), 54–61.

———, "The Socialization of the Russian Bureaucratic Elite, 1811–1917: Life at the Tsarskoe Selo Lyceum and the School of Jurisprudence," *Russian History*, v. 3 (1976), 1–32.

Sirotkin, V. G., "Russkaia pressa pervyi chetverti xix veka na inostrannykh iazykakh kak istoricheskii istochnik," *Istoriia SSSR*, 1976 (No. 4), 77–97.

Skvortsov, I. P., Bagalei, D. I., eds., *Meditsinskii fakul'tet Khar'kovskago universiteta za pervyia 100 let ego sushchestvovaniia 1805–1905*. Kharkov, 1905.

Sladkevich, N. G., ed., *Ocherki po istorii leningradskogo universiteta*. Leningrad, 1962.

Sliusarkskii, A. G., *V. N. Karazin: ego nauchnaia i obshchestvennaia deiatel'nost'*. Kharkov, 1955.

Smirnov, F. N., "A. P. Kunitsyn i dekabristy," *VMU*, 1961 (No. 5), 60–69.

Smoljan, Olga, *Friedrich Maximilian Klinger: Leben und Werke*. E. M. Arndt. trans., Weimar, 1962.

Snegirev, I. M., *Ivan Mikhailovich Snegirev i dnevnik ego vospominanii s 1821–1865 god*. A. Ivanovskii, ed., SPB, 1871.

Śniadecki, Jan, *Pisma Pedagogiczne*, Jan Hulewicz, ed., Warsaw, 1961.

———, *Wybór pism naukowych*, Stefen Drobot, ed., Cracow, 1954.

Solodkin, I. I., "Iz istorii kafedry ugolovnogo prava Peterburgskogo-Leningradskogo universiteta," *VLU*, 1969 (No. 5), 127–138.

———, "Ugolovno-pravovye vozzreniia A. P. Kunitsyna," *VLU*, 1966 (No. 11), 122–127.

Solov'ev, I. M., ed., *Russkie universitety v ikh ustavakh i vospominaniiakh sovremenikov*. SPB, 1914.

Spektorskii, E. V., *Stoletie kievskago universiteta Sv.Vladimira*. Belgrade, 1935.

Squire, P. S., *The Third Department: The Political Police in the Russia of Nicholas I*. Cambridge, 1968.

Starr, S. Frederick, *Decentralization and Self-Government in Russia 1830–70*. Princeton, 1972.

Steinger, Charles S., "Government Policy and the University of St. Petersburg 1819–1849." Ph.D., Ohio State University, 1971.

Sturdza, A. S., "O sud'be Pravoslavnoi Tserkvi Russkoi v Tsarstvovanie Imperatora Aleksandra I-go; iz zapisok A. S. Sturdzy," *RA*, 1876 (February), 266–288.

Sukhomlinov, M. I., *Izsledovaniia i stat'i po russkoi literature i prosveshcheniiu*, 2 v., SPB, 1889.

———, ed., "Delo o Sant-Peterburgskom Universitete v 1821 godu,"

Chteniia v Imperatorskom Obshchestve Istorii i Drevnostei Rossiiskikh pri Moskovskom Universitete. 1866 (3), Smes, 61–164.

Sverbeeva, D. N., *Zapiski Dmitriia Nikolaevicha Sverbeeva, 1799–1826*. Sof'ia Sverbeeva, ed., 2 v., Moscow, 1899.

Tabiś, Jan, *Polacy na uniwersytecie kijowskim 1834–1863*. Cracow, 1974

Thackeray, Frank W., *Antecedents of Revolution: Alexander I and the Polish Kingdom, 1815–1825*. Boulder, 1980.

Tikhii, N., *V. N. Karazin, ego zhizn' i obshchestvennaia diatel'nost'*. Kiev, 1905.

———, "V. N. Karazin, vinovnik uchrechdeniia universiteta v Khar'kove," *Zapiski Imperatorskago Khar'kovskago universiteta*, 1905 (No. 2), 1–80.

Tikhomandritskii, M. A., "Opyt istorii fizikomatematicheskago fakul'teta Imperatorskago Khar'kovskago universiteta za pervye 100 let ego suschchestvovania," *Zapiski Imperatorskago Khar'kovskago Universiteta*, 1905 (No. 1), 1–80.

Tikhomirov, M. N., *Istoriia moskovskogo universiteta*. 2 v. Moscow, 1955. I.

Tkachenko, A. M., *Rol' Khar'kovskogo universiteta v razvitii shkoly v pervom tridtsatiletii sushchestvovanniia universiteta 1805–1835 gg*. Avtoreferat dissertatsiia. Kharkov, 1950.

Tobien, Alex, "Die Aufhebung der Leibeigenschaft in Kurland," *Baltische Monatsschrift*, XLIV (1897), 129–145, 199–215.

Tolmachev, I. V., "Iakov Vasil'evich Tolmachev ordinarnyi professor SPB universiteta, 1779–1873, Avtobiograficheskaia zapiska," *RA*, 1892 (September), 699–724.

Torke, Hans J., "Continuity and Change in the Relations between Bureaucracy and Society in Russia 1613–1861," *Canadian Slavic Studies*, V (1971), 457–476.

———, "Das russische Beamtentum in der ersten Hälfte des 19 Jahrhunderts," *Forschungen zur Osteuropäischen Geschichte*, v. 13 (Berlin, 1967), 1–345.

Tret'iakov, M. P., "Imperatorskii Moskovskii Universitet v 1799–1830 v vospominaniiakh Mikhaila Prokhorovicha Tret'iakova," *RA*, 1892 (July), 105–131; (August), 307–345; (September), 533–553.

Truchim, Stefan, *Współpraca polsko-rosyjska nad organizacją szkolnictwa rosyjskiego w początkach xix wieku*. Lodz, 1960.

Tur, Ludwik, *Uniwersytet Wileński i jego znaczenie*. Lwow, 1903.

Turgenev, N. I., *Arkhiv Brat'ev Turgenevykh: Dnevniki i pis'ma Nikolaia Ivanovicha Turgeneva za 1806–1811 goda* (v. I); *za 1816–1824* (v. III). SPB, 1911, Petrograd, 1921.

Turner, R. Steven, "University Reformers and Professional Scholarship in

Germany 1760–1806," *The University in Society*, L. Stone, ed., 2 v., Princeton, 1974. II, 495–531.

Vladimirskii-Budanov, M. F., *Istoriia Imperatorskago universiteta Sv. Vladimira*. Kiev, 1884.

Voitolovskaia, E. L., *Komediia N. V. Gogolia "Revizor": Kommentarii*. Leningrad, 1971.

Vucinich, Alexander, *Science in Russian Culture: A History to 1860*. Stanford, 1963.

Walker, Franklin A., "Popular Response to Public Education in the Reign of Alexander I (1801–1825), *History of Education Quarterly* (Winter, 1984), 527–543.

Whiting, K. R., "Aleksei Andreevich Arakcheev." Ph.D., Harvard University, 1951.

Whittaker, Cynthia H., "The Ideology of Sergei Uvarov: An Interpretive Essay," *The Russian Review*, v. 37 (1978), 158–176.

———, "The Impact of the Oriental Renaissance in Russia: The Case of Sergej Uvarov," *Jahrbücher für Geschichte Osteuropas*, v. 26 (1978), 503–524.

———, *The Origins of Modern Russian Education: An Intellectual Biography of Count Sergei Uvarov, 1786–1855*. DeKalb, Ill., 1984.

Wieczynski, Joseph L., "Apostle of Obscurantism: the Archimandrite Photius of Russia (1792–1838), *Journal of Ecclesiastical History*, XXII (1971), 319–331.

———, "The Mutiny of the Semenovsky Regiment in 1820," *The Russian Review*, v. 29 (1970), 167–180.

Winter, Eduard, *August Ludwig v. Schlözer und Russland*. Berlin, 1961.

———, "Die Jesuiten in Russland 1772 bis 1820." *Forschen und Wirken: Festschrift zur 150-Jahrfeier der Humboldt Universität zu Berlin 1810–1960*. 3 v., Berlin, 1960, III, 167–190.

Wischnitzer, Markus, *Die Universität Göttingen and die Entwicklung der liberalen Ideen in Russland in erstern Viertel des 19 Jahrhunderts*. Berlin, 1907.

Wittram, Reinhard, *Baltische Geschichte*, Munich, 1954.

Wortman, Richard S., *The Development of a Russian Legal Consciousness*. Chicago, 1976.

Yaney, George L., "Law, Society and the Domestic Regime in Russia in Historical Perspective," *The American Political Science Review*, LIX (1965), 379–390.

———, *The Systematization of Russian Government: Social Evolution in the Domestic Administration of Imperial Russia 1811–1905*. Urbana, 1973.

Zacek, Judith Cohen, "The Lancaster School Movement in Russia," *SEER*, 45 (1967), 343–367.

————, "The Russian Bible Society 1812–1826." Ph.D., Columbia University, 1964.

Zagoskin, N. P., *Istoricheskaia zapiska o chetyrekh otdeleniiakh kazanskago universiteta za 1814–1827 gg.* Kazan, 1899.

————, *Istoriia Imperatorskago universiteta za pervyia sto let ego sushchestvovaniia 1804–1904.* 4 v., Kazan, 1902–1904.

————, *Materialy dlia istorii kafedr i uchrezhdenii imperatorskago kazanskago universiteta 1804–1826 gg.* Kazan, 1899.

————, ed., *Sputnik po kazani.* Kazan, 1895.

Zagurskii, L. N., *Opyt istorii iuridicheskago fakul'teta Imperatorskago Khar'kovskago universiteta.* Kharkov, 1906.

Zaionchkovskii, P. A., "Vyshaia biurokratiia nakanune krymskoi voiny." *Istoriia SSSR,* 1974 (No. 4), 154–164.

Zalenski, Stanislas, *Les Jesuites de la Russie-Blanche,* A. Vivier, trans., 2 v., Paris, 1886.

Zaleskii, V. F., *Istoriia prepodavaniia filosofii prava v kazanskom universitete v sviazi s vazhneishimi dannymi vneshnei istorii iuridicheskogo fakul'teta.* Kazan, 1903.

Zawadzki, W. H., "Adam Czartoryski: An Advocate of Slavonic Solidarity at the Congress of Vienna," *Oxford Slavonic Papers,* X (1977), 73–97.

Zhmuds'kyi, O. Z., *Istoriia Kyivs'kogo universytetu 1834–1959.* Kiev, 1959.

Zhukovich, P. (N.), "Ob osnovanii i ustroistve glavnoi dukhovnoi seminarii pri Vilenskom universitete 1803–1832 gg.," *Khristianskoe chtenie,* 1887 (No. 3–4), 237–286.

Zimmerman, Judith E., "The Uses and Misuses of Tsarist Educational Policy," *History of Education Quarterly,* v. 16 (1976), 487–494.

Zverev, V. M., "Dekabristy i filosofskie iskaniia v Rossii pervoi chetverti xix v.," *Dekabristy i russkaia kul'tura,* B. S. Meilakh, ed., Leningrad, 1975, 27–57.

————, "Filosofiia v Rossii do i posle 'suda' nad professorami Peterburgskogo universiteta," *VLU,* 1969 (No. 5), 97–106.

————, "Gnoselogicheskie vzgiady P. D. Lodiia," *VLU,* 1964 (No. 3), 97–107.

INDEX